Mastering OpenCV 4 with Python

A practical guide covering topics from image processing, augmented reality to deep learning with OpenCV 4 and Python 3.7

Alberto Fernández Villán

Packt>

BIRMINGHAM - MUMBAI

Mastering OpenCV 4 with Python

Copyright © 2019 Packt Publishing

Commissioning Editor: Richa Tripathi
Acquisition Editor: Alok Dhuri
Content Development Editor: Manjusha Mantri
Technical Editor: Riddesh Dawne
Copy Editor: Safis Editing
Project Coordinator: Prajakta Naik
Proofreader: Safis Editing
Indexer: Rekha Nair
Graphics: Jisha Chirayil
Production Coordinator: Shraddha Falebhai

First published: March 2019

Production reference: 1280319

Published by Packt Publishing Ltd.
Livery Place
35 Livery Street
Birmingham
B3 2PB, UK.

ISBN 978-1-78934-491-2

www.packtpub.com

`mapt.io`

Mapt is an online digital library that gives you full access to over 5,000 books and videos, as well as industry leading tools to help you plan your personal development and advance your career. For more information, please visit our website.

Why subscribe?

- Spend less time learning and more time coding with practical eBooks and Videos from over 4,000 industry professionals

- Improve your learning with Skill Plans built especially for you

- Get a free eBook or video every month

- Mapt is fully searchable

- Copy and paste, print, and bookmark content

Packt.com

Did you know that Packt offers eBook versions of every book published, with PDF and ePub files available? You can upgrade to the eBook version at `www.packt.com` and as a print book customer, you are entitled to a discount on the eBook copy. Get in touch with us at `customercare@packtpub.com` for more details.

At `www.packt.com`, you can also read a collection of free technical articles, sign up for a range of free newsletters, and receive exclusive discounts and offers on Packt books and eBooks.

Contributors

About the author

Alberto Fernández Villán is a software engineer with more than 12 years of experience in developing innovative solutions. In the last couple of years, he has been working in various projects related to monitoring systems for industrial plants, applying both Internet of Things (IoT) and big data technologies. He has a Ph.D. in computer vision (2017), a deep learning certification (2018), and several publications in connection with computer vision and machine learning in journals such as *Machine Vision and Applications, IEEE Transactions on Industrial Informatics, Sensors, IEEE Transactions on Industry Applications, IEEE Latin America Transactions,* and more. As of 2013, he is a registered and active user (*albertofernandez*) on the Q&A OpenCV forum.

About the reviewers

Wilson Choo is a computer vision engineer working on validating computer vision and deep learning algorithms on many different hardware configurations. His strongest skills include algorithm benchmarking, integration, app development, and test automation.

He is also a machine learning and computer vision enthusiast. He often researches trending CVDL algorithms and applies them to solve modern-day problems. Besides that, Wilson likes to participate in hackathons, where he showcases his ideas and competes with other developers. His favorite programming languages are Python and C++.

Vincent Kok is a maker and a software platform application engineer in the transportation industry. He graduated from USM with a MSc in embedded system engineering. Vincent actively involves himself with the developer community, as well as attending Maker Faire events held around the world, such as in Shenzhen in 2014, and in Singapore and Tokyo in 2015. Designing electronics hardware kits and giving soldering/Arduino classes for beginners are some of his favorite ways to spend his free time. Currently, his focus is in computer vision technology, software test automation, deep learning, and constantly keeping himself up to date with the latest technology.

Rubén Usamentiaga is a tenured associate professor in the department of computer science and engineering at the University of Oviedo. He received his M.S. and Ph.D. degrees in computer science from the University of Oviedo in 1999 and 2005, respectively. He has participated in 4 European projects, 3 projects of the National R&D Plan, 2 projects of the Regional Plan of the Principado of Asturias, and 14 contracts with companies. He is the author of more than 60 publications in JCR journals (25 of Q1) and more than 50 publications in international conferences. In addition, he has completed a 6-month research stay at the *Aeronautical Technology Center* and a 3-month research stay at the University of Laval in Quebec.

Arun Ponnusamy, works as a computer vision research engineer at an AI start-up in India. He is a lifelong learner, passionate about image processing, computer vision, and machine learning. He is an engineering graduate from PSG College of Technology, Coimbatore. He started his career at MulticoreWare Inc., where he spent most of his time on image processing, OpenCV, software optimization, and GPU computing.

Arun loves to understand computer vision concepts clearly and explain them in an intuitive way in his blog and in meetups. He has created an open source Python library for computer vision, named cvlib, which is aimed at simplicity and user friendliness. He is currently working on object detection, action recognition, and generative networks.

Packt is searching for authors like you

Table of Contents

Section 3: Machine Learning and Deep Learning in OpenCV

Preface

In a nutshell, this book is about computer vision using OpenCV, which is a computer vision (and also machine learning) library, and the Python programming language. You may be wondering why OpenCV and Python? That is really a good question, which we address in the first chapter of this book. To summarize, OpenCV is the best open source computer vision library (BSD license—it is free for both academic and commercial use), offering more than 2,500 optimized algorithms, including state-of-the-art computer vision algorithms, and it also has machine learning and deep learning support. OpenCV is written in optimized C/C++, but it provides Python wrappers. Therefore, this library can be used in your Python programs. In this sense, Python is considered the ideal language for scientific computing because it stimulates rapid prototyping and has a lot of prebuilt libraries for every aspect of your computer vision projects.

As introduced in the previous paragraph, there are many prebuilt libraries you can use in your projects. Indeed, in this book, we use lots of them, showing you that it's really easy to install and use new libraries. Libraries such as Matplotlib, scikit-image, SciPy, dlib, face-recognition, Pillow, cvlib, Keras, TensorFlow, and Flask will be used in this book to show you the potential of the Python ecosystem. If this is the first time that you're reading about these libraries, don't worry, because we introduce *hello world* examples for almost all of these libraries.

This book is a complete resource for creating advanced applications with Python and OpenCV using various techniques, such as facial recognition, target tracking, augmented reality, object detection, and classification, among others. In addition, this book explores the potential of machine learning and deep learning techniques in computer vision applications using the Python ecosystem.

It's time to dive deeper into the content of this book. We are going to introduce you to what this book covers, including a short paragraph talking about each chapter of the book. So, let's get started!

Who this book is for

This book is great for students, researchers, and developers with basic Python programming knowledge who are new to computer vision and who would like to dive deeper into this world. It's assumed that readers have some previous experience with Python. A basic understanding of image data (for example, pixels and color channels) would also be helpful, but is not necessary, because these concepts are covered in the book. Finally, standard mathematical skills are required.

What this book covers

Chapter 1, *Setting Up OpenCV*, shows how to install everything you need to start programming with Python and OpenCV. You'll also be introduced to general terminology and concepts to contextualize what you will learn, establishing and setting the bases in relation to the main concepts of computer vision using OpenCV.

Chapter 2, *Image Basics in OpenCV*, demonstrates how to start writing your first scripts, in order to introduce you to the OpenCV library.

Chapter 3, *Handling Files and Images*, shows you how to cope with files and images, which are necessary for building your computer vision applications.

Chapter 4, *Constructing Basic Shapes in OpenCV*, covers how to draw shapes—from basic ones to some that are more advanced—using the OpenCV library.

Chapter 5, *Image Processing Techniques*, introduces most of the common image processing techniques you will need for your computer vision projects.

Chapter 6, *Constructing and Building Histograms*, shows how to both create and understand histograms, which are a powerful tool for understanding image content.

Chapter 7, *Thresholding Techniques*, introduces the main thresholding techniques you will need for your computer vision applications as a key process of image segmentation.

Chapter 8, *Contour Detection, Filtering, and Drawing*, shows how to deal with contours, which are used for shape analysis and for both object detection and recognition.

Chapter 9, *Augmented Reality*, teaches you how to build your first augmented reality application.

Chapter 10, *Machine Learning with OpenCV*, introduces you to the world of machine learning. You will see how machine learning can be used in your computer vision projects.

Chapter 11, *Face Detection, Tracking, and Recognition*, demonstrates how to create face processing projects using state-of-the-art algorithms, in connection with face detection, tracking, and recognition.

Chapter 12, *Introduction to Deep Learning*, introduces you to the world of deep learning with OpenCV and also some deep learning Python libraries (TensorFlow and Keras).

Chapter 13, *Mobile and Web Computer Vision with Python and OpenCV*, shows how to create computer vision and deep learning web applications using Flask.

To get the most out of this book

With the aim of making the most of this book, you have to take into account two simple but key considerations:

1. Some basic knowledge of Python programming is assumed as all the scripts and examples in this book are in Python.
2. The NumPy and OpenCV-Python packages are highly interconnected (you will learn why in this book). In spite of NumPy examples being fully explained, the learning curve can be softened if some NumPy knowledge is acquired before starting this book.

Download the example code files

You can download the example code files for this book from your account at www.packt.com. If you purchased this book elsewhere, you can visit www.packt.com/support and register to have the files emailed directly to you.

You can download the code files by following these steps:

1. Log in or register at www.packt.com.
2. Select the **SUPPORT** tab.
3. Click on **Code Downloads & Errata**.
4. Enter the name of the book in the **Search** box and follow the onscreen instructions.

Once the file is downloaded, please make sure that you unzip or extract the folder using the latest version of:

- WinRAR/7-Zip for Windows
- Zipeg/iZip/UnRarX for Mac
- 7-Zip/PeaZip for Linux

The code bundle for the book is also hosted on GitHub at `https://github.com/PacktPublishing/Mastering-OpenCV-4-with-Python`. In case there's an update to the code, it will be updated on the existing GitHub repository.

We also have other code bundles from our rich catalog of books and videos available at `https://github.com/PacktPublishing/`. Check them out!

Download the color images

We also provide a PDF file that has color images of the screenshots/diagrams used in this book. You can download it here: `https://www.packtpub.com/sites/default/files/downloads/9781789344912_Color Images.pdf`.

Conventions used

There are a number of text conventions used throughout this book.

`CodeInText`: Indicates code words in text, database table names, folder names, filenames, file extensions, pathnames, dummy URLs, user input, and Twitter handles. Here is an example: "The code for `build_sample_image()` is provided next."

A block of code is set as follows:

```
channels = cv2.split(img)
    eq_channels = []
    for ch in channels:
        eq_channels.append(cv2.equalizeHist(ch))
```

When we wish to draw your attention to a particular part of a code block, the relevant lines or items are set in bold:

```
Hu moments (original): '[ 1.92801772e-01 1.01173781e-02 5.70258405e-05
1.96536742e-06 2.46949980e-12 -1.88337981e-07 2.06595472e-11]'
 Hu moments (rotation): '[ 1.92801772e-01 1.01173781e-02 5.70258405e-05
1.96536742e-06 2.46949980e-12 -1.88337981e-07 2.06595472e-11]'
 Hu moments (reflection): '[ 1.92801772e-01 1.01173781e-02 5.70258405e-05
1.96536742e-06 2.46949980e-12 -1.88337981e-07 -2.06595472e-11]'
```

Any command-line input or output is written as follows:

```
$ mkdir opencv-project
$ cd opencv-project
```

Bold: Indicates a new term, an important word, or words that you see on screen. For example, words in menus or dialog boxes appear in the text like this. Here is an example: "Select **System info** from the **Administration** panel."

 Warnings or important notes appear like this.

 Tips and tricks appear like this.

Get in touch

Feedback from our readers is always welcome.

General feedback: If you have questions about any aspect of this book, mention the book title in the subject of your message and email us at customercare@packtpub.com.

Errata: Although we have taken every care to ensure the accuracy of our content, mistakes do happen. If you have found a mistake in this book, we would be grateful if you would report this to us. Please visit www.packt.com/submit-errata, selecting your book, clicking on the Errata Submission Form link, and entering the details.

Piracy: If you come across any illegal copies of our works in any form on the internet, we would be grateful if you would provide us with the location address or website name. Please contact us at copyright@packt.com with a link to the material.

If you are interested in becoming an author: If there is a topic that you have expertise in, and you are interested in either writing or contributing to a book, please visit `authors.packtpub.com`.

Reviews

Please leave a review. Once you have read and used this book, why not leave a review on the site that you purchased it from? Potential readers can then see and use your unbiased opinion to make purchase decisions, we at Packt can understand what you think about our products, and our authors can see your feedback on their book. Thank you!

For more information about Packt, please visit `packt.com`.

Section 1: Introduction to OpenCV 4 and Python

In this first section of the book, you will be introduced to the OpenCV library. You will learn how to install everything you need to start programming with Python and OpenCV. Also, you will familiarize yourself with the general terminology and concepts to contextualize what you will learn, establishing the foundations you will need in order to grasp the main concepts of this book. Additionally, you will start writing your first scripts in order to get to grips with the OpenCV library, and you will also learn how to work with files and images, which are necessary for building your computer vision applications. Finally, you will see how to draw basic and advanced shapes using the OpenCV library.

The following chapters will be covered in this section:

- Chapter 1, *Setting Up OpenCV*
- Chapter 2, *Image Basics in OpenCV*
- Chapter 3, *Handling Files and Images*
- Chapter 4, *Constructing Basic Shapes in OpenCV*

Setting Up OpenCV

1

Mastering OpenCV 4 with Python will give you the knowledge to build projects involving **Open Source Computer Vision Library** (**OpenCV**) and Python. These two *technologies* (the first one is a programming language, while the second one is a computer vision and machine learning library) will be introduced. Also, you will learn why the combination of OpenCV and Python has the potential to build every kind of computer application. Finally, an introduction about the main concepts related to the content of this book will be provided.

In this chapter, you will be given step-by-step instructions to install everything you need to start programming with Python and OpenCV. This first chapter is quite long, but do not worry, because it is divided into easily assimilated sections, starting with general terminology and concepts, which assumes that the reader is new to this information. At the end of this chapter, you will be able to build your first project involving Python and OpenCV.

The following topics will be covered in this chapter:

- A theoretical introduction to the OpenCV library
- Installing Python OpenCV and other packages
- Running samples, documentation, help, and updates
- Python and OpenCV project structure
- First Python and OpenCV project

Technical requirements

This chapter and subsequent chapters are focused on Python (a programming language) and OpenCV (a computer vision library) concepts in connection with computer vision, machine learning, and deep learning techniques (among others). Therefore, Python (https://www.python.org/) and OpenCV (https://opencv.org/) should be installed on your computer. Moreover, some Python packages related to scientific computing and data science should also be installed (for example, NumPy (http://www.numpy.org/) or Matplotlib (https://matplotlib.org/)).

Additionally, it is recommended that you install an **integrated development environment** (**IDE**) software package because it facilitates computer programmers with software development. In this sense, a Python-specific IDE is recommended. The *de facto* Python IDE is PyCharm, which can be downloaded from https://www.jetbrains.com/pycharm/.

Finally, in order to facilitate GitHub activities (for example, cloning a repository), you should install a Git client. In this sense, GitHub provides desktop clients that include the most common repository actions. For an introduction to Git commands, check out https://education.github.com/git-cheat-sheet-education.pdf, where commonly used Git command-line instructions are summarized. Additionally, instructions for installing a Git client on your operating system are included.

The GitHub repository for this book, which contains all the supporting project files necessary to work through the book from the first chapter to the last, can be accessed at https://github.com/PacktPublishing/Mastering-OpenCV-4-with-Python.

Finally, it should be noted that the README file of the GitHub repository for Mastering OpenCV with Python includes the following, which is also attached here for the sake of completeness:

- Code testing specifications
- Hardware specifications
- Related books and products

Code testing specifications

Mastering OpenCV 4 with Python requires some installed packages, which you can see here:

- Chapter 1, *Setting Up OpenCV*: opencv-contrib-python
- Chapter 2, *Image Basics in OpenCV*: opencv-contrib-python and matplotlib

- Chapter 3, *Handling Files and Images*: `opencv-contrib-python` and `matplotlib`
- Chapter 4, *Constructing Basic Shapes in OpenCV*: `opencv-contrib-python` and `matplotlib`
- Chapter 5, *Image Processing Techniques*: `opencv-contrib-python` and `matplotlib`
- Chapter 6, *Constructing and Building Histograms*: `opencv-contrib-python` and `matplotlib`
- Chapter 7, *Thresholding Techniques*: `opencv-contrib-python`, `matplotlib`, `scikit-image`, and `scipy`
- Chapter 8, *Contours Detection, Filtering, and Drawing*: `opencv-contrib-python` and `matplotlib`
- Chapter 9, *Augmented Reality*: `opencv-contrib-python` and `matplotlib`
- Chapter 10, *Machine Learning with OpenCV*: `opencv-contrib-python` and `matplotlib`
- Chapter 11, *Face Detection, Tracking, and Recognition*: `opencv-contrib-python`, `matplotlib`, `dlib`, `face-recognition`, `cvlib`, `requests`, `progressbar`, `keras`, and `tensorflow`
- Chapter 12, *Introduction to Deep Learning*: `opencv-contrib-python`, `matplotlib`, `tensorflow`, and `keras`
- Chapter 13, *Mobile and Web Computer Vision with Python and OpenCV*: `opencv-contrib-python`, `matplotlib`, `flask`, `tensorflow`, `keras`, `requests`, and `pillow`

 Make sure that the version numbers of your installed packages are equal to, or greater than, versions specified here to ensure that the code examples run correctly.

If you want to install the exact versions this book was tested on, include the version when installing from `pip`, which is indicated as follows.

Run the following command to install the both main and contrib modules:

- Install `opencv-contrib-python`:

```
pip install opencv-contrib-python==4.0.0.21
```

It should be noted that OpenCV requires `numpy`. `numpy-1.16.1` has been installed when installing `opencv-contrib-python==4.0.0.21`.

Run the following command to install Matplotlib library:

- Install `matplotlib`:

```
pip install matplotlib==3.0.2
```

It should be noted that `matplotlib` requires `kiwisolver, pyparsing, six, cycler,` and `python-dateutil`.

`cycler-0.10.0, kiwisolver-1.0.1, pyparsing-2.3.1, python-dateutil-2.8.0,` and `six-1.12.0` have been installed when installing `matplotlib==3.0.2`.

Run the following command to install library which contains collections of algorithm for image processing:

- Install `scikit-image`:

```
pip install scikit-image==0.14.2
```

It should be noted that `scikit-image` requires `cloudpickle, decorator, networkx, numpy, toolz, dask, pillow, PyWavelets,` and `six`.

`PyWavelets-1.0.1, cloudpickle-0.8.0, dask-1.1.1, decorator-4.3.2, networkx-2.2, numpy-1.16.1, pillow-5.4.1, six-1.12.0,` and `toolz-0.9.0` have been installed when installing `scikit-image==0.14.2`.

If you need SciPy, you can install it with the following command:

- Install `scipy`:

```
pip install scipy==1.2.1
```

It should be noted that `scipy` requires `numpy`.

`numpy-1.16.1` has been installed when installing `scipy==1.2.1`.

Run the following command to install `dlib` library:

- Install `dlib`:

```
pip install dlib==19.8.1
```

To install the face recognition library, run the following command:

- Install `face-recognition`:

```
pip install face-recognition==1.2.3
```

It should be noted that `face-recognition` requires `dlib`, `Click`, `numpy`, `face-recognition-models`, and `pillow`.

`dlib-19.8.1`, `Click-7.0`, `face-recognition-models-0.3.0`, and `pillow-5.4.1` have been installed when installing `face-recognition==1.2.3`.

Run the following command to install open source computer vision library:

- Install `cvlib`:

```
pip install cvlib==0.1.8
```

To install requests library run the following command:

- Install `requests`:

```
pip install requests==2.21.0
```

It should be noted that `requests` requires `urllib3`, `chardet`, `certifi`, and `idna`.

`urllib3-1.24.1`, `chardet-3.0.4`, `certifi-2018.11.29`, and `idna-2.8` have been installed when installing `requests==2.21.0`.

Run the following command to install text progress bar library:

- Install `progressbar`:

```
pip install progressbar==2.5
```

Run the following command to install Keras library for deep learning:

- Install `keras`:

```
pip install keras==2.2.4
```

It should be noted that `keras` requires `numpy`, `six`, `h5py`, `keras-applications`, `scipy`, `keras-preprocessing`, and `pyyaml`.

h5py-2.9.0, keras-applications-1.0.7, keras-preprocessing-1.0.9, numpy-1.16.1 pyyaml-3.13, and scipy-1.2.1 six-1.12.0 have been installed when installing keras==2.2.4.

Run the following command to install TensorFlow library:

- Install tensorflow:

```
pip install tensorflow==1.12.0
```

It should be noted that TensorFlow requires termcolor, numpy, wheel, gast, six, setuptools, protobuf, markdown, grpcio, werkzeug, tensorboard, absl-py, h5py, keras-applications, keras-preprocessing, and astor.

termcolor-1.1.0, numpy-1.16.1, wheel-0.33.1, gast-0.2.2, six-1.12.0, setuptools-40.8.0, protobuf-3.6.1, markdown-3.0.1, grpcio-1.18.0, werkzeug-0.14.1, tensorboard-1.12.2, absl-py-0.7.0, h5py-2.9.0, keras-applications-1.0.7, keras-preprocessing-1.0.9, and astor-0.7.1 have been installed when installing tensorflow==1.12.0.

Run the following command to install Flask library:

- Install flask:

```
pip install flask==1.0.2
```

It should be noted that flask requires Werkzeug, click, itsdangerous, and MarkupSafe Jinja2.

Jinja2-2.10, MarkupSafe-1.1.1, Werkzeug-0.14.1, click-7.0, and itsdangerous-1.1.0 have been installed when installing flask==1.0.2.

Hardware specifications

The hardware specifications are as follows:

- 32-bit or 64-bit architecture
- 2+ GHz CPU
- 4 GB RAM
- At least 10 GB of hard disk space available

Understanding Python

Python is an interpreted high-level and general-purpose programming language with a dynamic type system and automatic memory management. The official home of the Python programming language is `https://www.python.org/`. The popularity of Python has risen steadily over the past decade. This is because Python is a very important programming language in some of today's most exciting and challenging technologies. **Artificial intelligence** (**AI**), machine learning, neural networks, deep learning, **Internet of Things** (**IoT**), and robotics (among others) rely on Python.

Here are some advantages of Python:

- Python is considered a perfect language for scientific computing, mainly for four reasons:
    - It is very easy to understand.
    - It has support (via packages) for scientific computing.
    - It removes many of the complexities other programming languages have.
    - It has a simple and consistent syntax.
- Python stimulates rapid prototyping because it helps in easy writing and execution of code. Indeed, Python can implement the same logic with as little as one-fifth of the code as compared to other programming languages.
- Python has a lot of prebuilt libraries (NumPy, SciPy, scikit-learn) for every need of your AI project. Python benefits from a rich ecosystem of libraries for scientific computing.
- It is an independent platform, which allows developers to save time in testing on different platforms.
- Python offers some tools, such as Jupyter Notebook, that can be used to share scripts in an easy and comfortable way. This is perfect in scientific computing because it stimulates collaboration in an interactive computational environment.

Introducing OpenCV

OpenCV is a C++ programming library, with real-time capabilities. As it is written in optimized C/C++, the library can profit from multi-core processing. A theoretical introduction about the OpenCV library is carried out in the next section.

In connection with the OpenCV library, here are some reasons for its popularity:

- Open source computer vision library
- OpenCV (BSD license—https://en.wikipedia.org/wiki/BSD_licenses) is free
- Specific library for image processing
- It has more than 2,500 optimized algorithms, including state-of-the-art computer vision algorithms
- Machine learning and deep learning support
- The library is optimized for performance
- There is a big community of developers using and supporting OpenCV
- It has C++, Python, Java, and MATLAB interfaces
- The library supports Windows, Linux, Android, and macOS
- Fast and regular updates (official releases now occur every six months)

Contextualizing the reader

In order to contextualize the reader, it is necessary to establish and set the bases in relation to the main concepts concerning the theme of this book. The last few years have seen considerable interest in AI and machine learning, specifically in the area of deep learning. These terms are used interchangeably and very often confused with each other. For the sake of completeness and clarification, these terms are briefly described next.

AI refers to a set of technologies that enable machines – computers or robotic systems – to process information in the same way humans would.

The term AI is commonly used as an umbrella for a machine technology in order to provide intelligence covering a wide range of methods and algorithms. **Machine Learning** is the process of programming computers to learn from historical data to make predictions on new data. Machine learning is a sub-discipline of AI and refers to statistical techniques that machines use on the basis of learned interrelationships. On the basis of data gathered or collected, algorithms are independently *learned* by computers. These algorithms and methods include support vector machine, decision tree, random forest, logistic regression, Bayesian networks, and neural networks.

Neural Networks are computer models for machine learning that are based on the structure and functioning of the biological brain. An artificial neuron processes a plurality of input signals and, in turn, when the sum of the input signals exceeds a certain threshold value, signals to further adjacent neurons will be sent. **Deep Learning** is a subset of machine learning that operates on large volumes of unstructured data, such as human speech, text, and images. A deep learning model is an artificial neural network that comprises multiple layers of mathematical computation on data, where results from one layer are fed as input into the next layer in order to classify the input data and/or make a prediction.

Therefore, these concepts are interdependent in a hierarchical way, AI being the broadest term and deep learning the most specific. This structure can be seen in the next diagram:

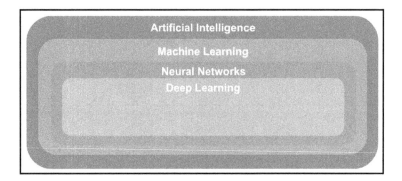

Computer vision is an interdisciplinary field of **Artificial Intelligence** that aims to give computers and other devices with computing capabilities a high-level understanding from both digital images and videos, including functionality for acquiring, processing, and analyzing digital images. This is why computer vision is, partly, another sub-area of **Artificial Intelligence**, heavily relying on machine learning and deep learning algorithms to build computer vision applications. Additionally, **Computer vision** is composed of several technologies working together—**Computer graphics**, **Image processing**, **Signal processing**, **Sensor technology**, **Mathematics**, or even **Physics**.

Therefore, the previous diagram can be completed to introduce the computer vision discipline:

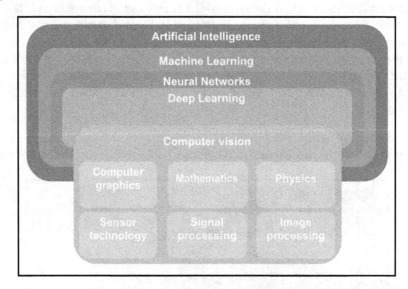

A theoretical introduction to the OpenCV library

OpenCV is a programming library with real-time computer vision capabilities and it is free for both academic and commercial use (BSD license). In this section, an introduction about the OpenCV library will be given, including its main modules and other useful information in connection with the library.

OpenCV modules

OpenCV (since version 2) is divided into several modules, where each module can be understood, in general, as being dedicated to one group of computer vision problems. This division can be seen in the next diagram, where the main modules are shown:

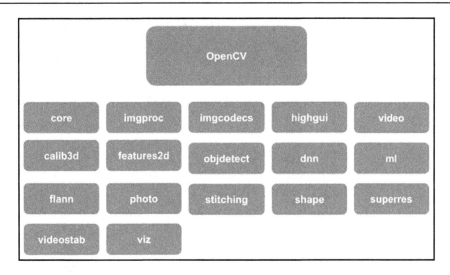

OpenCV modules are shortly described here:

- **core**: Core functionality. Core functionality is a module defining basic data structures and also basic functions used by all other modules in the library.
- **imgproc**: Image processing. An image-processing module that includes image filtering, geometrical image transformations, color space conversion, and histograms.
- **imgcodecs**: Image codecs. Image file reading and writing.
- **videoio**: Video I/O. An interface to video capturing and video codecs.
- **highgui**: High-level GUI. An interface to UI capabilities. It provides an interface to easily do the following:
    - Create and manipulate windows that can display/show images
    - Add trackbars to the windows, keyboard commands, and handle mouse events
- **video**: Video analysis. A video-analysis module including background subtraction, motion estimation, and object-tracking algorithms.
- **calib3d**: Camera calibration and 3D reconstruction. Camera calibration and 3D reconstruction covering basic multiple-view geometry algorithms, stereo correspondence algorithms, object pose estimation, both single and stereo camera calibration, and also 3D reconstruction.

- **features2d**: 2D features framework. This module includes feature detectors, descriptors, and descriptor matchers.
- **objdetect**: Object detection. Detection of objects and instances of predefined classes (for example, faces, eyes, people, and cars).
- **dnn**: **Deep neural network** (**DNN**) module. This module contains the following:
    - API for new layers creation
    - Set of built useful layers
    - API to construct and modify neural networks from layers
    - Functionality for loading serialized networks models from different deep learning frameworks
- **ml**: Machine learning. The **Machine Learning Library** (**MLL**) is a set of classes and methods that can be used for classification, regression, and clustering purposes.
- **flann**: Clustering and search in multi-dimensional spaces. **Fast Library for Approximate Nearest Neighbors** (**FLANN**) is a collection of algorithms that are highly suited for fast nearest-neighbor searches.
- **photo**: Computational photography. This module provides some functions for computational photography.
- **stitching**: Images stitching. This module implements a stitching pipeline that performs automatic panoramic image stitching.
- **shape**: Shape distance and matching. Shape distance and matching module that can be used for shape matching, retrieval, or comparison.
- **superres**: Super-resolution. This module contains a set of classes and methods that can be used for resolution enhancement.
- **videostab**: Video stabilization. This module contains a set of classes and methods for video stabilization.
- **viz**: 3D visualizer. This module is used to display widgets that provide several methods to interact with scenes and widgets.

OpenCV users

Regardless of whether you are a professional software developer or a novice programmer, the OpenCV library will be interesting for graduate students, researchers, and computer programmers in image-processing and computer vision areas. The library has gained popularity among scientists and academics because many state-of-the-art computer vision algorithms are provided by this library.

Additionally, it is often used as a teaching tool for both computer vision and machine learning. It should be taken into account that OpenCV is robust enough to support real-world applications. That is why OpenCV can be used for non-commercial and commercial products. For example, it is used by companies such as Google, Microsoft, Intel, IBM, Sony, and Honda. Research institutes in leading universities, such as MIT, CMU, or Stanford, provide support for the library. OpenCV has been adopted all around the world. It has more than 14 million downloads and more than 47,000 people in its community.

OpenCV applications

OpenCV is being used for a very wide range of applications:

- 2D and 3D feature toolkits
- Street view image stitching
- Egomotion estimation
- Facial-recognition system
- Gesture recognition
- Human-computer interaction
- Mobile robotics
- Motion understanding
- Object identification
- Automated inspection and surveillance
- Segmentation and recognition
- Stereopsis stereo vision – depth perception from two cameras
- Medical image analysis
- Structure from motion
- Motion tracking
- Augmented reality
- Video/image search and retrieval
- Robot and driverless car navigation and control
- Driver drowsiness and distraction detection

Why citing OpenCV in your research work

If you are using OpenCV in your research, it is recommended you cite the OpenCV library. This way, other researchers can better understand your proposed algorithms and reproduce your results for better credibility. Additionally, OpenCV will increase repercussion, resulting in a better computer vision library. The BibTex entry for citing OpenCV is shown in the following code:

```
@article{opencv_library,
  author = {Bradski, G.},
  citeulike-article-id = {2236121},
  journal = {Dr. Dobb's Journal of Software Tools},
  keywords = {bibtex-import},
  posted-at = {2008-01-15 19:21:54},
  priority = {4},
  title = {{The OpenCV Library}},
  year = {2000}
}
```

Installing OpenCV, Python, and other packages

OpenCV, Python, and AI-related packages can be installed on most operating systems. We will see how to install these packages by means of different approaches.

 Make sure you check out the different installation options before choosing the one that best suits your needs.

Additionally, at the end of this chapter, an introduction to Jupyter Notebook is given due to the popularity of these documents, which can be run to perform data analysis.

Installing Python, OpenCV, and other packages globally

In this section, you will see how to install Python, OpenCV, and any other package globally. Specific instructions are given for both Linux and Windows operating systems.

Installing Python

We are going to see how to install Python globally on both the Linux and Windows operating systems.

Installing Python on Linux

On Debian derivatives such as Ubuntu, use APT to install Python. Afterwards, it is recommended to upgrade the pip version. pip (https://pip.pypa.io/en/stable/) is the PyPA (https://packaging.python.org/guides/tool-recommendations/) recommended tool for installing Python packages:

```
$ sudo apt-get install python3.7

$ sudo pip install --upgrade pip
```

To verify that Python has been installed correctly, open a Command Prompt or shell and run the following command:

```
$ python3 --version
 Python 3.7.0
```

Installing Python on Windows

Go to https://www.python.org/downloads/. The default Python Windows installer is 32 bits. Start the installer. Select **Customize installation**:

On the next screen, all the optional features should be checked:

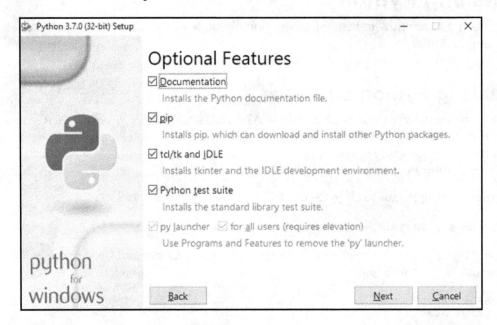

Finally, on the next screen, make sure to check **Add Python to environment variables** and **Precompile standard library**. Optionally, you can customize the location of the installation, for example, C:\Python37:

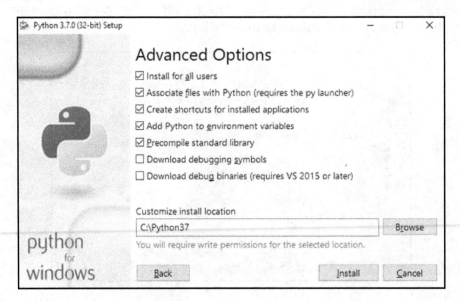

Press the **Install** button and, in a few minutes, the installation should be ready. On the last page of the installer, you should also press **Disable path length limit**:

To check whether Python has been installed properly, press and hold the *Shift* key and right-click with your mouse somewhere on your desktop. Select **Open command window here**. Alternatively, on Windows 10, use the lower-left search box to search for cmd. Now, write python in the command window and press the *Enter* key. You should see something like this:

You should also upgrade pip:

```
$ python -m pip install --upgrade pip
```

Installing OpenCV

Now, we are going to install OpenCV on both the Linux and Windows operating systems. First, we are going to see how to install OpenCV on Linux, and then how to install OpenCV on Windows.

Installing OpenCV on Linux

Ensure you have installed NumPy. To install NumPy, enter the following:

```
$ pip3 install numpy
```

Then install OpenCV:

```
$ pip3 install opencv-contrib-python
```

Additionally, we can install Matplotlib, which is a Python plotting library that produces quality figures:

```
$ pip3 install matplotlib
```

Installing OpenCV on Windows

Ensure you have installed NumPy. To install NumPy, enter the following:
```
$ pip install numpy
```

Then install OpenCV:

```
$ pip install opencv-contrib-python
```

Additionally, we can install Matplotlib:

```
$ pip install matplotlib
```

Testing the installation

One way to test the installation is to execute an OpenCV Python script. In order to do it, you should have two files, `logo.png` and `test_opencv_installation.py`, in a specific folder:

Open a cmd and go to the path where these two files are. Next, we can check the installation by typing the following:

```
python test_opencv_installation.py
```

You should see both the OpenCV RGB logo and the OpenCV grayscale logo:

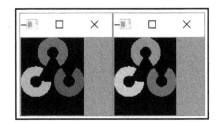

In that case, the installation has been successful.

Installing Python, OpenCV, and other packages with virtualenv

virtualenv (https://pypi.org/project/virtualenv/) is a very popular tool that creates isolated Python environments for Python libraries. virtualenv allows multiple Python projects that have different (and sometimes conflicting) requirements. In a technical way, virtualenv works by installing some files under a directory (for example, env/).

Additionally, `virtualenv` modifies the PATH environment variable to prefix it with a custom bin directory (for example, `env/bin/`). Additionally, an exact copy of the Python or Python3 binary is placed in this directory. Once this virtual environment is activated, you can install packages in the virtual environment using pip. `virtualenv` is also recommended by the PyPA (`https://packaging.python.org/guides/tool-recommendations/`). Therefore, we will see how to install OpenCV or any other packages using virtual environments.

Usually, pip and `virtualenv` are the only two packages you need to install globally. This is because, once you have installed both packages, you can do all your work inside a virtual environment. In fact, `virtualenv` is really all you need, because this package provides a copy of pip, which gets copied into every new environment you create.

Now, we will see how to install, activate, use, and deactivate virtual environments. Specific commands are given now for both Linux and Windows operating systems. We are not going to add a specific section for each of the operating systems, because the process is very similar in each one. Let's start installing `virtualenv`:

```
$ pip install virtualenv
```

Inside this directory (`env`), some files and folders are created with all you need to run your python applications. For example, the new python executable will be located at `/env/scripts/python.exe`. The next step is to create a new virtual environment. First, change the directory into the root of the project directory. The second step is to use the `virtualenv` command-line tool to create the environment:

```
$ virtualenv env
```

Here, `env` is the name of the directory you want to create your virtual environment inside. It is a common convention to call the directory you want to create your virtual environment inside `env`, and to put it inside your project directory. This way, if you keep your code at `~/code/myproject/`, the environment will be at `~/code/myproject/env/`.

The next step is to activate the `env` environment that you have just created using the command-line tool to execute the `activate` script, which is in the following location:

- `~/code/myprojectname/env/bin/activate` (Linux)
- `~/code/myprojectname/env/Scripts/activate` (Windows)

For example, under Windows, you should type the following:

```
$ ~/code/myprojectname/env/Scripts/activate
(env) $
```

Now you can install the required packages only for this activated environment. For example, if you want to install Django, which is a free and open source web framework, written in Python, you should type this:

```
(env)$ pip install Django
```

 Remember that this package will only be installed for the myprojectname project.

You can also deactivate the environment by executing the following:

```
$ deactivate
$
```

You should see that you have returned to your normal prompt, indicating that you are no longer in any virtualenv. Finally, if you want to delete your environment, just type the following:

```
$ rmvirtualenv test
```

Python IDEs to create virtual environments with virtualenv

In the next section, we are going to create virtual environments with PyCharm, which is a Python IDE. But before doing that, we are going to discuss IDEs. An IDE is a software application that facilitates computer programmers with software development. IDEs present a single program where all the development is done. In connection with Python IDEs, two approaches can be found:

- General editors and IDEs with Python support
- Python-specific editors and IDEs

In the first category (general IDEs), some examples should be highlighted:

- Eclipse + PyDev
- Visual Studio + Python Tools for Visual Studio
- Atom + Python extension

In the second category, here are some Python-specific IDEs:

- **PyCharm**: One of the best full-featured, dedicated IDEs for Python. PyCharm installs quickly and easily on Windows, macOS, and Linux platforms. It is the *de facto* Python IDE environment.
- **Spyder**: Spyder, which comes with the Anaconda package manager distribution, is an open source Python IDE that is highly suited for data science workflows.
- **Thonny**: Thonny is intended to be an IDE for beginners. It is available for all major platforms (Windows, macOS, Linux), with installation instructions on the site.

In this case, we are going to install PyCharm (the *de facto* Python IDE environment) Community Edition. Afterwards, we are going to see how to create virtual environments using this IDE. PyCharm can be downloaded from `https://www.jetbrains.com/pycharm/`. PyCharm can be installed on Windows, macOS, and Linux:

After the installation of PyCharm, we are ready to use it. Using PyCharm, we can create virtual environments in a very simple and intuitive way.

PyCharm makes it possible to use the `virtualenv` tool to create a project-specific isolated virtual environment. Additionally, the `virtualenv` tool comes bundled with PyCharm, so the user does not need to install it.

After opening Pycharm, you can click **Create New Project**. If you want to create a new environment, you should click on **Project Interpreter: New Virtualenv environment**. Then click on **New environment using Virtualenv**. This can be seen in the next screenshot:

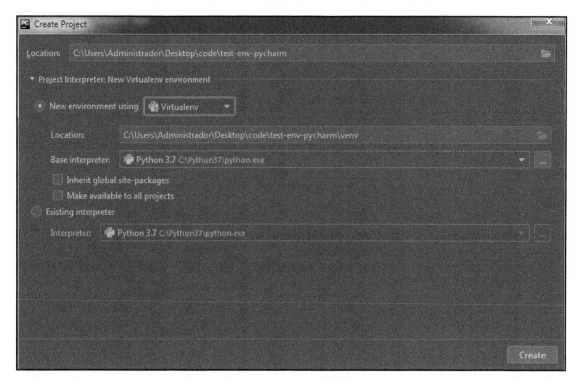

You should note that the virtual environment is named (by default in PyCharm) venv and located under the project folder. In this case, the project is named test-env-pycharm and the virtual environment, venv, is located at test-env-pycharm/venv. Additionally, you can see that the venv name can be changed according to your preferences.

When you click on the **Create** button, PyCharm loads the project and creates the virtual environment. You should see something like this:

After the project is created, you are ready to install a package with just a few clicks. Click on **File**, then click on **Settings...** (*Ctrl + Alt + S*). A new window will appear, showing something like this:

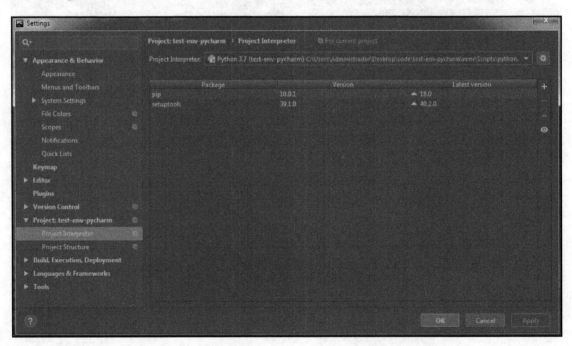

Now, click on **Project:** and select **Project Interpreter**. On the right-hand side of this screen, the installed packages are shown in connection with the selected **Project Interpreter**. You can change it on top of this screen. After selecting the appropriate interpreter (and, hence, the environment for your project), you can install a new package. To do so, you can search in the upper-left input box. In the next screenshot, you can see an example of searching for the numpy package:

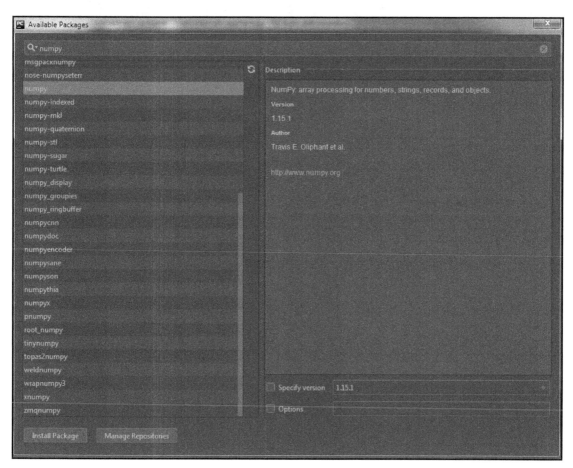

You can install the package (latest version by default) by clicking on **Install Package**. You can also specify a concrete version, as can be seen in the previous screenshot:

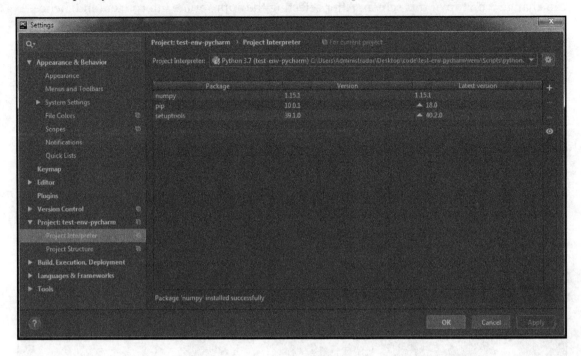

After the installation of this package, we can see that we now have three installed packages on our virtual environment. Additionally, it is very easy to change between environments. You should go to **Run/Debug Configurations** and click on **Python interpreter** to change between environments. This feature can be seen in the next screenshot:

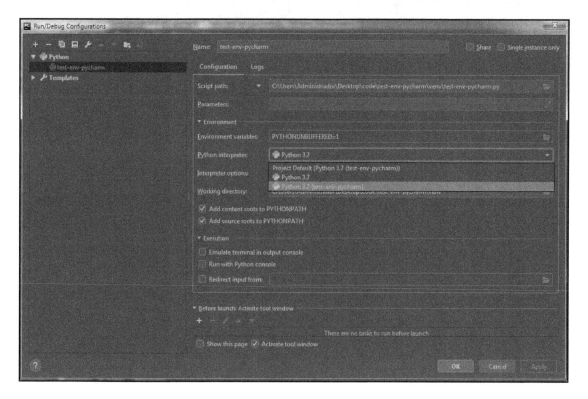

Finally, you may have noticed that, in the first step, of creating a virtual environment with PyCharm, options other than `virtualenv` are possible. PyCharm gives you the ability to create virtual environments using **Virtualenv**, **Pipenv**, and **Conda**:

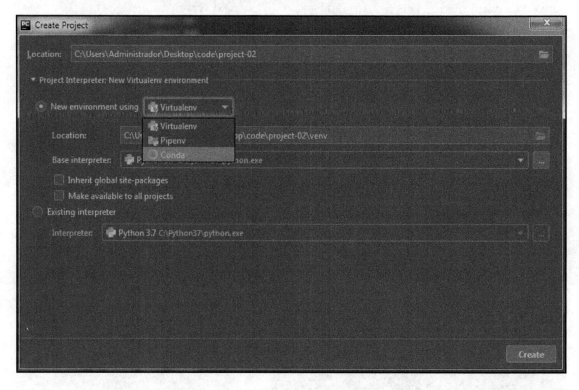

We previously introduced **Virtualenv** and how to work with this tool for creating isolated Python environments for Python libraries.

Pyenv (`https://github.com/pyenv/pyenv`) is used to isolate Python versions. For example, you may want to test your code against Python 2.6, 2.7, 3.3, 3.4, and 3.5, so you will need a way to switch between them.

Conda (`https://conda.io/docs/`) is an open source package management and environment management system (provides virtual environment capabilities) that runs on Windows, macOS, and Linux. Conda is included in all versions of Anaconda and Miniconda.

Since working with Anaconda/Miniconda and Conda may be of interest to readers, a quick introduction is given in the next subsection, but it is not necessary to run the code examples included in this book.

Anaconda/Miniconda distributions and conda package–and environment-management system

Conda (`https://conda.io/docs/`) is an open source package-management and environment-management system (provides virtual environment capabilities) that runs on many operating systems (for example, Windows, macOS, and Linux). Conda installs, runs, and updates packages and their dependencies. Conda can create, save, load, and switch between environments.

As conda is included in all versions of Anaconda and Miniconda, you should have already installed Anaconda or Miniconda.

Anaconda is a downloadable, free, open source, high-performance Python and R distribution. Anaconda comes with conda, conda build, Python, and more than 100 open source scientific packages and their dependencies. Using the conda install command, you can easily install popular open source packages for data science from the Anaconda repository. Miniconda is a small version of Anaconda, which includes only conda, Python, the packages they depend on, and a small number of other useful packages.

Installing Anaconda or Miniconda is easy. For the sake of simplicity, we are focusing on Anaconda. To install Anaconda, check the Acadonda installer for your operating system (https://www.anaconda.com/download/). Anaconda 5.2 can be installed in both Python 3.6 and Python 2.7 versions on Windows, macOS, and Linux:

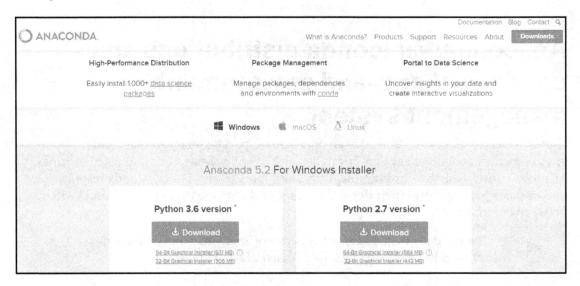

After you have finished installing, in order to test the installation, in Terminal or Anaconda Prompt, run the following command:

```
$ conda list
```

For a successful installation, a list of installed packages appears. As mentioned, Anaconda (and Miniconda) comes with conda, which is a simple package manager similar to apt-get on Linux. In this way, we can install new packages in Terminal using the following command:

```
$ conda install packagename
```

Here, packagename is the actual name of the package we want to install. Existing packages can be updated using the following command:

```
$ conda update packagename
```

We can also search for packages using the following command:

```
$ anaconda search -t conda packagename
```

This will bring up a whole list of packages available through individual users.
A package called `packagename` from a user called username can then be installed as follows:

```
$ conda install -c username packagename
```

Additionally, conda can be used to create and manage virtual environments. For example, creating a `test` environment and installing NumPy version 1.7 is as simple as typing the next command:

```
$ conda create --name test numpy=1.7
```

In a similar fashion as working with `virtualenv`, environments can be activated and deactivated. To do this on macOS and Linux, just run the following:

```
$ source activate test
  $ python
  . . .
$ source deactivate
```

On Windows, run the following:

```
$ activate test
  $ python
  . . .
$ deactivate
```

 See the conda cheat sheet PDF (1 MB) for a single-page summary of the most important information about using conda: `https://conda.io/docs/_downloads/conda-cheatsheet.pdf`.

Finally, it should be pointed out that we can work with conda under the PyCharm IDE, in a similar way as `virtualenv` to create and manage virtual environments, because PyCharm can work with both tools.

Packages for scientific computing, data science, machine learning, deep learning, and computer vision

So far, we have seen how to install Python, OpenCV, and a few other packages (`numpy` and `matplotlib`) from scratch, or using Anaconda distribution, which includes many popular data-science packages. In this way, some knowledge about the main packages for scientific computing, data science, machine learning, and computer vision is a key point because they offer powerful computational tools. Throughout this book, many Python packages will be used. Not all of the cited packages in this section will, but a comprehensive list is provided for the sake of completeness in order to show the potential of Python in topics related to the content of this book:

- **NumPy** (`http://www.numpy.org/`) provides support for large, multi-dimensional arrays. NumPy is a key library in computer vision because images can be represented as multi-dimensional arrays. Representing images as NumPy arrays has many advantages.
- **OpenCV** (`https://opencv.org/`) is an open source computer vision library.
- **Scikit-image** (`https://scikit-image.org/`) is a collection of algorithms for image processing. Images manipulated by scikit-image are simply NumPy arrays.
- The **Python Imaging Library** (**PIL**) (`http://www.pythonware.com/products/pil/`) is an image-processing library that provides powerful image-processing and graphics capabilities.
- **Pillow** (`https://pillow.readthedocs.io/`) is the friendly PIL fork by Alex Clark and contributors. The PIL adds image-processing capabilities to your Python interpreter.
- **SimpleCV** (`http://simplecv.org/`) is a framework for computer vision that provides key functionalities to deal with image processing.
- **Mahotas** (`https://mahotas.readthedocs.io/`) is a set of functions for image processing and computer vision in Python. It was originally designed for bioimage informatics. However, it is useful in other areas as well. It is completely based on numpy arrays as its datatype.
- **Ilastik** (`http://ilastik.org/`) is a user-friendly and simple tool for interactive image segmentation, classification, and analysis.
- **Scikit-learn** (`http://scikit-learn.org/`) is a machine learning library that features various classification, regression, and clustering algorithms.

- **SciPy** (https://www.scipy.org/) is a library for scientific and technical computing.
- **NLTK** (https://www.nltk.org/) is a suite of libraries and programs to work with human-language data.
- **spaCy** (https://spacy.io/) is an open-source software library for advanced natural language processing in Python.
- **LibROSA** (https://librosa.github.io/librosa/) is a library for both music and audio processing.
- **Pandas** (https://pandas.pydata.org/) is a library (built on top of NumPy) that provides high-level data computation tools and easy-to-use data structures.
- **Matplotlib** (https://matplotlib.org/) is a plotting library that produces publication-quality figures in a variety of formats.
- **Seaborn** (https://seaborn.pydata.org/) is a graphics library that is built on top of Matplotlib.
- **Orange** (https://orange.biolab.si/) is an open source machine learning and data-visualization toolkit for novices and experts.
- **PyBrain** (http://pybrain.org/) is a machine learning library that provides easy-to-use state-of-the-art algorithms for machine learning.
- **Milk** (http://luispedro.org/software/milk/) is a machine learning toolkit focused on supervised classification with several classifiers.
- **TensorFlow** (https://www.tensorflow.org/) is an open source machine learning and deep learning library.
- **PyTorch** (https://pytorch.org/) is an open source machine learning and deep learning library.
- **Theano** (http://deeplearning.net/software/theano/) is a library for fast mathematical expressions, evaluation, and computation, which has been compiled to run on both CPU and GPU architectures (a key point for deep learning).
- **Keras** (https://keras.io/) is a high-level deep learning library that can run on top of TensorFlow, CNTK, Theano, or Microsoft Cognitive Toolkit.
- **Django** (https://www.djangoproject.com/) is a Python-based free and open source web framework that encourages rapid development and clean, pragmatic design.
- **Flask** (http://flask.pocoo.org/) is a micro web framework written in Python based on Werkzeug and Jinja 2.

All these packages can be organized based on their main purpose:

- **To work with images**: NumPy, OpenCV, scikit-image, PIL Pillow, SimpleCV, Mahotas, ilastik
- **To work in text**: NLTK, spaCy, NumPy, scikit-learn, PyTorch
- **To work in audio**: LibROSA
- **To solve machine learning problem**: pandas, scikit-learn, Orange, PyBrain, Milk
- **To see data clearly**: Matplotlib, Seaborn, scikit-learn, Orange
- **To use deep learning**: TensorFlow, Pytorch, Theano, Keras
- **To do scientific computing**: SciPy
- **To integrate web applications**: Django, Flask

 Additional Python libraries and packages for AI and machine learning can be found at `https://python.libhunt.com/packages/artificial-intelligence`.

Jupyter Notebook

The Jupyter Notebook an open source web application that allows you to edit and run documents via a web browser. These documents, which are called Notebook documents (or notebooks), contain code (more than 40 programming languages, including Python, are supported) and rich text elements (paragraphs, equations, figures). The Jupyter Notebook can be executed on a local computer or can be installed on a remote server. You can start with notebooks, trying them online or installing the Jupyter Notebook.

Trying Jupiter Notebook online

First, go to `https://jupyter.org/try`. You will see something like this:

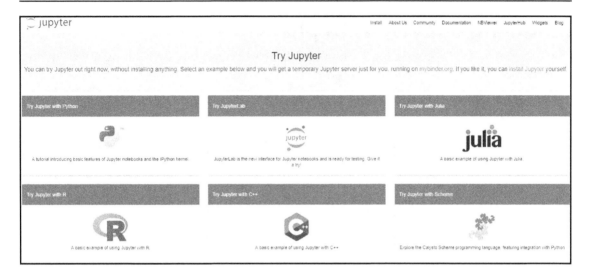

To try Jupyter with Python online, click on the Python option, or paste this URL into your web browser: `https://mybinder.org/v2/gh/ipython/ipython-in-depth/master?filepath=binder/Index.ipynb`. Once the page has loaded, you can start coding/loading notebooks.

Installing the Jupyter Notebook

To install Jupyter, you can follow the main steps at `http://jupyter.org/install.html`. Installing Jupyter Notebook can also be done using Anaconda or using Python's package manager, pip.

Installing Jupyter using Anaconda

It is strongly recommended you install Python and Jupyter using the Anaconda Distribution, which includes Python, the Jupyter Notebook, and other commonly used packages for scientific computing and data science. To install Jupyter using Anaconda, download Anaconda (`https://www.anaconda.com/distribution/`) and install it. This way, you have installed Jupyter Notebook. To run the notebook, run the following command in Command Prompt (Windows) or Terminal (macOS/Linux):

```
$ jupyter notebook
```

Installing Jupyter with pip

You can also install Jupyter using Python's package manager, pip, by running the following commands:

```
$ python -m pip install --upgrade pip
$ python -m pip install jupyter
```

At this point, you can start the notebook server by running the following command:

```
$ jupyter notebook
```

The previous command will show you some key information in connection with the notebook server, including the URL of the web application (which by default is `http://localhost:8888`). It will then open your default web browser to this URL. To start a specific notebook, the following command should be used:

```
$ jupyter notebook notebook.ipynb
```

This was a quick introduction to notebooks. In the next chapters, we are going to create some notebooks, so you will have the opportunity to play with them and gain full knowledge of this useful tool.

The OpenCV and Python project structure

The **project structure** is the way you organize all the files inside a folder in a way that the project best accomplishes the objectives. We are going to start with a `.py` script (`sampleproject.py`) that should be with other files in order to complete the information about this script – dependencies, license, how to install it, or how to test it. A common approach for structuring this basic project is as follows:

```
sampleproject/
|
├──── .gitignore
├──── sampleproject.py
├──── LICENSE
├──── README.rst
├──── requirements.txt
├──── setup.py
└──── tests.py
```

`sampleproject.py`—if your project is only a single Python source file, then put it into the directory and name it something related to your project.

The README (.rst or .md extension) is used to register the main properties of the project, which should cover, at least, the following:

- What your project does
- How to install it
- Example usage
- How to set up the dev environment
- How to ship a change
- Change log
- License and author info

A template you can use can be downloaded from this GitHub repository: https://github.com/dbader/readme-template. For further information, please see https://dbader.org/blog/write-a-great-readme-for-your-github-project.

The LICENSE.md document contains the applicable license. This is arguably the most important part of your repository, aside from the source code itself. The full license text and copyright claims should exist in this file. It is always a good idea to have one if you are distributing code. Typically, the **GNU General Public License (GPL)** (http://www.gnu.org/licenses/gpl.html) or the MIT license (https://opensource.org/licenses/MIT) are used in open source projects. You can check out http://choosealicense.com/ if you are not sure which license should be applied to your project.

A requirements.txt pip requirements file (https://pip.pypa.io/en/stable/user_guide/#requirements-files) should be placed at the root of the repository, which is used to specify the dependencies required to contribute to the project. The requirements.txt file can be generated using the following:

```
$ pip freeze > requirements.txt
```

To install these requirements, you can use the following command:

```
$ pip install -r requirements.txt
```

The setup.py file allows you to create packages you can redistribute. This script is meant to install your package on the end user's system, not to prepare the development environment as pip install -r < requirements.txt does. It is a key file because it defines information of your package (such as versioning, package requirements, and the project description).

The tests.py script contains the tests.

The `.gitignore` file tells Git what kind of files to ignore, such as IDE clutter or local configuration files. You can find sample `.gitignore` files for Python projects at `https://github.com/github/gitignore`.

Our first Python and OpenCV project

Based on the minimal project structure that was shown in the previous section, we are going to create our first Python and OpenCV project. This project has the following structure:

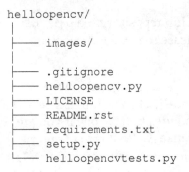

```
helloopencv/
|
├──── images/
|
├──── .gitignore
├──── helloopencv.py
├──── LICENSE
├──── README.rst
├──── requirements.txt
├──── setup.py
└──── helloopencvtests.py
```

`README.rst` (`.rst` extension) follows a basic structure, which was shown in the previous section. Python and **ReStructuredText** (**RST**) are deeply linked—RST is the format of docutils and sphinx (the *de facto* standard for documenting python code). RST is used both to document objects via docstrings, and to write additional documentation. If you go to the official Python documentation (`https://docs.python.org/3/library/stdtypes.html`), you can view the RST source of each page (`https://raw.githubusercontent.com/python/cpython/3.6/Doc/library/stdtypes.rst`). Using RST for the `README.rst` makes it directly compatible with the entire documentation setup. In fact, `README.rst` is often the cover page of a project's documentation.

There are some RST editors you can use to help you write the `README.rst`. You can also use some online editors. For example, the online Sphinx editor is a good choice (`https://livesphinx.herokuapp.com/`).

The `.gitignore` file specifies intentionally untracked files that Git should ignore (`https://git-scm.com/docs/gitignore`). `.gitignore` tells `git` which files (or patterns) Git should ignore. It is usually used to avoid committing transient files from your working directory that are not useful to other collaborators, such as compilation products and temporary files that IDEs create. Open `https://github.com/github/gitignore/blob/master/Python.gitignore` to see a `.gitignore` file that you can include in your Python projects.

setup.py (see the previous section for a deeper description), it is a Python file that is usually shipped with libraries or programs, also written in Python. Its purpose is to correctly install the software. A very complete example of this file can be seen at https://github.com/pypa/sampleproject/blob/master/setup.py, which is full of comments to help you understand how to adapt it to your needs. This file is proposed by the **Python Packaging Authority (PyPa)** (https://www.pypa.io/en/latest/). One key point is in connection with the *packages* option, as we can read in the aforementioned setup.py file.

You can just specify package directories manually here if your project is simple. Or you can use find_packages(). Alternatively, if you just want to distribute a single Python file, use the py_modules argument instead as follows, which will expect a file called my_module.py to exist, py_modules=["my_module"].

Therefore, in our case, py_modules =["helloopencv"] is used.

Additionally, setup.py allows you to easily install Python packages. Often it is enough to write the following:

```
$ python setup.py install
```

Therefore, if we want to install this simple package, we can write the previous command, python setup.py install, inside the helloopencv folder. For example, in Windows, run the following command:

```
C:\...\helloopencv>python setup.py install
```

You should see something like this:

```
running install
. . .
. . .
Installed c:\python37\lib\site-packages\helloopencv-0.1-py3.7.egg
Processing dependencies for helloopencv==0.1
. . .
. . .
Finished processing dependencies for helloopencv==0.1
```

When finished, helloopencv is installed in our system (like any other Python package). You can also install helloopencv with pip, pip install ., inside the helloopencv folder. For example, in Windows, run the following command:

```
C:\...\helloopencv>pip install .
```

You should see something like this:

```
Processing c:\...\helloopencv
...
...
Successfully installed helloopencv-0.1
```

This indicates that `helloopencv` has been installed successfully. To use this package, we can write a Python file and import the `helloopencv` package. Alternatively, we can perform a quick use of this package by importing it directly from the Python interpreter. Following this second approach, you can open Command Prompt, import the package, and make use of it. First, open Command Prompt, then type `python` to run the interpreter:

```
C:\...\helloopencv>python
Python 3.7.0 (v3.7.0:1bf9cc5093, Jun 27 2018, 04:06:47) [MSC v.1914 32 bit
(Intel)] on win32
Type "help", "copyright", "credits" or "license" for more information.
>>>
```

Once the interpreter is loaded, we can import the package:

```
>>> import helloopencv
helloopencv.py is being imported into another module
>>>
```

The `helloopencv.py is being imported into another module` output is a message from the `helloopencv` package (specifically from the `helloopencv.py` file) indicating that this file has been imported. Therefore, this message indicates that the module has been successfully imported. Once imported, we can make use of it. For example, we can call the `show_message` method:

```
>>> helloopencv.show_message()
'this function returns a message'
>>>
```

We can see that the result of calling this method is a message that is printed on the screen. This method is a simple way to know that everything has been installed correctly because it involves installing, importing, and making use of a function from the package. Furthermore, we can call a more useful method contained in the `helloopencv` package. You can, for example, call the `load_image` method to load an image from disk and afterwards, you can display it using the `show_image` method:

```
>>> image = helloopencv.load_image("C:/.../images/logo.png")
>>> helloopencv.show_image(image)
```

Here, the parameter of the `load_image` function is the path of an image from your computer. In this case, the `logo.png` image is loaded. After calling the `show_image` method, an image should be displayed. To close the window, a key must be pressed. Then you should be able to write in the interpreter again. To see all the methods that are available in the `helloopencv` package, you can open the `helloopencv.py` file with your favorite editor or IDE and have a look at it. In this Python file, you can see some methods that conform to our first Python project:

- `show_message()`: This function prints the `this function returns a message` message.
- `load_image()`: This function loads an image from its path.
- `show_image()`: This function shows an image once it has been loaded.
- `convert_to_grayscale()`: This function converts an image to grayscale once it has been loaded.
- `write_image_to_disk()`: This function saves an image on disk.

All of these methods perform simple and basic operations. Most of them make use of the OpenCV library, which is imported at the beginning of this file (`import cv2`). Do not worry about the Python code contained in this file, because only basic operations and calls to the OpenCV library are performed.

You can execute the `helloopencv.py` script without installing the package. To execute this file, you should run the `python helloopencv.py` command once Command Prompt is opened:

```
C:\...\helloopencv>python helloopencv.py
helloopencv.py is being run directly
```

After the execution of this file, the `helloopencv.py is being run directly` message will appear, which means that the file is executed directly and not imported from another module or package (or the Python interpreter). You can also see that an image is loaded and displayed. You can press any key to continue the execution. Once again, the grayscale version of the logo is displayed and any key should be pressed again to end the execution. The execution ends after the grayscale image is saved on the disk.

Lastly, the `helloopencvtests.py` file can be used for unit testing. Testing applications has become a standard skill for any competent developer. The Python community embraces testing, and the Python standard library has good built-in tools to support testing (`https://docs.python.org/3/library/unittest.html`).

In the Python ecosystem, there are a lot of testing tools. The two most common packages used for testing are nose (https://pypi.org/project/nose/) and pytest (https://pypi.org/project/pytest/). In this first Python project, we are going to use pytest for unit testing.

To execute the test, run the py.test -s -v helloopencvtests.py command once Command Prompt is opened:

```
C:\...\helloopencv>py.test -s -v helloopencvtests.py
============================== test session starts
==============================
 platform win32 -- Python 3.7.0, pytest-3.8.0, py-1.6.0, pluggy-0.7.1 --
c:\python37\python.exe
 cachedir: .pytest_cache
 collected 4 items
 helloopencvtests.py::test_show_message testing show_message
 PASSED
 helloopencvtests.py::test_load_image testing load_image
 PASSED
 helloopencvtests.py::test_write_image_to_disk testing
 write_image_to_disk
 PASSED
 helloopencvtests.py::test_convert_to_grayscale testing
test_convert_to_grayscale
 PASSED
=========================== 4 passed in 0.57 seconds
===========================
```

After the execution of the tests, you can see that four tests were executed. The PASSED message means that the tests were executed successfully. This is a quick introduction to unit testing in Python. Nevertheless, the full pytest documentation can be found at https://docs.pytest.org/en/latest/contents.html#toc.

Summary

In this first chapter, we covered the main steps to set up OpenCV and Python to build your computer vision projects. At the beginning of this chapter, we quickly looked at the main concepts in this book – Artificial Intelligence, machine learning, neural networks, and deep learning. Then we explored the OpenCV library, including the history of the library and its main modules. As OpenCV and other packages can be installed in many operating systems and in different ways, we covered the main approaches.

Specifically, we saw how to install Python, OpenCV, and other packages globally or in a virtual environment. In connection with the installation of the packages, we introduced Anaconda/Miniconda and Conda, because we can also create and manage virtual environments. Additionally, Anaconda/Miniconda comes with many open source scientific packages, including SciPy and NumPy.

We explored the main packages for scientific computing, data science, machine learning, and computer vision, because they offer powerful computational tools. Then we discussed the Python-specific IDEs, including PyCharm (the *de facto* Python IDE environment). PyCharm (and other IDEs) can help us create virtual environments in a very intuitive way. We also looked at Jupyter Notebooks, because it can be a good tool for the readers of this book. In the next chapters, more Jupyter Notebooks will be created to give you a better understanding of this useful tool. Finally, we explored an OpenCV and Python project structure, covering the main files that should be included. Then we built our first Python and OpenCV sample project, where we saw the commands to build, run, and test this project.

In the next chapter, you will start to write your first scripts as you get better acquainted with the OpenCV library. You will see some basic concepts necessary to start coding your computer vision projects (for example, understanding main image concepts, the coordinate system in OpenCV, and accessing and manipulating pixels in OpenCV).

Questions

1. What is a virtual environment?
2. What is the connection between pip, virtualenv, pipenv, Anaconda, and conda?
3. What is the Jupyter Notebook?
4. What are the main packages to work with computer vision in Python?
5. What does `pip install -r requirements.txt` do?
6. What is an IDE and why should you use one during the development of your projects?
7. Under what license is OpenCV published?

Further reading

The following references will help you dive deeper into concepts presented in this chapter:

- Python Machine Learning:
  - *Python Machine Learning*, by Sebastian Raschka: `https://www.packtpub.com/big-data-and-business-intelligence/python-machine-learning`

- Python Deep Learning:
  - *Python Deep Learning Projects*, by Rahul Kumar, Matthew Lamons: `https://www.packtpub.com/big-data-and-business-intelligence/python-deep-learning-projects`

Check out these references (mainly books) for more information on concepts that will be presented in future chapters of the book. Keep this list handy; it will be really helpful:

- *OpenCV Computer Vision with Python* (`https://www.packtpub.com/application-development/opencv-computer-vision-python`)
- *OpenCV: Computer Vision Projects with Python* (`https://www.packtpub.com/application-development/opencv-computer-vision-projects-python`)
- *Augmented Reality for Developers* (`https://www.packtpub.com/web-development/augmented-reality-developers`)
- *Deep Learning with Python and OpenCV* (`https://www.packtpub.com/big-data-and-business-intelligence/deep-learning-python-and-opencv`)
- *Deep Learning with Keras* (`https://www.packtpub.com/big-data-and-business-intelligence/deep-learning-keras`)
- *Getting Started with TensorFlow* (`https://www.packtpub.com/big-data-and-business-intelligence/getting-started-tensorflow`)
- *Mastering Flask Web Development - Second Edition* (`https://www.packtpub.com/web-development/mastering-flask-web-development-second-edition`)

Image Basics in OpenCV

2

Images are a key component in a computer vision project because they provide, in many cases, the input to work with. Therefore, understanding main image concepts is the basic knowledge you need to start coding your computer vision projects. Also, some of the OpenCV library peculiarities, such as the coordinate system or the BGR order (rather than RGB), will be introduced.

In this chapter, you will learn how to start writing your first scripts, which will introduce you to the OpenCV library. At the end of this chapter, you will have enough knowledge to start programming your first computer vision project in OpenCV and Python.

In this chapter, we will cover the following topics:

- A theoretical introduction to image basics
- Concepts of pixel, colors, channels, images, and color spaces
- The coordinate system in OpenCV
- Accessing and manipulating pixels in OpenCV in different color spaces (getting and setting)
- BGR order in OpenCV (rather than RGB)

Technical requirements

The technical requirements for this chapter are listed as follows:

- Python and OpenCV
- A Python-specific IDE
- The NumPy and Matplotlib packages
- Jupyter Notebook
- Git client

Further details about how to install these requirements can be found in `Chapter 1`, *Setting Up OpenCV*. The GitHub repository for Mastering OpenCV with Python, which contains all the supporting project files that are necessary to work through this book from the first chapter to the last, can be accessed at `https://github.com/PacktPublishing/Mastering-OpenCV-4-with-Python`.

A theoretical introduction to image basics

The main purpose of this section is to provide a theoretical introduction to image basics – these will be explained in detail in the next section. First, a quick introduction will be given to underline the importance of some of the difficulties you will encounter when developing the image-processing set in a computer vision project, and then some simple formulation will be introduced in connection with images.

Main problems in image processing

The first concept to introduce is related to images, which can be seen as a **two-dimensional** (**2D**) view of a 3D world. A digital image is a numeric representation, normally binary, of a 2D image as a finite set of digital values, which are called **pixels** (the concept of a pixel will be explained in detail in the *Concepts of pixels, colors, channels, images, and color spaces* section). Therefore, the goal of computer vision is to transform this 2D data into the following:

- A new representation (for example, a new image)
- A decision (for example, perform a concrete task)
- A new result (for example, correct classification of the image)
- Some useful information extraction (for example, object detection)

Computer vision may tackle common problems (or difficulties) when dealing with image-processing techniques:

- Ambiguous images because they are affected by perspective, which can produce changes in the visual appearance of the image. For example, the same object viewed from different perspectives can result in different images.
- Images commonly affected by many factors, such as illumination, weather, reflections, and movements.

- Objects in the image may also be occluded by other objects, making it difficult to detect or classify the occluded ones. Depending on the level of the occlusion, the required task (for example, classification of an image into some predefined categories) can be really challenging.

To put all of these difficulties together, imagine that you want to develop a face-detection system. This system should be robust enough to deal with changes in illumination or weather conditions. Additionally, the system should tackle the movements of the head, and could even deal with the fact that the user can be farther from or closer to the camera. It should be able to detect the head of the user with some degree of rotation in every axis (yaw, roll, and pitch). For example, many face-detection algorithms show good performance when the head is near frontal. However, they fail to detect a face if it's not frontal (for example, a face in profile). Moreover, you may want to detect the face even if the user is wearing glasses or sunglasses, which produces an occlusion in the eye region. When developing a computer vision project, you must take all of these factors into consideration. A good approximation is to have many test images to validate your algorithm by incorporating some difficulties. You can also classify your test images in connection with the main difficulty they have to easily detect the weak points of your algorithm.

Image-processing steps

Image processing includes the following three steps:

1. Get the image to work with. This process usually involves some functions so that you can read the image from different sources (camera, video stream, disk, online resources).
2. Process the image by applying image-processing techniques to achieve the required functionality (for example, detecting a cat in an image).
3. Show the result of the processing step (for example, drawing a bounding box in the image and then saving it to disk).

Furthermore, step two can be broken down into three processing levels:

- Low-level process
- Mid-level process
- High-level process

The **low-level process** usually takes an image as the input and then outputs another image. Example procedures that can be applied in this step include the following:

- Noise removal
- Image sharpening
- Illumination normalization
- Perspective correction

In connection with the face-detection example, the output image can be an illumination normalization image to deal with changes caused by sun reflections.

The **mid-level process** takes the preprocessed image to output some kind of representation of the image. Consider this as a collection of numbers (for example, a vector containing 100 numbers), which summarizes the main information of the image to be used for further processing. In connection with the face-detection example, the output could be a rectangle defined by a point (x,y), the width and the height containing the detected face.

The **high-level process** takes this vector of numbers (usually called **attributes**) and outputs the final result. For example, the input could be the detected face and the output could be the following:

- Face recognition
- Emotion recognition
- Drowsiness and distraction detection
- Remote heart rate measurement from the face

Images formulation

An image can be described as a 2D function, $f(x,y)$, where (x,y) are the spatial coordinates and the value of f at any point, (x,y), is proportional to the brightness or gray levels of the image. Additionally, when both (x,y) and brightness values of f are all finite discrete quantities, the image is called a **digital image**. Therefore, $f(x,y)$ takes the following values:

- $x \in [0, h-1]$, where h is the height of the image
- $y \in [0, w-1]$, where w is the width of the image
- $f(x,y) \in [0, L-1]$, where $L = 256$ (for an 8-bit image)

A color image can be represented in the same way, but we need to define three functions to represent the red, green, and blue values, respectively. Each of these three individual functions follows the same formulation as the $f(x,y)$ function that was defined for grayscale images. We will denote these three functions subindex R, G and B for the three formulations (for the color images) as $fR(x,y)$, $fG(x,y)$, and $fB(x,y)$.

A black and white image follows the same approximation in the way that only one function is required to represent the image. However, one key point is that $f(x,y)$ can only take two values. Usually, these values are 0 (black) and 255 (white).

These three types of images are commonly used in computer vision, so remember their formulation.

The following screenshot shows the three types of images (a color image, a grayscale image, and a black and white image):

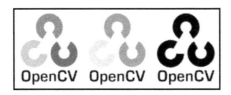

Remember that the digital image can be seen as an approximation of the real scene because $f(x,y)$ values are finite discrete quantities. Additionally, both grayscale and black and white images have only one sample per point (only one function is needed) and color images have three samples per point (three functions are needed—corresponding to the red, green, and blue components of the image).

Concepts of pixels, colors, channels, images, and color spaces

There are several different color models, but the most common one is the **Red, Green, Blue (RGB)** model, which will be used to explain some key concepts concerning digital images.

In Chapter 5, *Image Processing Techniques,* the main color models (also known as **color spaces**) will be fully explained.

The RGB model is an additive color model in which the primary colors *(R, G, B)* are mixed together to reproduce a broad range of colors. As we previously stated, in the RGB model, the primary colors are red, green, and blue.

Each primary color, *(R, G, B),* is usually called a channel, which is commonly represented as an integer value in the [0, 255] range. Therefore, each channel produces a total of 256 discrete values, which corresponds to the total number of bits that are used to represent the color channel value *(2^8=256)*. Additionally, since there are three different channels, this is called a **24-bit color depth**:

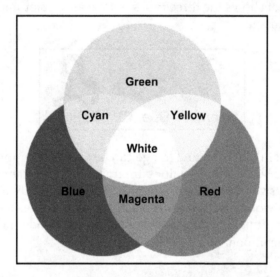

In the previous diagram, you can see the additive color property of the RGB color space:

- Adding red to green gives yellow
- Adding red to blue produces magenta
- Adding green to blue generates cyan
- Adding all three primary colors together produces white

As we previously stated and in connection with the RGB color model, a specific color is represented by red, green, and blue values, expressing the pixel value as an RGB triplet, *(r, g, b)*. A typical RGB color selector in a piece of graphics software is shown as follows. As you can imagine, each slider ranges from 0 to 255:

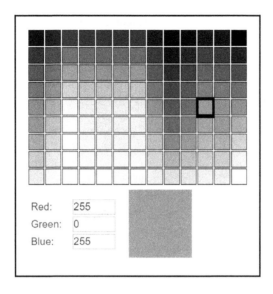

You can also see that adding pure red to pure blue produces a perfect magenta color. You can play with the RGB color chart at https://www.rapidtables.com/web/color/RGB_Color.html.

An image with a resolution of *800 × 1,200* is a grid with 800 columns and 1,200 rows, containing *800 × 1,200 = 960,000* pixels. It should be noted that knowing how many pixels are in an image does not indicate its physical dimensions (one pixel does not equal one millimeter). Instead, how *large* a pixel is (and hence, how large an image will be) will depend on the **pixels per inch** (**PPI**) that have been set for that image. A general rule of thumb is to have a PPI in the range of [200 - 400].

The basic equation for calculating PPI is as follows:
PPI = width(pixels)/width of image (inches)
PPI = height(pixels)/height of image (inches)
So, for example, if you want to print a 4 × 6 inch image, and your image is *800 × 1,200*, the PPI will be 200.

We will now look into file extensions.

File extensions

Although the images we are going to manipulate in OpenCV can be seen as rectangular arrays of RGB triplets (in the case of RGB images), they are not necessarily created, stored, or transmitted in that format. In this sense, some file formats, such as GIF, PNG, bitmaps, or JPEG, use different forms of compression (lossless or lossy) to represent images more efficiently.

In this way, and for the sake of completeness, a brief introduction to these image files is given here, with a special focus on the file formats supported by OpenCV. The following file formats (with the associated file extensions) are supported by OpenCV:

- **Windows bitmaps**: `*.bmp` and `*.dib`
- **JPEG files**: `*.jpeg`, `*.jpg`, and `*.jpe`
- **JPEG 2000 files**: `*.jp2`
- **Portable Network Graphics**: `*.png`
- **Portable image format**: `*.pbm`, `*.pgm`, and `*.ppm`
- **TIFF files**: `*.tiff` and `*.tif`

The **Bitmap image file (BMP)** or **device independent bitmap (DIB)** file format is a raster image file format that's used to store bitmap digital images. The BMP file format can deal with 2D digital images in various color depths and, optionally, with data compression, alpha channels, or color profiles.

Joint Photographic Experts Group (JPEG) is a raster image file format that's used to store images that have been compressed to store a lot of information in a small file.

JPEG 2000 is an image compression standard and coding system that uses wavelet-based compression techniques offering a high level of scalability and accessibility. In this way, JPEG 2000 compresses images with fewer artefacts than a regular JPEG.

Portable Network Graphics (PNG) is a compressed raster graphics file format, which was introduced in 1994 as an improved replacement for **Graphics Interchange Format (GIF)**.

The **portable pixmap format (PPM)**, the **portable bitmap format (PBM)**, and the **portable graymap format (PGM)** specify rules for exchanging graphics files. Several applications refer to these file formats collectively as the **portable anymap format (PNM)**. These files are a convenient and simple method of saving image data. Additionally, they are easy to read. In this sense, the PPM, PBM, and PGM formats are all designed to be as simple as possible.

Tagged Image File Format (TIFF) is an adaptable file format for handling images and data within a single file.

The lossless and lossy types of compression algorithms are applied to the image, resulting in images that are smaller than the uncompressed image. On the one hand, in lossless compression algorithms, the resulting image is equivalent to the original, meaning that after reversing the compression process, the resulting image is equivalent (equal) to the original. On the other hand, in lossy compression algorithms, the resulting image is not equivalent to the original, meaning that some details in the image are lost. In this sense, in many lossy compression algorithms, the level of compression can be adjusted.

The coordinate system in OpenCV

To show you the coordinate system in OpenCV and how to access individual pixels, we are going to show you a low-resolution image of the OpenCV logo:

This logo has a dimension of *20 × 18* pixels, that is, this image has 360 pixels. So, we can add the pixel count in every axis, as shown in the following image:

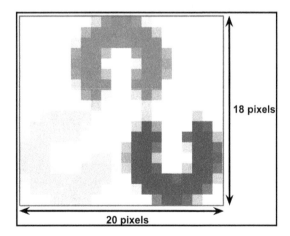

Now, we are going to look at the indexing of the pixels in the form *(x,y)*. Notice that pixels are zero-indexed, meaning that the upper left corner is at **(0, 0)**, not **(1, 1)**. Take a look at the following image, which indexes three individual pixels. As you can see, the upper left corner of the image is the coordinates of the origin. Moreover, *y* coordinates get larger as they go down:

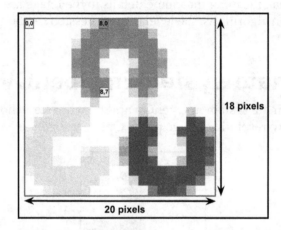

The information for an individual pixel can be extracted from an image in the same way as an individual element of an array is referenced in Python. In the next section, we are going to see how we can do this.

Accessing and manipulating pixels in OpenCV

In this section, you will learn how to access and read pixel values with OpenCV and how to modify them. Additionally, you will learn how to access the image properties. If you want to work with many pixels at a time, you need to create **Region of Image** (**ROI**). In this section, you will learn how to do this. Finally, you will learn how to split and merge images.

Remember that in Python, images are represented as NumPy arrays. Therefore, most of the operations that are included in these examples are related to NumPy, so a good understanding about the NumPy package is required to both understand the code included in these examples and to write optimized code with OpenCV.

Accessing and manipulating pixels in OpenCV with BGR images

Now, we are going to see how we can work with BGR images in OpenCV. OpenCV loads the color images so that the blue channel is the first, the green channel is the second, and the red channel is the third. Please see the *Accessing and manipulating pixels in OpenCV with grayscale images* section to fully understand this concept.

First, read the image to work with using the cv2.imread() function. The image should be in the working directory, or a full path to the image should be provided. In this case, we are going to read the logo.png image and store it in the img variable:

```
# The function cv2.imread() is used to read an image from the the working
directory
# Alternatively, you should provide a full path of the image:
# Load OpenCV logo image (in this case from the working directoy):
img = cv2.imread('logo.png')
```

After the image has been loaded in img, we will gain access to some properties of the image. The first property we are going to extract from the loaded image is shape, which will tell us the number of rows, columns, and channels (if the image is in color). We will store this information in the dimensions variable for future use:

```
# To get the dimensions of the image use img.shape
# img.shape returns a tuple of number of rows, columns and channels (if a
colour image)
# If image is grayscale, img.shape returns a tuple of number of rows and
columns.
# So, it can be used to check if loaded image is grayscale or color image.
# Get the shape of the image:
dimensions = img.shape
```

Another property is the size of the image (img.size is equal to the multiplication of *height × width × channels*):

```
# Total number of elements is obtained by img.size:
total_number_of_elements= img.size
```

The property image datatype is obtained by `img.dtype`. In this case, the image datatype is `uint8` (unsigned char), because values are in the [0 - 255] range:

```
# Image datatype is obtained by img.dtype.
# img.dtype is very important because a large number of errors is caused by
invalid datatype.
# Get the image datatype:
image_dtype = img.dtype
```

To display an image, we will use the `cv2.imshow()` function to show an image in a window. The window automatically fits to the image size. The first argument to this function is the window name and the second one is the image to be displayed. In this case, since the loaded image has been stored in the `img` variable, we will use this variable as the second argument:

```
# The function cv2.imshow() is used to display an image in a window
# The first argument of this function is the window name
# The second argument of this function is the image to be shown.
# Each created window should have different window names.
# Show original image:
cv2.imshow("original image", img)
```

After the image is displayed, the `cv2.waitKey()` function, which is a keyboard binding function, will wait for a specified number of milliseconds for any keyboard event. The argument is the time in milliseconds. If any key is pressed at that time, the program will continue. If the number of milliseconds is 0 (`cv2.waitKey(0)`), it will wait indefinitely for a keystroke. Therefore, this function will allow us to see the displayed window waiting for a keystroke:

```
# The function cv2.waitKey(), which is a keyboard binding function, waits
for any keyboard event.
# This function waits the value indicated by the argument (in
milliseconds).
# If any keyboard event is produced in this period of time, the program
continues its execution
# If the value of the argument is 0, the program waits indefinitely until a
keyboard event is produced:
cv2.waitKey(0)
```

To access (read) a pixel value, we need to provide the row and column of the desired pixel to the `img` variable, which contains the loaded image. For example, to get the value of the pixel (x=40, y=6), we would use the following code:

```
# A pixel value can be accessed by row and column coordinates.
# In case of BGR image, it returns an array of (Blue, Green, Red) values.
# Get the value of the pixel (x=40, y=6):
(b, g, r) = img[6, 40]
```

We have loaded the three pixel values in three variables, `(b,g,r)`. You can see here that OpenCV uses the BGR format for color images. Additionally, we can access one channel at a time. In this case, we will use row, column, and the index of the desired channel for indexing. For example, to get only the blue value of the pixel (x=40, y=6), we would use the following code:

```
# We can only  access one channel at a time.
# In this case, we will use row, column and the index of the desired
channel for indexing.
# Get only blue value of the pixel (x=40, y=6):
b = img[6, 40, 0]
```

The pixel values can be also modified in the same way. Remember that it is the `(b, g, r)` format. For example, to set the pixel (x=40, y=6) to red, perform the following:

```
# The pixel values can be also modified in the same way - (b, g, r) format:
img[6, 40] = (0, 0, 255)
```

Sometimes, you will have to deal with a certain region rather than one pixel. In this case, the ranges of the values should be provided instead of the individual values. For example, to get to the top-left corner of the image, enter the following:

```
# In this case, we get the top left corner of the image:
top_left_corner = img[0:50, 0:50]
```

The `top_left_corner` variable is another image (smaller than `img`), but we can play with it in the same way.

Accessing and manipulating pixels in OpenCV with grayscale images

Grayscale images have only one channel. Therefore, some differences are introduced when working with these images. We are going to highlight these differences here.

Again, we will use the `cv2.imread()` function to read an image. In this case, the second argument is needed because we want to load the image in grayscale. The second argument is a flag specifying the way the image should be read. The value that's needed for loading an image in grayscale is `cv2.IMREAD_GRAYSCALE`:

```
# The function cv2.imshow() is used to display an image in a window
# The first argument of this function is the window name
# The second argument of this function is the image to be shown.
# In this case, the second argument is needed because we want to load the
image in grayscale.
# Second argument is a flag specifying the way the image should be read.
# Value needed for loading an image in grayscale: 'cv2.IMREAD_GRAYSCALE'.
# load OpenCV logo image:
gray_img = cv2.imread('logo.png', cv2.IMREAD_GRAYSCALE)
```

In this case, we store the image in the `gray_img` variable. If we get the dimensions of the image (using `gray_img.shape`), we will get only two values that is, rows and columns. In grayscale images, the channel information is not provided:

```
# To get the dimensions of the image use img.shape
# If color image, img.shape returns returns a tuple of number of rows,
columns and channels
# If grayscale, returns a tuple of number of rows and columns.
# So, it can be used to check if the loaded image is grayscale or color
image.
# Get the shape of the image (in this case only two components!):
dimensions = gray_img.shape
```

`img.shape` will return the dimensions of the image in a tuple, like this—`(99, 82)`.

A pixel value can be accessed by row and column coordinates. In grayscale images, only one value is obtained (usually called the **intensity** of the pixel). For example, if we want to get the intensity of the pixel (x=40, y=6), we would use the following code:

```
# You can access a pixel value by row and column coordinates.
# For BGR image, it returns an array of (Blue, Green, Red) values.
# Get the value of the pixel (x=40, y=6):
i = gray_img[6, 40]
```

The pixel values of the image can be also modified in the same way. For example, if we want to change the value of the pixel (x=40, y=6) to black (intensity equals to 0), we would use the following code:

```
# You can modify the pixel values of the image in the same way.
# Set the pixel to black:
gray_img[6, 40] = 0
```

BGR order in OpenCV

We already mentioned that OpenCV uses the BGR color format instead of the RGB one. This can be seen in the following diagram, where you can see the order of the three channels:

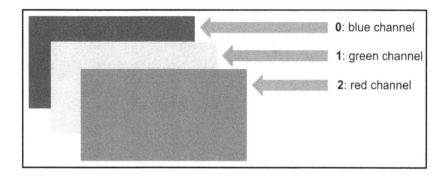

The pixel structure of a BGR image can be seen in the following diagram. In particular, we have detailed how to access **pixel (y=n, x=1)** for clarification purposes:

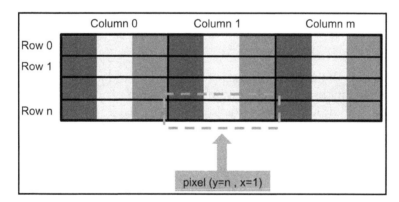

Initial developers at OpenCV chose the BGR color format (instead of the RGB one) because at the time, the BGR color format was very popular among software providers and camera manufacturers. For example, in Windows, when specifying a color value using COLORREF, they used the BGR format, `0x00bbggrr` (`https://docs.microsoft.com/es-es/windows/desktop/gdi/colorref`). In summary, BGR was chosen for historical reasons.

Additionally, other Python packages use the RGB color format. Therefore, we need to know how to convert an image from one format into the other. For example, Matplotlib uses the RGB color format. Matplotlib (`https://matplotlib.org/`) is the most popular 2D Python plotting library and offers you a wide variety of plotting methods. You can interact with the plotted images (for example, zoom into images and save them). Matplotlib can be used both in Python scripts or in the Jupyter Notebook. You can check out the Matplotlib documentation for further details (`https://matplotlib.org/contents.html`).

Therefore, a good choice for your projects is to show the images using the Matplotlib package instead of the functionality offered by OpenCV. Now we are going to see now how we can deal with the different color formats in the two libraries.

First of all, we load the image using the `cv2.imread()` function:

```
# Load image using cv2.imread:
img_OpenCV = cv2.imread('logo.png')
```

The image is stored in the `img_OpenCV` variable because the `cv2.imread()` function loads the image in BGR order. Then, we split the loaded image into its three channels, (b, g, r), using the `cv2.split()` function. The parameter of this function is the image we want to split:

```
# Split the loaded image into its three channels (b, g, r):
b, g, r = cv2.split(img_OpenCV)
```

The next step is to merge the channels again (in order to build a new image based on the information provided by the channels) but in a different order. We change the order of the b and r channels in order to follow the RGB format, that is, the one we need for Matplotlib:

```
# Merge again the three channels but in the RGB format:
img_matplotlib = cv2.merge([r, g, b])
```

At this point, we have two images (`img_OpenCV` and `img_matplotlib`), which are going to be plotted with both OpenCV and Matplotlib so that we can see the results. First of all, we will show these two images with Matplotlib.

To show the two images with Matplotlib in the same window, we will use `subplot`, which places multiple images within the same window. You have three parameters to use within `subplot`, for example `subplot(m,n,p)`. In this case, `subplot` handles plots in a m x n grid, where *m* establishes the number of rows, *n* establishes the number of columns, and *p* establishes where you want to place your plot in the grid. To show the images with Matplotlib, we will use `imshow`.

In this case, as we are showing two images horizontally, m = 1 and n = 2. We will be using p = 1 for the first subfigure (img_OpenCV) and p = 2 for the second subfigure (img_matplotlib):

```
# Show both images (img_OpenCV and img_matplotlib) using matplotlib
# This will show the image in wrong color:
plt.subplot(121)
plt.imshow(img_OpenCV)
# This will show the image in true color:
plt.subplot(122)
plt.imshow(img_matplotlib)
plt.show()
```

Therefore, the output you will get should be very similar to the output that's shown in the following diagram:

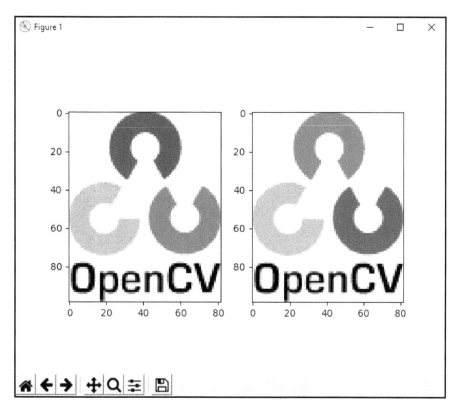

As you can see, the first subfigure shows the image in the wrong color (BGR order), while the second subfigure shows the image in true color (RGB order). In the same way, we will show the two images using `cv2.imshow()`:

```
# Show both images (img_OpenCV and img_matplotlib) using cv2.imshow()
# This will show the image in true color:
cv2.imshow('bgr image', img_OpenCV)
# This will show the image in wrong color:
cv2.imshow('rgb image', img_matplotlib)
cv2.waitKey(0)
cv2.destroyAllWindows()
```

The following screenshot shows what you will get from executing the previous code:

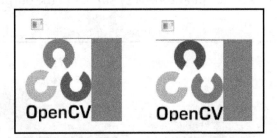

As expected, the screenshot shows the image in true color, while the second figure shows the image in the wrong color.

Additionally, if we want to show the two images in the same window, we can build a *full* image that contains the two images, concatenating them horizontally. To do so, we will use NumPy's `concatenate()` method. The parameters of this method are the two images to concatenate and the axis. In this case, `axis = 1` (to stack them horizontally):

```
# To stack horizontally (img_OpenCV to the left of img_matplotlib):
img_concats = np.concatenate((img_OpenCV, img_matplotlib), axis=1)
# Now, we show the concatenated image:
cv2.imshow('bgr image and rgb image', img_concats)
cv2.waitKey(0)
cv2.destroyAllWindows()
```

Check out the following screenshot to see the concatenated image:

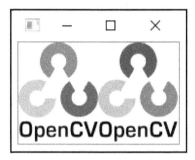

One consideration to take into account is that `cv2.split()` is a time-consuming operation. Depending on your needs, consider using NumPy indexing. For example, if you want to get one channel of the image, instead of using `cv2.split()` to get the desired channel, you can use NumPy indexing. See the following example to get the channels using NumPy indexing:

```
# Using numpy capabilities to get the channels and to build the RGB image
# Get the three channels (instead of using cv2.split):
B = img_OpenCV[:, :, 0]
G = img_OpenCV[:, :, 1]
R = img_OpenCV[:, :, 2]
```

Another consideration is that you can use NumPy for converting the image from BGR into RGB in a single instruction:

```
# Transform the image BGR to RGB using Numpy capabilities:
img_matplotlib = img_OpenCV[:, :, ::-1]
```

To summarize everything in this chapter, we have created two Jupiter Notebooks. In these notebooks, you can play with all of the concepts that have been introduced so far:

- `Getting-And-Setting-BGR.ipynb`
- `Getting-And-Setting-GrayScale.ipynb`

Taking advantage of the benefits notebook (and all of the information included in this chapter), no additional information is needed to play with them. So, go ahead and try it for yourself. Remember (see `Chapter 1`, *Setting Up OpenCV*) that to run the notebook, you need to run the following command at the Terminal (Mac/Linux) or Command Prompt (Windows):

```
$ jupyter notebook
```

This command will print information in connection with the notebook server, including the URL of the web application (by default, this URL is `http://localhost:8888`). Additionally, this command will also open your web browser pointing to this URL:

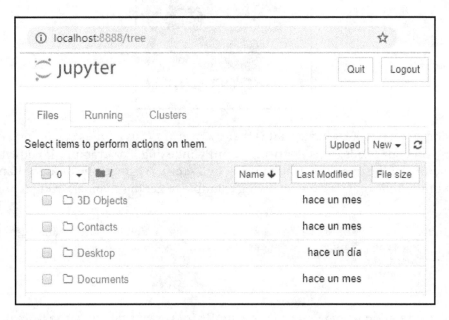

At this point, you are able to upload the `Getting-And-Setting-BGR.ipynb` and `Getting-And-Setting-GrayScale.ipynb` files by clicking on the **Upload** button (see the previous screenshot). These files use the `logo.png` image. Therefore, you should upload this image in the same way. After loading these three files, you should see these files loaded:

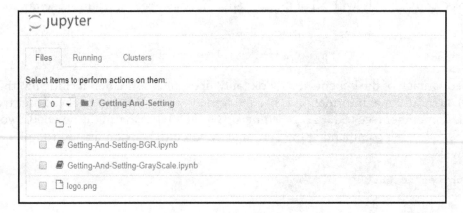

At this point, you can open these notebooks by clicking on them. You should see the content of the notebook, which is shown in the following screenshot:

Getting and Setting methods in Python Using OpenCV

Introduction

This notebook is going to teach you the basic concepts you will need for accessing and manipulating pixels in images using OpenCV and Python (getting and setting methods) with BGR images. The test image, which is going to be used in this example, corresponds to the OpenCV logo image. To display an image in notebooks make sure the cell is in Markdown mode and use the following code "![alt text] (imagename.png)" - without the blank space before the imagename. This image is displayed next:

OpenCV

So, let's start!

Load the image and see the properties of the loaded image

First of all, **import** the necessary packages:

```
In [16]:  #import required packages
          import cv2
```

Finally, you can start executing the loaded notebook document. You can execute the notebook step by step (one cell a time) by pressing *Shift + Enter*. Additionally, you can execute the whole notebook in a single step by clicking on the **Cell** | **Run All** menu. Moreover, you can also restart the kernel (the computational engine) by clicking on the **Kernel** | **Restart** menu.

> For more information on editing a notebook, check out `https://github.com/jupyter/notebook/blob/master/docs/source/examples/Notebook/Notebook%20Basics.ipynb`, which is also a notebook!

Summary

In this chapter, we looked at the key concepts related to images. Images constitute rich information that's necessary to build your computer vision projects. OpenCV uses the BGR color format instead of RGB, but some Python packages (for example, Matplotlib) use the latter format. Therefore, we have covered how to convert the image from one color format into the other.

Additionally, we have summarized the main functions and options to work with images:

- To access image properties
- Some OpenCV functions, such as
  `cv2.imread()`, `cv2.split()`, `cv2.merge()`, `cv2.imshow()`, `cv2.waitKey()`,
  and `cv2.destroyAllWindows()`
- How to get and set image pixels in both BGR and grayscale images

Finally, we included two notebooks, which let you play with all these concepts. Remember that once you have loaded the notebook, you can run it step by step by pressing *Shift + Enter* or run the notebook in a single step by clicking on the **Cell** | **Run All** menu.

In the next chapter, you will learn how to cope with files and images, which are necessary for building your computer vision applications.

Questions

1. What are the main image-processing steps?
2. What are the three processing levels?
3. What is the difference between a grayscale image and a black and white image?
4. What is a pixel?
5. What is image resolution?
6. What OpenCV functions do you use to perform the following actions?
    - Load (read) an image
    - Show an image
    - Wait for a keystroke
    - Split the channels
    - Merge the channels
7. What command do you use to run the Jupyter Notebook?
8. What color will you get with the following triplets?
    - B = 0, G = 255, R = 255
    - B = 255, G = 255, R = 0
    - B = 255, G = 0, R = 255
    - B = 255, G = 255, R = 255
9. Suppose that you have loaded an image in `img`. How do you check whether `img` is color or grayscale?

Further reading

The following references will help you dive deeper into the concepts that were presented in this chapter:

- For more information about Git, have a look at this book:

  Mastering Git, by Jakub Narębski (`https://www.packtpub.com/application-development/mastering-git`)

- For more on Jupyter Notebook:

  Jupyter Notebook for All – Part I, by Dan Toomey (`https://www.packtpub.com/big-data-and-business-intelligence/jupyter-notebook-for-all-part-1-video`)

3
Handling Files and Images

In any kind of project, coping with files and images is a key aspect. In this sense, many projects should work with files as forms of data input. Additionally, the project can generate some data after any kind of processing has been done, which can be outputted in the form of files or images. In computer vision, this information flow (input-processing-output) takes special relevance due to the inherent characteristics of these types of projects (for example, images to be processed and models that are generated by machine learning algorithms).

In this chapter, we are going to see how we can handle both files and images. You will learn how to cope with files and images, which are necessary for building computer vision applications.

More specifically, we will cover the following topics:

- A theoretical introduction to handling files and images
- Reading/writing images
- Reading camera frames and video files
- Writing a video file
- Playing with video capture properties

Technical requirements

The technical requirements for this chapter are listed as follows:

- Python and OpenCV
- A Python-specific IDE
- The NumPy and Matplotlib Python packages
- Git client

The GitHub repository for Mastering OpenCV with Python can be accessed at `https://github.com/PacktPublishing/Mastering-OpenCV-4-with-Python`.

An introduction to handling files and images

Before going deeper in handling files and images, we are going to give you an overview of what we will look at in this chapter. This overview is summarized in the following diagram:

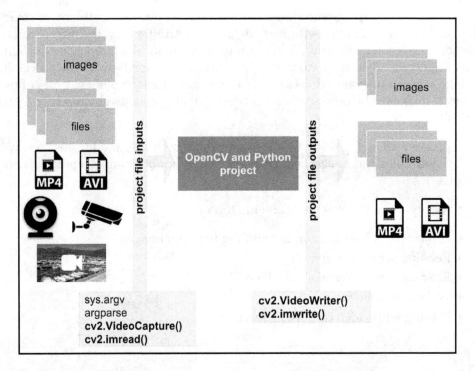

In the preceding diagram, you can see that a computer vision project (for example, an **OpenCV and Python project**) should deal with some input files (for example, **files** and **images**). Additionally, after some processing, the project can output some files (for example, **images** and **files**). So, in this chapter, we are going to see how to cope with these requirements and how to implement this flow (input-processing-output) properly.

A primary and necessary step to execute a program is to properly cope with command-line arguments, which are parameters that are given to a program or script containing some kind of *parameterized* information. For example, if you write a script to add two numbers, a common approach is to have two arguments, which are the two numbers that are necessary to perform the addition. In computer vision projects, **images** and different types of files are usually passed to the script as command-line arguments.

> Command-line arguments are a common and simple way to parameterize the execution of programs.

sys.argv

To handle command-line arguments, Python uses `sys.argv`. In this sense, when a program is executed, Python takes all the values from the command line and sets them in the `sys.argv` list. The first element of the list is the full path to the script (or the script name—it is operating system dependent), which is always `sys.argv[0]`. The second element of the list is the first argument to the script, which is `sys.argv[1]`, and so on. This can be seen in the following diagram, where the `sysargv_python.py` script is executed with two arguments:

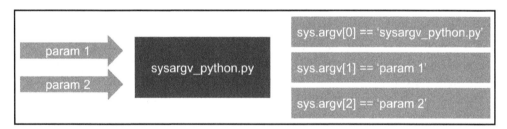

To see how `sys.argv` works, we are going to use the `sysargv_python.py` script:

```
# Import the required packages
import sys

# We will print some information in connection with sys.argv to see how it
works:
print("The name of the script being processed is:
'{}'".format(sys.argv[0]))
print("The number of arguments of the script is:
'{}'".format(len(sys.argv)))
print("The arguments of the script are: '{}'".format(str(sys.argv)))
```

If we execute this script without any parameter, we will see the following information:

```
The name of the script being processed is: 'sysargv_python.py'
The number of arguments of the script is: '1'
The arguments of the script are: '['sysargv_python.py']'
```

Additionally, if we execute this script with one parameter (for example, `sysargv_python.py OpenCV`), we will get the following information:

```
The name of the script being processed is: 'sysargv_python.py'
The number of arguments of the script is: '2'
The arguments of the script are: '['sysargv_python.py', 'OpenCV']'
```

As you can see, the first element, `sysargv_python.py` (`sys.argv[0]`), of the list is the script name. The second element, `OpenCV`, of the list (`sys.argv[1]`) is the first argument to our script.

 `argv[0]` is the script name, which is operating system dependent if it is a full pathname or not. See `https://docs.python.org/3/library/sys.html` for more information..

Argparse – command-line option and argument parsing

It should be taken into account that we should not handle `sys.argv` directly, mainly when our programs take complex parameters or multiple filenames. Alternatively, we should use Python's `argparse` library, which handles command-line arguments in a systematic way, making it accessible to write user-friendly command-line programs. In other words, Python has a module called `argparse` (`https://docs.python.org/3/library/argparse.html`) in the standard library for parsing command-line arguments. First, the program determines what arguments it requires. Then, `argparse` will work out how to parse these arguments to `sys.argv`. Also, `argparse` produces help and usage messages, and issues errors when invalid arguments are provided.

The minimum example to introduce this module is given here, `argparse_minimal.py`, which is shown as follows:

```
# Import the required packages
import argparse

# We first create the ArgumentParser object
# The created object 'parser' will have the necessary information
# to parse the command-line arguments into data types.
parser = argparse.ArgumentParser()

# The information about program arguments is stored in 'parser' and used
when parse_args() is called.
# ArgumentParser parses arguments through the parse_args() method:
parser.parse_args()
```

Running this script with no parameters results in nothing being displayed to `stdout`. However, if we include the `--help` (or `-h`) option, we will get the usage message of the script:

```
usage: argparse_minimal.py [-h]
optional arguments:
-h, --help show this help message and exit
```

Specifying any other parameters results in an error, for example:

```
argparse_minimal.py 6
usage: argparse_minimal.py [-h]
argparse_minimal.py: error: unrecognized arguments: 6
```

Therefore, we must call this script with the `-h` argument. In this way, the usage message information will be shown. No other possibilities are allowed as no arguments are defined. In this way, the second example to introduce `argparse` is to add a parameter, which can be seen in the `argparse_positional_arguments.py` example:

```
# Import the required packages
import argparse

# We first create the ArgumentParser object
# The created object 'parser' will have the necessary information
# to parse the command-line arguments into data types.
parser = argparse.ArgumentParser()

# We add a positional argument using add_argument() including a help
parser.add_argument("first_argument", help="this is the string text in
connection with first_argument")
```

```
# The information about program arguments is stored in 'parser'
# Then, it is used when the parser calls parse_args().
# ArgumentParser parses arguments through the parse_args() method:
args = parser.parse_args()

# We get and print the first argument of this script:
print(args.first_argument)
```

We added the `add_argument()` method. This method is used to specify what command-line options the program will accept. In this case, the `first_argument` argument is required. Additionally, the `argparse` module stores all the parameters, matching its name with the name of each added parameter—in this case, `first_argument`. Therefore, to obtain our parameter, we perform `args.first_argument`.

If this script is executed as `argparse_positional_arguments.py 5`, the output will be 5. However, if the script is executed without arguments as `argparse_positional_arguments.py`, the output will be as follows:

```
usage: argparse_positional_arguments.py [-h] first_argument
argparse_positional_arguments.py: error: the following arguments are
required: first_argument
```

Finally, if we execute the script with the -h option, the output will be as follows:

```
usage: argparse_positional_arguments.py [-h] first_argument
positional arguments:
 first_argument this is the string text in connection with first_argument
optional arguments:
 -h, --help show this help message and exit
```

By default, `argparse` treats the options we give it as strings. Therefore, if the parameter is not a string, the `type` option should be established. We will see the `argparse_sum_two_numbers.py` script adding two arguments and, hence, these two arguments are of the `int` type:

```
# Import the required packages
import argparse

# We first create the ArgumentParser object
# The created object 'parser' will have the necessary information
# to parse the command-line arguments into data types.
parser = argparse.ArgumentParser()

# We add 'first_number' argument using add_argument() including a help. The
type of this argument is int
parser.add_argument("first_number", help="first number to be added",
```

```
type=int)

# We add 'second_number' argument using add_argument() including a help The
type of this argument is int
parser.add_argument("second_number", help="second number to be added",
type=int)

# The information about program arguments is stored in 'parser'
# Then, it is used when the parser calls parse_args().
# ArgumentParser parses arguments through the parse_args() method:
args = parser.parse_args()
print("args: '{}'".format(args))

print("the sum is: '{}'".format(args.first_number + args.second_number))

# Additionally, the arguments can be stored in a dictionary calling vars()
function:
args_dict = vars(parser.parse_args())

# We print this dictionary:
print("args_dict dictionary: '{}'".format(args_dict))

# For example, to get the first argument using this dictionary:
print("first argument from the dictionary:
'{}'".format(args_dict["first_number"]))
```

If the script is executed without arguments, the output will be as follows:

```
argparse_sum_two_numbers.py
usage: argparse_sum_two_numbers.py [-h] first_number second_number
argparse_sum_two_numbers.py: error: the following arguments are required:
first_number, second_number
```

Additionally, if we execute the script with the –h option, the output will be as follows:

```
argparse_sum_two_numbers.py --help
usage: argparse_sum_two_numbers.py [-h] first_number second_number

positional arguments:
  first_number first number to be added
  second_number second number to be added

optional arguments:
  -h, --help show this help message and exit
```

It should be taken into account that in the previous example, we introduced the possibility of storing arguments in a dictionary by calling the `vars()` function:

```
# Additionally, the arguments can be stored in a dictionary calling vars()
function:
args_dict = vars(parser.parse_args())

# We print this dictionary:
print("args_dict dictionary: '{}'".format(args_dict))

# For example, to get the first argument using this dictionary:
print("first argument from the dictionary:
'{}'".format(args_dict["first_number"]))
```

For example, if this script is executed as `argparse_sum_two_numbers.py 5 10`, the output will be as follows:

```
args: 'Namespace(first_number=5, second_number=10)'
the sum is: '15'
args_dict dictionary: '{'first_number': 5, 'second_number': 10}'
first argument from the dictionary: '5'
```

This was a quick introduction to both `sys.argv` and `argparse`. An advanced introduction to `argparse` can be seen at `https://docs.python.org/3/howto/argparse.html`. Additionally, its docs are quite detailed and meticulous and have covered plenty of examples (`https://docs.python.org/3/library/argparse.html`). At this point, you can now learn how to read and write images using `argparse` in your OpenCV and Python programs, which will be shown in the *Reading and writing images* section.

Reading and writing images

In computer vision projects, images are commonly used as command-line arguments in our scripts. In the following sections, we are going to see how we can read and write images.

Reading images in OpenCV

The following example, `argparse_load_image.py`, shows you how to load an image:

```
# Import the required packages
import argparse
import cv2

# We first create the ArgumentParser object
```

```
# The created object 'parser' will have the necessary information
# to parse the command-line arguments into data types.
parser = argparse.ArgumentParser()

# We add 'path_image' argument using add_argument() including a help. The
# type of this argument is string (by default)
parser.add_argument("path_image", help="path to input image to be
displayed")

# The information about program arguments is stored in 'parser'
# Then, it is used when the parser calls parse_args().
# ArgumentParser parses arguments through the parse_args() method:
args = parser.parse_args()

# We can now load the input image from disk:
image = cv2.imread(args.path_image)

# Parse the argument and store it in a dictionary:
args = vars(parser.parse_args())

# Now, we can also load the input image from disk using args:
image2 = cv2.imread(args["path_image"])

# Show the loaded image:
cv2.imshow("loaded image", image)
cv2.imshow("loaded image2", image2)

# Wait until a key is pressed:
cv2.waitKey(0)

# Destroy all windows:
cv2.destroyAllWindows()
```

In this example, the required argument is path_image, which contains the path of the image we want to load. The path of the image is a string. Therefore, no type should be included in the positional argument because it is a string by default. Both args.path_image and args["path_image"] will contain the path of the image (two different ways of getting the value from the parameter), so we will use them as the parameter of the cv2.imread() function.

Reading and writing images in OpenCV

A common approach is to load an image, perform some kind of processing, and finally output this processed image (see `Chapter 2`, *Image Basics in OpenCV*, for a deeper explanation of these three steps). In this sense, the processed image can be saved to disk. In the following example, these three steps (load, processing, and save) are introduced. In this case, the processing step is very simple (convert the image into grayscale). This can be seen in the following example, `argparse_load_processing_save_image.py`:

```
# Import the required packages
import argparse
import cv2


# We first create the ArgumentParser object
# The created object 'parser' will have the necessary information
# to parse the command-line arguments into data types.
parser = argparse.ArgumentParser()


# Add 'path_image_input' argument using add_argument() including a help.
The type is string (by default):
parser.add_argument("path_image_input", help="path to input image to be
displayed")


# Add 'path_image_output' argument using add_argument() including a help.
The type is string (by default):
parser.add_argument("path_image_output", help="path of the processed image
to be saved")


# Parse the argument and store it in a dictionary:
args = vars(parser.parse_args())


# We can load the input image from disk:
image_input = cv2.imread(args["path_image_input"])


# Show the loaded image:
cv2.imshow("loaded image", image_input)


# Process the input image (convert it to grayscale):
gray_image = cv2.cvtColor(image_input, cv2.COLOR_BGR2GRAY)


# Show the processed image:
cv2.imshow("gray image", gray_image)


# Save the processed image to disk:
cv2.imwrite(args["path_image_output"], gray_image)


# Wait until a key is pressed:
```

```
cv2.waitKey(0)

# Destroy all windows:
cv2.destroyAllWindows()
```

In this previous example, there are two required arguments. The first one is `path_image_input`, which contains the path of the image we want to load. The path of the image is a string. Therefore, no type should be included in the positional argument because it is a string by default. The second one is `path_image_output`, which contains the path of the resulting image we want to save. In this example, the processing step consists of converting the loaded image into grayscale:

```
# Process the input image (convert it to grayscale)
gray_image = cv2.cvtColor(image_input, cv2.COLOR_BGR2GRAY)
```

It should be noted that the second argument, `cv2.COLOR_BGR2GRAY`, assumes that the loaded image is a BGR color image. If you have loaded an RGB color image and you want to convert it into grayscale, you should use `cv2.COLOR_RGB2GRAY`.

This is a very simple processing step, but it is included for the sake of simplicity. In future chapters, more elaborate processing algorithms will be shown.

Reading camera frames and video files

In some projects, you have to capture camera frames (for example, capture frames with the webcam of your laptop). In OpenCV, we have `cv2.VideoCapture`, which is a class for video capturing from different sources, such as image sequences, video files, and cameras. In this section, we are going to see some examples to introduce us to this class for capturing camera frames.

Reading camera frames

This first example, `read_camera.py`, shows you how to read frames from a camera that's connected to your computer. The required argument is `index_camera`, which indicates the index of the camera to read. If you have connected a webcam to your computer, it has an index of `0`. Additionally, if you have a second camera, you can select it by passing `1`. As you can see, the type of this parameter is `int`.

The first step to work with cv2.VideoCapture is to create an object to work with. In this case, the object is capture, and we call the constructor like this:

```
# We create a VideoCapture object to read from the camera (pass 0):
capture = cv2.VideoCapture(args.index_camera)
```

If index_camera is 0 (your first connected camera), it is equivalent to cv2.VideoCapture(0). To check whether the connection has been established correctly, we have the capture.isOpened() method, which returns False if the connection could not be established. In the same way, if the capture was initialized correctly, this method returns True.

To capture footage frame by frame from the camera, we call the capture.read() method, which returns the frame from the camera. This frame has the same structure as an image in OpenCV, so we can work with it in the same way. For example, to convert the frame into grayscale, do the following:

```
gray_frame = cv2.cvtColor(frame, cv2.COLOR_BGR2GRAY)
```

Additionally, capture.read() returns a bool. This bool indicates whether the frame has been correctly read from the capture object.

Accessing some properties of the capture object

Finally, you can access some properties of the capture object using capture.get(property_identifier). In this case, we get some properties, such as frame **width**, frame **height**, and **frames per second** (**fps**). If we call a property that is not supported, the returned value will be 0:

```
# Import the required packages
import cv2
import argparse

# We first create the ArgumentParser object
# The created object 'parser' will have the necessary information
# to parse the command-line arguments into data types.
parser = argparse.ArgumentParser()

# We add 'index_camera' argument using add_argument() including a help.
parser.add_argument("index_camera", help="index of the camera to read from", type=int)
args = parser.parse_args()

# We create a VideoCapture object to read from the camera (pass 0):
```

```
capture = cv2.VideoCapture(args.index_camera)

# Get some properties of VideoCapture (frame width, frame height and frames
per second (fps)):
frame_width = capture.get(cv2.CAP_PROP_FRAME_WIDTH)
frame_height = capture.get(cv2.CAP_PROP_FRAME_HEIGHT)
fps = capture.get(cv2.CAP_PROP_FPS)

# Print these values:
print("CV_CAP_PROP_FRAME_WIDTH: '{}'".format(frame_width))
print("CV_CAP_PROP_FRAME_HEIGHT : '{}'".format(frame_height))
print("CAP_PROP_FPS : '{}'".format(fps))

# Check if camera opened successfully
if capture.isOpened()is False:
    print("Error opening the camera")

# Read until video is completed
while capture.isOpened():
    # Capture frame-by-frame from the camera
    ret, frame = capture.read()

    if ret is True:
        # Display the captured frame:
        cv2.imshow('Input frame from the camera', frame)

        # Convert the frame captured from the camera to grayscale:
        gray_frame = cv2.cvtColor(frame, cv2.COLOR_BGR2GRAY)

        # Display the grayscale frame:
        cv2.imshow('Grayscale input camera', gray_frame)

        # Press q on keyboard to exit the program
        if cv2.waitKey(20) & 0xFF == ord('q'):
            break
    # Break the loop
    else:
        break

# Release everything:
capture.release()
cv2.destroyAllWindows()
```

Saving camera frames

This previous example can be easily modified to add a useful functionality. Imagine that you want to save some frames to disk when something interesting happens. In the following example, `read_camera_capture.py`, we are going to add this functionality. When the *C* key is pressed on the keyboard, we save the current frame to disk. We save both the BGR and the grayscale frames. The code that performs this functionality is shown here:

```
# Press c on keyboard to save current frame
if cv2.waitKey(20) & 0xFF == ord('c'):
    frame_name = "camera_frame_{}.png".format(frame_index)
    gray_frame_name = "grayscale_camera_frame_{}.png".format(frame_index)
    cv2.imwrite(frame_name, frame)
    cv2.imwrite(gray_frame_name, gray_frame)
    frame_index += 1
```

`ord('c')` returns the value representing the c character using eight bits. Additionally, the `cv2.waitKey()` value is bitwise AND using the & operator with `0xFF` to get only its last eight bits. Therefore, we can perform a comparison between these two 8-bit values. When the *C* key is pressed, we build the names for both frames. Then, we save the two images to disk. Finally, `frame_index` is incremented so that it's ready for the next frame to be saved. Check out `read_camera_capture.py` to see the full code of this script.

Reading a video file

`cv2.VideoCapture` also allows us to read a video file. Therefore, to read a video file, the path to the video file should be provided when creating the `cv2.VideoCapture` object:

```
# We first create the ArgumentParser object
# The created object 'parser' will have the necessary information
# to parse the command-line arguments into data types.
parser = argparse.ArgumentParser()

# We add 'video_path' argument using add_argument() including a help.
parser.add_argument("video_path", help="path to the video file")
args = parser.parse_args()

# Create a VideoCapture object. In this case, the argument is the video
# file name:
capture = cv2.VideoCapture(args.video_path)
```

Check out `read_video_file.py` to see the full example of how to read and display a video file using `cv2.VideoCapture`.

Reading from an IP camera

To finish with `cv2.VideoCapture`, we are going to see how we can read from an IP camera. Reading from an IP camera in OpenCV is very similar to reading from a file. In this sense, only the parameter to the constructor of `cv2.VideoCapture` should be changed. The good thing about this is that you do not need an IP camera in your local network to try this functionality. There are many public IP cameras you can try to connect. For example, we are going to connect to an IP public camera, which is placed at *Club Nàutic Port de la Selva – Costa Brava – Cap de Creus (Girona, Spain)*. The web page of this port is hosted at `https://www.cnps.cat/`. You can navigate to the webcam sections (`https://www.cnps.cat/webcams/`) to find some webcams to connect with.

Therefore, the only thing you have to modify is the parameter that's given to `cv2.VideCapture`. In this case, it's `http://217.126.89.102:8010/axis-cgi/mjpg/video.cgi`. If you execute this example (`read_ip_camera.py`), you should see something similar to the following screenshot, where both the BGR and the grayscale images that were obtained from the IP camera are shown:

Writing a video file

In this section, we are going to see how we can write to video files using `cv2.VideoWriter`. However some concepts (for example, fps, codecs, and video file formats) should be introduced first.

Calculating frames per second

In the *Reading camera frame and video files* section, we saw how we can get some properties from the `cv2.VideoCapture` object. fps is an important metric in computer vision projects. This metric indicates how many frames are processed per second. It is safe to say that a higher number of fps is better. However, the number of frames your algorithm should process every second will depend on the specific problem you have to solve. For example, if your algorithm should track and detect people walking down the street, 15 fps is probably enough. But if your goal is to detect and track cars going fast on a highway, 20-25 fps are probably necessary.

Therefore, it is important to know how to calculate the fps metric in your computer vision projects. In the following example, `read_camera_fps.py`, we are going to modify `read_camera.py` to output the number of fps. The key points are shown in the following code:

```
# Read until the video is completed, or 'q' is pressed
while capture.isOpened():
    # Capture frame-by-frame from the camera
    ret, frame = capture.read()

    if ret is True:
        # Calculate time before processing the frame:
        processing_start = time.time()

        # All the processing should be included here
        # ...
        # ...
        # End of processing

        # Calculate time after processing the frame
        processing_end = time.time()

        # Calculate the difference
        processing_time_frame = processing_end - processing_start

        # FPS = 1 / time_per_frame
        # Show the number of frames per second
        print("fps: {}".format(1.0 / processing_time_frame))

    # Break the loop
    else:
        break
```

First, we take the time before the processing is done:

```
processing_start = time.time()
```

Then, we take the time after all the processing is done:

```
processing_end = time.time()
```

Following that, we calculate the difference:

```
processing_time_frame = processing_end - processing_start
```

Finally, we calculate and print the number of fps:

```
print("fps: {}".format(1.0 / processing_time_frame))
```

Considerations for writing a video file

A video code is a piece of software that's used to both compress and decompress a digital video. Therefore, a codec can be used to convert an uncompressed video into a compressed one, or it can be used to convert a compressed video to an uncompressed one. The compressed video format usually follows a standard specification called **video compression specification** or **video coding format**. In this sense, OpenCV provides FOURCC, which is a 4-byte code that's used to specify the video codec. FOURCC stands for *four character code*. The list of all available codes can be seen at `http://www.fourcc.org/codecs.php`. It should be taken into account that the supported codecs are platform-dependent. This means that if you want to work with a specific codec, this codec should already be installed on your system. Typical codecs are DIVX, XVID, X264, and MJPG.

Additionally, a video file format is a type of file format that's used to store digital video data. Typical video file formats are AVI (`*.avi`), MP4 (`*.mp4`), QuickTime (`*.mov`), and Windows Media Video (`*.wmv`).

Finally, it should be taken into account that the right combination between video file formats (for example, `*.avi`) and FOURCC (for example, DIVX) is not straightforward. You will probably need to experiment and play with these values. Therefore, when creating a video file in OpenCV, you will have to take all of these factors into consideration.

The following diagram tries to summarize them:

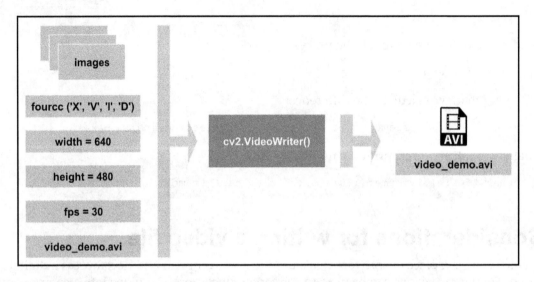

This diagram summarizes the main considerations you should take into account when creating a video file using `cv2.VideoWriter()` in OpenCV. In this diagram, the `video_demo.avi` video has been created. In this case, the FOURCC value is `XVID` and the video file format is `AVI` (`*.avi`). Finally, both the fps and the dimensions of every frame of the video should be established.

Additionally, the following example, `write_video_file.py`, writes a video file and it can also be helpful to play with these concepts. Some key points of this example are commented here. In this example, the required argument is the video file name (for example, `video_demo.avi`):

```
# We first create the ArgumentParser object
# The created object 'parser' will have the necessary information
# to parse the command-line arguments into data types.
parser = argparse.ArgumentParser()

# We add 'output_video_path' argument using add_argument() including a
help.
parser.add_argument("output_video_path", help="path to the video file to
write")
args = parser.parse_args()
```

We are going to take frames from the first camera that's connected to our computer. Therefore, we create the object accordingly:

```
# Create a VideoCapture object and pass 0 as argument to read from the
camera
capture = cv2.VideoCapture(0)
```

Next, we will get some properties from the capture object (frame width, frame height, and fps). We are going to use them to create our video file:

```
# Get some properties of VideoCapture (frame width, frame height and frames
per second (fps)):
frame_width = capture.get(cv2.CAP_PROP_FRAME_WIDTH)
frame_height = capture.get(cv2.CAP_PROP_FRAME_HEIGHT)
fps = capture.get(cv2.CAP_PROP_FPS)
```

Now, we specify the video codec using FOURCC, a four-byte code. Remember, it is platform-dependent. In this case, we define the codec as XVID:

```
# FourCC is a 4-byte code used to specify the video codec and it is
platform dependent!
# In this case, define the codec XVID
fourcc = cv2.VideoWriter_fourcc('X', 'V', 'I', 'D')
```

The following line also works:

```
# FourCC is a 4-byte code used to specify the video codec and it is
platform dependent!
# In this case, define the codec XVID
fourcc = cv2.VideoWriter_fourcc(*'XVID')
```

Then, we create the cv2.VideoWriter object, out_gray. We use the same properties as the input camera. The last argument is False so that we can write the video in grayscale. If we want to create the video in color, this last argument should be True:

```
# Create VideoWriter object. We use the same properties as the input
camera.
# Last argument is False to write the video in grayscale. True otherwise
(write the video in color)
out_gray = cv2.VideoWriter(args.output_video_path, fourcc, int(fps),
(int(frame_width), int(frame_height)), False)
```

We get frame by frame output from the capture object by using `capture.read()`. Each frame is converted into grayscale and written to the video file. We can show the frame, but this is not necessary to write the video. If *q* is pressed, the program ends:

```
# Read until video is completed or 'q' is pressed
while capture.isOpened():
    # Read the frame from the camera
    ret, frame = capture.read()
    if ret is True:

        # Convert the frame to grayscale
        gray_frame = cv2.cvtColor(frame, cv2.COLOR_BGR2GRAY)

        # Write the grayscale frame to the video
        out_gray.write(gray_frame)

        # We show the frame (this is not necessary to write the video)
        # But we show it until 'q' is pressed
        cv2.imshow('gray', gray_frame)
        if cv2.waitKey(1) & 0xFF == ord('q'):
            break
    else:
        break
```

Finally, we release everything (the `cv2.VideoCapture` and `cv2.VideWriter` objects, and we destroy the created windows):

```
# Release everything:
capture.release()
out_gray.release()
cv2.destroyAllWindows()
```

The full code for this example can be seen in the `write_video_file.py` file.

Playing with video capture properties

In some of the previous examples, we saw how to get some properties from the `cv2.VideoCapture` object. In this section, we are going to see how we can get all of the properties and understand how they work. Finally, we are going to use these properties to load a video file and output it backwards (showing the last frame of the video first and so on).

Getting all the properties from the video capture object

First, we create the `read_video_file_all_properties.py` script to show all the properties. Some of these properties only work when we're working with cameras (not with video files). In these cases, a 0 value is returned. Additionally, we have created the `decode_fourcc()` function, which converts the value that's returned by `capture.get(cv2.CAP_PROP_FOURCC)` as a string value that contains the int representation of the codec. In this sense, this value should be converted into a four-byte char representation to output the codec properly. Therefore, the `decode_fourcc()` function copes with this.

The code of this function is given as follows:

```python
def decode_fourcc(fourcc):
    """Decodes the fourcc value to get the four chars identifying it

    """
    fourcc_int = int(fourcc)

    # We print the int value of fourcc
    print("int value of fourcc: '{}'".format(fourcc_int))

    # We can also perform this in one line:
    # return "".join([chr((fourcc_int >> 8 * i) & 0xFF) for i in range(4)])

    fourcc_decode = ""
    for i in range(4):
        int_value = fourcc_int >> 8 * i & 0xFF
        print("int_value: '{}'".format(int_value))
        fourcc_decode += chr(int_value)
    return fourcc_decode
```

To explain how it works, the following diagram summarizes the main steps:

```
┌─────────────────────────────────────────────┐
│                                               │
│   capture.get(cv2.CAP_PROP_FOURCC)            │
│                                               │
│                    ↓                          │
│                                               │
│              828601953                        │
│                                               │
│                    ↓                          │
│                                               │
│   00110001011000110111011001100001            │
│                                               │
│                    ↓                          │
│                                               │
│   00110001-01100011-01110110-01100001         │
│                                               │
│                    ↓                          │
│                                               │
│              97-118-99-49                      │
│                                               │
│                    ↓                          │
│                                               │
│                 a-v-c-1                        │
│                                               │
└─────────────────────────────────────────────┘
```

As you can see, the first step is to obtain the int representation of the value that's returned by `capture.get(cv2.CAP_PROP_FOURCC)`, which is a string. Then, we iterate four times to get every eight bits and convert these eight bits into `int`. Finally, these `int` values are converted into `char` using the `chr()` function. It should be noted that we can perform this function in only one line of code, as follows:

```python
return "".join([chr((fourcc_int >> 8 * i) & 0xFF) for i in range(4)])
```

The `CAP_PROP_POS_FRAMES` property gives you the current frame of the video file and the `CAP_PROP_POS_MSEC` property gives you the timestamp of the current frame. We can also get the number of fps with the `CAP_PROP_FPS` property.
The `CAP_PROP_FRAME_COUNT` property gives you the total number of frames of the video file.

To get and print all the properties, use the following code:

```python
# Get and print these values:
print("CV_CAP_PROP_FRAME_WIDTH:
'{}'".format(capture.get(cv2.CAP_PROP_FRAME_WIDTH)))
print("CV_CAP_PROP_FRAME_HEIGHT :
'{}'".format(capture.get(cv2.CAP_PROP_FRAME_HEIGHT)))
print("CAP_PROP_FPS : '{}'".format(capture.get(cv2.CAP_PROP_FPS)))
```

```
print("CAP_PROP_POS_MSEC :
'{}'".format(capture.get(cv2.CAP_PROP_POS_MSEC)))
print("CAP_PROP_POS_FRAMES :
'{}'".format(capture.get(cv2.CAP_PROP_POS_FRAMES)))
print("CAP_PROP_FOURCC    :
'{}'".format(decode_fourcc(capture.get(cv2.CAP_PROP_FOURCC))))
print("CAP_PROP_FRAME_COUNT   :
'{}'".format(capture.get(cv2.CAP_PROP_FRAME_COUNT)))
print("CAP_PROP_MODE : '{}'".format(capture.get(cv2.CAP_PROP_MODE)))
print("CAP_PROP_BRIGHTNESS :
'{}'".format(capture.get(cv2.CAP_PROP_BRIGHTNESS)))
print("CAP_PROP_CONTRAST :
'{}'".format(capture.get(cv2.CAP_PROP_CONTRAST)))
print("CAP_PROP_SATURATION :
'{}'".format(capture.get(cv2.CAP_PROP_SATURATION)))
print("CAP_PROP_HUE : '{}'".format(capture.get(cv2.CAP_PROP_HUE)))
print("CAP_PROP_GAIN    : '{}'".format(capture.get(cv2.CAP_PROP_GAIN)))
print("CAP_PROP_EXPOSURE :
'{}'".format(capture.get(cv2.CAP_PROP_EXPOSURE)))
print("CAP_PROP_CONVERT_RGB :
'{}'".format(capture.get(cv2.CAP_PROP_CONVERT_RGB)))
print("CAP_PROP_RECTIFICATION :
'{}'".format(capture.get(cv2.CAP_PROP_RECTIFICATION)))
print("CAP_PROP_ISO_SPEED :
'{}'".format(capture.get(cv2.CAP_PROP_ISO_SPEED)))
print("CAP_PROP_BUFFERSIZE :
'{}'".format(capture.get(cv2.CAP_PROP_BUFFERSIZE)))
```

You can view the full code of this script in
the read_video_file_all_properties.py file.

Using the properties – playing a video backwards

To see how we can use the aforementioned properties, we are going to understand the
read_video_file_backwards.py script, which uses some of these properties to load a
video and output it backwards, showing the last frame of the video first and so on. We are
going to use the following properties:

- cv2.CAP_PROP_FRAME_COUNT: This property provides the total number of
  frames
- cv2.CAP_PROP_POS_FRAMES: This property provides the current frame

The first step is to get the index of the last frame:

```
# We get the index of the last frame of the video file
frame_index = capture.get(cv2.CAP_PROP_FRAME_COUNT) - 1
```

Therefore, we set the current frame to read to this position:

```
# We set the current frame position
capture.set(cv2.CAP_PROP_POS_FRAMES, frame_index)
```

This way, we can read this frame as usual:

```
# Capture frame-by-frame from the video file
ret, frame = capture.read()
```

Finally, we decrement the index in order to read the next frame from the video file:

```
# Decrement the index to read next frame
frame_index = frame_index - 1
```

The full code is provided in the `read_video_file_backwards.py` script. This script can be easily modified to save the resulting video playing backwards (not only showing it). This script is proposed in the *Question* section.

Summary

In this chapter, we saw that working with images and files is a key element of computer vision projects. A common approach in this kind of project is to load some images first, perform some processing, and then output the processed images. In this chapter, we reviewed this flow. Additionally, in connection with video streams, both `cv2.VideoCapture` and `cv2.VideoWriter` were covered. We also looked at the `cv2.VideoWriter` class for video writing. Two key aspects were reviewed when writing video files—video codecs (for example, DIVX) and video file formats (for example, AVI). To work with video codecs, OpenCV provides FOURCC, a four-byte code. Typical codecs are DIVX, XVID, X264, and MJPG, while typical video file formats are AVI (`*.avi`), MP4 (`*.mp4`), QuickTime (`*.mov`), and Windows Media Video (`*.wmv`).

We also reviewed the concept of fps and how to calculate it in our programs. Additionally, we looked at how to get all the properties of the `cv2.VideoCapture` object and how to use them to load a video and output it backwards, showing the last frame of the video first. Finally, we saw how to cope with command-line arguments. Python uses `sys.argv` to handle command-line arguments. When our programs take complex parameters or multiple filenames, we should use Python's argparse library.

In the next chapter, we are going to learn how to draw basic and more advanced shapes using the OpenCV library. OpenCV provides functions to draw lines, circles, rectangles, ellipses, text, and polylines. In connection with computer vision projects, it is a common approach to draw basic shapes in the image in order to do the following:

- Show some intermediate results of your algorithm (for example, bounding box of the detected objects)
- Show the final results of your algorithm (for example, the class of the detected objects, such as cars, cats, or dogs)
- Show some debugging information (for example, execution time)

Therefore, the next chapter can be of great help in connection with your computer vision algorithms.

Questions

1. What is `sys.argv[1]`?
2. Write a piece of code to add a `first_number` argument of the `int` type and include the help first number to be added using `parser.add_argument()`.
3. Write a piece of code to save the imagine `img` to disk with the name `image.png`.
4. Create the `capture` object using `cv2.VideoCapture()` to read from the first camera that's connected to your computer.
5. Create the object capture using `cv2.VideoCapture()` to read from the first camera connected to your computer and print the `CAP_PROP_FRAME_WIDTH` property.
6. Read an image and save it to disk with the same name but ending in `_copy.png` (for example, `logo_copy.png`).
7. Create a script (`read_video_file_backwards_save_video.py`) that loads a video file and creates another played backwards (containing the last frame of the video first and so on).

Further reading

The following references will help you dive deeper into argparse, which is a key point in your computer vision projects:

- *Parsing the command line with argparse* (`https://www.packtpub.com/mapt/book/application_development/9781783280971/16/ch16lvl1sec147/parsing-the-command-line-with-argparse`)
- *Using argparse to get command-line input* (`https://www.packtpub.com/mapt/book/application_development/9781786469250/5/ch05lvl1sec60/using-argparse-to-get-command-line-input`)

4
Constructing Basic Shapes in OpenCV

One basic functionality offered by OpenCV is drawing basic shapes. OpenCV provides functions to draw lines, circles, rectangles, ellipses, and so on. When building a computer vision project, you usually want to modify the image by drawing some shapes. For example, if you develop a face detection algorithm, you should draw a rectangle highlighting the detected faces in the computed image. Additionally, if you develop a face recognition algorithm, you should draw a rectangle highlighting the detected faces and also write some text showing the identity of the detected faces. And finally, it is a common approach to write some *debugging* information. You could show, for example, the number of detected faces (in order to see the performance of your face detection algorithm) or the processing time. In this chapter, you are going to see how to draw basic and more advanced shapes using the OpenCV library.

The following topics will be covered:

- A theoretical introduction to drawing in OpenCV
- Basic shapes—lines, rectangles, and circles
- Basic shapes (2)—clip and arrowed lines, ellipses, and polylines
- Drawing text
- Dynamic drawing with mouse events
- Advanced drawing

Technical requirements

The technical requirements are as follows:

- Python and OpenCV
- Python-specific IDE

- NumPy and Matplotlib packages
- Git client

For further details about how to install these, see `Chapter 1`, *Setting Up OpenCV*. The GitHub repository containing all the supporting project files necessary to work through the book from the first chapter to the last one can be accessed here: `https://github.com/PacktPublishing/Mastering-OpenCV-4-with-Python`.

A theoretical introduction to drawing in OpenCV

OpenCV provides many functions to draw basic shapes. Common basic shapes include lines, rectangles, and circles. However, with OpenCV we can draw more basic shapes. As mentioned briefly in the introduction, it is a common approach to draw basic shapes on the image in order to do the following:

- Show some intermediate results of your algorithm
- Show the final results of your algorithm
- Show some debugging information

In the next screenshot, you can see an image modified to include some useful information in connection with the two algorithms mentioned in the introduction (face detection and face recognition). In this way, you can process all the images in a directory and, afterward, you can see where your algorithm has detected wrong faces (false positives) or even missing faces (false negatives):

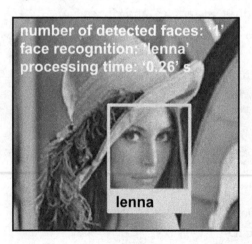

A **false positive** is an error where the result indicates the presence of a condition when in reality the condition is not satisfied (for example, a chair is classified as a face). A **false negative** is an error where the result indicates the absence of a condition when in reality the condition should be satisfied (for example, a face is not detected).

In this chapter, we are going to see how to draw some basic shapes and text in different colors. To introduce this and to review some concepts from previous chapters, we are going to show you two basic functionalities that we will be using in most of the examples in this chapter. The first functionality is building a `colors` dictionary, which defines the main colors to be used. In the next screenshot, you can see how it works:

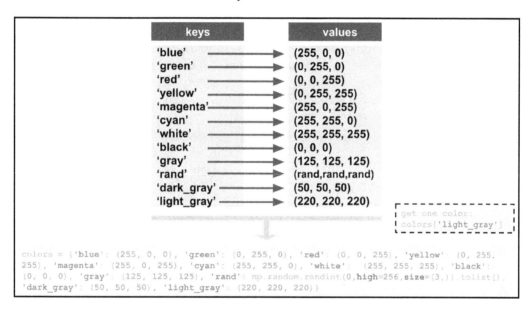

It should be pointed out that this dictionary is just for training and practicing purposes; for other purposes, there are other options that you can use. A common approach is to create a `constant.py` file to define the colors. Each color is defined by a constant:

```
"""
Common colors triplets (BGR space) to use in OpenCV
"""

BLUE = (255, 0, 0)
GREEN = (0, 255, 0)
RED = (0, 0, 255)
YELLOW = (0, 255, 255)
MAGENTA = (255, 0, 255)
```

```
CYAN = (255, 255, 0)
DARK_GRAY = (50, 50, 50)
...
```

The following code will enable you to use these constants:

```
import constant

# Getting red color:
print("red: '{}'".format(constant.RED))
```

Constants are usually specified in capital letters (for example, BLUE) and with underscores between the words (for example, DARK_GRAY).

Additionally, as we are going to plot the figures using Matplotlib, we have created a show_with_matplotlib() function with two arguments. The first one is the image we want to show, and the second is the title of the figure to plot. Therefore, the first step of this function converts the BGR image to RGB, because you have to show color images with Matplotlib. The second and final step of this function is to show the image using Matplotlib capabilities. To put these pieces together, the testing_colors.py script has been coded. In this script, we draw some lines, each one in a color of the dictionary.

The code to create the dictionary is shown here:

```
# Dictionary containing some colors
colors = {'blue': (255, 0, 0), 'green': (0, 255, 0), 'red': (0, 0, 255),
'yellow': (0, 255, 255), 'magenta': (255, 0, 255), 'cyan': (255, 255, 0),
'white': (255, 255, 255), 'black': (0, 0, 0), 'gray': (125, 125, 125),
'rand': np.random.randint(0, high=256, size=(3,)).tolist(), 'dark_gray':
(50, 50, 50), 'light_gray': (220, 220, 220)}
```

You can see that some predefined colors are included in this dictionary—blue, green, red, yellow, magenta, cyan, white, black, gray, a random one, gray, dark_gray, and light_gray. If you want to use a specific color (for example, magenta), you should perform the following:

```
colors['magenta']
```

Alternatively, you can use (255, 0, 255) to get the magenta color. But it is easier to use this dictionary rather than write triplets of numbers, because you do not need to memorize the addition properties of the RGB color space (adding blue—(255,0,0) and red—(0,0,255) gives magenta—(255, 0, 255)). Remember that you can use constant.py to perform this functionality.

If you do not know what these numbers are or represent, you should read `Chapter 2`, *Image Basics in OpenCV*, where these concepts are introduced.

In order to see how to use these two functionalities, which we use in most of the examples in this chapter (the `colors` function and the `show_with_matplotlib()` function), we have created the `testing_colors.py` script. If you execute it, you will see the next screenshot:

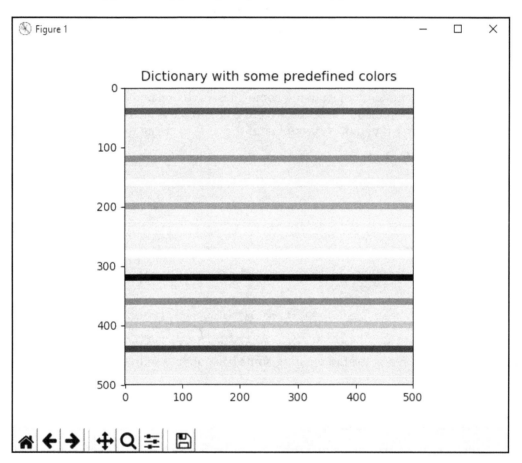

In this example, we have created an image of size *500 × 500*, with the 3 channels (we want a color image) and a `uint8` type (8-bit unsigned integers). We have created it with a black background:

```
# We create the canvas to draw: 400 x 400 pixels, 3 channels, uint8 (8-bit
unsigned integers)
# We set background to black using np.zeros()
image = np.zeros((500, 500, 3), dtype="uint8")
```

In this case, we want to set the background to light gray, not black. If you want to change the background, you can perform the following:

```
# If you want another background color, you can do the following:
image[:] = colors['light_gray']
```

Next, we add the functionality of drawing some lines, each one in a color of the dictionary. It should be noted that in the next section we are going to see how to create some basic shapes, so do not worry if you don't understand the code to create the lines:

```
# We draw all the colors to test the dictionary
# We draw some lines, each one in a color. To get the color, use
'colors[key]'
separation = 40
for key in colors:
cv2.line(image, (0, separation), (500, separation), colors[key], 10)
separation += 40
```

And finally, we draw the image using the created `show_with_matplotlib()` function:

```
# Show image:
show_with_matplotlib(image, 'Dictionary with some predefined colors')
```

The two arguments of `show_with_matplotlib()` are the image to plot and the title to show. So now we are ready to start creating some basic shapes with OpenCV and Python.

Drawing shapes

In this section, we are going to see how to draw shapes using OpenCV capabilities. Firstly, we will look at how to draw the basic shapes, and then we will focus on more advanced shapes.

Basic shapes – lines, rectangles, and circles

In the next example, we are going to see how to draw basic shapes in OpenCV. These basic shapes include lines, rectangles, and circles, which are the most common and simple shapes to draw. The first step is to create an image where the shapes will be drawn. To this end, a *400 × 400* image with the 3 channels (to properly display a BGR image) and a `uint8` type (8-bit unsigned integers) will be created:

```
# We create the canvas to draw: 400 x 400 pixels, 3 channels, uint8 (8-bit
unsigned integers)
# We set the background to black using np.zeros()
image = np.zeros((400, 400, 3), dtype="uint8")
```

We set the background to light gray using the `colors` dictionary:

```
# If you want another background color, you can do the following:
image[:] = colors['light_gray']
```

This canvas (or image) is shown in the next screenshot:

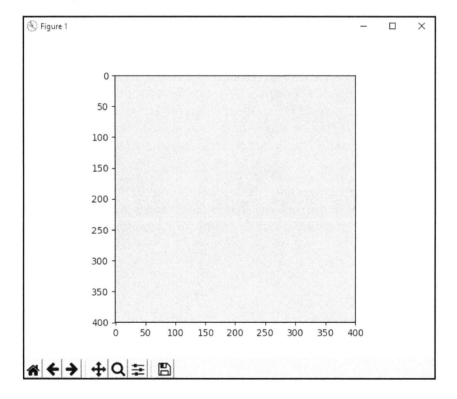

Now, we are ready to draw the basic shapes. It should be noted that most drawing functions that OpenCV provides have common parameters. For the sake of simplicity, these parameters are briefly introduced here:

- `img`: It is the image where the shape will be drawn.
- `color`: It is the color (BGR triplet) used to draw the shape.
- `thickness`: If this value is positive, it is the thickness of the shape outline. Otherwise, a filled shape will be drawn.
- `lineType`: It is the type of the shape boundary. OpenCV provides three types of line:
    - `cv2.LINE_4`: This means four-connected lines
    - `cv2.LINE_8`: This means eight-connected lines
    - `cv2.LINE_AA`: This means an anti-aliased line
- `shift`: This indicates the number of fractional bits in connection with the coordinates of some points defining the shape.

In connection with the aforementioned parameters, the `cv2.LINE_AA` option for `lineType` produces a much better quality drawing (for example, when drawing text), but it is slower to draw. So, this consideration should be taken into account. Both the eight-connected and the four-connected lines, which are non-antialiased lines, are drawn with the Bresenham algorithm. For the anti-aliased line type, the Gaussian filtering algorithm is used. Additionally, the `shift` parameter is necessary because many drawing functions can't deal with sub-pixel accuracy. For simplicity in our examples, we are going to work with integer coordinates. Therefore, this value will be set to 0 (`shift = 0`). However to give you a complete understanding, an example of how to use the `shift` parameter will also be provided.

 Remember that, for all the examples included in this section, a canvas has been created to draw all the shapes. This canvas is a *400 x 400* pixel image, with a light gray background. See the previous screenshot, which shows this canvas.

Drawing lines

The first function we are going to see is `cv2.line()`. The signature is as follows:

```
img = line(img, pt1, pt2, color, thickness=1, lineType=8, shift=0)
```

This function draws a line on the `img` image connecting `pt1` and `pt2`:

```
cv2.line(image, (0, 0), (400, 400), colors['green'], 3)
cv2.line(image, (0, 400), (400, 0), colors['blue'], 10)
cv2.line(image, (200, 0), (200, 400), colors['red'], 3)
cv2.line(image, (0, 200), (400, 200), colors['yellow'], 10)
```

After coding these lines, we call the `show_with_matplotlib(image, 'cv2.line()')` function. The result is shown in the next screenshot:

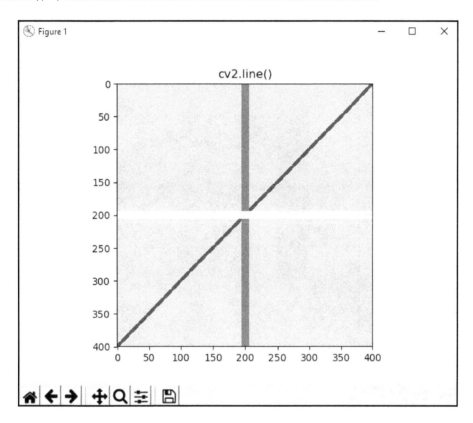

Drawing rectangles

The signature for the `cv2.rectangle()` function is as follows:

```
img = rectangle(img, pt1, pt2, color, thickness=1, lineType=8, shift=0)
```

This function draws a rectangle given the two opposite corners, pt1 and pt2:

```
cv2.rectangle(image, (10, 50), (60, 300), colors['green'], 3)
cv2.rectangle(image, (80, 50), (130, 300), colors['blue'], -1)
cv2.rectangle(image, (150, 50), (350, 100), colors['red'], -1)
cv2.rectangle(image, (150, 150), (350, 300), colors['cyan'], 10)
```

After drawing these rectangles, we call the show_with_matplotlib(image, 'cv2.rectangle()') function. The result is shown in the next screenshot:

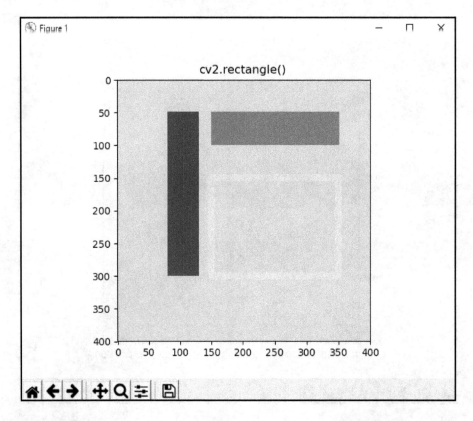

Remember that negative values (for example, -1) for the thickness parameter mean that a filled shape will be drawn.

Drawing circles

The signature for the cv2.circle() function is as follows:

```
img = circle(img, center, radius, color, thickness=1, lineType=8, shift=0)
```

This function draws a circle with a `radius` radius centered in the `center` position. Some circles are defined in the following code:

```
cv2.circle(image, (50, 50), 20, colors['green'], 3)
cv2.circle(image, (100, 100), 30, colors['blue'], -1)
cv2.circle(image, (200, 200), 40, colors['magenta'], 10)
cv2.circle(image, (300, 300), 40, colors['cyan'], -1)
```

After drawing these circles, we call the `show_with_matplotlib(image, 'cv2.circle()')` function. The result is shown in the next screenshot:

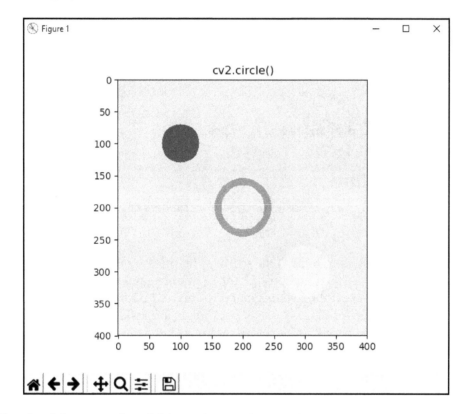

The full code of the examples of this section can be seen in `basic_drawing.py`.

Understanding advanced shapes

In this section, we are going to see how to draw clip lines, arrowed lines, ellipses, and polylines. These shapes are not as straightforward to draw as the shapes we saw in the previous section, but they are simple to understand. The first step is to create an image where the shapes will be drawn. For this, a *300 × 300* image with the 3 channels (to properly display a BGR image) and a `uint8` type (8-bit unsigned integers) will be created:

```
# We create the canvas to draw: 300 x 300 pixels, 3 channels, uint8 (8-bit
unsigned integers)
# We set the background to black using np.zeros()
image = np.zeros((300, 300, 3), dtype="uint8")
```

We set the background to light gray using the `colors` dictionary:

```
# If you want another background color, you can do the following:
image[:] = colors['light_gray']
```

At this point, we can start drawing the new shapes.

Drawing a clip line

The signature for the `cv2.clipLine()` function is as follows as follows:

```
retval, pt1, pt2 = clipLine(imgRect, pt1, pt2)
```

The `cv2.clipLine()` function returns the segment (defined by the `pt1` and `pt2` output points) inside the rectangle (the function *clips* the segment against the defined rectangle). In this sense, `retval` is `False`, if the two original `pt1` and `pt2` points are both outside the rectangle. Otherwise (some of the two `pt1` or `pt2` points are inside the rectangle) this function returns `True`. This can be more clearly seen with the next piece of code:

```
cv2.line(image, (0, 0), (300, 300), colors['green'], 3)
cv2.rectangle(image, (0, 0), (100, 100), colors['blue'], 3)
ret, p1, p2 = cv2.clipLine((0, 0, 100, 100), (0, 0), (300, 300))
if ret:
    cv2.line(image, p1, p2, colors['yellow'], 3)
```

In the next screenshot, you can see the resultant figure after executing this piece of code:

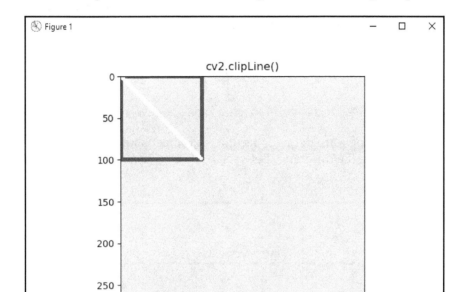

As you can see, the line segment defined by the p1 and p2 points is shown in yellow, *clipping* the original line segment against the rectangle. In this case, ret is True because at least one of the points is inside the rectangle and this is the reason why the yellow segment, defined by pt1 and pt2, is drawn.

Drawing arrows

The signature for this function is as follows:

```
cv.arrowedLine(img, pt1, pt2, color, thickness=1, lineType=8, shift=0,
tipLength=0.1)
```

This function allows you to create an arrow, which points from the first point defined by pt1 to the second point defined by pt2. The length of the arrow tip can be controlled by the tipLength parameter, which is defined in relation to the segment length (distance between pt1 and pt2):

```
cv2.arrowedLine(image, (50, 50), (200, 50), colors['red'], 3, 8, 0, 0.1)
cv2.arrowedLine(image, (50, 120), (200, 120), colors['green'], 3,
cv2.LINE_AA, 0, 0.3)
cv2.arrowedLine(image, (50, 200), (200, 200), colors['blue'], 3, 8, 0, 0.3)
```

As you can see, three arrows are defined. See the next screenshot, where these arrows are plotted. Additionally, see the difference between cv2.LINE_AA (you can also write 16) and 8 (you can also write cv2.LINE_8):

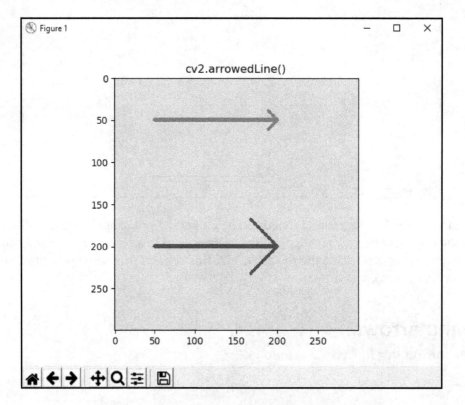

TIP

In this example, we have combined (on purpose to call your attention) both enums (for example, cv2.LINE_AA) or writing the value directly (for example, 8) in connection with the lineType parameter. This is definitely not a good idea, because it could confuse you. One criterion should be established and maintained throughout all your code.

Drawing ellipses

The signature for this function is as follows:

```
cv2.ellipse(img, center, axes, angle, startAngle, endAngle, color,
thickness=1, lineType=8, shift=0)
```

This function allows you to create different types of ellipses. The `angle` parameter (in degrees) allows you to rotate the ellipse. The `axes` parameter controls the size of the ellipse corresponding to half the size of the axes. If a full ellipse is required, `startAngle = 0` and `endAngle = 360`. Otherwise, you should adjust these parameters to the required elliptic arc (in degrees). You can also see that, by passing the same value for the axes, you can draw a circle:

```
cv2.ellipse(image, (80, 80), (60, 40), 0, 0, 360, colors['red'], -1)
cv2.ellipse(image, (80, 200), (80, 40), 0, 0, 360, colors['green'], 3)
cv2.ellipse(image, (80, 200), (10, 40), 0, 0, 360, colors['blue'], 3)
cv2.ellipse(image, (200, 200), (10, 40), 0, 0, 180, colors['yellow'], 3)
cv2.ellipse(image, (200, 100), (10, 40), 0, 0, 270, colors['cyan'], 3)
cv2.ellipse(image, (250, 250), (30, 30), 0, 0, 360, colors['magenta'], 3)
cv2.ellipse(image, (250, 100), (20, 40), 45, 0, 360, colors['gray'], 3)
```

These ellipses can be seen in the next screenshot:

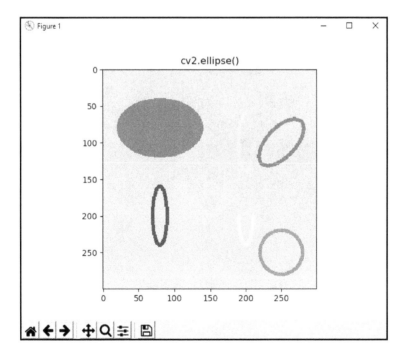

Drawing polygons

The signature for this function is as follows:

```
cv2.polylines(img, pts, isClosed, color, thickness=1, lineType=8, shift=0)
```

This function allows you to create polygonal curves. Here the key parameter is `pts`, where the array defining the polygonal curve should be provided. The shape of this parameter should be `(number_vertex, 1, 2)`. So a common approach is to define it by using `np.array` to create the coordinates (of the `np.int32` type) and, afterward, reshape it to match the aforementioned shape. For example, to create a triangle, the code will look like this:

```
# These points define a triangle
pts = np.array([[250, 5], [220, 80], [280, 80]], np.int32)
# Reshape to shape (number_vertex, 1, 2)
pts = pts.reshape((-1, 1, 2))
# Print the shapes: this line is not necessary, only for visualization
print("shape of pts '{}'".format(pts.shape))
# this gives: shape of pts '(3, 1, 2)'
```

Another important parameter is `isClosed`. If this parameter is `True`, the polygon will be drawn closed. Otherwise, a line segment between the first and last vertex will not be plotted, resulting in an open polygon. For a complete explanation, in order to draw a closed triangle, the code is given next:

```
# These points define a triangle
pts = np.array([[250, 5], [220, 80], [280, 80]], np.int32)
# Reshape to shape (number_vertex, 1, 2)
pts = pts.reshape((-1, 1, 2))
# Print the shapes: this line is not necessary, only for visualization
print("shape of pts '{}'".format(pts.shape))
# Draw this poligon with True option
cv2.polylines(image, [pts], True, colors['green'], 3)
```

In the same way, we have coded pentagons and rectangles, which can be seen in the next screenshot:

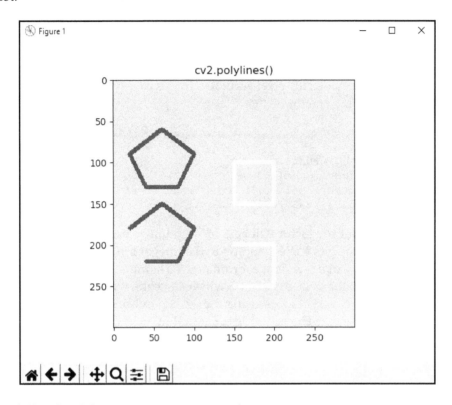

To see the full code of this section, you can see the `basic_drawing_2.py` script.

Shift parameter in drawing functions

Some of the previous functions (the ones with the `shift` parameter) can work with sub-pixel accuracy in connection with the pixel coordinates. To cope with this, you should pass the coordinates as fixed-point numbers, which are encoded as integers.

 A fixed-point number means that there is a specific (fixed) number of digits (bits) reserved for both the integer (on the left of the decimal point) and the fractional parts (on the right of the decimal point).

Therefore, the shift parameter allows you to specify the number of the fractional bits (on the right of the decimal point). In the end, the real point coordinates are calculated as follows:

$$Point(x, y) \rightarrow Point2f(x^{-shift}, y^{-shift})$$

For example, this piece of code draws two circles with a radius of 300. One of them uses a value of `shift` = 2 to provide sub-pixel accuracy. In this case, you should multiply both the origin and the radius by a factor of 4 (2 $^{shift=2}$):

```
shift = 2
factor = 2 ** shift
print("factor: '{}'".format(factor))
cv2.circle(image, (int(round(299.99 * factor)), int(round(299.99 *
factor))), 300 * factor, colors['red'], 1, shift=shift)
cv2.circle(image, (299, 299), 300, colors['green'], 1)
```

If `shift` = 3, the value for the factor will be 8 (2$^{shift=3}$), and so on. Multiplying by powers of 2 is the same as shifting the bits corresponding to the integer binary representations to the left by one. This way you can draw float coordinates. To summarize this point, we can also create a wrapper function for `cv2.circle()`, which can cope with float coordinates—`draw_float_circle()`—using the `shift` argument property. The key code for this example is shown next. The full code is defined in the `shift_parameter.py` script:

```
def draw_float_circle(img, center, radius, color, thickness=1, lineType=8,
shift=4):
    """Wrapper function to draw float-coordinate circles

    """
    factor = 2 ** shift
    center = (int(round(center[0] * factor)), int(round(center[1] *
factor)))
    radius = int(round(radius * factor))
    cv2.circle(img, center, radius, color, thickness, lineType, shift)

draw_float_circle(image, (299, 299), 300, colors['red'], 1, 8, 0)
draw_float_circle(image, (299.9, 299.9), 300, colors['green'], 1, 8, 1)
draw_float_circle(image, (299.99, 299.99), 300, colors['blue'], 1, 8, 2)
draw_float_circle(image, (299.999, 299.999), 300, colors['yellow'], 1, 8,
3)
```

lineType parameter in drawing functions

Another common parameter is `lineType`, which can take three different values. We have previously commented on the differences between these three types. In order to see it more clearly, you can see the next screenshot, where we have plotted three lines with the same thickness and inclination: `yellow = cv2.LINE_4`, `red = cv2.LINE_AA`, and `green = cv2.LINE_8`. To see the full code of this example, you can check the `basic_line_types.py` script:

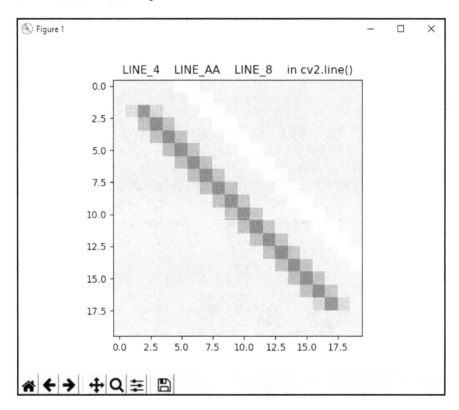

In the previous screenshot you can clearly see the difference when drawing a line with the three different line types.

Writing text

OpenCV can also be used to render text in images. In this section, we will see how to draw text by using the cv2.putText() function. Additionally, we will see all the available fonts you can use. Lastly, we will see some OpenCV functions in connection with text drawing.

Drawing text

The cv2.putText() function has the following signature:

```
img = cv.putText( img, text, org, fontFace, fontScale, color, thickness=1,
lineType= 8, bottomLeftOrigin=False)
```

This function draws the provided text string starting at the org coordinate (upper-left corner if bottomLeftOrigin = False and lower-left corner otherwise) using the font type provided by fontFace and the fontScale factor. In connection with this example, you can see that the last provided parameter, which is lineType, takes the three different values available in OpenCV (cv2.LINE_4, cv2.LINE_8, and cv2.LINE_AA). In this way, you can see the difference better when plotting these types. Remember that cv2.LINE_AA gives much better quality (an anti-aliased line type), but it is slower to draw than the other two types. The key code to draw some text is given next. The full code for this example can be seen in the text_drawing.py script:

```
# We draw some text on the image:
cv2.putText(image, 'Mastering OpenCV4 with Python', (10, 30),
cv2.FONT_HERSHEY_SIMPLEX, 0.9, colors['red'], 2, cv2.LINE_4)
cv2.putText(image, 'Mastering OpenCV4 with Python', (10, 70),
cv2.FONT_HERSHEY_SIMPLEX, 0.9, colors['red'], 2, cv2.LINE_8)
cv2.putText(image, 'Mastering OpenCV4 with Python', (10, 110),
cv2.FONT_HERSHEY_SIMPLEX, 0.9, colors['red'], 2, cv2.LINE_AA)

# Show image:
show_with_matplotlib(image, 'cv2.putText()')
```

In the next screenshot, you can see the result:

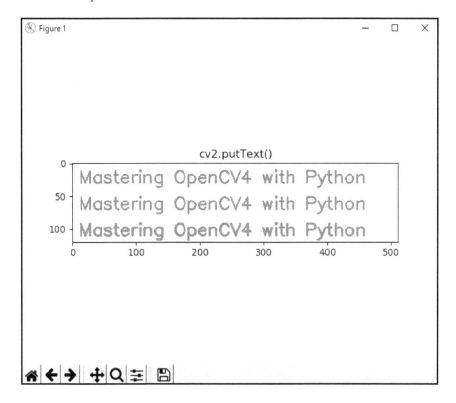

In this example, the background color is set to white. To perform this functionality, you can do the following:

```
image.fill(255)
```

Using all OpenCV text fonts

All the available fonts in OpenCV are as follows:

- FONT_HERSHEY_SIMPLEX = 0
- FONT_HERSHEY_PLAIN = 1
- FONT_HERSHEY_DUPLEX = 2
- FONT_HERSHEY_COMPLEX = 3
- FONT_HERSHEY_TRIPLEX = 4
- FONT_HERSHEY_COMPLEX_SMALL = 5

- FONT_HERSHEY_SCRIPT_SIMPLEX = 6
- FONT_HERSHEY_SCRIPT_COMPLEX = 7

In connection with this, we have coded the `text_drawing_fonts.py` script, which plots all the available fonts. As all these fonts are in the (0-7) range, we can iterate and call the `cv2.putText()` function, varying the `color`, `fontFace`, and `org` parameters. We have also plotted lowercase and uppercase versions of these fonts. The key piece of code to perform this functionality is as follows:

```
position = (10, 30)
for i in range(0, 8):
    cv2.putText(image, fonts[i], position, i, 1.1, colors[index_colors[i]],
2, cv2.LINE_4)
    position = (position[0], position[1] + 40)
    cv2.putText(image, fonts[i].lower(), position, i, 1.1,
colors[index_colors[i]], 2, cv2.LINE_4)
    position = (position[0], position[1] + 40)
```

The resultant screenshot is shown next:

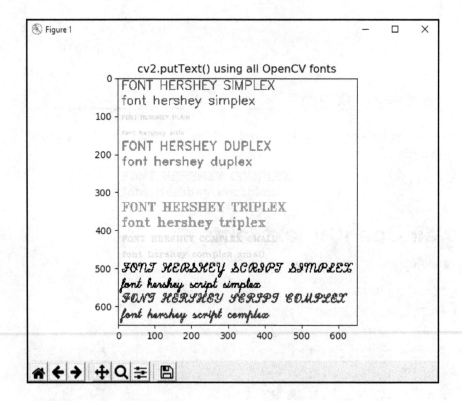

In the previous screenshot, you can see all available fonts in OpenCV (both in lowercase and uppercase versions). Therefore, you can use this screenshot as a reference for easily check what font you want to use in your project.

More functions related to text

OpenCV provides more functions in connection with text drawing. It should be noted that these functions are not for drawing text, but they can be used to *complement* the aforementioned `cv2.putText()` function, and they are commented as follows. The first function we are going to see is `cv2.getFontScaleFromHeight()`. The signature for this function is as follows:

```
retval = cv2.getFontScaleFromHeight(fontFace, pixelHeight, thickness=1)
```

This function returns the font scale (`fontScale`), which is a parameter to use in the `cv2.putText()` function, to achieve the provided height (in pixels) and taking into account both the font type (`fontFace`) and `thickness`.

The second function is `cv2.getTextSize()`:

```
retval, baseLine = cv2.getTextSize(text, fontFace, fontScale, thickness)
```

This function can be used to get the text size (width and height) based on the following arguments—text to draw, the font type (`fontFace`), `scale`, and `thickness`. This function returns `size` and `baseLine`, which corresponds to the *y* coordinate of the baseline relative to the bottom of the text. The next piece of code shows you the key aspects to see this functionality. The full code is available in the `text_drawing_bounding_box.py` script:

```
# assign parameters to use in the drawing functions
font = cv2.FONT_HERSHEY_SIMPLEX
font_scale = 2.5
thickness = 5
text = 'abcdefghijklmnopqrstuvwxyz'
circle_radius = 10

# We get the size of the text
ret, baseline = cv2.getTextSize(text, font, font_scale, thickness)

# We get the text width and text height from ret
text_width, text_height = ret

# We center the text in the image
text_x = int(round((image.shape[1] - text_width) / 2))
```

```
text_y = int(round((image.shape[0] + text_height) / 2))

# Draw this point for reference:
cv2.circle(image, (text_x, text_y), circle_radius, colors['green'], -1)

# Draw the rectangle (bounding box of the text)
cv2.rectangle(image, (text_x, text_y + baseline), (text_x + text_width -
thickness, text_y - text_height),
              colors['blue'], thickness)

# Draw the circles defining the rectangle
cv2.circle(image, (text_x, text_y + baseline), circle_radius,
colors['red'], -1)
cv2.circle(image, (text_x + text_width - thickness, text_y - text_height),
circle_radius, colors['cyan'], -1)

# Draw the baseline line
cv2.line(image, (text_x, text_y + int(round(thickness/2))), (text_x +
text_width - thickness, text_y +
int(round(thickness/2))), colors['yellow'], thickness)
# Write the text centered in the image
cv2.putText(image, text, (text_x, text_y), font, font_scale,
colors['magenta'], thickness)
```

The output of this example is given in the next screenshot:

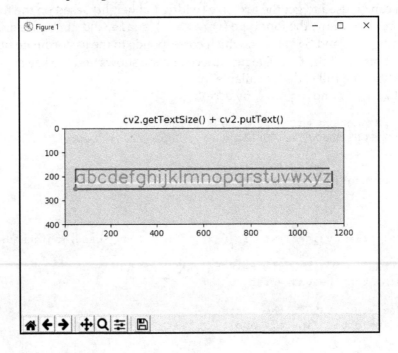

Pay attention to how the three little points (red, cyan, and green) are drawn and also to how the yellow baseline is shown.

Dynamic drawing with mouse events

In this section, you will learn how to perform dynamic drawing using mouse events. We are going to see some examples in increasing order of complexity.

Drawing dynamic shapes

Th next example gives you an introduction into how to handle mouse events with OpenCV. The cv2.setMouseCallback() function performs this functionality. The signature for this method is as follows:

```
cv2.setMouseCallback(windowName, onMouse, param=None)
```

This function establishes the mouse handler for the window named windowName. The onMouse function is the callback function, which is called when a mouse event is performed (for example, double-click, left-button down, left-button up, among others). The optional param parameter is used to pass additional information to the callback function.

So the first step is to create the callback function:

```
# This is the mouse callback function:
def draw_circle(event, x, y, flags, param):
    if event == cv2.EVENT_LBUTTONDBLCLK:
        print("event: EVENT_LBUTTONDBLCLK")
        cv2.circle(image, (x, y), 10, colors['magenta'], -1)

    if event == cv2.EVENT_MOUSEMOVE:
        print("event: EVENT_MOUSEMOVE")

    if event == cv2.EVENT_LBUTTONUP:
        print("event: EVENT_LBUTTONUP")

    if event == cv2.EVENT_LBUTTONDOWN:
        print("event: EVENT_LBUTTONDOWN")
```

The draw_circle() function receives the specific event and the coordinates *(x, y)* for every mouse event. In this case, when a left double-click (cv2.EVENT_LBUTTONDBLCLK) is performed, we draw a circle in the corresponding *(x, y)* coordinates on the event.

Additionally, we have also printed some messages in order to see other produced events, but we do not use them to perform any additional actions.

The next step is to create a named window. In this case, we named it Image mouse. This named window is where the mouse callback function will be associated with:

```
# We create a named window where the mouse callback will be established
cv2.namedWindow('Image mouse')
```

And finally, we set (or activate) the mouse callback function to the function we created before:

```
# We set the mouse callback function to 'draw_circle'
cv2.setMouseCallback('Image mouse', draw_circle)
```

In summary, when a left double-click is performed, a filled magenta circle is drawn centered at the *(x, y)* position of the performed double-click. The full code for this example can be seen in the mouse_drawing.py script.

Drawing both text and shapes

In this example, we are combining both mouse events and drawing text. In this sense, some text is rendered to show how to use the mouse events to perform specific actions. To better understand this example, in the next screenshot you can see the rendered text:

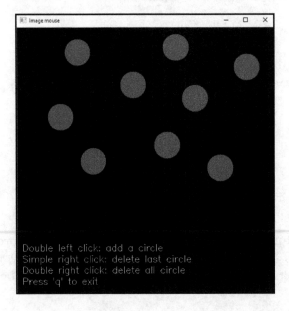

You can do the following:

- Add a circle using the double left-click
- Delete the last added circle using a simple left-click
- Delete all circles using the double right-click

To perform this functionality, we create a list called `circles`, where we maintain the current circles selected by the user. Additionally, we also create a *backup* image with the rendered text. When a mouse event is produced, we add or delete the circles from the `circles` list. Afterward, when drawing, we draw only the current circles from the list. So, for example, when the user performs a simple right-click, the last added circle is deleted from the list. The full code is provided in the `mouse_drawing_circles_and_text.py` script.

Event handling with Matplotlib

You can see in the previous example that we have not used Matplotlib to show the image. This is because Matplotlib can also deal with event handling and picking. Therefore, you can use Matplotlib capabilities to capture mouse events. There are more events that we can connect with Matplotlib (`https://matplotlib.org/users/event_handling.html`). For example, in connection with the mouse, we can connect with the following events—`button_press_event`, `button_release_event`, `motion_notify_event`, and `scroll_event`.

We are going to show a simple example in order to render a circle when a mouse click is performed connecting with the `button_press_event` event:

```
# 'button_press_event' is a MouseEvent where a mouse botton is click
(pressed)
# When this event happens the function 'click_mouse_event' is called:
figure.canvas.mpl_connect('button_press_event', click_mouse_event)
```

We have also to define the event listener for the `button_press_event` event:

```
# We define the event listener for the 'button_press_event':
def click_mouse_event(event):
    # (event.xdata, event.ydata) contains the float coordinates of the
mouse click event:
    cv2.circle(image, (int(round(event.xdata)), int(round(event.ydata))),
30, colors['blue'], cv2.FILLED)
    # Call 'update_image()' method to update the Figure:
    update_img_with_matplotlib()
```

Therefore, when a mouse click is performed, a `blue` circle is shown. It should be noted that we have coded the `update_img_with_matplotlib()` function. In the previous examples, we have used `show_with_matplotlib()`. The `show_with_matplotlib()` function is used to display an image using Matplotlib, while `update_img_with_matplotlib()` is used to update an existing figure. The full code for this example can be seen in the `matplotlib_mouse_events.py` script.

Advanced drawing

In this section, we are going to see how to combine some of the aforementioned functions to draw basic shapes in OpenCV (for example, lines, circles, rectangles, and text, among others) to render a more advanced drawing. To put all these pieces together, we have built an analog clock to show you the current time (hour, minutes, and seconds). For this, two scripts are coded:

- `analog_clock_values.py`
- `analog_clock_opencv.py`

The `analog_clock_opencv.py` script draws an analog clock, using `cv.line()`, `cv.circle()`, `cv.rectangle()`, and `cv2.putText()`. In this script, we first draw the static drawing. In this sense, you can see that there are two arrays containing *fixed* coordinates:

```
hours_orig = np.array(
    [(620, 320), (580, 470), (470, 580), (320, 620), (170, 580), (60, 470),
(20, 320), (60, 170), (169, 61), (319, 20),
    (469, 60), (579, 169)])

hours_dest = np.array(
    [(600, 320), (563, 460), (460, 562), (320, 600), (180, 563), (78, 460),
(40, 320), (77, 180), (179, 78), (319, 40),
    (459, 77), (562, 179)])
```

These arrays are necessary to render the hour markings, as they define the origin and destiny of the lines for every hour of the clock. So, these markings are drawn as follows:

```
for i in range(0, 12):
    cv2.line(image, array_to_tuple(hours_orig[i]),
array_to_tuple(hours_dest[i]), colors['black'], 3)
```

Additionally, a big circle is drawn, corresponding to the shape of the analog clock:

```
cv2.circle(image, (320, 320), 310, colors['dark_gray'], 8)
```

Finally, we draw the rectangle containing the `Mastering OpenCV 4 with Python` text, which will be rendered inside the clock:

```
cv2.rectangle(image, (150, 175), (490, 270), colors['dark_gray'], -1)
cv2.putText(image, "Mastering OpenCV 4", (150, 200), 1, 2,
colors['light_gray'], 1, cv2.LINE_AA)
cv2.putText(image, "with Python", (210, 250), 1, 2, colors['light_gray'],
1, cv2.LINE_AA)
```

Once this static information is drawn in the image, we copy it to the `image_original` image:

```
image_original = image.copy()
```

To draw the dynamic information, several steps are performed:

1. Get the hour, minute, and second from the current time:

```
# Get current date:
date_time_now = datetime.datetime.now()
# Get current time from the date:
time_now = date_time_now.time()
# Get current hour-minute-second from the time:
hour = math.fmod(time_now.hour, 12)
minute = time_now.minute
second = time_now.second
```

2. Transform these values (hour, minute, and second) to angles:

```
# Get the hour, minute and second angles:
second_angle = math.fmod(second * 6 + 270, 360)
minute_angle = math.fmod(minute * 6 + 270, 360)
hour_angle = math.fmod((hour*30) + (minute/2) + 270, 360)
```

3. Draw the lines corresponding to the hour, minute, and second needles:

```
# Draw the lines corresponding to the hour, minute and second needles:
second_x = round(320 + 310 * math.cos(second_angle * 3.14 / 180))
second_y = round(320 + 310 * math.sin(second_angle * 3.14 / 180))
cv2.line(image, (320, 320), (second_x, second_y), colors['blue'], 2)

minute_x = round(320 + 260 * math.cos(minute_angle * 3.14 / 180))
minute_y = round(320 + 260 * math.sin(minute_angle * 3.14 / 180))
cv2.line(image, (320, 320), (minute_x, minute_y), colors['blue'], 8)
```

```
hour_x = round(320 + 220 * math.cos(hour_angle * 3.14 / 180))
hour_y = round(320 + 220 * math.sin(hour_angle * 3.14 / 180))
cv2.line(image, (320, 320), (hour_x, hour_y), colors['blue'], 10)
```

4. Finally, a small circle is drawn, corresponding to the point where the three needles join:

```
cv2.circle(image, (320, 320), 10, colors['dark_gray'], -1)
```

In the next screenshot, you can see how the analog clock looks:

The `script analog_clock_values.py` script calculates the fixed coordinates for both the `hours_orig` and `hours_dest` arrays. To calculate the *(x, y)* coordinates for the hour markings, we use the parametric equation of a circle, as can be seen in the next screenshot:

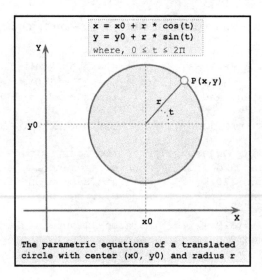

The parametric equations of a translated circle with center (x0, y0) and radius r

We have followed the equation in the previous screenshot to calculate the coordinates for the 12 points *P(x, y)* at every 30 degrees and starting at 0 degrees (0, 30, 60, 90, 120, 150, 180, 210, 240, 270, 300, and 330) with two different radii. This way, we are able to define the coordinates for the lines defining the hour markings. The code to calculate these coordinates is as follows:

```
radius = 300
center = (320, 320)

for x in (0, 30, 60, 90, 120, 150, 180, 210, 240, 270, 300, 330):
    x_coordinate = center[0] + radius * math.cos(x * 3.14/180)
    y_coordinate = center[1] + radius * math.sin(x * 3.14/180)
    print("x: {} y: {}".format(round(x_coordinate), round(y_coordinate)))

for x in (0, 30, 60, 90, 120, 150, 180, 210, 240, 270, 300, 330):
    x_coordinate = center[0] + (radius - 20) * math.cos(x * 3.14/180)
    y_coordinate = center[1] + (radius - 20) * math.sin(x * 3.14/180)
    print("x: {} y: {}".format(round(x_coordinate), round(y_coordinate)))
```

The full code for this script can be seen in `analog_clock_values.py`. It should be noted that we could have included the code to calculate these coordinates inside the other script, but it can be a good exercise for you to do it.

Summary

In this chapter, we reviewed the functionality OpenCV offers in connection with drawing shapes and text. In connection with shapes, we have seen how to draw very basic shapes (lines, rectangles, and circles), and also more advanced shapes (clip lines, arrows, ellipses, and polygons). In connection with text, we have seen how to draw it and how to render all the available fonts in the OpenCV library. Additionally, we have also covered how to capture mouse events and use them to perform specific actions (for example, drawing a point associated with the *(x, y)* coordinates of the performed mouse event). Finally, we rendered an analog clock, trying to summarize all the previous concepts of this chapter.

In the next chapter, we are going to see the main concepts concerning image processing techniques. We will also tackle how to perform basic image transformations (for example, translation, rotation, resizing, flipping, and cropping). Another key aspect is how to perform basic arithmetic with images such as bitwise operations (AND, OR, XOR, and NOT). Finally, we are going to cover an introduction to the main color spaces and color maps.

Questions

1. Which parameter should you configure properly to draw a filled shape (for example, circle or rectangle)?
2. Which parameter should you configure properly to draw anti-aliased line types?
3. Create a diagonal line starting at *(0,0)* and ending at *(512,512)*.
4. Render the text *Hello OpenCV* using the parameters you want.
5. Draw a polygon (with the shape of a circle) using 12 points.
6. Draw a rectangle using the mouse events with Matplotlib events when a double left-click is performed.
7. Try to draw this very simple meme generator using the `lenna.png` image as background:

Further reading

The following references will help you dive deeper into Matplotlib:

- *Mastering matplotlib* by Duncan M. McGreggor (`https://www.packtpub.com/big-data-and-business-intelligence/mastering-matplotlib`)
- *Matplotlib for Python Developers* by Benjamin Keller (`https://www.packtpub.com/big-data-and-business-intelligence/matplotlib-python-developers-video`)

Section 2: Image Processing in OpenCV

2

In this second section of the book, you will dive deeper into the OpenCV library. More specifically, you will see most of the common image processing techniques you will need in your computer vision projects. Additionally, you will see how to both create and understand histograms, which are powerful tools used to better understand image content. Furthermore, you will see the main thresholding techniques you will need in your computer vision applications as a key part of image segmentation. Also, you will see how to deal with contours, which are used for shape analysis and both object detection and recognition. Finally, you will learn how to build your first augmented reality applications.

The following chapters will be covered in this section:

- Chapter 5, *Image Processing Techniques*
- Chapter 6, *Constructing and Building Histograms*
- Chapter 7, *Thresholding Techniques*
- Chapter 8, *Contour Detection, Filtering, and Drawing*
- Chapter 9, *Augmented Reality*

Image Processing Techniques

5

Image processing techniques are the core of your computer vision projects. They can be seen as useful key tools, which you can use to complete various tasks. In other words, image processing techniques are like building blocks that should be kept in mind when processing your images. Therefore, a basic understanding of image processing is required if you are to work with computer vision projects.

In this chapter, you will learn most of the common image processing techniques you need. These will be complemented by the other image processing techniques covered in the next three chapters of this book (histograms, thresholding techniques, contour detection, and filtering).

In this chapter, the following topics will be covered:

- Splitting and merging channels
- Geometric transformations of images—translation, rotation, scaling, affine transformation, perspective transformation, and cropping
- Arithmetic with images—bitwise operations (AND, OR, XOR, and NOT) and masking
- Smoothing and sharpening techniques
- Morphological operations
- Color spaces
- Color maps

Technical requirements

The technical requirements for this chapter are listed as follows:

- Python and OpenCV
- A Python-specific IDE
- The NumPy and Matplotlib packages
- A Git client

For further details on how to install these requirements, see Chapter 1, *Setting Up OpenCV*. The GitHub repository, *Mastering OpenCV 4 with Python*, containing all the supporting project files necessary to work through this book from the first chapter to the last one, can be accessed at: https://github.com/PacktPublishing/Mastering-OpenCV-4-with-Python.

Splitting and merging channels in OpenCV

Sometimes, you have to work with specific channels on multichannel images. To do this, you have to split the multichannel image into several single-channel images. Additionally, once the processing has been done, you may want to create one multichannel image from different single-channel images. In order to both split and merge channels, you can use the cv2.split() and cv2.merge() functions, respectively. The cv2.split() function splits the source multichannel image into several single-channel images.
The cv2.merge() function merges several single-channel images into a multichannel image.

In the next example, splitting_and_merging.py, you will learn how to work with these two aforementioned functions. Using the cv2.split() function, if you want to get the three channels from a loaded BGR image, then you should use the following code:

```
(b, g, r) = cv2.split(image)
```

Using the cv2.merge() function, if you want to build the BGR image again from its three channels, then you should use the following code:

```
image_copy = cv2.merge((b, g, r))
```

You should remember that `cv2.split()` is a time-consuming operation, and so you should only use it if strictly necessary; otherwise, you can use the NumPy functionality to work with specific channels. For example, if you want to get the blue channel of the image, you can do the following:

```
b = image[:, :, 0]
```

Additionally, you can eliminate (set to 0), some of the channels of a multichannel image. The resulting image will have the same number of channels, but with the 0 value in the corresponding channel; for example, if you want to eliminate the blue channel of a BGR image, you can use the following code:

```
image_without_blue = image.copy()
image_without_blue[:, :, 0] = 0
```

If you execute the `splitting_and_merging.py` script, you will see the following screenshot:

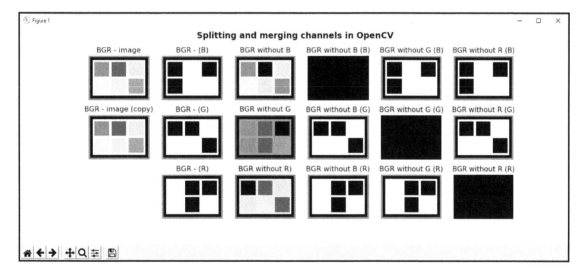

In order to understand this screenshot, you should remember the additive properties of the RGB color space. For example, in connection with the subplot **BGR without B**, you can see that most of it is yellow. This is because green and red values yield yellow. Another key feature that you can see is the black subplots corresponding to the specific channels that we have set to 0.

Geometric transformations of images

In this section the first, an introduction to the main geometric transformations of images will be covered. We will look at some examples the of scaling, translation, rotation, affine transformation, perspective transform, and cropping of images. The two key functions to perform these geometric transformations are `cv2.warpAffine()` and `cv2.warpPerspective()`. The `cv2.warpAffine()` function transforms the source image by using the following *2 x 3 M* transformation matrix:

$$dst(x, y) = src(M11x + M12y + M13, M21x + M22y + M23)$$

The `cv2.warpPerspective()` function transforms the source image using the following *3 x 3* transformation matrix:

$$dst(x,y) = src((M11x + M12y + M13)/(M31x + M32y + M33), (M21x + M22y + M23)/(M31xM32y + M33))$$

In the next subsections, we will learn about the most common geometric transformation techniques, which we will learn more about when we look at the `geometric_image_transformations.py` script.

Scaling an image

When scaling an image, you can call `cv2.resize()` with a specific size, and the scaling factors (`fx` and `fy`) will be calculated based on the provided size, as shown in the following code:

```
resized_image = cv2.resize(image, (width * 2, height * 2),
interpolation=cv2.INTER_LINEAR)
```

On the other hand, you can provide both the `fx` and `fy` values. For example, if you want to shrink the image by a factor of 2, you can use the following code:

```
dst_image = cv2.resize(image, None, fx=0.5, fy=0.5,
interpolation=cv2.INTER_AREA)
```

If you want to enlarge the image, the best approach is to use the `cv2.INTER_CUBIC` interpolation method (a time-consuming interpolation method) or `cv2.INTER_LINEAR`. If you want to shrink the image, the general approach is to use `cv2.INTER_LINEAR`.

The five interpolation methods provided with OpenCV are `cv2.INTER_NEAREST` (nearest neighbor interpolation), `cv2.INTER_LINEAR` (bilinear interpolation), `cv2.INTER_AREA` (resampling using pixel area relation), `cv2.INTER_CUBIC` (bicubic interpolation), and `cv2.INTER_LANCZOS4` (sinusoidal interpolation).

Translating an image

In order to translate an object, you need to create the *2 x 3* transformation matrix by using the NumPy array with float values providing the translation in both the *x* and *y* directions in pixels, as shown in the following code:

```
M = np.float32([[1, 0, x], [0, 1, y]])
```

This gives the following *M* transformation matrix:

$$M = \begin{bmatrix} 1 & 0 & t_x \\ 0 & 1 & t_y \end{bmatrix}$$

Once this matrix has been created, the `cv2.warpAffine()` function is called, as shown in the following code:

```
dst_image = cv2.warpAffine(image, M, (width, height))
```

The `cv2.warpAffine()` function transforms the source image using the *M* matrix provided. The third `(width, height)` argument establishes the size of the output image.

 Remember that `image.shape` returns `(width, height)`.

For example, if we want to translate an image with `200` pixels in the *x* direction and `30` pixels in the *y* direction, we use the following:

```
height, width = image.shape[:2]
M = np.float32([[1, 0, 200], [0, 1, 30]])
dst_image = cv2.warpAffine(image, M, (width, height))
```

Note that the translation can be also negative, as shown in the following code:

```
M = np.float32([[1, 0, -200], [0, 1, -30]])
dst_image = cv2.warpAffine(image, M, (width, height))
```

Rotating an image

In order to rotate the image, we make use of the `cv.getRotationMatrix2D()` function to build the *2 x 3* transformation matrix. This matrix rotates the image at the desired angle (in degrees), where positive values indicate a counterclockwise rotation. Both the `center` of rotation and the `scale` factor can also be adjusted. Using these elements in our example, the following transformation matrix is calculated:

$$\begin{bmatrix} \alpha & \beta & (1-\alpha) \cdot center.x - \beta \cdot center.y \\ -\beta & \alpha & \beta \cdot center.x + (1-\alpha) \cdot center.y \end{bmatrix}$$

This expression has the following values:

$$\alpha = scale \cdot cos\theta, \beta = scale \cdot sin\theta$$

The following example builds the *M* transformation matrix to rotate 180 degrees with respect to the center of the image with a scale factor of 1 (without scaling). Afterwards, this *M* matrix is applied to the image, as follows:

```
height, width = image.shape[:2]
M = cv2.getRotationMatrix2D((width / 2.0, height / 2.0), 180, 1)
dst_image = cv2.warpAffine(image, M, (width, height))
```

Affine transformation of an image

In an affine transformation, we first make use of the `cv2.getAffineTransform()` function to build the *2 x 3* transformation matrix, which will be obtained from the input image and the corresponding coordinates in the transformed image. Finally, this *M* matrix is passed to `cv2.warpAffine()`, as follows:

```
pts_1 = np.float32([[135, 45], [385, 45], [135, 230]])
pts_2 = np.float32([[135, 45], [385, 45], [150, 230]])
M = cv2.getAffineTransform(pts_1, pts_2)
dst_image = cv2.warpAffine(image_points, M, (width, height))
```

An **affine transformation** is a transformation where points, straight lines, and planes are preserved. Additionally, the parallel lines will remain parallel after this transformation. However, an affine transformation does not preserve both the distance and angles between points.

Perspective transformation of an image

In order to correct the perspective (also known as **perspective transformation**), you will need to create the transformation matrix by making use of the `cv2.getPerspectiveTransform()` function, where a *3 x 3* matrix is constructed. This function needs four pairs of points (coordinates of a quadrangle in both the source and output image) and calculates a perspective transformation matrix from these points. Then, the *M* matrix is passed to `cv2.warpPerspective()`, where the source image is transformed by applying the specified matrix with a specified size, as shown in the following code:

```
pts_1 = np.float32([[450, 65], [517, 65], [431, 164], [552, 164]])
pts_2 = np.float32([[0, 0], [300, 0], [0, 300], [300, 300]])
M = cv2.getPerspectiveTransform(pts_1, pts_2)
dst_image = cv2.warpPerspective(image, M, (300, 300))
```

Cropping an image

To crop the image, we will make use of NumPy slicing, as shown in the following code:

```
dst_image = image[80:200, 230:330]
```

As mentioned before, the code for these geometric transformations corresponds to the `geometric_image_transformations.py` script.

Image filtering

In this section, we are going to tackle how to blur and sharpen images, applying both several filters and custom-made kernels. Additionally, we will look at some common kernels that we can use to perform other image-processing functionalities.

Applying arbitrary kernels

OpenCV provides the `cv2.filter2D()` function in order to apply an arbitrary kernel to an image, convolving the image with the provided kernel. In order to see how this function works, we should first build the kernel that we will use later. In this case, a *5 x 5* kernel will be used, as shown in the following code:

```
kernel_averaging_5_5 = np.array([[0.04, 0.04, 0.04, 0.04, 0.04], [0.04,
0.04, 0.04, 0.04, 0.04], [0.04, 0.04, 0.04, 0.04, 0.04],[0.04, 0.04, 0.04,
0.04, 0.04], [0.04, 0.04, 0.04, 0.04, 0.04]])
```

This corresponds to a *5 x 5* averaging kernel. Additionally, you can also create the kernel like this:

```
kernel_averaging_5_5 = np.ones((5, 5), np.float32) / 25
```

Then we apply the kernel to the source image by applying the aforementioned function, as shown in the following code:

```
smooth_image_f2D = cv2.filter2D(image, -1, kernel_averaging_5_5)
```

Now we have seen a way to apply an arbitrary kernel to an image. In the previous example, an averaging kernel was created to smooth the image. There are other ways to perform image smoothing (also known as **image blurring**) without having to create the kernel. Instead, some other parameters could be provided to the corresponding OpenCV function. In the `smoothing_techniques.py` script, you can see the full code for this previous example and for the next subsection.

Smoothing images

As previously mentioned, in the `smoothing_techniques.py` script you will see other common filtering techniques to perform a smoothing operation. Smoothing techniques are commonly used to reduce noise, and additionally, these techniques can also be applied to reduce the pixelated effect in low-resolution images. These techniques are commented as follows.

You can see the output of this script in the following screenshot:

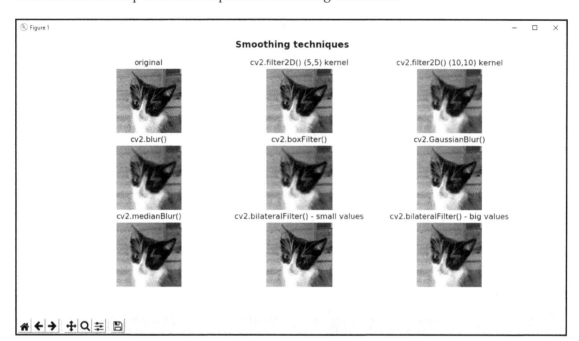

In the preceding screenshot, you can see the effect of applying common kernels in image processing.

Averaging filter

You can use both `cv2.blur()` and `cv2.boxFilter()` to perform an averaging by convolving the image with a kernel, which can be unnormalized in the case of `cv2.boxFilter()`. They simply take the average of all the pixels under the kernel area and replace the central element with this average. You can control the kernel size and the anchor kernel (by default `(-1,-1)`, meaning that the anchor is located at the kernel center). When the `normalize` parameter (by default `True`) of `cv2.boxFilter()` is equal to `True`, both functions perform the same operation. In this way, both functions smooth an image using the kernel, as shown in the following expression:

$$K = \alpha \begin{bmatrix} 1 & 1 & 1 & \cdots & 1 & 1 \\ 1 & 1 & 1 & \cdots & 1 & 1 \\ \cdots & & & & & \\ 1 & 1 & 1 & \cdots & 1 & 1 \end{bmatrix}$$

In the case of the `cv2.boxFilter()` function:

$$\alpha = \texttt{ksize.width*ksize.height}, \textit{when } \texttt{normalize=true}; 1 \textit{ otherwise}$$

In the case of the `cv2.blur()` function:

$$\alpha = \texttt{ksize.width*ksize.height}$$

In other words, `cv2.blur()` always uses a normalized box filter, as shown in the following code:

```
smooth_image_b = cv2.blur(image, (10, 10))
smooth_image_bfi = cv2.boxFilter(image, -1, (10, 10), normalize=True)
```

In the preceding code, the two lines of code are equivalent.

Gaussian filtering

OpenCV provides the `cv2.GaussianBlur()` function, which blurs an image by using a Gaussian kernel. This kernel can be controlled using the following parameters: `ksize` (kernel size), `sigmaX` (standard deviation in the x-direction of the Gaussian kernel), and `sigmaY` (standard deviation in the y-direction of the Gaussian kernel). In order to know which kernel has been applied, you can make use of the `cv2.getGaussianKernel()` function.

For example, in the following line of code, `cv2.GaussianBlur()` blurs the image using a Gaussian kernel of size `(9, 9)`:

```
smooth_image_gb = cv2.GaussianBlur(image, (9, 9), 0)
```

Median filtering

OpenCV provides the `cv2.medianBlur()` function, which blurs the image with a median kernel, as shown in the following code:

```
smooth_image_mb = cv2.medianBlur(image, 9)
```

This filter can be applied to reduce the salt-and-pepper noise of an image.

Bilateral filtering

The `cv2.bilateralFilter()` function can be applied to the input image in order to apply a bilateral filter. This function can be applied to reduce noise while keeping the edges sharp, as shown in the following code:

```
smooth_image_bf = cv2.bilateralFilter(image, 5, 10, 10)
```

It should be noted that all the previous filters tend to smooth all the images including their edges.

Sharpening images

In connection with this last function, there are some options you can try in order to sharpen the edges of your images. One simple approach is to perform what is known as **unsharp masking**, where an unsharp, or smoothed, version of an image is subtracted from the original image. In the following example, a Gaussian smoothing filter has been applied first and the resulting image is subtracted from the original image:

```
smoothed = cv2.GaussianBlur(img, (9, 9), 10)
unsharped = cv2.addWeighted(img, 1.5, smoothed, -0.5, 0)
```

Another option is to use a specific kernel for sharpening edges and then apply the `cv2.filter2D()` function. In the `sharpening_techniques.py` script, there are some defined kernels that can be applied for this purpose. The output of this script is shown in the following screenshot:

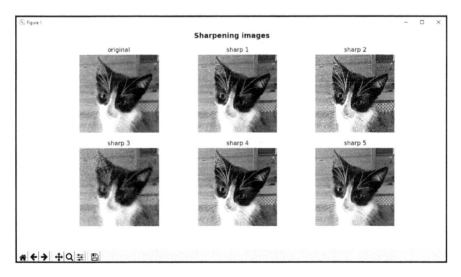

In the preceding screenshot, you can see the effect of applying different sharpening kernels, which can be seen in the `sharpening_techniques.py` script.

Common kernels in image processing

We have seen that the kernels have a great impact on the resulting image. In the `filter_2D_kernels.py` script, there are some defined common kernels to use for different purposes—edge detection, smoothing, sharpening, or embossing, among others. As a reminder, in order to apply a specific kernel, the `cv2.filter2D()` function should be used. The output of this script is shown in the following screenshot:

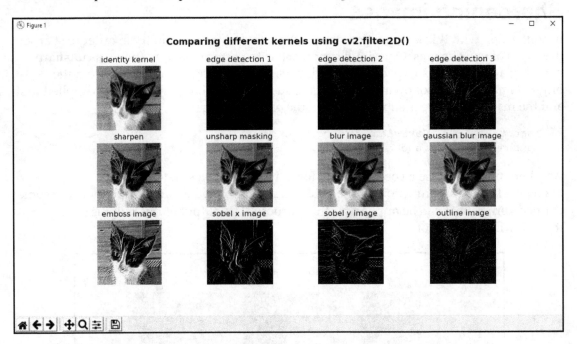

You can see the effect of applying different kernels using the `cv2.filter2D()` function, which can be used to apply a specific kernel.

Creating cartoonized images

As previously mentioned, `cv2.bilateralFilter()` can be applied to reduce noise while preserving the sharp edges. However, this filter can produce both intensity plateaus (the staircase effect) and false edges (gradient reversal) in the filtered image. While this can be taken into account in your filtered images (there are several improvements to the bilateral filter that deals with these artifacts), it can be very cool to create cartoonized images. The full code can be seen in `cartoonizing.py`, but in this section we will look at a brief description.

The process to cartoonize images is quite simple and it is performed in the `cartonize_image()`. function. First of all, the sketch of the image is constructed (see the `sketch_image()` function), which is based on the edges of the image. There are other edge detectors to use, but in this case, the Laplacian operator is used. Before calling the `cv2.Laplacian()` function, we reduce the noise by smoothing the image by means of the `cv2.medianBlur()` median filter. Once the edges have been obtained, the resulting image is thresholded by applying `cv2.threshold()`. We will look at thresholding techniques in the next chapter, but in this example this function gives us a binary image from the given grayscale image corresponding to the output of the `sketch_image()` function. You can play with the threshold value (in this case fixed to `70`) in order to see how this value controls the number of black pixels (corresponding to the detected edges) appearing in the resulting image. If this value is small (for example, `10`) many black border pixels will appear. If this value is big (for example, `200`), few black border pixels will be outputted. To get a cartoonized effect, we call the `cv2.bilateralFilter()` function with big values (for example, `cv2.bilateralFilter(img, 10, 250, 250)`). The final step is to put together the sketch image and the output of the bilateral filter using `cv2.bitwise_and()` with the sketch image as the mask in order to set these values to the output. If desired, the output can also be converted to grayscale. Note that the `cv2.bitwise_and()` function is a bitwise operation, which we will see in the next section.

For the sake of completeness, OpenCV offers a similar functionality, and is also tested in this script. It works using the following filters:

- `cv2.pencilSketch()`: This filter produces a pencil sketch line drawing (similar to our `sketch_image()` function).
- `cv2.stylization()`: This filter can be applied to produce a wide variety of nonphotorealistic effects. In this case, we apply `cv2.stylization()` in order to get the cartoonized effect (similar to our `cartonize_image()` function).

The output corresponding to the `cartoonizing.py` script is shown in the following screenshot:

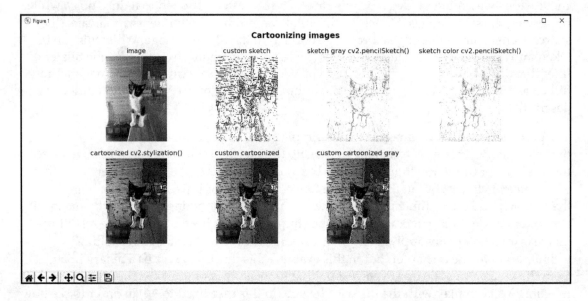

As you can see, the `cartonize_image()` function can also output a grayscale image calling `cv2.cvtColor()` to convert the image from BGR to grayscale.

Arithmetic with images

In this section, we will learn about some common arithmetic operations that can be performed on images, such as bitwise operations, addition, and subtraction, among others. In connection with these operations, one key point to take into account is the concept of saturation arithmetic, which is explained in the following subsection.

Saturation arithmetic

Saturation arithmetic is a type of arithmetic operation where the operations are limited to a fixed range by restricting the maximum and minimum values that the operation can take. For example, certain operations on images (for example, color space conversions, interpolation techniques, and so on) can produce values out of the available range. Saturation arithmetic is used in order to solve this.

For example, to store *r*, which can be the result of performing a certain operation to an 8-bit image (values ranged from 0 to 255), the following equation is applied:

$$I(x, y) = min(max(round(r), 0), 255)$$

This concept can be seen in the following saturation_arithmetic.py script:

```
x = np.uint8([250])
y = np.uint8([50])
# 250+50 = 300 => 255:
result_opencv = cv2.add(x, y)
print("cv2.add(x:'{}' , y:'{}') = '{}'".format(x, y, result_opencv))
# 250+50 = 300 % 256 = 44
result_numpy = x + y
print("x:'{}' + y:'{}' = '{}'".format(x, y, result_numpy))
```

In OpenCV, the values are clipped to ensure that they will never fall outside the range [0, 255]. This is called a **saturated operation**. In NumPy, the values are wrapped around. This is also called a **modulo operation**.

Image addition and subtraction

Image addition and subtraction can be performed with the cv2.add() and cv2.subtract() functions, respectively. These functions sum/subtraction the per-element sum/subtract of two arrays. These function can also be used to sum/subtract an array and a scalar. For example, if we want to add 60 to all the pixels of the image, we first have to build the image to add to the original, using the following code:

```
M = np.ones(image.shape, dtype="uint8") * 60
```

Then, we perform the addition, using the following code:

```
added_image = cv2.add(image, M)
```

Another possibility is to create a scalar and add it to the original image. For example, if we want to add 110 to all the pixels of the image, we first have to build the scalar using the following code:

```
scalar = np.ones((1, 3), dtype="float") * 110
```

Then, we perform the addition using the following code:

```
added_image_2 = cv2.add(image, scalar)
```

In the case of subtraction, the procedure is the same, but instead, we call the `cv2.subtract()` function. The full code for this script can be seen in `arithmetic.py`. The output of this script can be seen in the following screenshot:

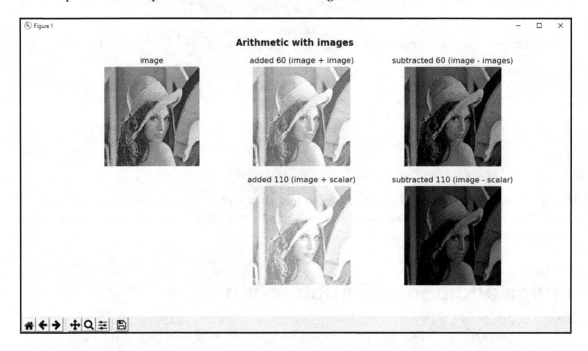

In the preceding screenshot, you can clearly see the effect of adding and subtracting a predefined value (computed in two different ways, but showing the same results). When we add a value, the image will be lighter, and when we subtract a value, it will be darker.

Image blending

Image blending is also **image addition**, but different weights are given to the images, giving an impression of transparency. In order to do this, the `cv2.addWeighted()` function will be used. This function is commonly used to get the output from the `Sobel` operator.

The `Sobel` operator is used for edge detection, where it creates an image emphasizing edges. The `Sobel` operator uses two 3 × 3 kernels, which are convolved with the original image in order to calculate approximations of the derivatives, capturing both horizontal and vertical changes, as shown in the following code:

```
# Gradient x is calculated:
# the depth of the output is set to CV_16S to avoid overflow
# CV_16S = one channel of 2-byte signed integers (16-bit signed integers)
gradient_x = cv2.Sobel(gray_image, cv2.CV_16S, 1, 0, 3)
gradient_y = cv2.Sobel(gray_image, cv2.CV_16S, 0, 1, 3)
```

Therefore, after the horizontal and vertical changes have been calculated, they can be blended into an image by using the aforementioned function, as follows:

```
# Conversion to an unsigned 8-bit type:
abs_gradient_x = cv2.convertScaleAbs(gradient_x)
abs_gradient_y = cv2.convertScaleAbs(gradient_y)

# Combine the two images using the same weight:
sobel_image = cv2.addWeighted(abs_gradient_x, 0.5, abs_gradient_y, 0.5, 0)
```

This can be seen in the `arithmetic_sobel.py` script. The output of this script can be seen in the following screenshot:

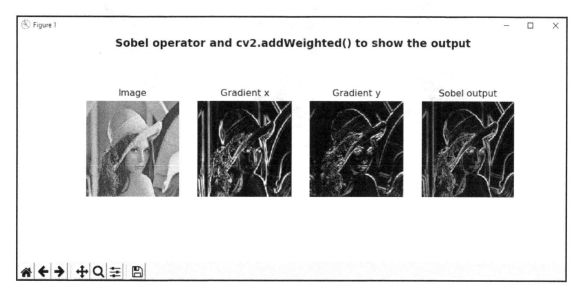

In the preceding screenshot, the output of the `Sobel` operator is shown, including both the horizontal and vertical changes.

Bitwise operations

There are some operations that can be performed at bit level using bitwise operators, which can be used to manipulate the values for comparison and calculations. These bitwise operations are simple, and are quick to calculate. This means that they are a useful tool when working on images.

Bitwise operations include AND, OR, NOT, and XOR.

- **Bitwise AND**: `bitwise_and = cv2.bitwise_and(img_1, img_2)`
- **Bitwise OR**: `bitwise_xor = cv2.bitwise_xor(img_1, img_2)`
- **Bitwise XOR**: `bitwise_xor = cv2.bitwise_xor(img_1, img_2)`
- **Bitwise NOT**: `bitwise_not_1 = cv2.bitwise_not(img_1)`

In order to explain how these operations work, look at the output of the `bitwise_operations.py` script in the following screenshot:

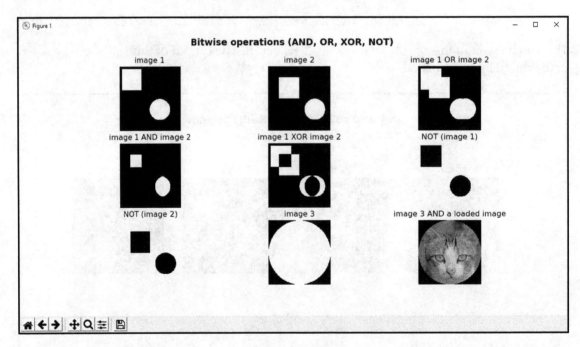

In order to play with bitwise operations further, you can look at the
following `bitwise_operations_images.py` script, where two images are loaded and
some bitwise operations (AND and OR) are performed. It should be noted that the images
ought to have the same shape:

```
# Load the original image (250x250):
image = cv2.imread('lenna_250.png')

# Load the binary image (but as a GBR color image - with 3 channels)
(250x250):
binary_image = cv2.imread('opencv_binary_logo_250.png')

# Bitwise AND
bitwise_and = cv2.bitwise_and(image, binary_image)

# Bitwise OR
bitwise_or = cv2.bitwise_or(image, binary_image)
```

The output can be seen in the following screenshot:

In the previous screenshot you can see the resulting images when performing bitwise
operations (AND, OR).

Morphological transformations

Morphological transformations are operations that are normally performed on binary images and based on the image shape. The exact operation is determined by a kernel-structuring element, which decides the nature of the operation. Dilation and erosion are the two basic operators in the area of morphological transformations. Additionally, opening and closing are two important operations, which are derived from the two aforementioned operations (dilation and erosion). Finally, there are three other operations that based on the difference between some of these previous operations.

All of these morphological transformations are described in the following subsections, and the `morphological_operations.py` script shows the output when applying these transformations to some test images. The key points will also be commented on.

Dilation operation

The main effect of a dilation operation on a binary image is to gradually expand the boundary regions of the foreground object. This means the areas of the foreground object will become larger while holes within those regions shrink. The details of operation are shown in the following code:

```
dilation = cv2.dilate(image, kernel, iterations=1)
```

Erosion operation

The main effect of an erosion operation on a binary image is to gradually erode away the boundary regions of the foreground object. This means that the areas of the foreground object will become smaller, and the holes within those areas will get bigger. You can see the details of this operation in the following code:

```
erosion = cv2.erode(image, kernel, iterations=1)
```

Opening operation

An opening operation performs an erosion followed by a dilation using the same structuring element (or kernel) for both operations. In this way, erosion can be applied to eliminate small groups of undesirable pixels (for example, salt-and-pepper noise).

Erosion will affect all regions of the image indiscriminately. By performing a dilation operation after the erosion, we will reduce some of these effects. You can see the details of this operation in the following code:

```
opening = cv2.morphologyEx(image, cv2.MORPH_OPEN, kernel)
```

Closing operation

Like its opposite, the closing operator can be derived from erosion and dilation operations. In this case, the operation performs a dilation followed by an erosion. A dilation operation is commonly used to fill small holes in images. However, the dilation operation will also make small groups of undesirable pixels bigger. By applying the erosion operation on the image after the dilation, some of this effect will be reduced. You can see the details of this operation in the following code:

```
closing = cv2.morphologyEx(image, cv2.MORPH_CLOSE, kernel)
```

Morphological gradient operation

A morphological gradient operation is defined as the difference between the dilation and erosion of the input image:

```
morph_gradient = cv2.morphologyEx(image, cv2.MORPH_GRADIENT, kernel)
```

Top hat operation

A top hat operation is defined as the difference between the input image and the opening of the image. You can see the details of this operation in the following code:

```
top_hat = cv2.morphologyEx(image, cv2.MORPH_TOPHAT, kernel)
```

Black hat operation

A black hat operation is defined as the difference between the input image and the closing of the input image. You can see the details of this operation in the following code:

```
black_hat = cv2.morphologyEx(image, cv2.MORPH_BLACKHAT, kernel)
```

Structuring element

In connection with the structuring element, OpenCV provides
the `cv2.getStructuringElement()` function.

This function outputs the desired kernel (a NumPy array of type `uint8`). Two parameters
should be passed to this function—the shape and the size of the kernel. OpenCV provides
the following three shapes:

- **Rectangular kernel**: `cv2.MORPH_RECT`
- **Elliptical kernel**: `cv2.MORPH_ELLIPSE`
- **Cross-shaped kernel**: `cv2.MORPH_CROSS`

Applying morphological transformations to images

In the `morphological_operations.py` script, we play with different kernel sizes and
shapes, morphological transformations, and images. We will describe some of the key
points of this script in this section.

First of all, the `build_kernel()` function returns the specific kernel to use in the
morphological transformation based on both the kernel type and size. Secondly,
the `morphological_operations` dictionary contains all the implemented morphological
operations. If we print the dictionary, the output will be as follows:

```
index: '0', key: 'erode', value: '<function erode at 0x0C1F8228>'
index: '1', key: 'dilate', value: '<function dilate at 0x0C1F8390>'
index: '2', key: 'closing', value: '<function closing at 0x0C1F83D8>'
index: '3', key: 'opening', value: '<function opening at 0x0C1F8420>'
index: '4', key: 'gradient', value: '<function morphological_gradient at
0x0C1F8468>'
index: '5', key: 'closing|opening', value: '<function closing_and_opening
at 0x0C1F8348>'
index: '6', key: 'opening|closing', value: '<function opening_and_closing
at 0x0C1F84B0>'
```

In other words, the key of the dictionary identifies the morphological operation to use and
the value is the function to call when the corresponding key is used. For example, if we
want to call the `erode` operation, we must perform the following:

```
result = morphological_operations['erode'](image, kernel_type, kernel_size)
```

In the preceding code `image`, `kernel_type`, and `kernel_size` are the parameters of the `erode` function (in fact, they are the parameters for all the functions of the dictionary).

The `apply_morphological_operation()` function applies all the morphological operations defined in the dictionary to the array of images. Finally, the `show_images()` function is called, where all the images contained in the array are plotted. Specific implementation details can be seen in the source code of the `morphological_operations.py` script, which contains plenty of comments.

The script plots four figures, where different kernel types and sizes are tested. For example, in the following screenshot, you can see the output when a kernel size of *(3, 3)* and a rectangular kernel (`cv2.MORPH_RECT`) are used:

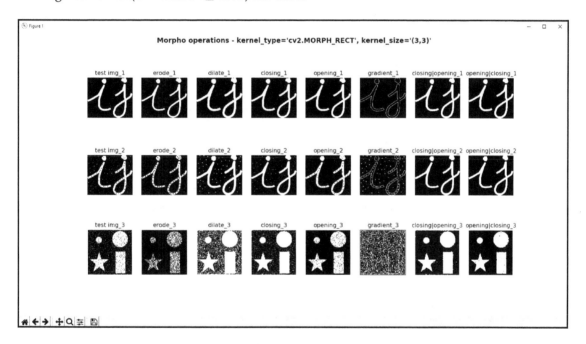

As you can see in the preceding screenshot, morphological operations are a useful technique when preprocessing the images because you can get rid of some noise, which can disturb the proper processing of the images. Additionally, morphological operations can also be used to deal with imperfections in the structure of the image.

Color spaces

In this section, the basics of popular color spaces will be covered. These color spaces are—RGB, CIE L*a*b*, HSL and HSV, and YCbCr.

OpenCV provides more than 150 color-space conversion methods to perform the user's required conversions. In the following example, the conversions are performed from an image loaded in the RGB (BGR in OpenCV) to the other color spaces (for example, HSV, HLS, or YCbCr).

Showing color spaces

The **RGB** color space is an additive color space, where a specific color is represented by red, green, and blue values. Human vision works in a similar way, so this color space is an appropriate way to display computer graphics.

The **CIELAB** color space (also known as **CIE L*a*b*** or simply *LAB*) represents a specific color as three numerical values, where L* represents the lightness, a* represents the green-red components, and b* represents the blue-yellow components. This color space is also used in some image processing algorithms.

Hue, saturation, lightness (HSL) and **hue, saturation, value (HSV)** are two color spaces, where only one channel (H) is used to describe the color, making it very intuitive to specify the color. In these color models, the separation of the luminance component has some advantages when applying image processing techniques.

YCbCr is a family of color spaces used in video and digital photography systems, representing colors in terms of the chroma components (Y) and two chrominance components/chroma (Cb and Cr). This color space is very popular in image segmentation, based on the color model derived from the YCbCr image.

In the `color_spaces.py` script, an image is loaded in the BGR color space and converted into the aforementioned color spaces. In this script, the key function is `cv2.cvtColor()`, which converts an input image of one color space into another.

In the case of transformations to/from the RGB color space, the order of the channels should be specified explicitly (BGR or RGB). For example:

```
image = cv2.imread('color_spaces.png')
```

```
hsv_image = cv2.cvtColor(image, cv2.COLOR_BGR2HSV)
```

Note that we have used `cv2.COLOR_BGR2HSV` and not `cv2.COLOR_RGB2HSV`.

The full code for this script can be seen in `color_space.py`. The output can be seen in the following screenshot:

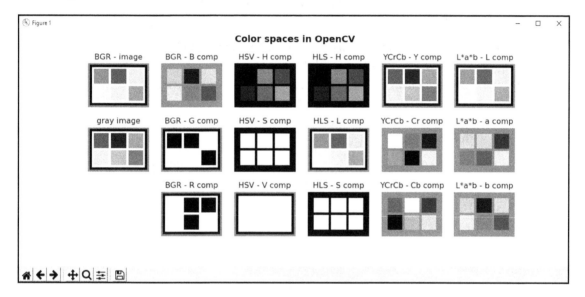

As shown in the preceding screenshot, the BGR image is converted into the HSV, HLS, YCrCb, and L*a*b* color spaces. All the components (channels) for each color space are also shown.

Skin segmentation in different color spaces

The aforementioned color spaces can be used in different image processing tasks and techniques. For example, the `skin_segmentation.py` script implements different algorithms to perform skin segmentation working in different color spaces (YCrCb, HSV, and RGB). This script also loads several test images to see how these algorithms work.

The key functions in this script are `cv2.cvtColor()`, which we have already mentioned on, and `cv2.inRange()`, which checks whether the elements contained in an array lie between the elements of two other arrays (the lower boundary array and the upper boundary array).

Therefore, we use the `cv2.inRange()` function to segment the colors corresponding to the skin. As you can see, the values defined for these two arrays (lower and upper boundaries) play a critical role in the performance of the segmentation algorithms. In this way, a wide investigation has been carried out in order to set them properly. In this example, the values are obtained from the following research papers:

- *RGB-H-CbCr Skin Color Model for Human Face Detection* by Nusirwan Anwar, Abdul Rahman, K. C. Wei, and John See
- *Skin segmentation algorithm based on the YCrCb color space* by Shruti D Patravali, Jyoti Waykule, and Apurva Katre
- *Face Segmentation Using Skin-Color Map in Videophone Applications* by D. Chai and K.N. Ngan

The `skin_detectors` dictionary has been built to apply all the skin segmentation algorithms to the test images. If we print it, the output will be as follows:

```
index: '0', key: 'ycrcb', value: '<function skin_detector_ycrcb at
0x07B8C030>'
index: '1', key: 'hsv', value: '<function skin_detector_hsv at 0x07B8C0C0>'
index: '2', key: 'hsv_2', value: '<function skin_detector_hsv_2 at
0x07B8C108>'
index: '3', key: 'bgr', value: '<function skin_detector_bgr at 0x07B8C1E0>'
```

You can see that there are four skin detectors defined. In order to call a skin segmentation detector (for example, `skin_detector_ycrcb`), you must perform the following:

```
detected_skin = skin_detectors['ycrcb'](image)
```

The output of the script can be seen in the following screenshot:

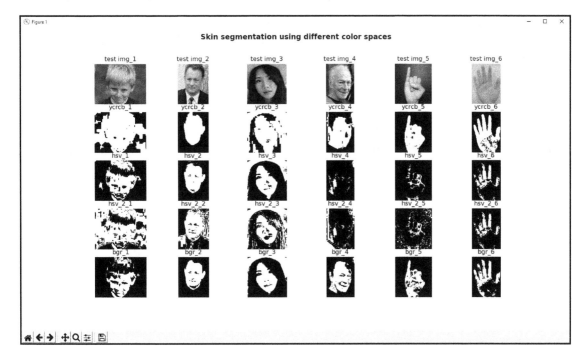

You can see the effect of applying different skin segmentation algorithms using several test images to see how these algorithms work under different conditions.

Color maps

In many computer vision applications, the output of your algorithm is a grayscale image. However, human eyes are not good at observing changes in grayscale images. They are more sensitive when appreciating changes in color images, therefore a common approach is to transform (recolor) the grayscale images into a pseudocolor equivalent image.

Color maps in OpenCV

In order to perform this transformation, OpenCV has several color maps to enhance visualization. The `cv2.applyColorMap()` function applies a color map on the given image. The `color_map_example.py` script loads a grayscale image and applies the `cv2.COLORMAP_HSV` color map, as shown in the following code:

```
img_COLORMAP_HSV = cv2.applyColorMap(gray_img, cv2.COLORMAP_HSV)
```

Finally, we are going to apply all the color maps to the same grayscale image and plot them in the same figure. This can be seen in the `color_map_all.py` script. The color maps that OpenCV has defined are listed as follows:

- `COLORMAP_AUTUMN = 0`
- `COLORMAP_BONE = 1`
- `COLORMAP_JET = 2`
- `COLORMAP_WINTER = 3`
- `COLORMAP_RAINBOW = 4`
- `COLORMAP_OCEAN = 5`
- `COLORMAP_SUMMER = 6`
- `COLORMAP_SPRING = 7`
- `COLORMAP_COOL = 8`
- `COLORMAP_HSV = 9`
- `COLORMAP_HOT = 11`
- `COLORMAP_PINK = 10`
- `COLORMAP_PARULA = 12`

The `color_map_all.py` script applies all these color maps to a grayscale image. The output of this script can be seen in the following screenshot:

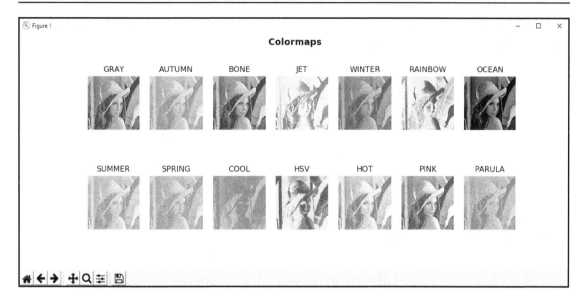

In the previous screenshot, you can see the effect of applying all the predefined color maps to a grayscale image with the objective of enhancing the visualization.

Custom color maps

You can also apply custom color maps to an image. This functionality can be achieved in several ways.

The first approach is to define a color map that maps the 0 to 255 grayscale values to 256 colors. This can be done by creating an 8-bit color image of size *256 x 1* in order to store all the created colors. After that, you map the grayscale intensities of the image to the defined colors by means of a lookup table. In order to achieve this, you can do one of the following:

- Make use of the `cv2.LUT()` function
- Map the grayscale intensities of the image to the defined colors so you can make use of `cv2.applyColorMap()`

One key point is to store the created colors when creating the 8-bit color image of size *256 x 1*. If you are going to use `cv2.LUT()`, the image should be created as follows:

```
lut = np.zeros((256, 3), dtype=np.uint8)
```

If you are going to use `cv2.cv2.applyColorMap()`, then it should be as follows:

```
lut = np.zeros((256, 1, 3), dtype=np.uint8)
```

The full code for this can be seen in `color_map_custom_values.py`. The output of this script can be seen in the following screenshot:

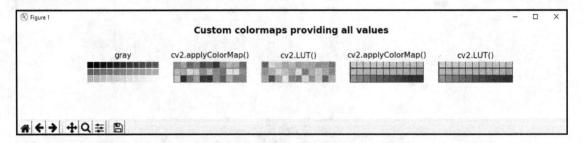

The second approach to define a color map is to provide only some key colors and then *interpolate* the values in order to get all the necessary colors to build the lookup table. The `color_map_custom_key_colors.py` script shows how to achieve this.

The `build_lut()` function builds the lookup table based on these key colors. Based on five color points, this function calls `np.linspace()` to get all the 64 evenly spaced colors calculated over the interval, each defined by two color points. To understand this better, look at the following screenshot:

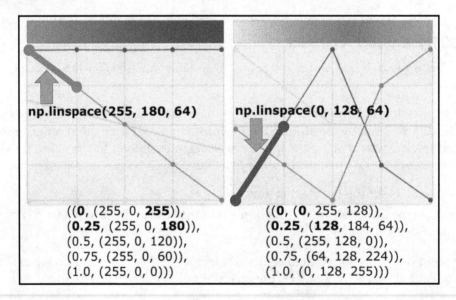

In this screenshot, you can see, for example, how to calculate all the 64 evenly spaced colors for two line segments (see the green and blue highlighted segments).

Finally,in order to build the lookup table for the following five key color points (`(0,  (0, 255, 128))`,`(0.25,  (128, 184, 64))`,`(0.5,  (255, 128, 0))`,`(0.75,  (64, 128, 224))`, and `(1.0,  (0, 128, 255))`), the following calls to `np.linspace()` are performed:

```
blue : np.linspace('0', '128', '64' - '0' = '64')
green : np.linspace('255', '184', '64' - '0' = '64')
red : np.linspace('128', '64', '64' - '0' = '64')
blue : np.linspace('128', '255', '128' - '64' = '64')
green : np.linspace('184', '128', '128' - '64' = '64')
red : np.linspace('64', '0', '128' - '64' = '64')
blue : np.linspace('255', '64', '192' - '128' = '64')
green : np.linspace('128', '128', '192' - '128' = '64')
red : np.linspace('0', '224', '192' - '128' = '64')
blue : np.linspace('64', '0', '256' - '192' = '64')
green : np.linspace('128', '128', '256' - '192' = '64')
red : np.linspace('224', '255', '256' - '192' = '64')
```

The output of the `color_map_custom_key_colors.py` script can be seen in the next screenshot:

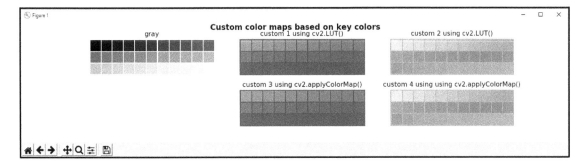

In the previous screenshot, you can see the effect of applying two custom color maps to a grayscale image.

Showing the legend for the custom color map

Finally, one interesting functionality is to provide the legend when showing your custom color map. This can be achieved with the `color_map_custom_legend.py` script.

In order to build the legend image, the `build_lut_image()` function performs this functionality. We first call the `build_lut()` function in order to get the lookup table. Then, we call `np.repeat()` in order to replicate this lookup table several times (this operation is repeated `height` times). Note that the shape of the lookup table is (256, 3). We want the shape of the output image to be `height`, 256, and 3, and so we can use `np.repeat()` together with `np.newaxis()`, like this:

```
image = np.repeat(lut[np.newaxis, ...], height, axis=0)
```

The output of this script can be seen in the following screenshot:

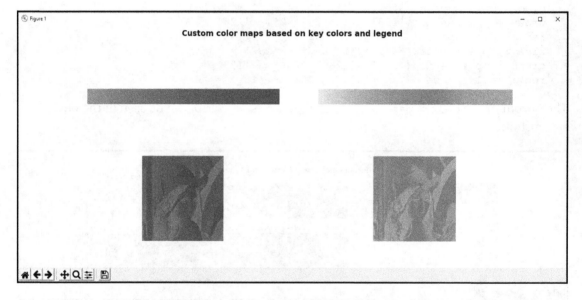

In the preceding screenshot, you can see the effect of applying two custom color maps to a grayscale image and showing the legend for each color map.

Summary

In this chapter, we reviewed most of the common image processing techniques you need in your computer vision projects. In the next three chapters (Chapter 6, *Constructing and Building Histograms*, Chapter 7, *Thresholding Techniques,* and Chapter 8, *Contour Detection, Filtering, and Drawing*), the most common image processing techniques will be reviewed.

In Chapter 6, *Constructing and Building Histograms*, you will learn how to both create and understand histograms, which are a powerful technique that is used to better understand image content.

Questions

1. Which function splits a multichannel into several single-channel images?
2. Which function merges several single-channel images into a multichannel image?
3. Translate an image 150 pixels in the *x* direction and 300 pixels in the *y* direction.
4. Rotate an image named img by 30 degrees with respect to the center of the image with a scale factor of 1.
5. Build a *5 x 5* averaging kernel and apply it to an image using cv2.filter2D().
6. Add 40 to all the pixels in a grayscale image.
7. Apply the COLORMAP_JET color map to a grayscale image.

Further reading

The following reference will help you dive deeper into image processing techniques in OpenCV:

- *Learning Image Processing with OpenCV* by Gloria Bueno García et al. (https://www.packtpub.com/application-development/learning-image-processing-opencv)

6
Constructing and Building Histograms

Histograms are a powerful technique used to better understand image content. For example, many cameras display in real time the histogram of the scene that is being captured in order to adjust some parameters of the camera acquisition (for example, exposure time, brightness, or contrast) with the purpose of capturing appropriate images and helping detect image acquisition issues.

In this chapter, you will see how to create and understand histograms.

This chapter will tackle the main concepts concerning histograms, and the following topics will be covered:

- A theoretical introduction to histograms
- Grayscale histograms
- Color histograms
- Custom visualizations of histograms
- Comparing OpenCV, NumPy, and Matplotlib histograms
- Histogram equalization
- Adaptive histogram equalization
- Comparing CLAHE and histogram equalization
- Histogram comparison

Technical requirements

The technical requirements are as follows:

- Python and OpenCV
- Python-specific IDE
- NumPy and Matplotlib packages
- Git client

Further details about how to install these requirements are discussed in Chapter 1, *Setting Up OpenCV*. The GitHub repository for *Mastering OpenCV 4 with Python*, containing all the supporting project files necessary to work through the book from the first chapter to the last one, can be accessed at this URL: https://github.com/PacktPublishing/Mastering-OpenCV-4-with-Python.

A theoretical introduction to histograms

An image histogram is a type of histogram that reflects the tonal distribution of the image, plotting the number of pixels for each tonal value. The number of pixels for each tonal value is also called **frequency**. Therefore, a histogram for a grayscale image with intensity values in the range [0, K-1] would contain exactly K entries. For example, in the case of 8-bit grayscale images, K = 256 (2^8 = 256), and hence, the intensity values are in the range [0, 255]. Each entry of the histogram is defined as follows:

$$h(i) = number of pixels with intensity i (i \epsilon [0, 255])$$

For example, *h(80) = number of pixels with intensity 80.*

In the next screenshot, you can see that the image (left) has 7 distinct gray levels. The gray levels are: 30, 60, 90, 120, 150, 180 and 210. The histogram (right) shows how many times (frequency) each tonal value appears in the image. In this case, as each region is *50 x 50* pixels in size (2,500 pixels), the frequency will be 2,500 for the aforementioned gray level values, and 0 otherwise:

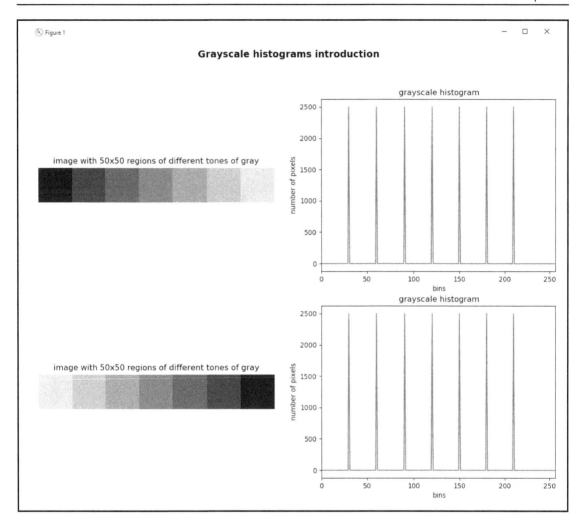

Note that histograms show only statistical information and not the location of pixels. That is why the histograms for both images are exactly the same.

The `histogram_introduction.py` script plots the figure as shown previously. In this script, the `build_sample_image()` function builds the first image (up) and the `build_sample_image_2()` function builds the second image (down) by making use of NumPy operations. The code for `build_sample_image()` is provided next:

```
def build_sample_image():
    """Builds a sample image with 50x50 regions of different tones of
gray"""

    # Define the different tones. In this case: 60, 90, 120, ..., 210
    # The end of interval (240) is not included
    tones = np.arange(start=60, stop=240, step=30)

    # Initialize result withe the first 50x50 region with 30-intensity
level
    result = np.ones((50, 50, 3), dtype="uint8") * 30

    # Build the image concatenating horizontally the regions:
    for tone in tones:
        img = np.ones((50, 50, 3), dtype="uint8") * tone
        result = np.concatenate((result, img), axis=1)

    return result
```

And here, note the code for `build_sample_image2()`:

```
def build_sample_image_2():
    """Builds a sample image with 50x50 regions of different tones of gray
    flipping the output of build_sample_image()
    """

    # Flip the image in the left/right direction:
    img = np.fliplr(build_sample_image())
    return img
```

The NumPy operations that have been used to build these images (`np.ones()`, `np.arange()`, `np.concatenate()`, and `np.fliplr()`) are described briefly in the following:

- `np.ones()`: Returns an array of a given shape and type filled with the value of 1. In this case, shape—`(50, 50, 3)`, and `dtype="uint8"`.
- `np.arange()`: Returns evenly spaced values within a given interval, taking into account the provided step. The end of the interval (`240` in this case) is not included.

- np.concatenate(): Joins a sequence of arrays along an existing axis; in this case, axis=1 to concatenate the images horizontally.
- np.fliplr(): Flips the array in the left/right direction.

The functionality to calculate and show histograms will be covered in the next sections.

Histogram terminology

Before going deeper into histograms and how to construct and visualize them by using the OpenCV (and also NumPy and Matplotlib) functions related to histograms, we need to understand some terminologies in connection with histograms:

- bins: The histograms in the previous screenshot show the number of pixels (frequency) for every tonal value, ranging from 0 to 255. Each of these 256 values is called a **bin** in histogram terminology. The number of bins can be selected as desired. Common values are 8, 16, 32, 64, 128, 256. OpenCV uses histSize to refer to bins.
- range: This is the range of intensity values we want to measure. Normally, it is [0,255], corresponding to all the tonal values (0 corresponds to black and 255 corresponds to white).

Grayscale histograms

OpenCV provides the cv2.calcHist() function in order to calculate the histogram of one or more arrays. Therefore, this function can be applied to single-channel images (for example, grayscale images) and to multi-channel images (for example, BGR images).

In this section, we are going to see how to calculate histograms for grayscale images. The signature for this function is as follows:

```
cv2.calcHist(images, channels, mask, histSize, ranges[, hist[,
accumulate]])
```

To this, the following applies:

- images: It represents the source image of type uint8 or float32 provided as a list (example, [gray_img]).

- `channels`: It represents the index of the channel for which we calculate the histogram provided as a list (for example, `[0]` for grayscale images, or `[0],[1],[2]` for multi-channel images to calculate the histogram for the first, second, or third channel, respectively).
- `mask`: It represents a mask image to calculate the histogram of a specific region of the image defined by the mask. If this parameter is equal to `None`, the histogram will be calculated with no mask and the full image will be used.
- `histSize`: It represents the number of `bins` provided as a list (for example, `[256]`).
- `ranges`: It represents the range of intensity values we want to measure (for example, `[0,256]`).

Grayscale histograms without a mask

Therefore, the code for calculating the histogram for a full grayscale image (without a mask) is as follows:

```
image = cv2.imread('lenna.png')
gray_image = cv2.cvtColor(image, cv2.COLOR_BGR2GRAY)
hist = cv2.calcHist([gray_image], [0], None, [256], [0, 256])
```

In this case, `hist` is a `(256, 1)` array. Each value (bin) of the array corresponds to the number of pixels (frequency) with the corresponding tone value.

To plot histograms with Matplotlib, you can use `plt.plot()`, providing the histogram and the color to show the histogram (example, `color='m'`). The following color abbreviations are supported—`'b'`—blue, `'g'`—green, 'r'—red, `'c'`—cyan, `'m'`—magenta, `'y'`—yellow, `'k'`—black, and `'w'`—white. The full code for this example can be seen in the `grayscale_histogram.py` script.

We commented in the introduction that histograms can be used to reveal or detect image acquisition issues. The following example will show you how to detect image brightness issues. The brightness of a grayscale image can be defined as the average intensity of all the pixels of the image given by the following formulation:

$$Brightness = \frac{1}{m \cdot n} \sum_{x=1}^{m} \sum_{y=1}^{n} I(x,y)$$

Here, *I(x, y)* is the tone value for a specific pixel of the image.

Therefore, if the average tone of an image is high (for example, `220`), this means that most pixels of the image will be very close to the white color. On the contrary, if the average tone on an image is low (for example, `30`) this means that most pixels of the image will be very close to the black color.

In the aforementioned script, `grayscale_histogram.py`, we will see how to change the brightness of an image and how the histogram changes.

In this script, which has already been introduced in order to show how a histogram can be calculated and shown for a grayscale image, we also performed some basic math on the grayscale-loaded image. Specifically, we have performed both image addition and subtraction in order to add/subtract a specific quantity to or from the gray level intensity of every pixel of the image. This can be performed with the `cv2.add()` and `cv2.subtract()` functions.

> We covered how to perform arithmetic with images in Chapter 5, *Image Processing Techniques*. Therefore, in you have any doubts in connection with this, you can review the previous chapter.

In this way, the average brightness level of the image can be shifted. This can be seen in the next screenshot, corresponding to the output of the script:

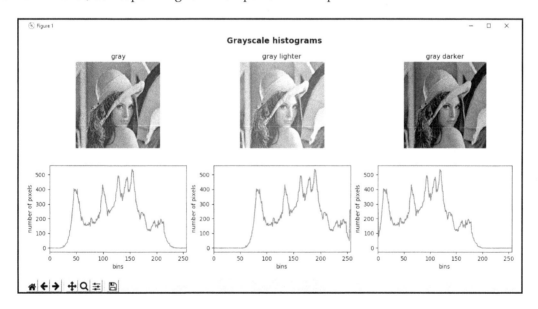

In this specific case, we have added/subtracted 35 to/from every pixel of the original image, and then calculated the histogram for the resulting images:

```
# Add 35 to every pixel on the grayscale image (the result will look
lighter) and calculate histogram
M = np.ones(gray_image.shape, dtype="uint8") * 35
added_image = cv2.add(gray_image, M)
hist_added_image = cv2.calcHist([added_image], [0], None, [256], [0, 256])

# Subtract 35 from every pixel (the result will look darker) and calculate
histogram
subtracted_image = cv2.subtract(gray_image, M)
hist_subtracted_image = cv2.calcHist([subtracted_image], [0], None, [256],
[0, 256])
```

As you can see, the central grayscale image corresponds to the image where 35 is added to every pixel of the original image, resulting in a lighter image. In this image, the histogram appears shifted to the right, in the sense that there are no pixels with intensities in the range [0-35]. On the contrary, the grayscale image on the right corresponds to the image where 35 is subtracted from every pixel of the original image, resulting in a darker image. The histogram appears shifted to the left, in the sense that there are no pixels with intensities in the range [220-255].

Grayscale histograms with a mask

To see how to apply a mask, see the grayscale_histogram_mask.py script, where a mask is created and used to calculate a histogram by using the previously created mask. In order to create the mask, the following line is necessary:

```
mask = np.zeros(gray_image.shape[:2], np.uint8)
mask[30:190, 30:190] = 255
```

Therefore, the mask consists of a black image with the same dimensions as the loaded image, and with the white ones corresponding to the regions where we want to calculate the histogram.

Afterwards, the cv2.calcHist() function is called passing the created mask:

```
hist_mask = cv2.calcHist([gray_image], [0], mask, [256], [0, 256])
```

The output of this script can be seen in the following screenshot:

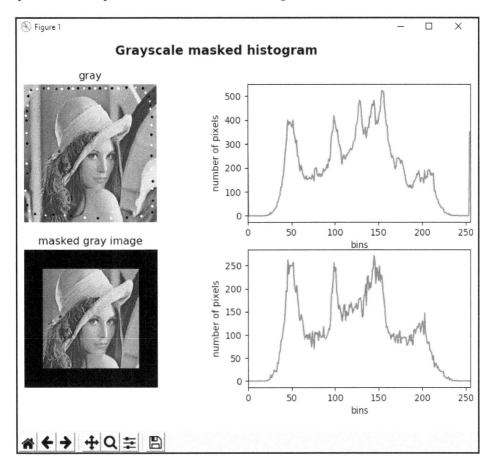

As you can see, we have modified the image to add some small black and white circles with 0 and 255 grayscale intensities (in other words, black and white circles), respectively. This can be seen in the first histogram, which has two picks in `bins=0` and `255`. However, these picks do not appear in the resulting histogram of the masked image because they are not being taken into account when the histogram is calculated, because the mask was applied.

Color histograms

In this section, we will see how to calculate color histograms. The script that performs this functionality is color_histogram.py. In the case of a multi-channel image (for example, a BGR image), the process of calculating the color histogram involves calculating the histogram in each of the channels. In this case, we have created a function to calculate the histogram from a three-channel image:

```
def hist_color_img(img):
    """Calculates the histogram from a three-channel image"""

    histr = []
    histr.append(cv2.calcHist([img], [0], None, [256], [0, 256]))
    histr.append(cv2.calcHist([img], [1], None, [256], [0, 256]))
    histr.append(cv2.calcHist([img], [2], None, [256], [0, 256]))
    return histr
```

It should be noted that we could have created a for loop or a similar approach in order to call the cv2.calcHist() function three times. But, for the sake of simplicity, we have performed the three calls indicating the different channels explicitly. In this case, as we are loading BGR images, the calls are as follows:

- **Calculate histogram for the blue channel**: cv2.calcHist([img], [0], None, [256], [0, 256])
- **Calculate histogram for the green channel**: cv2.calcHist([img], [1], None, [256], [0, 256])
- **Calculate histogram for the red channel**: cv2.calcHist([img], [1], None, [256], [0, 256])

Therefore, in order to calculate the color histogram of an image, note the following:

```
image = cv2.imread('lenna.png')
hist_color = hist_color_img(image)
```

In this script, we have also made use of `cv2.add()` and `cv2.subtract()` to modify the brightness of the loaded BGR image and see how the histogram changes. In this case, `15` has been added/subtracted to every pixel of the original BGR image. This can be seen in the next screenshot corresponding to the output of the `color_histogram.py` script:

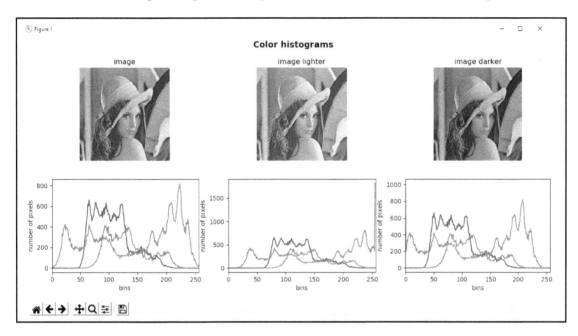

Custom visualizations of histograms

In order to visualize histograms, we have made use of the `plt.plot()` function. If we want to visualize a histogram by using only OpenCV capabilities, there is no OpenCV function to draw histograms. In this case, we have to make use of OpenCV primitives (for example, `cv2.polylines()` and `cv2.rectangle()`, among others) to create some (basic) functionality for plotting histograms. In the `histogram_custom_visualization.py` script, we have created the `plot_hist()` function, which performs this functionality. This function creates a BGR color image, plotting the histogram in it. The code for this function is as follows:

```
def plot_hist(hist_items, color):
    """Plots the histogram of a image"""

    # For visualization purposes we add some offset:
    offset_down = 10
```

```
        offset_up = 10

        # This will be used for creating the points to visualize (x-
coordinates):
        x_values = np.arange(256).reshape(256, 1)

        canvas = np.ones((300, 256, 3), dtype="uint8") * 255
        for hist_item, col in zip(hist_items, color):
            # Normalize in the range for proper visualization:
            cv2.normalize(hist_item, hist_item, 0 + offset_down, 300 -
offset_up, cv2.NORM_MINMAX)
            # Round the normalized values of the histogram:
            around = np.around(hist_item)
            # Cast the values to int:
            hist = np.int32(around)
            # Create the points using the histogram and the x-coordinates:
            pts = np.column_stack((x_values, hist))
            # Draw the points:
            cv2.polylines(canvas, [pts], False, col, 2)
            # Draw a rectangle:
            cv2.rectangle(canvas, (0, 0), (255, 298), (0, 0, 0), 1)

        # Flip the image in the up/down direction:
        res = np.flipud(canvas)

        return res
```

This function receives the histogram and builds the *(x, y)* points, `pts` for every element of the histogram, where the *y* value represents the frequency of the *x* element of the histogram. These points, `pts`, are drawn by using the `cv2.polylines()` function, which we have seen in Chapter 4, *Constructing Basic Shapes in OpenCV*. This function draws a polygonal curve based on the `pts` array. Finally, the image is flipped vertically because the *y* values are upside down. In the next screenshot, we can compare the visualization using `plt.plot()` and our custom function:

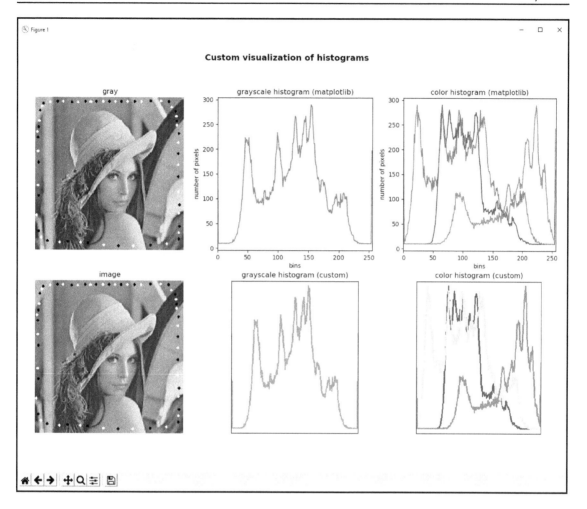

Comparing OpenCV, NumPy, and Matplotlib histograms

We have already seen that OpenCV provides the `cv2.calcHist()` function to calculate histograms. Additionally, NumPy and Matplotlib offer similar functions for the creation of histograms. In the `comparing_opencv_numpy_mpl_hist.py` script, we are comparing these functions for performance purposes. In this sense, we are going to see how to create histograms with OpenCV, NumPy, and Matplotlib, and then measure the execution time for each one and plot the results in a figure.

With the purpose of measuring the execution time, we are using `timeit.default_timer` because it provides the best clock available on your platform and version of Python automatically. In this way, we import it at the beginning of the script:

```
from timeit import default_timer as timer
```

The way we use the timer is summarized here:

```
start = timer()
# ...
end = timer()
execution_time = start - end
```

It should be taken into account that `default_timer()` measurements can be affected by other programs running on the same machine at the same time. Therefore, the best approach to performing accurate timing is to repeat it several times and take the best time.

In order to calculate the histograms, we are going to use the following functions:

- `cv2.calcHist()` provided by OpenCV
- `np.histogram()` provided by NumPy
- `plt.hist()` provided by Matplotlib

Hence, the code for calculating the execution for each of the aforementioned functions is provided as follows:

```
start = timer()
# Calculate the histogram calling cv2.calcHist()
hist = cv2.calcHist([gray_image], [0], None, [256], [0, 256])
end = timer()
exec_time_calc_hist = (end - start) * 1000

start = timer()
# Calculate the histogram calling np.histogram():
hist_np, bins_np = np.histogram(gray_image.ravel(), 256, [0, 256])
end = timer()
exec_time_np_hist = (end - start) * 1000

start = timer()
# Calculate the histogram calling plt.hist():
(n, bins, patches) = plt.hist(gray_image.ravel(), 256, [0, 256])
end = timer()
exec_time_plt_hist = (end - start) * 1000
```

We multiply the value to get milliseconds (rather than seconds). The output for the `comparing_opencv_numpy_mpl_hist.py` script can be seen in the following screenshot:

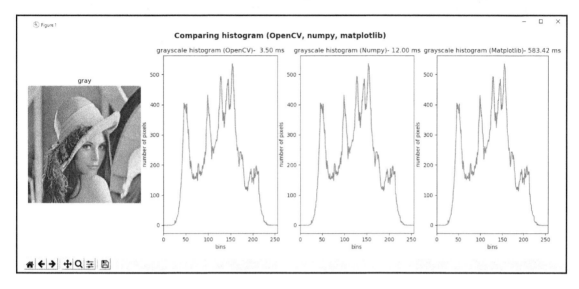

As can be seen, `cv2.calcHist()` is faster than both `np.histogram()` and `plt.hist()`. Therefore, for performance purposes, you can use the OpenCV function.

Histogram equalization

In this section, we will see how to perform histogram equalization using the OpenCV function, `cv2.equalizeHist()`, and how to apply it to both grayscale and color images. The `cv2.equalizeHist()` function normalizes the brightness and also increases the contrast of the image. Therefore, the histogram of the image is modified after applying this function. In the next subsections, we will explore both the original and the modified histogram in order to see how it is changed.

Grayscale histogram equalization

Using the `cv2.equalizeHist()` function with the purpose of equalizing the contrast of a given grayscale image is pretty easy:

```
image = cv2.imread('lenna.png')
gray_image = cv2.cvtColor(image, cv2.COLOR_BGR2GRAY)
gray_image_eq = cv2.equalizeHist(gray_image)
```

In the `grayscale_histogram_equalization.py` script, we apply histogram equalization to three images. The first one is the original grayscale image. The second one is the original image but modified, in the sense that we have added 35 to every pixel of the image. The third one is the original image but modified, in the sense that we have subtracted 35 from every pixel of the image. We have also calculated histograms before and after the equalization of the histogram. Finally, all of these images are plotted. The output of this script can be seen in the following screenshot:

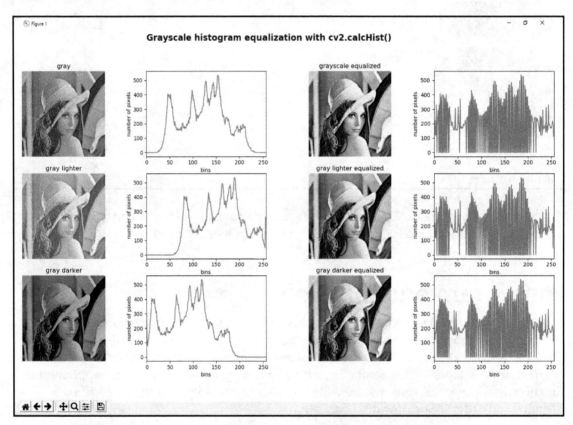

In the previous screenshot, we can see that the three equalized images are really very similar and this fact can also be reflected in the equalized histograms, where all three of them are also very similar. This is because histogram equalization tends to normalize the brightness (and also increase the contrast) of images.

Color histogram equalization

Following the same approach, we can perform histogram equalization in color images. We have to say this is not the best approach for histogram equalization in color images and we will see how to perform it correctly. Therefore, this first (*and incorrect*) version applies histogram equalization to each channel of the BGR images. This approach can be seen in the following code:

```
def equalize_hist_color(img):
    """Equalize the image splitting the image applying cv2.equalizeHist()
to each channel and merging the results"""

    channels = cv2.split(img)
    eq_channels = []
    for ch in channels:
    eq_channels.append(cv2.equalizeHist(ch))

    eq_image = cv2.merge(eq_channels)
    return eq_image
```

We have created the `equalize_hist_color()` function, which splits the BGR image by using `cv2.split()` and applies the `cv2.equalizeHist()` function to each channel. Finally, we merge all the resulting channels using `cv2.merge()`. We have applied this function to three different images. The first one is the original BGR image. The second one is the original image but modified in the sense that we have added `15` to every pixel of the image. The third one is the original image but modified in the sense that we have subtracted `15` from every pixel of the image. We have also calculated histograms before and after the equalization of the histogram.

Finally, all of these images are plotted. The output of the
`color_histogram_equalization.py` script can be seen in the following screenshot:

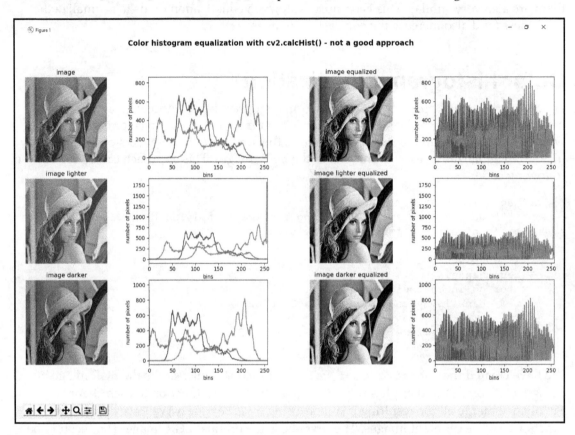

We have commented that equalizing the three channels is not a good approach because the color shade changes dramatically. This is due to the additive properties of the BGR color space. As we are changing both the brightness and the contrast in the three channels independently, this can lead to new color shades appearing in the image when merging the equalized channels. This issue can be seen in the previous screenshot.

A better approach is to convert the BGR image to a color space containing a luminance/intensity channel (Yuv, Lab, HSV, and HSL). Then, we apply histogram equalization only on the luminance channel and, finally, perform inverse transformation, that is, we merge the channels and convert them back to the BGR color space.

This approach can be seen in the `color_histogram_equalization_hsv.py` script, where the `equalize_hist_color_hsv()` function will perform this functionality:

```
def equalize_hist_color_hsv(img):
    """Equalize the image splitting the image after HSV conversion and
applying cv2.equalizeHist()
    to the V channel, merging the channels and convert back to the BGR
color space
    """

    H, S, V = cv2.split(cv2.cvtColor(img, cv2.COLOR_BGR2HSV))
    eq_V = cv2.equalizeHist(V)
    eq_image = cv2.cvtColor(cv2.merge([H, S, eq_V]), cv2.COLOR_HSV2BGR)
    return eq_image
```

The output can be seen in the following screenshot:

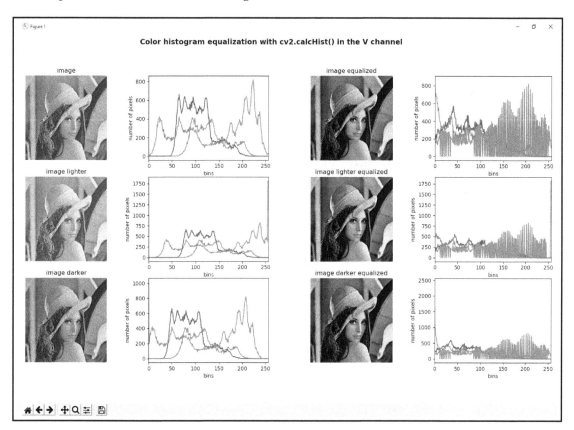

As can be seen, obtained the results obtained after equalizing only the V channel of the HSV image are much better than equalizing all the channels of the BGR image. As we commented, this approach is also valid for a color space containing a luminance/intensity channel (Yuv, Lab, HSV, and HSL). This will be seen in the next section.

Contrast Limited Adaptive Histogram Equalization

In this section, we are going to see how to apply **contrast limited adaptive histogram equalization** (**CLAHE**) to equalize images, which is a variant of **adaptive histogram equalization** (**AHE**), in which contrast amplification is limited. The noise in relatively homogeneous regions of the image is overamplified by AHE, while CLAHE tackles this problem by limiting the contrast amplification. This algorithm can be applied to improve the contrast of images. This algorithm works by creating several histograms of the original image, and uses all of these histograms to redistribute the lightness of the image.

In the `clahe_histogram_equalization.py` script, we are applying CLAHE to both grayscale and color images. When applying CLAHE, there are two parameters to tune. The first one is `clipLimit`, which sets the threshold for contrast limiting. The default value is 40. The second one is `tileGridSize`, which sets the number of *tiles* in the row and column. When applying CLAHE, the image is divided into small blocks called **tiles** (*8 x 8* by default) in order to perform its calculations.

To apply CLAHE to a grayscale image, we must perform the following:

```
clahe = cv2.createCLAHE(clipLimit=2.0)
gray_image_clahe = clahe.apply(gray_image)
```

Additionally, we can also apply CLAHE to color images, very similar to the approach commented in the previous section for the contrast equalization of color images, where the results after equalizing only the luminance channel of an HSV image are much better than equalizing all the channels of the BGR image.

In this section, we are going to create four functions in order to equalize the color images by using CLAHE only on the luminance channel of different color spaces:

```
def equalize_clahe_color_hsv(img):
    """Equalize the image splitting after conversion to HSV and applying
CLAHE
    to the V channel and merging the channels and convert back to BGR
    """
```

```
    cla = cv2.createCLAHE(clipLimit=4.0)
    H, S, V = cv2.split(cv2.cvtColor(img, cv2.COLOR_BGR2HSV))
    eq_V = cla.apply(V)
    eq_image = cv2.cvtColor(cv2.merge([H, S, eq_V]), cv2.COLOR_HSV2BGR)
    return eq_image


def equalize_clahe_color_lab(img):
    """Equalize the image splitting after conversion to LAB and applying
CLAHE
    to the L channel and merging the channels and convert back to BGR
    """

    cla = cv2.createCLAHE(clipLimit=4.0)
    L, a, b = cv2.split(cv2.cvtColor(img, cv2.COLOR_BGR2Lab))
    eq_L = cla.apply(L)
    eq_image = cv2.cvtColor(cv2.merge([eq_L, a, b]), cv2.COLOR_Lab2BGR)
    return eq_image


def equalize_clahe_color_yuv(img):
    """Equalize the image splitting after conversion to YUV and applying
CLAHE
    to the Y channel and merging the channels and convert back to BGR
    """

    cla = cv2.createCLAHE(clipLimit=4.0)
    Y, U, V = cv2.split(cv2.cvtColor(img, cv2.COLOR_BGR2YUV))
    eq_Y = cla.apply(Y)
    eq_image = cv2.cvtColor(cv2.merge([eq_Y, U, V]), cv2.COLOR_YUV2BGR)
    return eq_image


def equalize_clahe_color(img):
    """Equalize the image splitting the image applying CLAHE to each
channel and merging the results"""

    cla = cv2.createCLAHE(clipLimit=4.0)
    channels = cv2.split(img)
    eq_channels = []
    for ch in channels:
        eq_channels.append(cla.apply(ch))

    eq_image = cv2.merge(eq_channels)
    return eq_image
```

The output for this script can be seen in the next screenshot, where we compare the result after applying all these functions to a test image:

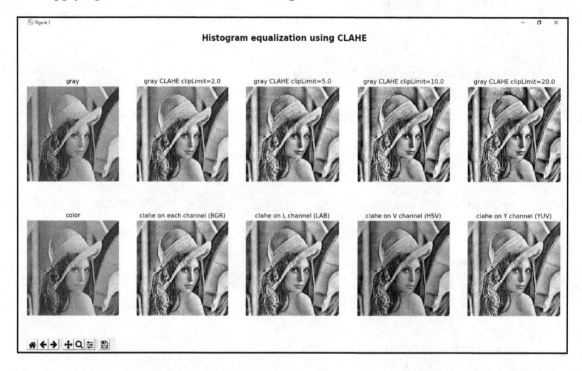

In the previous screenshot, we can see the result after applying CLAHE on a test image by varying the `clipLimit` parameter. Additionally, we can see the different results after applying CLAHE on the luminance channel in different color spaces (LAB, HSV, and YUV). Finally, we can see the wrong approach of applying CLAHE on the three channels of the BGR image.

Comparing CLAHE and histogram equalization

For the sake of completeness, in the `comparing_hist_equalization_clahe.py` script, you can see how both CLAHE and histogram equalization (`cv2.equalizeHist()`) work on the same image, visualizing both the resulting image and the resulting histogram.

This can be seen in the following screenshot:

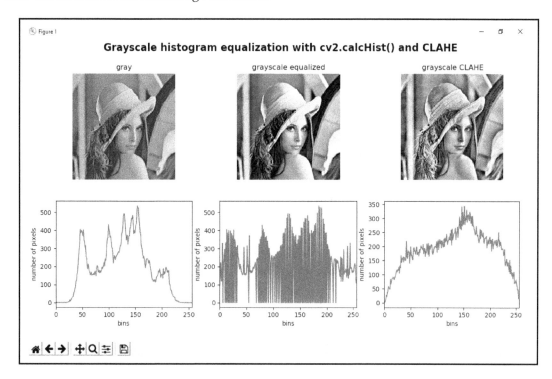

It is safe to say that CLAHE gives better results and performance than applying histogram equalization in many situations. In this sense, CLAHE is commonly used as the first step in many computer vision applications (for example, face processing, among others).

Histogram comparison

One interesting functionality offered by OpenCV in connection with histograms is the `cv2.compareHist()` function, which can be used to get a numerical parameter expressing how well two histograms match each other. In this sense, as histograms reflect the intensity distributions of the pixel values in the image, this function can be used to compare images. As previously commented, the histograms show only statistical information and not the location of pixels. Therefore, a common approach for image comparison is to divide the image into a certain number of regions (commonly with the same size), calculate the histogram for each region, and, finally, concatenate all the histograms to create the feature representation of the image. In this example, for simplicity, we are not going to divide the image into a certain number of regions, so only one region (the full image) will be used.

The signature for the `cv2.compareHist()` function is as follows:

```
cv2.compareHist(H1, H2, method)
```

Here, `H1` and `H2` are the histograms being compared, and `method` establishes the comparison method.

OpenCV offers four different metrics (methods) to compute the matching:

- `cv2.HISTCMP_CORREL`: This metric computes the correlation between the two histograms. This metric returns values in the range `[-1, 1]`, where 1 means a perfect match and -1 is no match at all.
- `cv2.HISTCMP_CHISQR`: This metric computes the chi-squared distance between the two histograms. This metric returns values in the range `[0, unbounded]`, where 0 means a perfect match and a mismatch is unbounded.
- `cv2.HISTCMP_INTERSECT`: This metric computes the intersection between the two histograms. This metric returns values in the range `[0,1]` if the histograms are normalized, where 1 means a perfect match and 0 no match at all.
- `cv2.HISTCMP_BHATTACHARYYA`: This metric computes the Bhattacharyya distance between the two histograms. This metric returns values in the range `[0,1]`, where 0 is a perfect match and 1 no match at all.

In the `compare_histograms.py` script, we first load four images, and then we calculate the similarity among all these images and a test image using all the metrics commented previously.

The four images that we are using are as follows:

- `gray_image.png`: This image corresponds to a grayscale image.
- `gray_added_image.png`: This image corresponds to the original image, but modified in the sense that we have added 35 to every pixel of the image.
- `gray_subtracted_image.png`: This image corresponds to the original image, but modified in the sense that we have subtracted 35 to every pixel of the image.
- `gray_blurred.png`: This image corresponds to the original image but modified with a blur filter (`cv2.blur(gray_image, (10, 10))`).

The test (or query) image is also `gray_image.png`. The output for this example can be seen in the next screenshot:

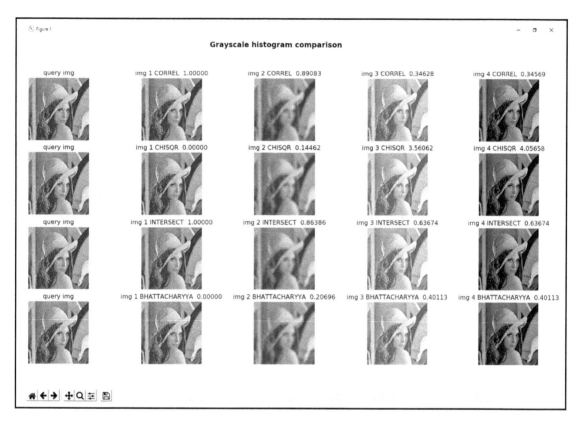

As you can see, `img 1` gives the best results (a perfect match in all the metrics) because it is the same image. Additionally, `img 2` also gives very good performance metrics. It makes sense because `img 2` is a smoothed version of the query image. Finally, `img 3` and `img 4` give poor performance metrics because the histogram is shifted.

Summary

In this chapter, all the main concepts related to histograms have been reviewed. In this sense, we have seen what a histogram represents and how it can be calculated by using OpenCV, NumPy, and Matplotlib functions. Additionally, we have seen the difference between grayscale and color histograms, showing how to calculate and show both types. Histogram equalization is also an important factor when working with histograms, and we have seen how to perform histogram equalization to both grayscale and color images. Finally, a histogram comparison can also be very helpful in order to perform an image comparison. We have seen the four metrics OpenCV provides to measure the similarity between two histograms.

In connection with the next chapter, the main thresholding techniques (simple thresholding, adaptive thresholding, and Otsu's thresholding, among others) will be covered in relation to what you will need in your computer vision applications as a key part of image segmentation.

Questions

1. What is an image histogram?
2. Calculate the histogram of a grayscale image using 64 bins.
3. Add 50 to every pixel on a grayscale image (the result will look lighter) and calculate the histogram.
4. Calculate the red channel histogram of a BGR image without a mask.
5. What functions do OpenCV, NumPy, and Matplotlib provide for calculating histograms?
6. Modify the `grayscale_histogram.py` script to compute the brightness of these three images (`gray_image`, `added_image`, and `subtracted_image`). Rename the script to `grayscale_histogram_brightness.py`.
7. Modify the `comparing_hist_equalization_clahe.py` script to show the execution time of both `cv2.equalizeHist()` and CLAHE. Rename it to `comparing_hist_equalization_clahe_time.py`.

Further reading

The reference listed here will help you delve more deeply into image processing techniques in OpenCV:

- *Learning Image Processing with OpenCV* by Gloria Bueno García et al (`https://www.packtpub.com/application-development/learning-image-processing-opencv`)

Thresholding Techniques 7

Image segmentation is a key process in many computer vision applications. It is commonly used to partition an image into different regions that, ideally, correspond to real-world objects extracted from the background. Therefore, image segmentation is an important step in image recognition and content analysis. Image thresholding is a simple, yet effective, image segmentation method, where the pixels are partitioned depending on their intensity value, and so, it can be used to partition an image into a foreground and background.

In this chapter, you will learn the importance of thresholding techniques in your computer vision projects. The main thresholding techniques that OpenCV (and also the scikit-image image processing library) provides, which you will need in your computer vision applications as a key part of image segmentation, will be reviewed.

The main sections of this chapter are as follows:

- Introducing thresholding techniques
- Simple thresholding technique
- Adaptive thresholding technique
- Otsu's thresholding algorithm
- Triangle thresholding algorithm
- Thresholding color images
- Thresholding algorithms using scikit-image

Technical requirements

The technical requirements are listed as follows:

- Python and OpenCV.
- A Python-specific IDE.
- The NumPy and Matplotlib packages.

- The scikit-image image processing library (optional for the last section of this chapter. See the *Thresholding algorithms using scikit-image* section to know how to install it for Conda-based distributions). See the following instructions in order to install it using `pip`.
- The SciPy library (This is optional for the last section of this chapter) is also required. See the following instructions in order to install it using `pip`.
- A Git client.

Further details about how to install these requirements are covered in Chapter 1, *Setting Up OpenCV*. The GitHub repository for *Mastering OpenCV 4 with Python*, containing all the supporting project files necessary to work through the book from the first chapter to the last one, can be accessed at `https://github.com/PacktPublishing/Mastering-OpenCV-4-with-Python`.

Installing scikit-image

To install scikit-image (`https://pypi.org/project/scikit-image/`) use the following command:

```
$ pip install scikit-image
```

Alternatively, you can also install scikit-image for Conda-based distributions, as detailed in the specific section where this library is used.

To check if the installation has been performed correctly, just open a Python shell and try to import the `scikit-image` library as follows:

```
python
import skimage
```

Installing SciPy

To install SciPy (`https://pypi.org/project/scipy/`) use the following command:

```
$ pip install scipy
```

To check if the installation has been performed correctly, just open a Python shell and try to import the `scipy` library as follows:

```
python
import scipy
```

Remember that the recommended approach is to install packages in virtual environments. See `Chapter 1`, *Setting Up OpenCV*, in order to see how to create and manage virtual environments.

Introducing thresholding techniques

Thresholding is a simple, yet effective method for image partitioning into a foreground and background. The objective of image segmentation is to modify the representation of an image into another representation that is easier to process. For example, image segmentation is commonly used to extract objects from the background based on some properties of the object (for example, color, edges, or histogram). The simplest thresholding methods replace each pixel in the source image with a black pixel if the pixel intensity is less than some predefined constant (the threshold value), or a white pixel, if the pixel intensity is greater than the threshold value.

OpenCV provides the `cv2.threshold()` function to threshold images. We will see this function in further detail in the next subsections of this chapter.

In the `thresholding_introduction.py` script, we are applying the `cv2.threshold()` function with some predefined threshold values—0, 50, 100, 150, 200, and 250—in order to see how different thresholded images change.

For example, to threshold an image with the threshold value of `thresh = 50`, the code is as follows:

```
ret1, thresh1 = cv2.threshold(gray_image, 50, 255, cv2.THRESH_BINARY)
```

Here, `thresh1` is the thresholded image, which is a black-and-white image. Pixels with an intensity of less than 50 will be black, and pixels with an intensity greater than 50 will be white.

Another example can be seen in the following code, where `thresh5` corresponds to the thresholded image:

```
ret5, thresh5 = cv2.threshold(gray_image, 200, 255, cv2.THRESH_BINARY)
```

In this case, pixels with an intensity of less than 200 will be black, and pixels with an intensity greater than 200 will be white.

The output for the aforementioned script can be seen in the following screenshot:

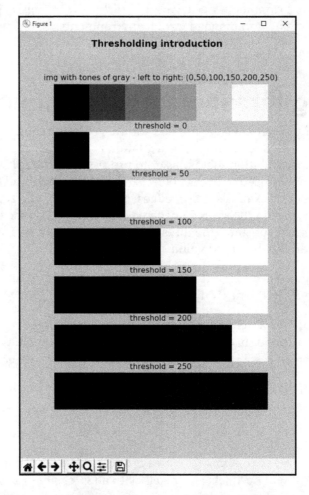

In this screenshot, you can see the source image, which is a sample image with some equally-sized regions filled with different tones of gray. More specifically, these tones of gray are 0, 50, 100, 150, 200, and 250. The build_sample_image() function builds this sample image as follows:

```
def build_sample_image():
    """Builds a sample image with 50x50 regions of different tones of
gray"""

    # Define the different tones.
    # The end of interval is not included
    tones = np.arange(start=50, stop=300, step=50)
```

```
# print(tones)

# Initialize result with the first 50x50 region with 0-intensity level
result = np.zeros((50, 50, 3), dtype="uint8")

# Build the image concatenating horizontally the regions:
for tone in tones:
    img = np.ones((50, 50, 3), dtype="uint8") * tone
    result = np.concatenate((result, img), axis=1)

return result
```

The NumPy operations that have been used to build this
sample image (np.ones(), np.zeros(), np.arange(), np.concatenate(),
and np.fliplr()) are described briefly as follows:

- np.ones(): This returns an array of a given shape and type filled with ones; in this case, a shape of (50, 50, 3), and dtype="uint8".
- np.zeros(): This returns an array of a given shape and type filled with zeros; in this case, a shape of (50, 50, 3), and dtype="uint8".
- np.arange(): This returns evenly spaced values within a given interval, taking into account the provided step. The end of the interval (300, in this case) is not included.
- np.concatenate(): This joins a sequence of arrays along an existing axis, in this case, axis=1, to concatenate the images horizontally.

After the sample image is built, the next step is to threshold it with different threshold values. In this case, the threshold values are 0, 50, 100, 150, 200, and 250.

You will see that the threshold values are the same as the different tones of gray in the sample image. The code for thresholding the sample image with different thresholding values is as follows:

```
ret1, thresh1 = cv2.threshold(gray_image, 0, 255, cv2.THRESH_BINARY)
ret2, thresh2 = cv2.threshold(gray_image, 50, 255, cv2.THRESH_BINARY)
ret3, thresh3 = cv2.threshold(gray_image, 100, 255, cv2.THRESH_BINARY)
ret4, thresh4 = cv2.threshold(gray_image, 150, 255, cv2.THRESH_BINARY)
ret5, thresh5 = cv2.threshold(gray_image, 200, 255, cv2.THRESH_BINARY)
ret6, thresh6 = cv2.threshold(gray_image, 250, 255, cv2.THRESH_BINARY)
```

You can see how the resulting black-and-white image changes after thresholding, according to the thresholding value and the different tones of gray of the sample image.

After thresholding an image, the common output is a black-and-white image. In the previous chapters, the background of the screenshots was also white. In this chapter, for proper visualization, we have changed the background of the screenshot to a `silver` color using `fig.patch.set_facecolor('silver')`.

Simple thresholding

In order to perform simple thresholding, OpenCV provides the `cv2.threshold()` function that was briefly introduced in the previous section. The signature for this method is as follows:

```
cv2.threshold(src, thresh, maxval, type, dst=None) -> retval, dst
```

The `cv2.threshold()` function applies a fixed-level thresholding to the `src` input array (multiple-channel, 8-bit or 32-bit floating point). The fixed level is adjusted by the `thresh` parameter, which sets the threshold value. The `type` parameter sets the thresholding type, which will be further explained in the next subsection.

Different types are as follows:

- `cv2.THRESH_BINARY`
- `cv2.THRESH_BINARY_INV`
- `cv2.THRESH_TRUNC`
- `cv2.THRESH_TOZERO`
- `cv2.THRESH_TOZERO_INV`
- `cv2.THRESH_OTSU`
- `cv2.THRESH_TRIANGLE`

Additionally, the `maxval` parameter sets the maximum value to use only with the `cv2.THRESH_BINARY` and `cv2.THRESH_BINARY_INV` thresholding types. Finally, the input image should be single channel only in the `cv2.THRESH_OTSU` and `cv2.THRESH_TRIANGLE` thresholding types.

In this section, we will examine all the possible configurations to understand all of these parameters.

Thresholding types

The types of thresholding operation are described according to its formulation. Take into account that *src* is the source (original) image, and *dst* corresponds to the destination (result) image after thresholding. In this sense, *src(x, y)* will correspond to the intensity of the pixel *(x, y)* of the source image, and *dst(x, y)* will correspond to the intensity of the pixel *(x, y)* of the destination image.

Here is the formula for cv2.THRESH_BINARY:

$$\texttt{dst}(x, y) = \begin{cases} \texttt{maxval} \; if \, \texttt{src} \, (x, y) \, > \, \texttt{thresh} \\ 0 \; otherwise \end{cases}$$

So, if the intensity of the pixel *src(x, y)* is higher than thresh, then the new pixel intensity is set to a maxval parameter. Otherwise, the pixels are set to 0.

Here is the formula for cv2.THRESH_BINARY_INV:

$$\texttt{dst}(x, y) = \begin{cases} 0 \; if \, \texttt{src} \, (x, y) \, > \, \texttt{thresh} \\ \texttt{maxval} \; otherwise \end{cases}$$

So, if the intensity of the pixel *src(x, y)* is higher than thresh, then the new pixel intensity is set to 0. Otherwise, it is set to maxval.

Here is the formula for cv2.THRESH_TRUNC:

$$\texttt{dst}(x, y) = \begin{cases} \texttt{threshold} \; if \, \texttt{src} \, (x, y) \, > \, \texttt{thresh} \\ \texttt{src} \, (x, y) \; otherwise \end{cases}$$

So, if the intensity of the pixel *src(x, y)* is higher than thresh, then the new pixel intensity is set to threshold. Otherwise, it is set to *src(x, y)*.

Here is the formula for cv2.THRESH_TOZERO:

$$\texttt{dst}(x, y) = \begin{cases} \texttt{src} \, (x, y) \; if \, \texttt{src} \, (x, y) \, > \, \texttt{thresh} \\ 0 \; otherwise \end{cases}$$

So, if the intensity of the pixel *src(x, y)* is higher than thresh, the new pixel value will be set to *src(x, y)*. Otherwise, it is set to 0.

Here is the formula for cv2.THRESH_TOZERO_INV:

$$dst(x, y) = \begin{cases} 0 \ if \ \text{src} \ (x, y) > \text{thresh} \\ \text{src} \ (x, y) \ otherwise \end{cases}$$

So, if the intensity of the pixel *src(x, y)* is greater than thresh, the new pixel value will be set to 0. Otherwise, it is set to *src(x, y)*.

Also, the special cv2.THRESH_OTSU and cv2.THRESH_TRIANGLE values can be combined with one of the values previously introduced (cv2.THRESH_BINARY, cv2.THRESH_BINARY_INV, cv2.THRESH_TRUNC, cv2.THRESH_TOZERO, and cv2.THRESH_TOZERO_INV). In these cases (cv2.THRESH_OTSU and cv2.THRESH_TRIANGLE), the thresholding operation (implemented only for 8-bit images) computes the optimal threshold value instead of the specified thresh value. It should be noted that the thresholding operation returns the computed optimal threshold value.

The thresholding_simple_types.py script helps you understand the aforementioned types. We use the same sample image introduced in the previous section, and we perform a thresholding operation with a fixed threshold value (thresh = 100) with all the previous types.

The key code to perform this is as follows:

```
ret1, thresh1 = cv2.threshold(gray_image, 100, 255, cv2.THRESH_BINARY)
ret2, thresh2 = cv2.threshold(gray_image, 100, 220, cv2.THRESH_BINARY)
ret3, thresh3 = cv2.threshold(gray_image, 100, 255, cv2.THRESH_BINARY_INV)
ret4, thresh4 = cv2.threshold(gray_image, 100, 220, cv2.THRESH_BINARY_INV)
ret5, thresh5 = cv2.threshold(gray_image, 100, 255, cv2.THRESH_TRUNC)
ret6, thresh6 = cv2.threshold(gray_image, 100, 255, cv2.THRESH_TOZERO)
ret7, thresh7 = cv2.threshold(gray_image, 100, 255, cv2.THRESH_TOZERO_INV)
```

As previously mentioned, the maxval parameter sets the maximum value to use only with the cv2.THRESH_BINARY and cv2.THRESH_BINARY_INV thresholding types. In this example, we have set the value of maxval to 255 and 220 for the cv2.THRESH_BINARY and cv2.THRESH_BINARY_INV types in order to see how the thresholded image changes in both cases. The output of this script can be seen in the next screenshot:

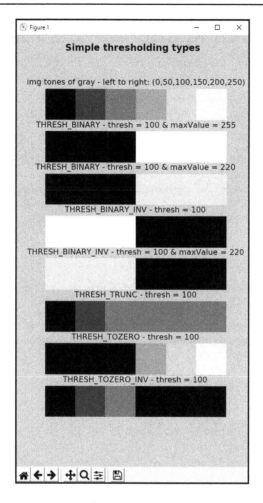

In the previous screenshot, you can see both the original grayscale image and the result of each of the seven thresholding operations that were performed. Additionally, you can see the effect of the `maxval` parameter, used only with the `cv2.THRESH_BINARY` and `cv2.THRESH_BINARY_INV` thresholding types. More specifically, see, for example, the difference between the first and second thresholding operation results – white versus gray in the result images – and also the difference between the third and fourth thresholding operation results – white versus gray in the result images.

Simple thresholding applied to a real image

In the previous examples, we have applied the simple thresholding operation to a custom-made image in order to see how the different parameters work. In this section, we are going to apply `cv2.threshold()` to a real image. The `thresholding_example.py` script performs this. We applied the `cv2.threshold()` function with different thresholding values as follows – $60, 70, 80, 90, 100, 110, 120, 130$:

```
ret1, thresh1 = cv2.threshold(gray_image, 60, 255, cv2.THRESH_BINARY)
ret2, thresh2 = cv2.threshold(gray_image, 70, 255, cv2.THRESH_BINARY)
ret3, thresh3 = cv2.threshold(gray_image, 80, 255, cv2.THRESH_BINARY)
ret4, thresh4 = cv2.threshold(gray_image, 90, 255, cv2.THRESH_BINARY)
ret5, thresh5 = cv2.threshold(gray_image, 100, 255, cv2.THRESH_BINARY)
ret6, thresh6 = cv2.threshold(gray_image, 110, 255, cv2.THRESH_BINARY)
ret7, thresh7 = cv2.threshold(gray_image, 120, 255, cv2.THRESH_BINARY)
ret8, thresh8 = cv2.threshold(gray_image, 130, 255, cv2.THRESH_BINARY)
```

And finally, we show the thresholded images as follows:

```
show_img_with_matplotlib(cv2.cvtColor(thresh1, cv2.COLOR_GRAY2BGR),
"threshold = 60", 2)
show_img_with_matplotlib(cv2.cvtColor(thresh2, cv2.COLOR_GRAY2BGR),
"threshold = 70", 3)
show_img_with_matplotlib(cv2.cvtColor(thresh3, cv2.COLOR_GRAY2BGR),
"threshold = 80", 4)
show_img_with_matplotlib(cv2.cvtColor(thresh4, cv2.COLOR_GRAY2BGR),
"threshold = 90", 5)
show_img_with_matplotlib(cv2.cvtColor(thresh5, cv2.COLOR_GRAY2BGR),
"threshold = 100", 6)
show_img_with_matplotlib(cv2.cvtColor(thresh6, cv2.COLOR_GRAY2BGR),
"threshold = 110", 7)
show_img_with_matplotlib(cv2.cvtColor(thresh7, cv2.COLOR_GRAY2BGR),
"threshold = 120", 8)
show_img_with_matplotlib(cv2.cvtColor(thresh8, cv2.COLOR_GRAY2BGR),
"threshold = 130", 9)
```

The output of this script can be seen in the following screenshot:

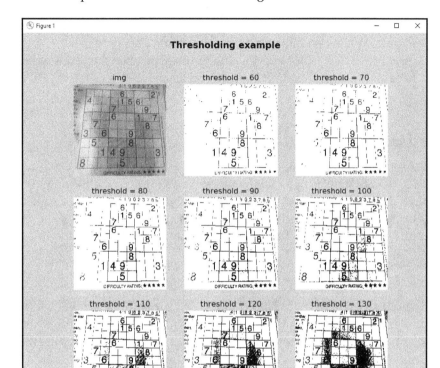

As you can see, the threshold value plays a critical role when thresholding images using `cv2.threshold()`. Suppose that your image-processing algorithm tries to recognize the digits inside the grid. If the threshold value is low (for example, `threshold = 60`), there are some digits missing in the thresholded image. On the other hand, if the threshold value is high (for example, `threshold = 120`), there are some digits occluded by black pixels. Therefore, establishing a global threshold value for the entire image is quite difficult. Moreover, if the image is affected by different illumination conditions, this task is almost impossible. This is why other thresholding algorithms can be applied to threshold the images. In the next section, the adaptive thresholding algorithm will be introduced.

Finally, you can see in the code snippet that we have created several thresholded images (one by one) with fixed threshold values. This can be optimized by creating an array containing the threshold values (using `np.arange()`) and iterating over the created array to call `cv.threshold()` for every value of the array. See the *Questions* section, because this optimization is proposed as an exercise.

Adaptive thresholding

In the previous section, we have applied `cv2.threshold()` using a global threshold value. As we could see, the obtained results were not very good due to the different illumination conditions in the different areas of the image. In these cases, you can try adaptive thresholding. In OpenCV, the adaptive thresholding is performed by the `cv2.adaptiveThreshold()` function. The signature for this method is as follows:

```
adaptiveThreshold(src, maxValue, adaptiveMethod, thresholdType, blockSize,
C[, dst]) -> dst
```

This function applies an adaptive threshold to the `src` array (8-bit single-channel image). The `maxValue` parameter sets the value for the pixels in the `dst` image for which the condition is satisfied. The `adaptiveMethod` parameter sets the adaptive thresholding algorithm to use:

- `cv2.ADAPTIVE_THRESH_MEAN_C`: The `T(x, y)` threshold value is calculated as the mean of the `blockSize x blockSize` neighborhood of `(x, y)` minus the `C` parameter
- `cv2.ADAPTIVE_THRESH_GAUSSIAN_C`: The `T(x, y)` threshold value is calculated as the weighted sum of the `blockSize x blockSize` neighborhood of `(x, y)` minus the `C` parameter

The `blockSize` parameter sets the size of the neighborhood area used to calculate a threshold value for the pixel, and it can take the values `3, 5, 7, . . .` and so forth.

The `C` parameter is just a constant subtracted from the means or weighted means (depending on the adaptive method set by the `adaptiveMethod` parameter). Commonly, this value is positive, but it can be zero or negative. Finally, the `thresholdType` parameter sets the `cv2.THRESH_BINARY` or `cv2.THRESH_BINARY_INV` thresholding types.

According to the following formula where *T(x, y)* is the threshold calculated for each pixel, the `thresholding_adaptive.py` script applies adaptive thresholding to a test image using
the `cv2.ADAPTIVE_THRESH_MEAN_C` and `cv2.ADAPTIVE_THRESH_GAUSSIAN_C` methods:

- Here is the formula for `cv2.THRESH_BINARY`:

$$\mathtt{dst}(x, y) = \begin{cases} \texttt{maxValue} \; if \, \texttt{src}\,(x, y) > \texttt{T(x,y)} \\ 0 \; otherwise \end{cases}$$

- Here is the formula for `cv2.THRESH_BINARY_INV`:

$$\mathtt{dst}(x, y) = \begin{cases} 0 \; if \, \texttt{src}\,(x, y) > \texttt{T(x,y)} \\ \texttt{maxValue} \;\; otherwise \end{cases}$$

The output of this script can be seen in the following screenshot:

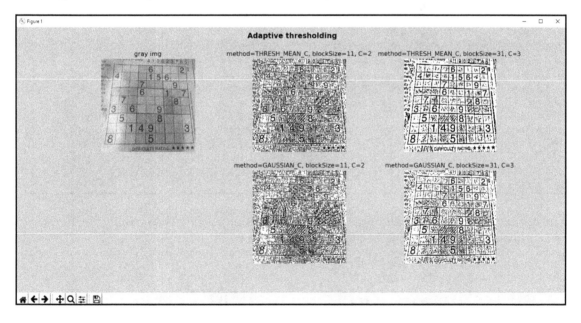

In the previous screenshot, you can see the output after applying `cv2.adaptiveThreshold()` with different parameters. As previously mentioned, if your task is to recognize the digits, the adaptive thresholding can give you better thresholded images. However, as you can also see, a lot of noise appears in the image. In order to deal with it, you can apply some smoothing operations (see `Chapter 5`, *Image Processing Techniques*).

In this case, we can apply a bilateral filter, because it is highly useful in noise removal while maintaining sharp edges. In order to apply a bilateral filter, OpenCV provides the `cv2.bilateralFilter()` function. Therefore, we can apply the function before thresholding the image as follows:

```
gray_image = cv2.bilateralFilter(gray_image, 15, 25, 25)
```

The code for this example can be seen in the `thresholding_adaptive_filter_noise.py` script. The output can be seen in the following screenshot:

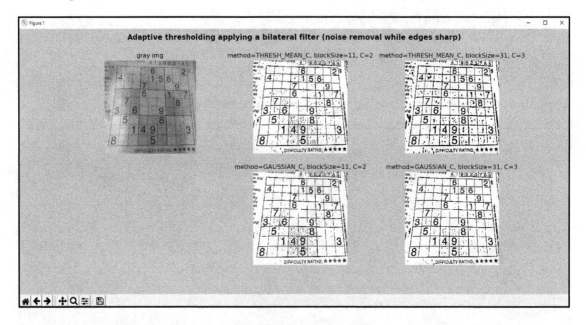

You can see that applying a smoothing filter is a good solution to deal with noise. In this case, a bilateral filter is applied because we want to keep the edges sharp.

Otsu's thresholding algorithm

As we saw in previous sections, the simple thresholding algorithm applies an arbitrary global threshold value. In this case, what we need to do is experiment with different thresholding values and look at the thresholded images in order to see if the result satisfies our necessities. However, this approach can be very tedious.

One solution is to use the adaptive thresholding that OpenCV provides by means of the `cv2.adapativeThreshold()` function. When applying adaptive thresholding in OpenCV, there is no need to set a thresholding value, which is a good thing.

However, two parameters should be established correctly: the `blockSize` parameter and the `C` parameter. Another approach is to use Otsu's binarization algorithm, which is a good approach when dealing with bimodal images. A bimodal image can be characterized by its histogram containing two peaks. Otsu's algorithm automatically calculates the optimal threshold value that separates both peaks by maximizing the variance between two classes of pixels. Equivalently, the optimal threshold value minimizes the intra-class variance. Otsu's binarization algorithm is a statistical method, because it relies on statistical information derived from the histogram (for example, mean, variance, or entropy). In order to compute Otsu's binarization in OpenCV, we make use of the `cv2.threshold()` function as follows:

```
ret, th = cv2.threshold(gray_image, 0, 255, cv2.THRESH_BINARY +
cv2.THRESH_OTSU)
```

In this case, there is no need to set a threshold value because Otsu's binarization algorithm calculates the optimal threshold value, that is why `thresh = 0`.
The `cv2.THRESH_OTSU` flag indicates that Otsu's algorithm will be applied. Additionally, in this case, this flag is combined with `cv2.THRESH_BINARY`. In fact, it can be combined with `cv2.THRESH_BINARY`, `cv2.THRESH_BINARY_INV`, `cv2.THRESH_TRUNC`, `cv2.THRESH_TOZERO`, and `cv2.THRESH_TOZERO_INV`. This function returns the thresholded image, `th`, and the thresholded value, `ret`.

In the `thresholding_otsu.py` script, we have applied this algorithm to a sample image. The output can be seen in the following screenshot. We have modified the `show_hist_with_matplotlib_gray()` function to add an extra parameter that corresponds to the optimal threshold value calculated by Otsu's algorithm. In order to draw this threshold value, we draw a line establishing the *x* coordinate with the `t` threshold value as follows:

```
plt.axvline(x=t, color='m', linestyle='--')
```

The output of the `thresholding_otsu.py` script can be seen in the following screenshot:

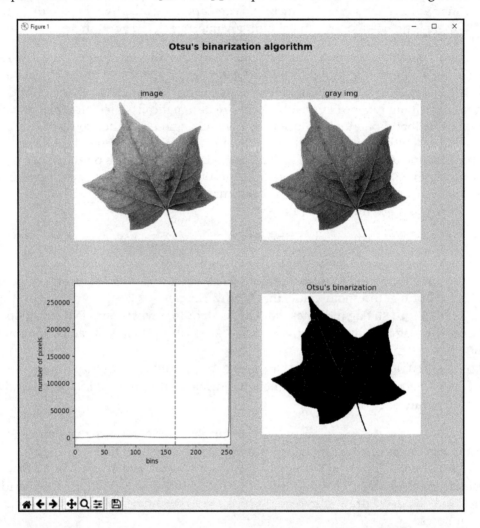

In the previous screenshot, we can see that the image is free of noise with a white background and a very well-defined green leaf. However, noise can affect the thresholding algorithm and we should deal with it properly. For example, in the previous section, we perform a bilateral filter in order to filter out some noise and preserve the edges. In the next example, we are going to add some noise to the leaf image, in order to see how the thresholding algorithm can be affected. This can be seen in the `thresholding_otsu_filter_noise.py` script. In this script, we apply Otsu's binarization algorithm before and after applying a Gaussian filter in order to see how the thresholded image changes drastically.

This can be seen in the following screenshot:

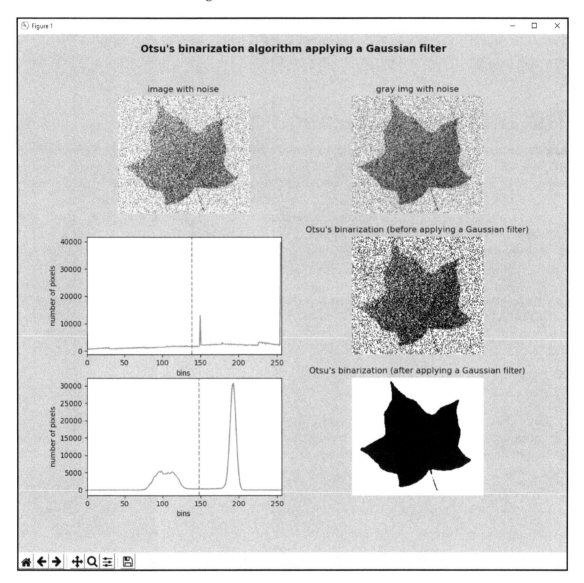

As we can see, if we do not apply a smoothing filter (a Gaussian filter, in this case), the thresholded image is also full of noise. However, applying a Gaussian filter is a good solution to filter the noise properly. Moreover, the filtered image is bimodal. This fact can be seen in the histogram corresponding to the filtered image. In this case, Otsu's binarization algorithm can segment the leaf properly.

The triangle binarization algorithm

Another automatic thresholding algorithm is the **triangle algorithm**, which is considered a shape-based method because it analyzes the structure (or *shape*) of the histogram (for example, trying to find valleys, peaks, and other *shape* histogram features). This algorithm works in three steps. In the first step, a line is calculated between the maximum of the histogram at b_{max} on the gray level axis and the lowest value b_{min} on the gray level axis. In the second step, the distance from the line (calculated in the first step) to the histogram for all the values of b $[b_{min}\text{-}b_{max}]$ is calculated. Finally, in the third step, the level where the distance between the histogram and the line is maximal is chosen as the threshold value.

The way to use the triangle binarization algorithm in OpenCV is very similar to Otsu's algorithm. In fact, only one flag should be changed properly. In case of Otsu's binarization, the cv2.THRESH_OTSU flag was set. In the case of the triangle binarization algorithm, the flag is cv2.THRESH_TRIANGLE, as follows:

```
ret1, th1 = cv2.threshold(gray_image, 0, 255, cv2.THRESH_BINARY +
cv2.THRESH_TRIANGLE)
```

In the next screenshot, you can see the output when applying the triangle binarization algorithm to a noise image (the same image that was used in Otsu's binarization example in the previous section). The full code for this example can be seen in the thresholding_triangle_filter_noise.py script:

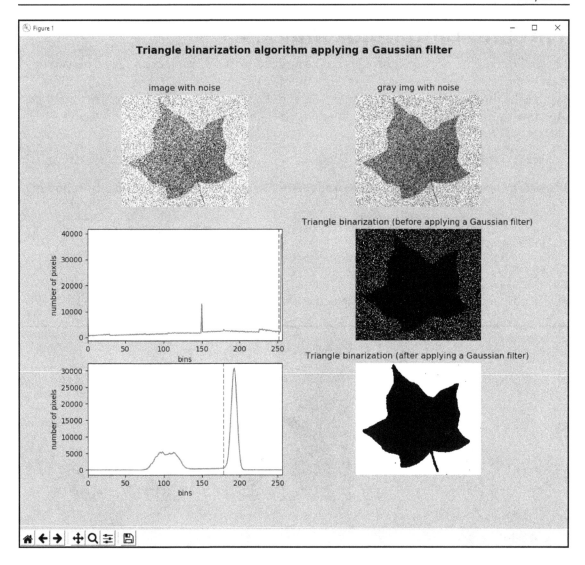

You can see that applying a Gaussian filter is a good solution to filter the noise. This way, the triangle binarization algorithm can segment the leaf properly.

Thresholding color images

The cv2.threshold() function can also be applied to multi-channel images. This can be seen in the thresholding_bgr.py script. In this case, the cv2.threshold() function applies the thresholding operation in each of the channels of the BGR image. This produces the same result as applying this function in each channel and merging the thresholded channels:

```
ret1, thresh1 = cv2.threshold(image, 150, 255, cv2.THRESH_BINARY)
```

Therefore, the preceding line of code produces the same result as performing the following:

```
(b, g, r) = cv2.split(image)
ret2, thresh2 = cv2.threshold(b, 150, 255, cv2.THRESH_BINARY)
ret3, thresh3 = cv2.threshold(g, 150, 255, cv2.THRESH_BINARY)
ret4, thresh4 = cv2.threshold(r, 150, 255, cv2.THRESH_BINARY)
bgr_thresh = cv2.merge((thresh2, thresh3, thresh4))
```

The result can be seen in the following screenshot:

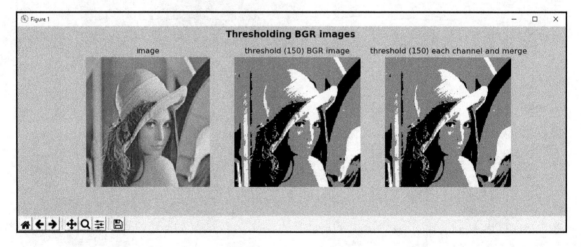

Although you can perform `cv2.threshold()` on multi-channel images (for example, BGR images), this operation can produce weird results. For example, in the resulting image, as each channel can take only two values (0 and 255 in this case), the final image has only 2^3 possible colors. In the next screenshot, we also apply this color thresholding to another test image:

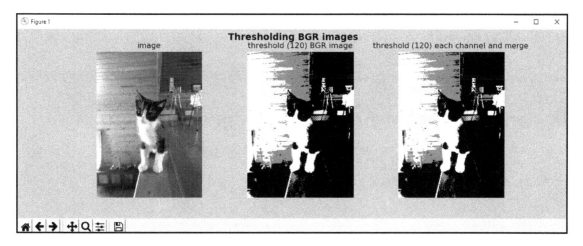

As shown in the previous screenshot, the output image has only 2^3 possible colors. Therefore, you should take this into account when performing thresholding operations in BGR images.

Thresholding algorithms using scikit-image

As we mentioned in `Chapter 1`, *Setting Up OpenCV*, there are other packages that can be used for scientific computing, data science, machine learning, deep learning, and computer vision. In connection with computer vision, scikit-image is a collection of algorithms for image processing (`https://scikit-image.org/`). Images manipulated by scikit-image are NumPy arrays.

In this section, we will make use of scikit-image capabilities in connection with thresholding techniques. So, if you want to replicate the results obtained here, the first step is to install it. See `https://scikit-image.org/download.html` in order to install scikit-image properly on your operating system. Here, we are going to install it with conda, which is an open source package management system (and also an environment management system). See `Chapter 1`, *Setting Up OpenCV*, in order to see how to install Anaconda/Miniconda distributions and conda. To install scikit-image for conda-based distributions (Anaconda, Miniconda), execute the following code:

```
conda install -c conda-forge scikit-image
```

Introducing thresholding with scikit-image

In order to test scikit-image, we are going to threshold a test image using Otsu's binarization algorithm. In order to try this method, the first step is to import the required packages. In this case, in connection with scikit-image as follows:

```
from skimage.filters import threshold_otsu
from skimage import img_as_ubyte
```

The key code to apply Otsu's binarization algorithm with scikit-image is the following:

```
thresh = threshold_otsu(gray_image)
binary = gray_image > thresh
binary = img_as_ubyte(binary)
```

The `threshold_otsu(gray_image)` function returns the threshold value based on Otsu's binarization algorithm. Afterwards, with this value, the binary image is constructed (dtype= `bool`), which should be converted to 8-bit unsigned integer format (dtype= `uint8`) for proper visualization. The `img_as_ubyte()` function is used for this purpose. The full code for this example can be seen in the `thresholding_scikit_image_otsu.py` script.

The output can be seen in the following screenshot:

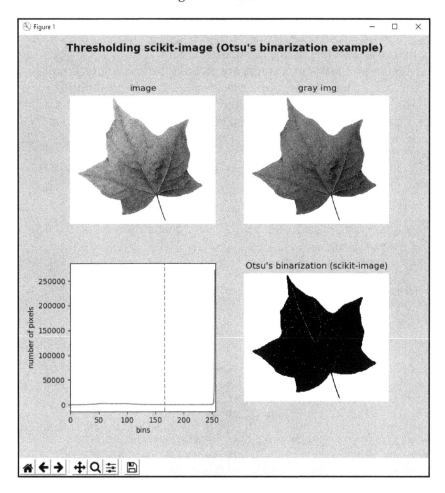

We will now try out some thresholding techniques with scikit-image.

Trying out more thresholding techniques with scikit-image

We are going to threshold a test image comparing Otsu's, triangle, Niblack's, and Sauvola's thresholding techniques. Otsu and triangle are global thresholding techniques, while Niblack and Sauvola are local thresholding techniques. Local thresholding techniques are considered a better approach when the background is not uniform. For more information about Niblack's and Sauvola's thresholding algorithms, see *An Introduction to Digital Image Processing (1986)* and *Adaptive document image binarization (2000)*, respectively. The full code for this example can be seen in
the `thresholding_scikit_image_techniques.py` script. In order to try these methods, the first step is to import the required packages. In this case, in connection with scikit-image as follows:

```
from skimage.filters import (threshold_otsu, threshold_triangle,
threshold_niblack, threshold_sauvola)
from skimage import img_as_ubyte
```

In order to perform the thresholding operations with scikit-image, we call each thresholding method
(`threshold_otsu()`, `threshold_niblack()`, `threshold_sauvola()`,
and `threshold_triangle()`):

```
# Trying Otsu's scikit-image algorithm:
thresh_otsu = threshold_otsu(gray_image)
binary_otsu = gray_image > thresh_otsu
binary_otsu = img_as_ubyte(binary_otsu)

# Trying Niblack's scikit-image algorithm:
thresh_niblack = threshold_niblack(gray_image, window_size=25, k=0.8)
binary_niblack = gray_image > thresh_niblack
binary_niblack = img_as_ubyte(binary_niblack)

# Trying Sauvola's scikit-image algorithm:
thresh_sauvola = threshold_sauvola(gray_image, window_size=25)
binary_sauvola = gray_image > thresh_sauvola
binary_sauvola = img_as_ubyte(binary_sauvola)

# Trying triangle scikit-image algorithm:
thresh_triangle = threshold_triangle(gray_image)
binary_triangle = gray_image > thresh_triangle
binary_triangle = img_as_ubyte(binary_triangle)
```

The output can be seen in the next screenshot:

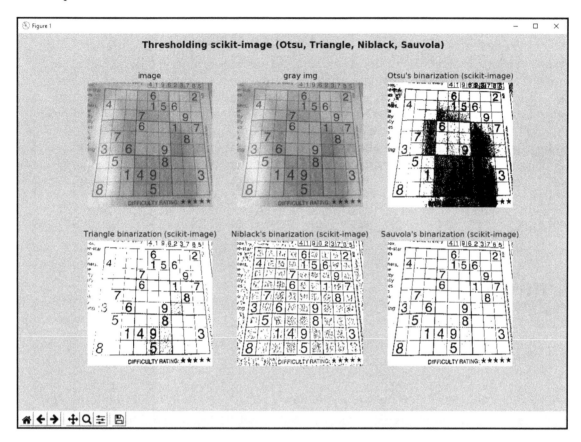

As you can see, local thresholding methods can provide better results when the background is not uniform. Indeed, these methods can be applied for text recognition. Finally, scikit-image comes with more thresholding techniques that you can try. If necessary, consult the API documentation to see all available methods at `http://scikit-image.org/docs/dev/api/api.html`.

Summary

In this chapter, we have reviewed the main thresholding techniques you can use to threshold your images. Thresholding techniques can be used for many computer vision tasks (for example, text recognition and image segmentation, among others). Both simple and adaptive thresholding techniques have been reviewed. Additionally, we have seen how to apply Otsu's binarization algorithm and the triangle algorithm to automatically select a global threshold for thresholding your images. Finally, we have seen how to use different thresholding techniques using scikit-image. In this sense, two global thresholding techniques (Otsu's and triangle algorithms) and two local thresholding techniques (Niblack's and Sauvola's algorithms) have been applied to a test image.

In Chapter 8, *Contour Detection, Filtering, and Drawing*, we will see how to deal with contours, which are very useful tools for shape analysis and object detection and recognition.

Questions

1. Apply a thresholding operation using cv2.threshold() with a threshold value of 100 and using the cv2.THRESH_BINARY thresholding type.
2. Apply an adaptive thresholding operation using cv2.adapativeThreshold() ,cv2.ADAPTIVE_THRESH_MEAN_C, C=2 and blockSize=9.
3. Apply Otsu's thresholding using the cv2.THRESH_BINARY thresholding type.
4. Apply triangle thresholding using the cv2.THRESH_BINARY thresholding type.
5. Apply Otsu's thresholding using scikit-image.
6. Apply triangle thresholding using scikit-image.
7. Apply Niblack's thresholding using scikit-image.
8. Apply Sauvola's thresholding using scikit-image and a window size of 25.
9. Modify the thresholding_example.py script in order to make use of np.arange(), with the purpose of defining the threshold values to apply to the cv2.threshold() function. Afterwards, call the cv2.threshold() function with the defined threshold values and store all the thresholded images in an array. Finally, show all the images in the array calling show_img_with_matplotlib() for each one. Rename the script to thresholding_example_arange.py.

Further reading

The following reference will help you dive deeper into thresholding and other image processing techniques:

- *Python 3.x for Computer Vision* by Saurabh Kapur (`https://www.packtpub.com/application-development/python-3x-computer-vision-video-0`)

8
Contour Detection, Filtering, and Drawing

A contour can be defined as a sequence of points defining the boundary of an object in an image. Therefore, contours convey key information about the object boundary, encoding the main information about the object shape. This information serves as the basis of image descriptors (for example, SIFT, Fourier descriptors or shape context, among others) and it can be used for shape analysis and object detection and recognition.

In this chapter, you will see how to deal with contours, which are used for shape analysis and object detection and recognition.

In this chapter, key points in connection with contours will be tackled in the following topics:

- An introduction to contours
- Compressing contours
- Image moments
- More functionality related to contours
- Filtering contours
- Recognizing contours
- Matching contours

Technical requirements

The technical requirements are listed as follows:

- Python and OpenCV
- Python-specific IDE

- NumPy and Matplotlib packages
- Git client

Further details about how to install these requirements are in Chapter 1, *Setting Up OpenCV*. The GitHub repository for *Mastering OpenCV 4 with Python* containing all the supporting project files, which are necessary to work through the book from the first chapter to the last one, can be accessed in the next URL: https://github.com/PacktPublishing/Mastering-OpenCV-4-with-Python/.

An introduction to contours

Contours can be seen as a curve joining all the points along the boundary of a certain shape. As they define the boundary of the shape, an analysis of these points can reveal key information for shape analysis and object detection and recognition. OpenCV provides many functions to properly detect and process contours. However, before diving into these functions, we are going to see the structure of a sample contour. For example, the following function simulates detecting a contour in a hypothetical image:

```python
def get_one_contour():
 """Returns a 'fixed' contour"""

 cnts = [np.array(
 [[[600, 320]], [[563, 460]], [[460, 562]], [[320, 600]], [[180, 563]],
 [[78, 460]], [[40, 320]], [[77, 180]], [[179, 78]], [[319, 40]], [[459,
 77]], [[562, 179]]], dtype=np.int32)]
 return cnts
```

As you can see, a contour is an array composed of many points of the np.int32 type (integers in the range [-2147483648, 2147483647]). Now, we can call this function to get this array of contours. In this case, this array has only one detected contour:

```python
contours = get_one_contour()
print("'detected' contours: '{}' ".format(len(contours)))
print("contour shape: '{}'".format(contours[0].shape))
```

At this point, we can apply all the functions that OpenCV provides to play with contours. Note that it is interesting to define the get_one_contour() function because it provides you with a simple way to have a contour ready to use in order to debug and test further functionality in connection with contours. In many situations, detected contours in a real image have hundreds of points, making it really difficult to debug your code. Therefore, keep this function handy.

In order to complete this introduction to contours, OpenCV provides
`cv2.drawContours()`, which draws a contour outline in the image. Therefore, we can call
this function to see what this contour is like. Additionally, we have also coded
the `draw_contour_points()` function, which draws the points of the contour in the
image. Also, we have used the `np.squeeze()` function in order to get rid of one-
dimensional arrays like using `[1,2,3]` instead of `[[[1,2,3]]]`. For example, if we print
the contour defined in the previous function, we will get the following:

```
[[[600 320]]
 [[563 460]]
 [[460 562]]
 [[320 600]]
 [[180 563]]
 [[ 78 460]]
 [[ 40 320]]
 [[ 77 180]]
 [[179 78]]
 [[319 40]]
 [[459 77]]
 [[562 179]]]
```

After performing the following line of code:

```
squeeze = np.squeeze(cnt)
```

If we print `squeeze`, we will get the following output:

```
[[600 320]
 [563 460]
 [460 562]
 [320 600]
 [180 563]
 [ 78 460]
 [ 40 320]
 [ 77 180]
 [179 78]
 [319 40]
 [459 77]
 [562 179]]
```

At this point, we can iterate over all the points of this array.

Hence, the code for the `draw_contour_points()` function is as follows:

```
def draw_contour_points(img, cnts, color):
    """Draw all points from a list of contours"""

    for cnt in cnts:
        squeeze = np.squeeze(cnt)

        for p in squeeze:
            p = array_to_tuple(p)
            cv2.circle(img, p, 10, color, -1)

    return img
```

Another consideration is that in the previous function, we have used the `array_to_tuple()` function, which converts an array into a tuple:

```
def array_to_tuple(arr):
    """Converts array to tuple"""

    return tuple(arr.reshape(1, -1)[0])
```

This way, the first point of the contour, `[600 320]`, is transformed into `(600, 320)`, which is ready to use inside `cv2.circle()` as its center. The full code for this previous introduction to contours can be seen in `contours_introduction.py`. The output of this script can be seen in the next screenshot:

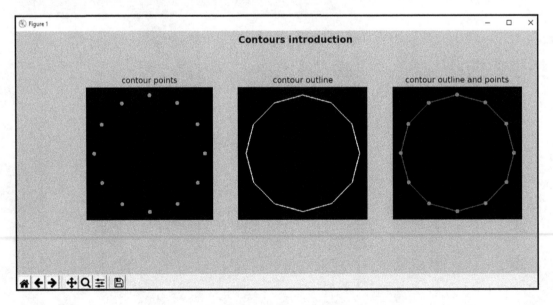

With the purpose of completing this introduction to contours, we also have coded a script, `contours_introduction_2.py`. Here, we have coded functions, `build_sample_image()` and `build_sample_image_2()`. These functions draw basic shapes in the image and their objective is to provide some predictable (or predefined) shapes.

These two functions have the same purpose as the defined `get_one_contour()` function in the previous script, that is, they help us understand key concepts related to contours. The code for the `build_sample_image()` function is as follows:

```
def build_sample_image():
    """Builds a sample image with basic shapes"""

    # Create a 500x500 gray image (70 intensity) with a rectangle and a
    circle inside:
    img = np.ones((500, 500, 3), dtype="uint8") * 70
    cv2.rectangle(img, (100, 100), (300, 300), (255, 0, 255), -1)
    cv2.circle(img, (400, 400), 100, (255, 255, 0), -1)

    return img
```

As you can see, this function draws two filled shapes (one rectangle and one circle). Therefore, this function creates an image with two (external) contours. The code for the `build_sample_image_2()` function is as follows:

```
def build_sample_image_2():
    """Builds a sample image with basic shapes"""

    # Create a 500x500 gray image (70 intensity) with a rectangle and a
    circle inside (with internal contours):
    img = np.ones((500, 500, 3), dtype="uint8") * 70
    cv2.rectangle(img, (100, 100), (300, 300), (255, 0, 255), -1)
    cv2.rectangle(img, (150, 150), (250, 250), (70, 70, 70), -1)
    cv2.circle(img, (400, 400), 100, (255, 255, 0), -1)
    cv2.circle(img, (400, 400), 50, (70, 70, 70), -1)
```

This function draws two filled rectangles (one inside another) and two filled circles (one inside another). This function creates an image with two external and two internal contours.

In `contours_introduction_2.py`, after the image has been *loaded,* we convert it to grayscale and thresholded in order to get a binary image. This binary image will be later used to find contours using the `cv2.findContours()` function. As seen previously, the created images only have circles and squares. Therefore, calling `cv2.findContours()` will find all these created contours. The signature for the `cv2.findContours()` method is as follows:

```
cv2.findContours(image, mode, method[, contours[, hierarchy[, offset]]]) ->
image, contours, hierarchy
```

OpenCV provides `cv2.findContours()`, which can be used to detect contours in binary images (for example, the resulting image after a thresholding operation). This function implements the algorithm defined in the paper *Topological Structural Analysis of Digitized Binary Images by Border Following.* It should be noted that before OpenCV 3.2, the source image would have been modified and since OpenCV 3.2, the source image is no longer modified after calling this function. The source image is treated as a binary image, where non-zero pixels are treated as ones. This function returns the detected contours containing, for each one, all the retrieved points defining the boundary.

The retrieved contours can be outputted in different modes—`cv2.RETR_EXTERNAL` (outputs only external the contours), `cv2.RETR_LIST` (outputs all the contours without any hierarchical relationship), and `cv2.RETR_TREE` (outputs all the contours by establishing a hierarchical relationship). The output vector `hierarchy` contains information about this hierarchical relationship, providing an entry for each detected contour. For each ith contour `contours[i]`, `hierarchy[i][j]` with j in the range `[0,3]` contains the following:

- `hierarchy[i][0]`: Index of the next contour at the same hierarchical level
- `hierarchy[i][1]`: Index of the previous contour at the same hierarchical level
- `hierarchy[i][2]`: Index of the first child contour
- `hierarchy[i][3]`: Index of the parent contour

A negative value in `hierarchy[i][j]` means that there is no next (j=0), no previous (j=1), no child (j=2), or no parent (j=3) contour. Finally, the `method` parameter sets the approximation method used when retrieving the points concerning each detected contour. This parameter is further explained in the next section.

If we execute the `contours_introduction_2.py` script, we can see the following screen:

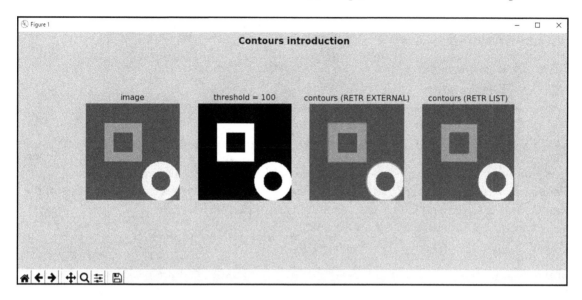

In this screenshot, external (`cv2.RETR_EXTERNAL`) and both external and internal (`cv2.RETR_LIST`) are calculated by calling `cv2.findContours()`.

Compressing contours

Detected contours can be compressed to reduce the number of points. In this sense, OpenCV provides several methods to reduce the number of points. This can be set with the parameter `method`. Additionally, this compression can be disabled by setting the flag to `cv2.CHAIN_APPROX_NONE`, where all boundary points are stored; hence, no compression is performed.

The `cv2.CHAIN_APPROX_SIMPLE` method can be used to compress the detected contours because it compresses horizontal, vertical, and diagonal segments of the contour, preserving only endpoints. For example, if we use `cv2.CHAIN_APPROX_SIMPLE` to compress the contour of a rectangle, it will only be composed of four points.

Finally, OpenCV provides two more flags for compressing contours based on the Teh-Chin algorithm, which is a non-parametric method. The first step of this algorithm determines the **region of support** (**ROS**) for each point based on its local properties.

Next, the algorithm computes measures of relative significance of each point. Finally, dominant points are detected by a process of non-maxima suppression. They use three different measures of significance, corresponding to different degrees of accuracy of discrete curvature measures:

- K-cosine measure
- K-curvature measure
- One curvature measure (k = 1 of 2))

Therefore, in connection with the discrete curvature measures, OpenCV provides two flags—`cv2.CHAIN_APPROX_TC89_L1` and `cv2.CHAIN_APPROX_TC89_KCOS`. For a deeper explanation of this algorithm, you can see the publication *On the Detection of Dominant Points on Digital Curves (1989)*. Just for clarification, `_CT89_` encodes the initial letters of the name's authors (Teh and Chin) and, also, the year of publication (1989).

In `contours_approximation_method.py`, the four aforementioned flags (`cv2.CHAIN_APPROX_NONE`, `cv2.CHAIN_APPROX_SIMPLE`, `cv2.CHAIN_APPROX_TC89_L1`, and `cv2.CHAIN_APPROX_TC89_KCOS`) for the `method` parameter are used to encode the two detected contours in the image. The output of this script can be seen in the next screenshot:

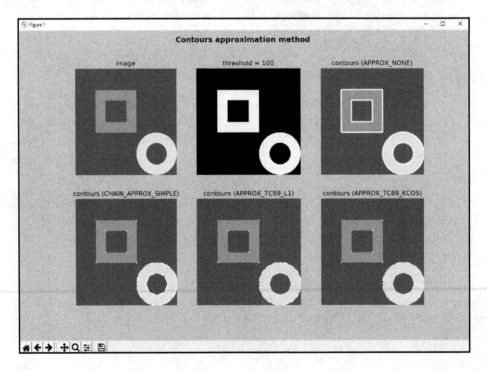

As can be seen, the points defining the contour are shown in white, showing how the four methods (cv2.CHAIN_APPROX_NONE, cv2.CHAIN_APPROX_SIMPLE, cv2.CHAIN_APPROX_TC89_L1, and cv2.CHAIN_APPROX_TC89_KCOS) compress the detected contours for the two provided shapes.

Image moments

In mathematics, a moment can be seen as a specific quantitative measure of a function shape. An image moment can be seen as a weighted average of image pixel intensities, or a function of such moments, encoding some interesting properties. In this sense, image moments are useful to describe some properties of the detected contours (for example, the center of mass of the object, or the area of the object, among others).

cv2.moments() can be used to calculate all the moments up to the third order of a vector shape or a rasterized shape.

The signature for this method is as follows:

```
retval = cv.moments(array[, binaryImage])
```

Therefore, in order to calculate the moments for a detected contour (for example, the first detected contour), perform the following:

```
M = cv2.moments(contours[0])
```

If we print M, we get the following information:

```
{'m00': 235283.0, 'm10': 75282991.16666666, 'm01': 75279680.83333333,
'm20': 28496148988.333332, 'm11': 24089788592.25, 'm02': 28492341886.0,
'm30': 11939291123446.25, 'm21': 9118893653727.8, 'm12': 9117775940692.967,
'm03': 11936167227424.852, 'mu20': 4408013598.184406, 'mu11':
2712402.277420044, 'mu02': 4406324849.628765, 'mu30': 595042037.7265625,
'mu21': -292162222.4824219, 'mu12': -592577546.1586914, 'mu03':
294852334.5449219, 'nu20': 0.07962727021646843, 'nu11':
4.8997396280458296e-05, 'nu02': 0.07959676431294238, 'nu30':
2.2160077537124397e-05, 'nu21': -1.0880470778779139e-05, 'nu12':
-2.2068296922023203e-05, 'nu03': 1.0980653771087236e-05}
```

As you can see, there are three different types of moment (m_{ji}, mu_{ji}, nu_{ji}).

The spatial moments m_{ji} are computed as follows:

$$\text{m}_{ji} = \sum_{x,y} \left(\texttt{array}(x,y) \cdot x^j \cdot y^i \right)$$

The central moments mu_{ji} are computed as follows:

$$mu_{ji} = \sum_{x,y} \left(\mathtt{array}(x, y) \cdot (x - \bar{x})^j \cdot (y - \bar{y})^i \right)$$

Here, the following applies:

$$\bar{x} = \frac{\mathtt{m}_{10}}{\mathtt{m}_{00}}, \quad \bar{y} = \frac{\mathtt{m}_{01}}{\mathtt{m}_{00}}$$

The preceding equation corresponds to the mass center.

Central moments are, by definition, invariant with respect to translations. Therefore, central moments are suited to describing the form of the object. However, a disadvantage of both spatial and central moments is their dependency on the size of the object. They are not scale-invariant.

Normalized central moments nu_{ij} are computed as follows:

$$nu_{ji} = \frac{mu_{ji}}{\mathtt{m}_{00}^{(i+j)/2+1}}$$

Normalized central moments are, by definition, invariants to both translation and scale.

The value for the next moments is calculated as follows:

$mu_{00} = m_{00}$, $nu_{00} = 1$, $nu_{10} = mu_{10} = mu_{01} = mu_{10} = 0$

Hence, these moments are not stored.

Moments are usually classified by their order, which is calculated based on the sum $(j+i)$ of indices j, i of the moment m_{ji}.

In the next subsections, further information about image moments will be given. More specifically, some object features based on moments (for example, center, eccentricity or the area of the contour, among others) will be computed. Additionally, Hu moment invariants will also be seen. Finally, Zernike moments are also introduced.

Some object features based on moments

As previously discussed, moments are features computed from contours allowing a geometrical reconstruction of the object. Despite not having a direct understandable geometrical meaning, some interesting geometrical properties and parameters can be calculated based on moments.

In `contours_analysis.py`, we will first calculate the moments for a detected contour and, afterwards, some object features will be computed:

```
M = cv2.moments(contours[0])
print("Contour area: '{}'".format(cv2.contourArea(contours[0])))
print("Contour area: '{}'".format(M['m00']))
```

As you can see, the moment `m00` gives the area of the contour, which is equivalent to function `cv2.contourArea()`. In order to calculate the centroid of the contour, you must perform the following:

```
print("center X : '{}'".format(round(M['m10'] / M['m00'])))
print("center Y : '{}'".format(round(M['m01'] / M['m00'])))
```

Roundness κ is the measure of how closely a contour approaches the contour of a perfect circle. The roundness of the contour can be calculated according to the next formula:

$$\kappa = \frac{P^2}{A \cdot 4 \cdot \pi}$$

`P` is the perimeter of the contour and `A` is the corresponding area. In the case of a perfect circle, the result will be 1; the higher the obtained value, the less circular it will be.

This can be calculated with `roundness()` function:

```
def roundness(contour, moments):
    """Calculates the roundness of a contour"""

    length = cv2.arcLength(contour, True)
    k = (length * length) / (moments['m00'] * 4 * np.pi)
    return k
```

Eccentricity (also called **elongation**) is a measure of how elongated a contour can be. The eccentricity ε can directly be derived from the semi-major and semi-minor axes a and b from the object, according to the next formula:

$$\varepsilon = \sqrt{\frac{a^2 - b^2}{b^2}}$$

Therefore, one approach to calculating the eccentricity of a contour is to calculate the ellipse that fits the contour and, afterwards, derive a and b from the calculated ellipse; finally, we calculate ε according to the previous formula.

The next code performs this:

```
def eccentricity_from_ellipse(contour):
    """Calculates the eccentricity fitting an ellipse from a contour"""

    (x, y), (MA, ma), angle = cv2.fitEllipse(contour)

    a = ma / 2
    b = MA / 2

    ecc = np.sqrt(a ** 2 - b ** 2) / a
    return ecc
```

Another approach is to calculate the eccentricity using contour moments via the next formula:

$$\varepsilon = \sqrt{1 - \frac{\dfrac{(mu20+mu02)}{2} - \sqrt{\dfrac{4 \cdot mu11^2 + (mu20+mu02)^2}{2}}}{\dfrac{(mu20+mu02)}{2} + \sqrt{\dfrac{4 \cdot mu11^2 + (mu20+mu02)^2}{2}}}}$$

This can be performed with `eccentricity_from_moments()`:

```
def eccentricity_from_moments(moments):
    """Calculates the eccentricity from the moments of the contour"""

    a1 = (moments['mu20'] + moments['mu02']) / 2
    a2 = np.sqrt(4 * moments['mu11'] ** 2 + (moments['mu20'] -
moments['mu02']) ** 2) / 2
    ecc = np.sqrt(1 - (a1 - a2) / (a1 + a2))
    return ecc
```

In order to complete the features that can be used to describe a contour, additional properties can be calculated. For example, the aspect ratio can be easily calculated based on the dimensions of the minimal bounding rectangle, calculated with `cv2.boundingRect()`. The aspect ratio is the ratio of width to height of the bounding rectangle of the contour:

```
def aspect_ratio(contour):
    """Returns the aspect ratio of the contour based on the dimensions of
the bounding rect"""
```

```
x, y, w, h = cv2.boundingRect(contour)
res = float(w) / h
return res
```

As previously discussed, all these properties are calculated in the `contours_analysis.py` script. The output of this script can be seen in the next screenshot:

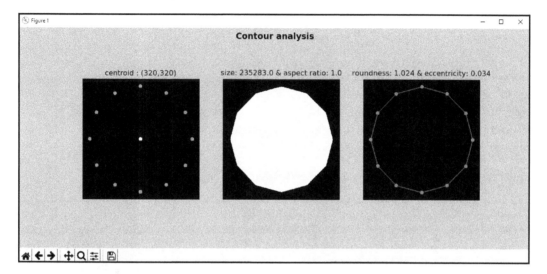

In the previous screenshot, the contour analysis is shown by printing all the properties calculated in the script.

 In the previous example, only moments up to the second order were used to calculate simple object features. In order to get a more precise description of complex objects, higher-order moments, or more complex moments (for example, Zernike, Legendre) should be used. In this sense, the more complex the object is, the higher the order of the moments should be calculated in order to minimize errors reconstructing the object from the moments. See the *Simple Image Analysis by Moments* publication for further information.

To complete this section, the script `contours_ellipses.py` is also coded. In this script, we first build an image to use. In this case, different ellipses are drawn in the image. This is performed with `build_image_ellipses()`. In this case, six ellipses are drawn using OpenCV function `cv2.ellipse()`. Afterwards, the contours of the drawn ellipses are detected in the thresholded image and some features are calculated. More specifically, both roundness and eccentricity are calculated. In the resulting image, only the eccentricity is shown.

In the next screenshot, the output of this script can be seen. As you can see, the eccentricity value is drawn centered in the centroid of each contour. This functionality is performed with function `get_position_to_draw()`:

```
def get_position_to_draw(text, point, font_face, font_scale, thickness):
    """Gives the coordinates to draw centered"""

    text_size = cv2.getTextSize(text, font_face, font_scale, thickness)[0]
    text_x = point[0] - text_size[0] / 2
    text_y = point[1] + text_size[1] / 2
    return round(text_x), round(text_y)
```

This function returns the *x, y* coordinates to draw `text` centered at the position `point` with the specific characteristics of the `text` to draw which are necessary to calculate the `text` size—font is set by the parameter `font_face`, font scale is set by the parameter `font_scale` and thickness is set by the parameter `thickness`.

The output of this script can be seen in the next screenshot:

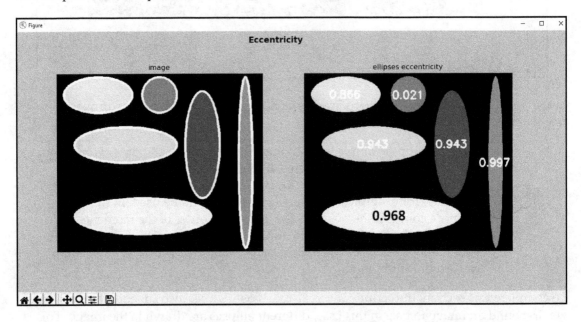

As can be seen, eccentricity, which is calculated using the aforementioned function, `eccentricity_from_moments()`, is shown. It should be noted that we have calculated the eccentricity using the two provided formulas, obtaining very similar results.

Hu moment invariants

Hu moment invariants are invariant with respect to translation, scale, and rotation and all the moments (except the seventh one) are invariant to reflection. In the case of the seventh one, the sign has been changed by reflection, which enables it to distinguish mirror images. OpenCV provides `cv2.HuMoments()` to calculate the seven Hu moment invariants.

The signature for this method is as follows:

```
cv2.HuMoments(m[, hu]) → hu
```

Here, `m` corresponds to the moments calculated with `cv2.moments()`. The output `hu` corresponds to the seven Hu invariant moments.

The seven Hu moment invariants are defined as follows:

$$hu[0] = \eta_{20} + \eta_{02}$$

$$hu[1] = (\eta_{20} - \eta_{02})^2 + 4\eta_{11}^2$$

$$hu[2] = (\eta_{30} - 3\eta_{12})^2 + (3\eta_{21} - \eta_{03})^2$$

$$hu[3] = (\eta_{30} + \eta_{12})^2 + (\eta_{21} + \eta_{03})^2$$

$$hu[4] = (\eta_{30} - 3\eta_{12})(\eta_{30} + \eta_{12})[(\eta_{30} + \eta_{12})^2 - 3(\eta_{21} + \eta_{03})^2] + (3\eta_{21} - \eta_{03})(\eta_{21} + \eta_{03})[3(\eta_{30} + \eta_{12})^2 - (\eta_{21} + \eta_{03})^2]$$

$$hu[5] = (\eta_{20} - \eta_{02})[(\eta_{30} + \eta_{12})^2 - (\eta_{21} + \eta_{03})^2] + 4\eta_{11}(\eta_{30} + \eta_{12})(\eta_{21} + \eta_{03})$$

$$hu[6] = (3\eta_{21} - \eta_{03})(\eta_{21} + \eta_{03})[3(\eta_{30} + \eta_{12})^2 - (\eta_{21} + \eta_{03})^2] - (\eta_{30} - 3\eta_{12})(\eta_{21} + \eta_{03})[3(\eta_{30} + \eta_{12})^2 - (\eta_{21} + \eta_{03})^2]$$

η_{ji} stands for nu_{ji}.

In the `contours_hu_moments.py` script, the seven Hu moment invariants are calculated. As stated before, we must first calculate the moments by using `cv2.moments()`. In order to calculate the moments, the parameter can be both a vector shape and an image. Besides, if the `binaryImage` parameter is true (only used for images), all non-zero pixels in the input image will be treated as 1's. In this script, we calculate moments using both a vector shape and an image. Finally, with the calculated moments, we will compute the Hu moment invariants.

The key code is explained next. We first load the image, transform it to grayscale, and apply `cv2.threshold()` to get a binary image:

```
# Load the image and convert it to grayscale:
image = cv2.imread("shape_features.png")
gray_image = cv2.cvtColor(image, cv2.COLOR_BGR2GRAY)

# Apply cv2.threshold() to get a binary image
ret, thresh = cv2.threshold(gray_image, 70, 255, cv2.THRESH_BINARY)
```

At this point, we compute the moments by using the thresholded image. Afterward, the centroid is calculated and, finally, the Hu moment invariants are calculated:

```
# Compute moments:
M = cv2.moments(thresh, True)
print("moments: '{}'".format(M))

# Calculate the centroid of the contour based on moments:
x, y = centroid(M)

# Compute Hu moments:
HuM = cv2.HuMoments(M)
print("Hu moments: '{}'".format(HuM))
```

Now, we repeat the procedure, but in this case, the contour is passed instead of the binary image. Therefore, we first calculate the coordinates of the contour in the binary image:

```
# Find contours
contours, hierarchy = cv2.findContours(thresh, cv2.RETR_EXTERNAL,
cv2.CHAIN_APPROX_NONE)

# Compute moments:
M2 = cv2.moments(contours[0])
print("moments: '{}'".format(M2))

# Calculate the centroid of the contour based on moments:
x2, y2 = centroid(M2)

# Compute Hu moments:
HuM2 = cv2.HuMoments(M2)
print("Hu moments: '{}'".format(HuM2))
```

Finally, the centroids are shown as follows:

```
print("('x','y'): ('{}','{}')".format(x, y))
print("('x2','y2'): ('{}','{}')".format(x2, y2))
```

As you can see, the computed moments, the Hu moment invariants, and the centroids are pretty similar but not the same. For example, the obtained centroids are as follows:

```
('x','y'): ('613','271')
('x2','y2'): ('613','270')
```

As you can see, the y coordinate differs by one pixel. The reason for this is limited raster resolution. The moments estimated for a contour are a little different from the moments calculated for the same rasterized contour. The output for this script can be seen in the next screenshot, where both centroids are shown in order to highlight this small difference in the y coordinate:

In `contours_hu_moments_properties.py`, we load three images. The first one is the original. The second one corresponds with the original but is rotated 180 degrees. The third one corresponds to a vertical reflection of the original. This can be seen in the output of the script. Additionally, we print the computed Hu moment invariants derived from the three aforementioned images.

The first step of this script is to load the images using `cv2.imread()` and convert them to grayscale by making use of `cv2.cvtColor()`. The second step is to apply `cv2.threshold()` to get the binary image. Finally, Hu moments are computed using `cv2.HuMoments()`:

```
# Load the images (cv2.imread()) and convert them to grayscale
(cv2.cvtColor()):
image_1 = cv2.imread("shape_features.png")
image_2 = cv2.imread("shape_features_rotation.png")
image_3 = cv2.imread("shape_features_reflection.png")
gray_image_1 = cv2.cvtColor(image_1, cv2.COLOR_BGR2GRAY)
gray_image_2 = cv2.cvtColor(image_2, cv2.COLOR_BGR2GRAY)
gray_image_3 = cv2.cvtColor(image_3, cv2.COLOR_BGR2GRAY)

# Apply cv2.threshold() to get a binary image:
ret_1, thresh_1 = cv2.threshold(gray_image_1, 70, 255, cv2.THRESH_BINARY)
ret_2, thresh_2 = cv2.threshold(gray_image_2, 70, 255, cv2.THRESH_BINARY)
ret_2, thresh_3 = cv2.threshold(gray_image_3, 70, 255, cv2.THRESH_BINARY)

# Compute Hu moments cv2.HuMoments():
HuM_1 = cv2.HuMoments(cv2.moments(thresh_1, True)).flatten()
HuM_2 = cv2.HuMoments(cv2.moments(thresh_2, True)).flatten()
HuM_3 = cv2.HuMoments(cv2.moments(thresh_3, True)).flatten()

# Show calculated Hu moments for the three images:
print("Hu moments (original): '{}'".format(HuM_1))
print("Hu moments (rotation): '{}'".format(HuM_2))
print("Hu moments (reflection): '{}'".format(HuM_3))

# Plot the images:
show_img_with_matplotlib(image_1, "original", 1)
show_img_with_matplotlib(image_2, "rotation", 2)
show_img_with_matplotlib(image_3, "reflection", 3)

# Show the Figure:
plt.show()
```

The computed Hue moment invariants are as follows:

```
Hu moments (original): '[ 1.92801772e-01 1.01173781e-02 5.70258405e-05
1.96536742e-06 2.46949980e-12 -1.88337981e-07 2.06595472e-11]'
 Hu moments (rotation): '[ 1.92801772e-01 1.01173781e-02 5.70258405e-05
1.96536742e-06 2.46949980e-12 -1.88337981e-07 2.06595472e-11]'
 Hu moments (reflection): '[ 1.92801772e-01 1.01173781e-02 5.70258405e-05
1.96536742e-06 2.46949980e-12 -1.88337981e-07 -2.06595472e-11]'
```

You can see that the computed Hu moment invariants are the same in the three cases, with the exception of the seventh one. This difference is highlighted in bold in the output shown previously. As you can see, the sign is changed.

The following screenshot shows the three images used to compute Hu moment invariants:

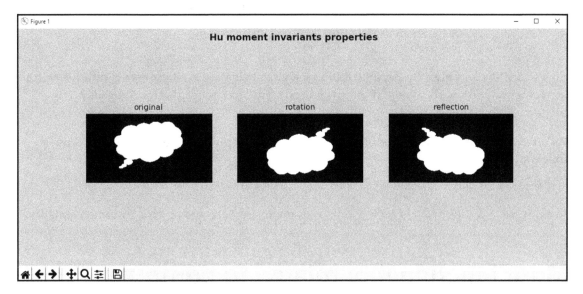

Zernike moments

Moments have been used in image processing and object classification and recognition since Hu introduced them. From this publication on, more powerful moment techniques in connection with moments have been developed.

A remarkable example is **Zernike moments**. Teague proposed Zernike moments based on the basis set of orthogonal Zernike polynomials. OpenCV provides no functions to compute Zernike moments. However, other Python packages can be used for this purpose.

In this sense, the `mahotas` package provides the `zernike_moments()` function, which can be used to compute Zernike moments. The signature of `zernike_moments()` is as follows:

```
mahotas.features.zernike_moments(im, radius, degree=8,
cm={center_of_mass(im)})
```

This function computes the Zernike moments on a circle of `radius` centered around `cm` (or the center of mass of the image if `cm` is not used). The maximum degree to use is set by `degree` (by default 8).

As an example, if we use the default values, we can compute the Zernike moments as follows:

```
moments = mahotas.features.zernike_moments(image, 21)
```

In this case, a radius of 21 is used. Zernike moments feature vector is of 25-dimensionality.

More functionality related to contours

So far, we have seen some contour properties derived from image moments (for example, centroid, area, roundness, or eccentricity, among others). Additionally, OpenCV provides some interesting functionality related to contours that can be also used to further describe contours.

In `contours_functionality.py`, we mainly use five OpenCV functions related to contours and one function that computes the extreme points of a given contour.

Before describing what each of these functions computes, it is preferable to show the output of this script, because the resulting image can help us understand each of the aforementioned functions:

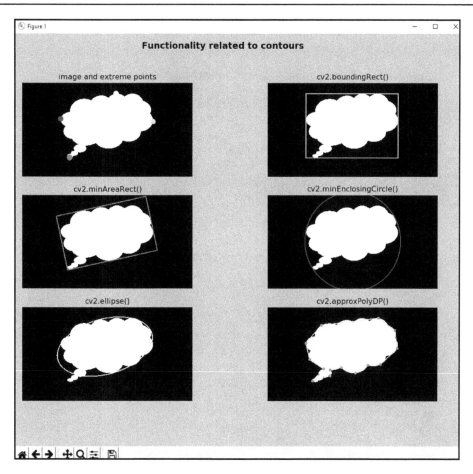

cv2.boundingRect() returns the minimal bounding rectangle enclosing all the points of the contour:

```
x, y, w, h = cv2.boundingRect(contours[0])
```

cv2.minAreaRect() returns the minimal rotated (if necessary) rectangle enclosing all the points of the contour:

```
rotated_rect = cv2.minAreaRect(contours[0])
```

In order to extract the four points of the rotated rectangle, you can use the cv2.boxPoints() function, which returns the four vertices of the rotated rectangle:

```
box = cv2.boxPoints(rotated_rect)
```

`cv2.minEnclosingCircle()` returns the minimal circle (it returns the center and radius) enclosing all the points of the contour:

```
(x, y), radius = cv2.minEnclosingCircle(contours[0])
```

`cv2.fitEllipse()` returns the ellipse that fits (with the minimum least square errors) all the points of the contour:

```
ellipse = cv2.fitEllipse(contours[0])
```

`cv2.approxPolyDP()` returns a contour approximation of the given contour, based on the given precision. This function uses the Douglas-Peucker algorithm.

The `epsilon` parameter establishes the precision, determining the maximum distance between the original curve and its approximation. Therefore, the resulting contour is a decimated contour similar to the given contour with fewer points:

```
approx = cv2.approxPolyDP(contours[0], epsilon, True)
```

`extreme_points()` calculates the four extreme points defining a given contour:

```python
def extreme_points(contour):
    """Returns extreme points of the contour"""

    index_min_x = contour[:, :, 0].argmin()
    index_min_y = contour[:, :, 1].argmin()
    index_max_x = contour[:, :, 0].argmax()
    index_max_y = contour[:, :, 1].argmax()

    extreme_left = tuple(contour[index_min_x][0])
    extreme_right = tuple(contour[index_max_x][0])
    extreme_top = tuple(contour[index_min_y][0])
    extreme_bottom = tuple(contour[index_max_y][0])

    return extreme_left, extreme_right, extreme_top, extreme_bottom
```

`np.argmin()` returns the indices of the minimum values along an axis. The indices corresponding to the first occurrence are returned in the case of multiple occurrences of the minimum values. `np.argmax()` returns the indices of the maximum values. Once the indices are calculated (for example, `index`), we will get the corresponding component of the array (for example, `contour[index]`—`[[ 40 320]]`) and we access the first component (for example, `contour[index][0]`—`[ 40 320]`). Finally we convert it to a tuple (for example, `tuple(contour[index][0])`—`(40,320)`).

As you can see, you can perform these calculations in a more compact way:

```
index_min_x = contour[:, :, 0].argmin()
extreme_left = tuple(contour[index_min_x][0])
```

This code can be rewritten as follows:

```
extreme_left = tuple(contour[contour[:, :, 0].argmin()][0])
```

Filtering contours

In previous sections, we have seen how to calculate the size of a detected contour. The size of a detected contour can be calculated based on image moments or using the OpenCV function `cv2.contourArea()`. In this example, we are going to sort the detected contours based on the computed size for each one.

Therefore, the `sort_contours_size()` function is key:

```
def sort_contours_size(cnts):
    """ Sort contours based on the size"""

    cnts_sizes = [cv2.contourArea(contour) for contour in cnts]
    (cnts_sizes, cnts) = zip(*sorted(zip(cnts_sizes, cnts)))
    return cnts_sizes, cnts
```

Before explaining the code of this function, we are going to introduce some key points. The * operator can be used in conjunction with `zip()` to unzip the list:

```
coordinate = ['x', 'y', 'z']
value = [5, 4, 3]
result = zip(coordinate, value)
print(list(result))
c, v =  zip(*zip(coordinate, value))
print('c =', c)
print('v =', v)
```

The output is as follows:

```
[('x', 5), ('y', 4), ('z', 3)]
c = ('x', 'y', 'z')
v = (5, 4, 3)
```

Let's incorporate the `sorted` function:

```
coordinate = ['x', 'y', 'z']
value = [5, 4, 3]
```

```
print(sorted(zip(value, coordinate)))
c, v = zip(*sorted(zip(value, coordinate)))
print('c =', c)
print('v =', v)
```

The output is as follows:

```
[(3, 'z'), (4, 'y'), (5, 'x')]
c = (3, 4, 5)
v = ('z', 'y', 'x')
```

Therefore, the `sort_contours_size()` function sorts the contours based on the size. Also, the script outputs the ordering number in the center of the contour. The output of `contours_sort_size.py` can be seen in the next screenshot:

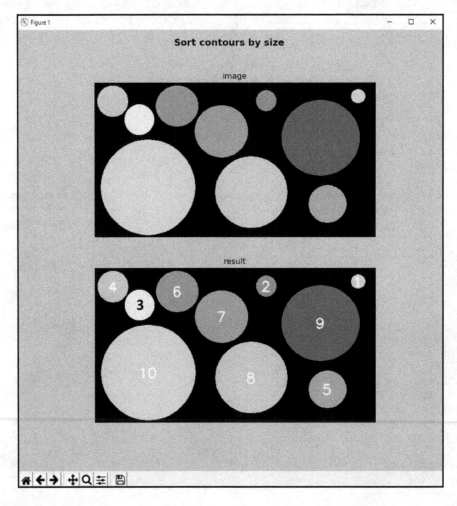

As you can see, in the upper part of the screenshot the original image is shown, while in the bottom part of the screenshot the original image has been modified to include the ordering number in the center of each contour.

Recognizing contours

We have previously introduced `cv2.approxPolyDP()`, which can be used to approximate one contour with another with fewer points using the Douglas-Peucker algorithm. A key parameter in this function is `epsilon`, which sets the approximation accuracy. In `contours_shape_recognition.py`, we will make use of `cv2.approxPolyDP()` in order to recognize the contours (for example, triangle, square, rectangle, pentagon, or hexagon, among others) based on the number of detected vertices in the decimated contour (the output of `cv2.approxPolyDP()`). In order to decimate the number of points, given a certain contour, we first compute the perimeter of the contour. Based on the perimeter, the `epsilon` parameter is established. This way, the decimated contour is invariant to scale. The epsilon parameter is calculated as follows:

```
epsilon = 0.03 * perimeter
```

The constant `0.03` is established after several tests. For example, if this constant is bigger (for example, `0.1`), the epsilon parameter will also be bigger and, hence, the approximation accuracy will be decreased.

This results in a contour with fewer points, and missing vertices are obtained. Therefore, recognition of the contours is performed incorrectly because it is based on the number of detected vertices. On the other hand, if this constant is smaller (for example, `0.001`), the epsilon parameter will also be smaller and, hence, the approximation accuracy will increased, resulting in an approximation contour with more points. In this situation, the recognition of the contours is also performed incorrectly because false vertices are obtained.

The output of the `contours_shape_recognition.py` script can be seen in the next screenshot:

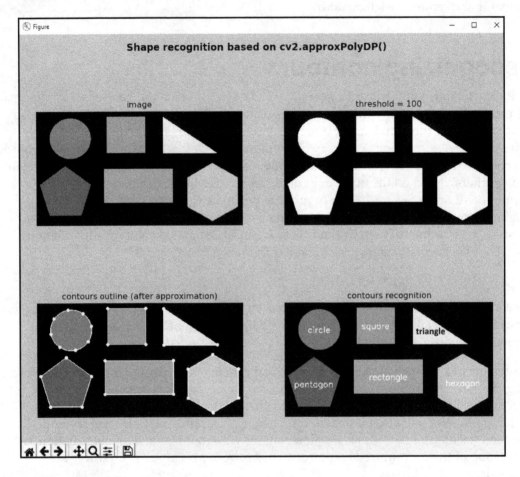

In the previous screenshot, the key steps (thresholding, contour approximation, and **contour recognition**) are shown.

Matching contours

Hu moment invariants can be used for both object matching and recognition. In this section, we are going to see how to match contours based on Hu moment invariants. OpenCV provides `cv2.matchShapes()`, which can be used to compare two contours using three comparison methods. All these methods use Hu moment invariants. The three implemented methods are `cv2.CONTOURS_MATCH_I1`, `cv2.CONTOURS_MATCH_I2`, and `cv2.CONTOURS_MATCH_I3`.

If *A* denotes the first object and *B* denotes the second object, then the following applies:

$$m_i^A = \text{sign}(h_i^A) \cdot \log h_i^A$$
$$m_i^B = \text{sign}(h_i^B) \cdot \log h_i^B$$

h_i^A, h_i^B are the Hu moments of *A* and *B*, respectively.

Finally, see the following:

- `cv2.CONTOURS_MATCH_I1`:

$$I_1(A, B) = \sum_{i=1...7} \left| \frac{1}{m_i^A} - \frac{1}{m_i^B} \right|$$

- `cv2.CONTOURS_MATCH_I2`:

$$I_2(A, B) = \sum_{i=1...7} \left| m_i^A - m_i^B \right|$$

- `cv2.CONTOURS_MATCH_I3`:

$$I_2(A, B) = \sum_{i=1...7} \left| m_i^A - m_i^B \right|$$

In `contours_matching.py`, we are making use of `cv2.matchShapes()` to match several contours against a perfect circle contour.

First of all, we draw a perfect circle in an image by using the OpenCV function `cv2.circle()`. This is going to be the reference image. In order to build this image, `build_circle_image()` is called. Afterwards, we load the image `match_shapes.png`, where many different shapes are drawn. Once the two images are ready, the next step is to find contours in each of the two aforementioned images:

1. Convert them to grayscale by using `cv2.cvtColor()`
2. Binarize them by using `cv2.threshold()`
3. Find contours by using `cv2.findContours()`

At this point, we are ready to compare all the contours extracted from `match_shapes.png` against the contour extracted from the image built using the `build_circle_image()` function:

```
for contour in contours:
    # Compute the moment of contour:
    M = cv2.moments(contour)

    # The center or centroid can be calculated as follows:
    cX = int(M['m10'] / M['m00'])
    cY = int(M['m01'] / M['m00'])

    # We match each contour against the circle contour using the three
matching modes:
    ret_1 = cv2.matchShapes(contours_circle[0], contour,
cv2.CONTOURS_MATCH_I1, 0.0)
    ret_2 = cv2.matchShapes(contours_circle[0], contour,
cv2.CONTOURS_MATCH_I2, 0.0)
    ret_3 = cv2.matchShapes(contours_circle[0], contour,
cv2.CONTOURS_MATCH_I3, 0.0)

    # Get the positions to draw:
    (x_1, y_1) = get_position_to_draw(str(round(ret_1, 3)), (cX, cY),
cv2.FONT_HERSHEY_SIMPLEX, 1.2, 3)
    (x_2, y_2) = get_position_to_draw(str(round(ret_2, 3)), (cX, cY),
cv2.FONT_HERSHEY_SIMPLEX, 1.2, 3)
    (x_3, y_3) = get_position_to_draw(str(round(ret_3, 3)), (cX, cY),
cv2.FONT_HERSHEY_SIMPLEX, 1.2, 3)

    # Write the obtainted scores in the result images:
    cv2.putText(result_1, str(round(ret_1, 3)), (x_1, y_1),
cv2.FONT_HERSHEY_SIMPLEX, 1.2, (255, 0, 0), 3)
    cv2.putText(result_2, str(round(ret_2, 3)), (x_2, y_2),
cv2.FONT_HERSHEY_SIMPLEX, 1.2, (0, 255, 0), 3)
    cv2.putText(result_3, str(round(ret_3, 3)), (x_3, y_3),
cv2.FONT_HERSHEY_SIMPLEX, 1.2, (0, 0, 255), 3)
```

The output of the `contours_matching.py` script can be seen in the following screenshot:

As it can be seen, image `result_1` displays matching scores using the matching mode `cv2.CONTOURS_MATCH_I1`, image `result_2` displays matching scores using the matching mode `cv2.CONTOURS_MATCH_I2` and, finally, `result_3` displays matching scores using the matching mode `cv2.CONTOURS_MATCH_I3`.

Summary

In this chapter, we have reviewed the main functionality OpenCV provides in connection with contours. Additionally, we have also coded some useful functions when comparing and describing contours. Moreover, we have also provided some interesting functionality that can be helpful when debugging your code. In this sense, functions for both creating reduced contours and creating images with simple shapes are provided. With this chapter we have finished four chapters related to image processing techniques—Chapter 5, *Image Processing Techniques*, reviewed key points in image processing; Chapter 6, *Constructing and Building Histograms*, introduced histograms; Chapter 7, *Thresholding Techniques*, covered thresholding techniques; and finally, in this chapter, we have explained how to deal with contours.

In the next chapter, we are going to supply an introduction to augmented reality, which is one of the hottest trends at present and can be defined as an improved version of reality, where the view of the real world is enhanced with superimposed computer-generated elements.

Questions

1. What function should you use if you want to detect contours in a binary image?
2. What four flags does OpenCV provide for compressing contours?
3. What function does OpenCV provide to compute image moments?
4. What moment provides the size of the contour?
5. What function does OpenCV provide to calculate the seven Hu moment invariants?
6. What function should you use if you want to get a contour approximation of a given contour?
7. The `extreme_points()` function defined in the `contour_functionality.py` script can be rewritten in a more compact way as explained in this chapter. Therefore, rewrite it accordingly.
8. What function should you use if you want to match contours using Hu moment invariants as features?

Further reading

The following references will help you dive deeper into contours and other image processing techniques:

- *Python 3.x for Computer Vision by Saurabh Kapur* (2017) (`https://www.packtpub.com/application-development/python-3x-computer-vision-video-0`)
- *OpenCV: Computer Vision Projects with Python* (2016) (`https://www.packtpub.com/application-development/opencv-computer-vision-projects-python`)

Augmented Reality

9

Augmented reality is one of the hottest trends at present. The concept of augmented reality can be defined as an improved version of reality, where the view of the real world is enhanced with superimposed computer-generated elements (for example, images, videos, or 3D models, among others). In order to overlay and integrate digital information—augmenting reality, different types of techniques can be used, mainly location-based and recognition-based approaches.

In this chapter, we will cover the main concepts related to augmented reality and we will also code some interesting applications in order to see the potential of this technology. In this chapter, you will learn how to build your first augmented reality applications. At the end of this chapter, you will have the knowledge to create your augmented reality applications using OpenCV.

The main sections of this chapter are the following:

- An introduction to augmented reality
- Markerless-based augmented reality
- Marker-based augmented reality
- Snapchat-based augmented reality
- QR code detection

Technical requirements

The technical requirements are listed here:

- Python and OpenCV
- Python-specific IDE
- NumPy and Matplotlib packages
- Git client

Further details about how to install these requirements are commented on in `Chapter 1,` *Setting Up OpenCV*.

The GitHub repository for *Mastering OpenCV 4 with Python*, containing all of the supporting project files necessary to work through this book, from the first chapter to the last, can be accessed in the next URL: `https://github.com/PacktPublishing/Mastering-OpenCV-4-with-Python/`.

An introduction to augmented reality

Location-based and recognition-based augmented reality are the two main types of augmented reality. Both types try to derive where the user is looking. This information is key in the augmented reality process, and relies on properly calculating the camera pose estimation. In order to accomplish this task, the two types are briefly described as follows:

- **Location-based augmented reality** relies on detecting the user's location and orientation by reading data from several sensors, that are very common in smartphone devices (for example, GPS, digital compass, and accelerometer) to derive where the user is looking. This information is used to superimpose computer-generated elements on the screen.
- On the other hand, **recognition-based augmented reality** uses image processing techniques to derive where the user is looking. Obtaining the camera pose from images necessitates finding the correspondences between known points in the environment, and their corresponding camera projections. In order to find these correspondences, two main approaches can be found in the literature:
  - **Marker-based pose estimation**: This approach relies on using planar markers (those based on square markers have gained popularity, especially in the augmented reality field) to compute the camera pose from their four corners. One major disadvantage of using square markers is in connection with the computation of the camera pose, which relies on the accurate determination of the four corners of the marker. This task can be very difficult in the case of occlusion. However, some approaches based on detection of markers can also deal with occlusion really well. This is the case of ArUco.

- **Markerless-based pose estimation**: When the scene cannot be prepared using markers to derive pose estimation, the objects, that are naturally present in the image can be used for pose estimation. Once a set of n 2D points and their corresponding 3D coordinates have been calculated, the pose of the camera is estimated by solving the **Perspective-n-Point** (**PnP**) problem. Due to these methods relying on point matching techniques, the input data is seldom exempt from outliers. This is why robust techniques to outliers (for example, RANSAC) can be used in the pose estimation process.

In the next screenshot, the two aforementioned approaches (marker-based and markerless-based augmented reality) are shown in connection with image processing techniques:

In the preceding screenshot, on the left side, you can see an example of the marker-based approach, where the marker is used to compute the camera pose from their four corners. Additionally, on the right side, you can see an example of the markerless-based approach, where the €50 note is used to compute the camera pose. Both approaches are explained in the following sections.

Markerless-based augmented reality

As commented before, camera pose estimation can be derived from images to find the correspondences between known points in the environment and their camera projections. In this section, we will see how to extract features from the images to derive the camera pose. Based on these features and their matching, we will see how to finally derive camera pose estimation, which is then used to overlay and integrate digital information.

Feature detection

A feature can be described as a small patch in the image, which is invariant (as much as possible) to image scaling, rotation, and illumination. This way, the same feature can be detected from different images of the same scene with different perspectives. Therefore, a good feature should be the following:

- Repeatable and precise (the same feature should be extracted from different images of the same object)
- Distinctive to the image (images with different structures will not have this feature)

OpenCV provides many algorithms and techniques to detect features in images. They include the following:

- **Harris Corner Detection**
- **Shi-Tomasi Corner Detection**
- **Scale Invariant Feature Transform (SIFT)**
- **Speeded-Up Robust Features (SURF)**
- **Features from Accelerated Segment Test (FAST)**
- **Binary Robust Independent Elementary Features (BRIEF)**
- **Oriented FAST and Rotated BRIEF (ORB)**

In the `feature_detection.py` script, we will use ORB for feature detection and description in images. This algorithm comes from OpenCV Labs, and it is described in the publication *ORB: An efficient alternative to SIFT or SURF (2011)*. ORB is basically a combination of FAST keypoint detector and BRIEF descriptor, with key modifications to enhance the performance. The first step is to detect `keypoints`.

ORB detects the `keypoints` (by default `500`) using a modified `FAST-9` (circle with a `radius` = `9` pixel, and it stores orientation of the detected `keypoints`). Once the `keypoints` are detected, the next step is to compute the descriptors in order to obtain the information associated with each detected keypoint. ORB uses a modified `BRIEF-32` descriptor to obtain the description for each detected keypoint. For example, a descriptor for a detected `keypoints` looks like this:

```
[103 4 111 192 86 239 107 66 141 117 255 138 81 92 62 101 123 148 91 62 3
177 61 205 31 12 129 68 165 203 116 116]
```

So, the first point is to create the ORB detector:

```
orb = cv2.ORB_create()
```

The next step is to detect the `keypoints` in the loaded image:

```
keypoints = orb.detect(image, None)
```

Once the `keypoints` are detected, the next step is to compute the descriptors of the detected `keypoints`:

```
keypoints, descriptors = orb.compute(image, keypoints)
```

Note that you can also perform `orb.detectAndCompute(image, None)` to both detect the `keypoints` and compute the descriptors of the detected `keypoints`. Finally, we can draw the detected `keypoints` using the `cv2.drawKeypoints()` function:

```
image_keypoints = cv2.drawKeypoints(image, keypoints, None, color=(255, 0, 255), flags=0)
```

The output of this script can be seen in the next screenshot:

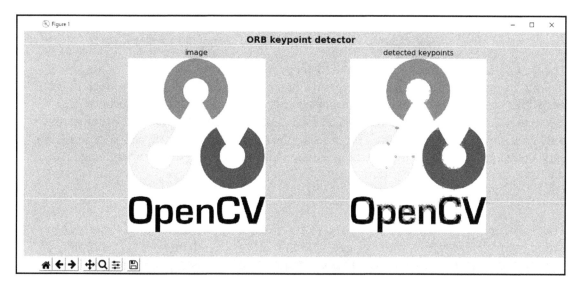

As it can be seen, the result on the right shows the detect ORB keypoints, which have been detected by the ORB keypoint detector.

Feature matching

In the next example, we are going to see how to match the detected features. OpenCV provides two matchers, as follows:

- **Brute-Force (BF) matcher**: This matcher takes each descriptor computed for each detected feature in the first set and it is matched with all other descriptors in the second set. Finally, it returns the match with the closest distance.
- **Fast Library for Approximate Nearest Neighbors (FLANN) matcher**: This matcher works faster than the BF matcher for large datasets. It contains optimized algorithms for nearest neighbor search.

In the `feature_matching.py` script, we will use BF matcher to see how to match the detected features. So, the first step is to both detect `keypoints` and compute the descriptors:

```
orb = cv2.ORB_create()
keypoints_1, descriptors_1 = orb.detectAndCompute(image_query, None)
keypoints_2, descriptors_2 = orb.detectAndCompute(image_scene, None)
```

The next step is to create the BF matcher object using `cv2.BFMatcher()`:

```
bf_matcher = cv2.BFMatcher(cv2.NORM_HAMMING, crossCheck=True)
```

The first parameter, `normType`, sets the distance measurement to use `cv2.NORM_L2` by default. In case of using ORB descriptors (or other binary-based descriptors such as BRIEF or BRISK), the distance measurement to use is `cv2.NORM_HAMMING`. The second parameter, `crossCheck` (which is `False` by default), can be set to `True` in order to return only consistent pairs in the matching process (the two features in both sets should match each other). Once created, the next step is to match the detected descriptors using the `BFMatcher.match()` method:

```
bf_matches = bf_matcher.match(descriptors_1, descriptors_2)
```

The `descriptors_1` and `descriptors_2` are the descriptors that should have been previously calculated; this way, we get the best matches in two images. At this point, we can sort the matches in ascending order of their distance:

```
bf_matches = sorted(bf_matches, key=lambda x: x.distance)
```

Finally, we can draw the matches using the `cv2.drawMatches()` function. In this case, only the first `20` matches (for the sake of visibility) are shown:

```
result = cv2.drawMatches(image_query, keypoints_1, image_scene,
keypoints_2, bf_matches[:20], None, matchColor=(255, 255, 0),
singlePointColor=(255, 0, 255), flags=0)
```

The `cv2.drawMatches()` function concatenates two images horizontally, and draws lines from the first to the second image showing the matches.

The output of the `feature_matching.py` script can be seen in the next screenshot:

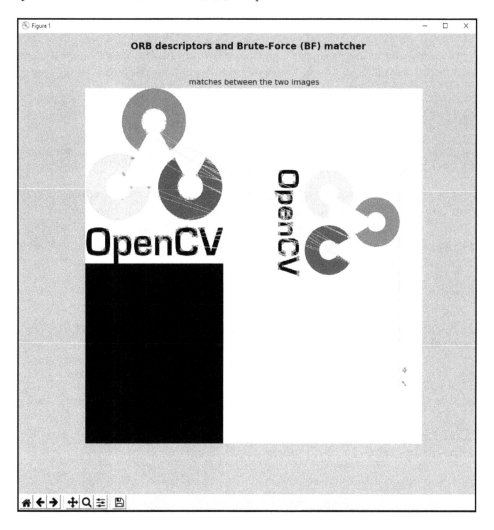

As you can see in the previous screenshot, the matches between both images (`image_query`, `image_scene`) are drawn.

Feature matching and homography computation to find objects

In order to complete this section, we are going to see the final step to find objects. Once the features are matched, the next step is to find a perspective transformation between the location of the matched `keypoints` in the two images using the `cv2.findHomography()` function.

OpenCV provides several methods to compute the homography matrix—RANSAC, Least-Median (`LMEDS`), and PROSAC (`RHO`). In this example, we are using RANSAC, shown as follows:

```
M, mask = cv2.findHomography(pts_src, pts_dst, cv2.RANSAC, 5.0)
```

Here, `pts_src` are the location of the matched key points in the source image, and `pts_dst` are the locations of the matched `keypoints` in the query image.

The fourth parameter, `ransacReprojThreshold`, sets the maximum reprojection error to treat a point pair as an inlier. In this case, if the reprojection error is bigger than `5.0`, the corresponding point pair is considered an outlier. This function computes and returns the perspective transformation matrix, `M`, between the source and the destination planes defined by the `keypoints` locations.

Finally, based on the perspective transformation matrix, `M`, we will calculate the four corners of the object in the query image. In order to do this, we will calculate the four corners of the original image based on its shape, and transform them to get the destination corners using the `cv2.perspectiveTransform()` function:

```
pts_corners_dst = cv2.perspectiveTransform(pts_corners_src, M)
```

Here, `pts_corners_src` contains the four corners of the original image, and `M` is the perspective transformation matrix; the `pts_corners_dst` output contains the four corners of the object in the query image. We can use the `cv2.polyline()` function to draw the outline of the detected object:

```
img_obj = cv2.polylines(image_scene, [np.int32(pts_corners_dst)], True, (0, 255, 255), 10)
```

Finally, we can also draw the matches using the `cv2.drawMatches()` function, as follows:

```
img_matching = cv2.drawMatches(image_query, keypoints_1, img_obj,
keypoints_2, best_matches, None, matchColor=(255, 255, 0),
singlePointColor=(255, 0, 255), flags=0)
```

The output of the `feature_matching_object_recognition.py` script can be seen in the next screenshot:

In the preceding screenshot, you can see both the feature matching and the homography computation, which are two key steps for object recognition.

Marker-based augmented reality

In this section, we are going to see how marker-based augmented reality works. There are many libraries, algorithms, or packages that you can use to both generate and detect markers. In this sense, one that provides state-of-the-art performance in detecting markers is ArUco.

ArUco automatically detects the markers and corrects possible errors. Additionally, ArUco proposes a solution to the occlusion problem by combining multiple markers with an occlusion mask, which is calculated by color segmentation.

As previously commented, pose estimation is a key process in augmented reality applications. Pose estimation can be performed based on markers. The main benefit of using markers is that they can be both efficiently and robustly detected in the image where the four corners of the marker can be accurately derived. Finally, the camera pose can be obtained from the previously calculated four corners of the marker. Therefore, in next subsections, we will see how to create marker-based augmented reality applications, starting from creating both markers and dictionaries.

Creating markers and dictionaries

The first step when using ArUco is the creation of markers and dictionaries. Firstly, an **ArUco marker** is a square marker composed of external and internal cells (also called **bits**). The external cells are set to black, creating an external border that can be fast and robustly detected. The remaining cells (the internal cells) are used for coding the marker. ArUco markers can also be created with different sizes. The size of the marker indicates the number of internal cells related to the internal matrix. For example, a marker size of 5×5 (n=5) is composed of 25 internal cells. Additionally, you can also set the number of bits in the marker border.

Secondly, a dictionary of markers is the set of markers considered to be used in a specific application. While previous libraries considered only fixed dictionaries, ArUco proposes an automatic method for generating the markers with the desired number of them and with the desired number of bits. In this sense, ArUco includes some predefined dictionaries covering many configurations in connection with the number of markers and the marker sizes.

The first step to consider when creating your marker-based augmented reality application is to print the markers to use.

In the `aruco_create_markers.py` script, we are creating some markers ready to print. The first step is to create the dictionary object. ArUco has some predefined dictionaries: `DICT_4X4_50 = 0`, `DICT_4X4_100 = 1`, `DICT_4X4_250 = 2`, `DICT_4X4_1000 = 3`, `DICT_5X5_50 = 4`, `DICT_5X5_100 = 5`, `DICT_5X5_250 = 6`, `DICT_5X5_1000 = 7`, `DICT_6X6_50 = 8`, `DICT_6X6_100 = 9`, `DICT_6X6_250 = 10`, `DICT_6X6_1000 = 11`, `DICT_7X7_50 = 12`, `DICT_7X7_100 = 13`, `DICT_7X7_250 = 14`, and `DICT_7X7_1000 = 15`.

In this case, we will create a dictionary using the `cv2.aruco.Dictionary_get()` function composed of 250 markers. Each marker will have a size of *7 x 7* (n=7):

```
aruco_dictionary = cv2.aruco.Dictionary_get(cv2.aruco.DICT_7X7_250)
```

At this point, a marker can be drawn using the `cv2.aruco.drawMarker()` function, which returns the marker ready to be printed. The first parameter of `cv2.aruco.drawMarker()` is the `dictionary` object. The second parameter is the marker `id`, which ranges between 0 and 249, because our dictionary has 250 markers. The third parameter, `sidePixels`, is the size (in pixels) of the created marker image. The fourth (optional, by default 1) parameter is `borderBits`, which sets the number of bits in the marker borders.

So, in this example, we are going to create three markers varying the number of bits in the marker borders:

```
aruco_marker_1 = cv2.aruco.drawMarker(dictionary=aruco_dictionary, id=2,
sidePixels=600, borderBits=1)
aruco_marker_2 = cv2.aruco.drawMarker(dictionary=aruco_dictionary, id=2,
sidePixels=600, borderBits=2)
aruco_marker_3 = cv2.aruco.drawMarker(dictionary=aruco_dictionary, id=2,
sidePixels=600, borderBits=3)
```

These marker images can be saved on disk (using `cv2.imwrite()`):

```
cv2.imwrite("marker_DICT_7X7_250_600_1.png", aruco_marker_1)
cv2.imwrite("marker_DICT_7X7_250_600_2.png", aruco_marker_2)
cv2.imwrite("marker_DICT_7X7_250_600_3.png", aruco_marker_3)
```

In the `aruco_create_markers.py` script, we also show the created markers. The output can be seen in the next screenshot:

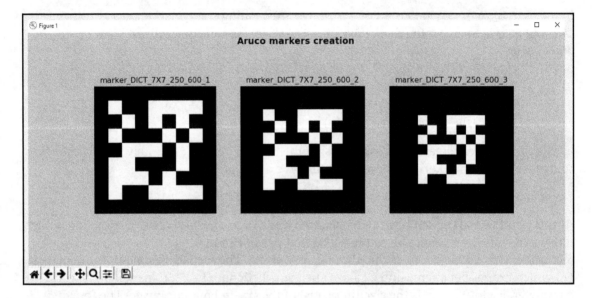

In the preceding screenshot, the three created markers are shown.

Detecting markers

You can use the `cv2.aruco.detectMarkers()` function to detect the markers in an image:

```
corners, ids, rejected_corners = cv2.aruco.detectMarkers(gray_frame,
aruco_dictionary, parameters=parameters)
```

The first parameter of `cv2.aruco.detectMarkers()` is the grayscale image where the markers are going to be detected. The second parameter is the dictionary object, which should have been previously created. The third parameter establishes all of the parameters that can be customized during the detection process. This function returns the following information:

- The list of corners of the detected markers is returned. For each marker, its four corners (top-left, top-right, bottom-right, and bottom-left) are returned.
- The list of the identifiers of the detected markers is returned.

- The list of rejected candidates is returned, which is composed of all of the squares that have been found, but they do not have a proper codification. This list of rejected candidates is useful for debugging purposes. Each rejected candidate is composed of its four corners.

The `aruco_detect_markers.py` script detects markers from the webcam. First, the markers are detected using the aforementioned `cv2.aruco.detectMarkers()` function and, then, we will draw both the detected markers and the rejected candidates using `cv2.aruco.drawDetectedMarkers()` function, as follows:

```
# Draw detected markers:
frame = cv2.aruco.drawDetectedMarkers(image=frame, corners=corners,
ids=ids, borderColor=(0, 255, 0))
# Draw rejected markers:
frame = cv2.aruco.drawDetectedMarkers(image=frame,
corners=rejected_corners, borderColor=(0, 0, 255))
```

If you execute the `aruco_detect_markers.py` script, detected markers will be drawn with a green border, while the rejected candidates will be drawn with a red border, as shown in the following screenshot:

In the preceding screenshot, you can see that a marker (with id=2) is detected, which is drawn with a green border. Additionally, you can also see two rejected candidates with a red border.

Camera calibration

Before obtaining the camera pose using the detected markers, it is necessary to know the calibration parameters of the camera. In this sense, ArUco provides the necessary calibration procedures to perform this task. Note that the calibration procedure is only performed once because the camera optics are not modified. The main function to use in the calibration process is `cv2.aruco.calibrateCameraCharuco()`.

The aforementioned function calibrates a camera using a set of corners from several views extracted from a board. When the calibration process is finished, this function returns the camera matrix (a *3 x 3* floating-point camera matrix) and a vector containing the distortion coefficients. More specifically, the *3 x 3* matrix encodes both the focal distances and the camera center coordinates (also known as **intrinsic parameters**). The distortion coefficients model the distortion produced by the camera.

The signature of the function is as follows:

```
calibrateCameraCharuco(charucoCorners, charucoIds, board, imageSize,
cameraMatrix, distCoeffs[, rvecs[, tvecs[, flags[, criteria]]]]) -> retval,
cameraMatrix, distCoeffs, rvecs, tvecs
```

Here, `charucoCorners` is a vector containing the detected charuco corners, `charucoIds` is the list of identifiers, `board` represents the board layout, and `imageSize` is the input image size. The output vector, `rvecs`, contains a vector of rotation vectors estimated for each board view and `tvecs` is a vector of translation vectors estimated for each pattern view. As previously commented, the camera matrix, `cameraMatrix`, and the distortion coefficients, `distCoeffs`, are also returned.

The board is created using the `cv2.aruco.CharucoBoard_create()` function:

The signature is as follows:

```
CharucoBoard_create(squaresX, squaresY, squareLength, markerLength,
dictionary) -> retval
```

Here, `squareX` is the number of squares in the *x* direction, `squaresY` is the number of squares in *y* direction, `squareLength` is the chessboard square side length (normally in meters), `markerLength` is the marker side length (same units as `squareLength`), and `dictionary` sets the first markers in the dictionary to use in order to create the markers inside the board. For example, in order to create a board, we can use the following lines of code:

```
dictionary = cv2.aruco.Dictionary_get(cv2.aruco.DICT_7X7_250)
board = cv2.aruco.CharucoBoard_create(3, 3, .025, .0125, dictionary)
img = board.draw((200 * 3, 200 * 3))
```

The created board can be seen in the next screenshot:

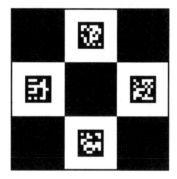

This board will be later used by the `cv2.aruco.calibrateCameraCharuco()` function in the calibration process:

```
cal = cv2.aruco.calibrateCameraCharuco(all_corners, all_ids, board,
image_size, None, None)
```

Once the calibration process has been finished, we will save both the camera matrix and the distortion coefficients to disk. To do so, we use pickle, which can be used for serializing and de-serializing a Python object structure.

After the calibration procedure has been finished, we can now perform camera pose estimation.

The `aruco_camera_calibration.py` script carries out the calibration procedure. Note that this script can be used to both create the board and perform the calibration procedure, by making use of the previously created and printed board.

Camera pose estimation

In order to estimate camera pose, the `cv2.aruco.estimatePoseSingleMarkers()` function can be used, which estimates the pose for single markers. The pose is composed of a rotation and a translation vector. The signature is as follows:

```
cv.aruco.estimatePoseSingleMarkers( corners, markerLength, cameraMatrix,
distCoeffs[, rvecs[, tvecs[, _objPoints]]] ) ->  rvecs, tvecs, _objPoints
```

Here, `cameraMatrix` and `distCoeffs` are the camera matrix and the distortion coefficients, respectively; they should be provided with the values obtained after the calibration process. The `corners` parameter is a vector containing the four corners of each detected marker. The `markerLength` parameter is the length of the marker side. Note that the returning translation vector will be in the same unit. This function returns `rvecs` (rotation vector), `tvecs` (translation vector) for each detected markers, and `_objPoints` (an array of object points of all of the detected marker corners).

The marker coordinate system is centered on the middle of the marker. Therefore, the coordinates of the four corners of the marker (in its own coordinate system) are the following:

- `(-markerLength/2, markerLength/2, 0)`
- `(markerLength/2, markerLength/2, 0)`
- `(markerLength/2, -markerLength/2, 0)`
- `(-markerLength/2, -markerLength/2, 0)`

Finally, ArUco also provides the `cv.aruco.drawAxis()` function, which can be used to draw the system axis for each detected marker.

The signature is as follows:

```
cv.aruco.drawAxis( image, cameraMatrix, distCoeffs, rvec, tvec, length ) ->
image
```

All parameters have been previously introduced in the previous functions, except the `length` parameter, which sets the length of the drawn axis (in the same unit as `tvec`). The output of the script `aruco_detect_markers_pose.py` can be seen in the next screenshot:

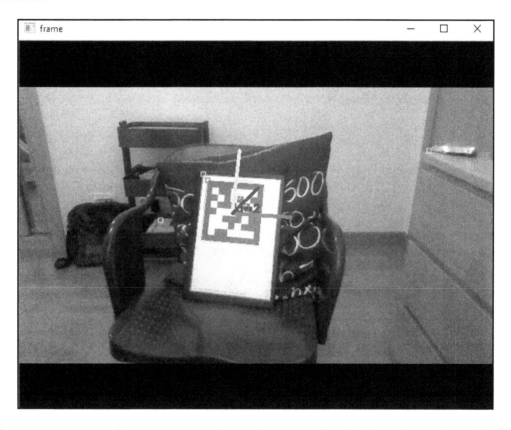

In the previous screenshot you can see that only one marker has been detected and also the system axis for this marker has been drawn.

Camera pose estimation and basic augmentation

At this point, we can overlay some images, shapes, or 3D models in order to see a complete augmented reality application. In this first example, we are going to overlay a rectangle with the size of the marker. The code to perform this functionality is the following:

```
if ids is not None:
    # rvecs and tvecs are the rotation and translation vectors respectively
    rvecs, tvecs, _ = cv2.aruco.estimatePoseSingleMarkers(corners, 1,
```

```
cameraMatrix, distCoeffs)

    for rvec, tvec in zip(rvecs, tvecs):
        # Define the points where you want the image to be overlaid
(remember: marker coordinate system):
        desired_points = np.float32(
            [[-1 / 2, 1 / 2, 0], [1 / 2, 1 / 2, 0], [1 / 2, -1 / 2, 0], [-1
/ 2, -1 / 2, 0]])

        # Project the points:
        projected_desired_points, jac = cv2.projectPoints(desired_points,
rvecs, tvecs, cameraMatrix, distCoeffs)

        # Draw the projected points:
        draw_points(frame, projected_desired_points)
```

The first step is to define the points where we want to overlay the image or model. As we want to overlay the rectangle over the detected markers, these coordinates are `[[-1 / 2, 1 / 2, 0], [1 / 2, 1 / 2, 0], [1 / 2, -1 / 2, 0], [-1 / 2, -1 / 2, 0]]`.

Remember, we must define these coordinates in the marker coordinate system. The next step is to project these points using the `cv2.projectPoints()` function:

```
projected_desired_points, jac = cv2.projectPoints(desired_points, rvecs,
tvecs, cameraMatrix, distCoeffs)
```

And finally, we draw these points using the `draw_points()` function:

```
def draw_points(img, pts):
    """ Draw the points in the image"""

    pts = np.int32(pts).reshape(-1, 2)
    img = cv2.drawContours(img, [pts], -1, (255, 255, 0), -3)
    for p in pts:
        cv2.circle(img, (p[0], p[1]), 5, (255, 0, 255), -1)

    return img
```

The output of the `aruco_detect_markers_draw_square.py` script can be seen in the next screenshot:

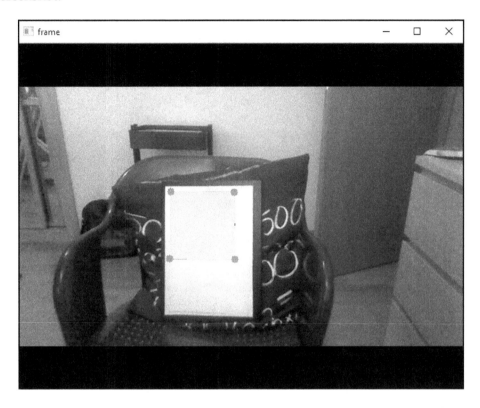

In the preceding screenshot, you can see that a cyan rectangle has been overlaid over the detected marker. Also, you can see the four corners of the rectangle, which are drawn in magenta.

Camera pose estimation and more advanced augmentation

The `aruco_detect_markers_draw_square.py` script can be easily modified in order to overlay a more advanced augmentation.

In this case, we are going to overlay the image of a tree, which can be seen in the next screenshot:

To perform this augmentation, we have coded the draw_augmented_overlay() function, as shown in the following:

```
def draw_augmented_overlay(pts_1, overlay_image, image):
    """Overlay the image 'overlay_image' onto the image 'image'"""

    # Define the squares of the overlay_image image to be drawn:
    pts_2 = np.float32([[0, 0], [overlay_image.shape[1], 0],
[overlay_image.shape[1], overlay_image.shape[0]], [0,
overlay_image.shape[0]]])

    # Draw border to see the limits of the image:
    cv2.rectangle(overlay_image, (0, 0), (overlay_image.shape[1],
overlay_image.shape[0]), (255, 255, 0), 10)

    # Create the transformation matrix:
    M = cv2.getPerspectiveTransform(pts_2, pts_1)

    # Transform the overlay_image image using the transformation matrix M:
    dst_image = cv2.warpPerspective(overlay_image, M, (image.shape[1],
image.shape[0]))
    # cv2.imshow("dst_image", dst_image)

    # Create the mask:
```

```
    dst_image_gray = cv2.cvtColor(dst_image, cv2.COLOR_BGR2GRAY)
    ret, mask = cv2.threshold(dst_image_gray, 0, 255,
cv2.THRESH_BINARY_INV)

    # Compute bitwise conjunction using the calculated mask:
    image_masked = cv2.bitwise_and(image, image, mask=mask)
    # cv2.imshow("image_masked", image_masked)

    # Add the two images to create the resulting image:
    result = cv2.add(dst_image, image_masked)
    return result
```

The `draw_augmented_overlay()` function first defines the squares of the overlay image. Then, the transformation matrix is calculated, which is used to transform the overlay image obtaining the `dst_image` image. Next, we create the `mask` and compute the bitwise operation using the previously created `mask` to obtain the `image_masked` image. The final step is to perform the addition between `dst_image` and `image_masked` in order to obtain the `result` image, which is finally returned.

The output of the `aruco_detect_markers_augmented_reality.py` script can be seen in the next screenshot:

To overlay more complex and advanced 3D models, OpenGL can be used. **Open Graphics Library (OpenGL)** is a cross-platform API for rendering 2D and 3D models.

In this sense, PyOpenGL (http://pyopengl.sourceforge.net/) is the most common and standard cross-platform Python binding to OpenGL.

Snapchat-based augmented reality

In this section, we are going to see how to create some funny Snapchat-based filters. In this case, we are going to create two filters. The first one overlays a big moustache between the nose and mouth on the detected face. The second one overlays a pair of glasses on the detected face.

In the following subsections, you will see how to achieve this functionality.

Snapchat-based augmented reality OpenCV moustache overlay

In the `snapchat_augmeted_reality_moustache.py` script, we overlay a moustache on the detected face. Images are continuously captured from the webcam. We have also included the possibility to use a test image instead of the images captured from the webcam. This can be useful in order to debug the algorithm. Before explaining the key steps of this script, we are going to see the next screenshot, which is the output of the algorithm when the test image is used:

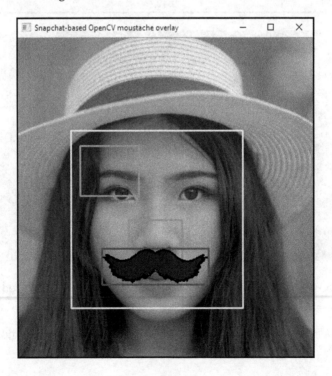

The first step is to detect all of the faces in the image. As you can see, the cyan rectangle indicates the position and size of the detected face in the image. The next step of the algorithm is to iterate over all detected faces in the image, searching for noses inside its region. The magenta rectangles indicate the detected noses in the image. Once we have detected the nose, the next step is to adjust the region where we want to overlay the moustache, which is calculated based on both the position and size of the nose previously calculated. In this case, the blue rectangle indicates the position where the moustache will be overlaid. You can also see there are two detected noses in the image, and there is only one moustache overlaid. This is because a basic check is performed in order to know whether the detected nose is valid. Once we have detected a valid nose, the moustache is overlaid, and we continue iterating over the detected faces if left, or another frame will be analyzed.

Therefore, in this script, both faces and noses are detected. To detect these objects, two classifiers are created, one for detecting faces, and the other one for detecting noses. To create these classifiers, the following code is necessary:

```
face_cascade = cv2.CascadeClassifier("haarcascade_frontalface_default.xml")
nose_cascade = cv2.CascadeClassifier("haarcascade_mcs_nose.xml")
```

Once the classifiers have been created, the next step is to detect these objects in the image. In this case, the cv2.detectMultiScale() function is used. This function detects objects of different sizes in the input grayscale image and returns the detected objects as a list of rectangles. For example, in order to detect faces, the following code can be used:

```
faces = face_cascade.detectMultiScale(gray, 1.3, 5)
```

At this point, we iterate over the detected faces, trying to detect noses:

```
# Iterate over each detected face:
for (x, y, w, h) in faces:
    # Draw a rectangle to see the detected face (debugging purposes):
    # cv2.rectangle(frame, (x, y), (x + w, y + h), (255, 255, 0), 2)

    # Create the ROIS based on the size of the detected face:
    roi_gray = gray[y:y + h, x:x + w]
    roi_color = frame[y:y + h, x:x + w]

    # Detects a nose inside the detected face:
    noses = nose_cascade.detectMultiScale(roi_gray)
```

Once the noses are detected, we iterate over all detected noses, and calculate the region where the moustache will be overlaid. A basic check is performed in order to filter out false nose positions. In case of success, the moustache will be overlaid over the image based on the previously calculated region:

```python
for (nx, ny, nw, nh) in noses:
    # Draw a rectangle to see the detected nose (debugging purposes):
    # cv2.rectangle(roi_color, (nx, ny), (nx + nw, ny + nh), (255, 0, 255), 2)

    # Calculate the coordinates where the moustache will be placed:
    x1 = int(nx - nw / 2)
    x2 = int(nx + nw / 2 + nw)
    y1 = int(ny + nh / 2 + nh / 8)
    y2 = int(ny + nh + nh / 4 + nh / 6)

    if x1 < 0 or x2 < 0 or x2 > w or y2 > h:
        continue

    # Draw a rectangle to see where the moustache will be placed (debugging purposes):
    # cv2.rectangle(roi_color, (x1, y1), (x2, y2), (255, 0, 0), 2)

    # Calculate the width and height of the image with the moustache:
    img_moustache_res_width = int(x2 - x1)
    img_moustache_res_height = int(y2 - y1)

    # Resize the mask to be equal to the region were the glasses will be placed:
    mask = cv2.resize(img_moustache_mask, (img_moustache_res_width, img_moustache_res_height))
    mask_inv = cv2.bitwise_not(mask)
    img = cv2.resize(img_moustache, (img_moustache_res_width, img_moustache_res_height))

    # Take ROI from the BGR image:
    roi = roi_color[y1:y2, x1:x2]

    # Create ROI background and ROI foreground:
    roi_bakground = cv2.bitwise_and(roi, roi, mask=mask_inv)
    roi_foreground = cv2.bitwise_and(img, img, mask=mask)

    # Show both roi_bakground and roi_foreground (debugging purposes):
    # cv2.imshow('roi_bakground', roi_bakground)
    # cv2.imshow('roi_foreground', roi_foreground)

    # Add roi_bakground and roi_foreground to create the result:
    res = cv2.add(roi_bakground, roi_foreground)
```

```
# Set res into the color ROI:
roi_color[y1:y2, x1:x2] = res

break
```

A key point is the `img_moustache_mask` image. This image is created using the alpha channel of the image to overlay.

This way, only the foreground of the overlaid image will be drawn in the image. In the following screenshot, you can see the created moustache mask based on the alpha channel of the overlay image:

To create this mask, we perform the following:

```
img_moustache = cv2.imread('moustache.png', -1)
img_moustache_mask = img_moustache[:, :, 3]
```

The output of the `snapchat_augmeted_reality_moustache.py` script can be seen in the next screenshot:

All the moustaches included in the following screenshot can be used in your augmented reality applications:

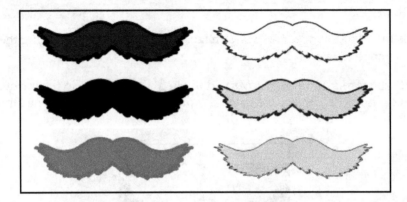

Indeed, we have also created the `moustaches.svg` file, where these six different moustaches have been included.

Snapchat-based augmented reality OpenCV glasses overlay

In a similar fashion, we have also coded the `snapchat_agumeted_reality_glasses.py` script to overlay a pair of glasses on the eyes region of the detected face. In this case, in order to detect the eyes in the image, the eye-pair detector is used.

Therefore, the classifier should be created accordingly:

```
eyepair_cascade = cv2.CascadeClassifier("haarcascade_mcs_eyepair_big.xml")
```

In the next screenshot, you can see the output of the algorithm when the test image is used:

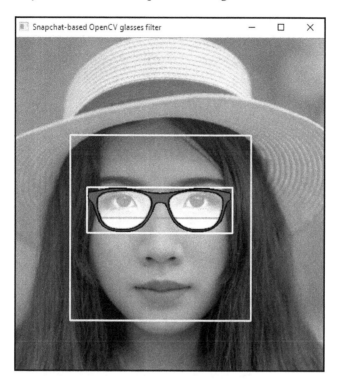

The cyan rectangle indicates the position and size of the detected face in the image. The magenta rectangles indicate the detected eye-pair in the image. The yellow rectangle indicates the position where the glasses will be overlaid, which is calculated based on both the position and size of the eye-pair region. As you can see, some transparency has been added to the glasses overlaid image in order to make them more realistic.

This can also be seen in the glasses image mask, which is shown in the next screenshot:

The output of the `snapchat_augmeted_reality_glasses.py` script can be seen in the next screenshot:

All of these glasses can be seen in the following screenshot:

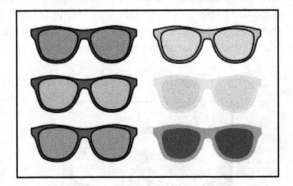

Finally, we have also created the `glasses.svg` file, where six different glasses have been included. Therefore, you can play and use all of these glasses in your augmented reality applications.

QR code detection

To complete this chapter, we are going to learn how to detect QR codes in images. This way, QR codes can also be used as markers for our augmented reality applications. The `cv2.detectAndDecode()` function both detects and decodes a QR code in the image containing the QR code. The image can be grayscale or color (BGR).

This function returns the following:

- An array of vertices of the found QR code is returned. This array can be empty if the QR code is not found.
- The rectified and binarized QR code is returned.
- The data associated with this QR code is returned.

In the `qr_code_scanner.py` script, we make use of the aforementioned function to detect and decode QR codes. The key points are commented next.

First, the image is loaded, as follows:

```
image = cv2.imread("qrcode_rotate_45_image.png")
```

Next, we create the QR code detector with the following code:

```
qr_code_detector = cv2.QRCodeDetector()
```

Then, we apply the `cv2.detectAndDecode()` function, as follows:

```
data, bbox, rectified_qr_code = qr_code_detector.detectAndDecode(image)
```

We check whether the QR code is found before decoding the data and show the detection by using the `show_qr_detection()` function:

```
if len(data) > 0:

    print("Decoded Data : {}".format(data))
    show_qr_detection(image, bbox)
```

The `show_qr_detection()` function draws both the lines and the corners of the detected QR code:

```
def show_qr_detection(img, pts):
    """Draws both the lines and corners based on the array of vertices of
the found QR code"""

    pts = np.int32(pts).reshape(-1, 2)
```

```
    for j in range(pts.shape[0]):
        cv2.line(img, tuple(pts[j]), tuple(pts[(j + 1) % pts.shape[0]]),
(255, 0, 0), 5)

    for j in range(pts.shape[0]):
        cv2.circle(img, tuple(pts[j]), 10, (255, 0, 255), -1)
```

The output of the `qr_code_scanner.py` script can be seen in the next screenshot:

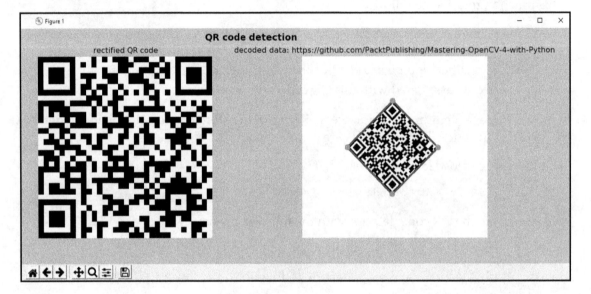

In the preceding screenshot, you can see the rectified and binarized QR code (left), and the detected marker (right), with a blue border, and magenta square points highlighting the detection.

Summary

In this chapter, we looked at an introduction to augmented reality. We coded several examples to see how to build both marker and markerless augmented reality applications. Additionally, we saw how to overlay simple models (shapes or images, among others).

As commented previously, to overlay more complex models, PyOpenGL (standard OpenGL bindings for Python) can be used. In this chapter, for the sake of simplification, this library is not tackled.

We have also seen how to create some funny Snapchat-based filters. It should be noted that in Chapter 11, *Face Detection, Tracking, and Recognition*, more advanced algorithms for both face detection, tracking, and location of facial landmarks will be covered. Therefore, Snapchat-based filters coded in this chapter can be easily modified to include a more robust pipeline to derive the position where both the glasses and the moustache should be overlaid. Finally, we have seen how to detect QR codes, which can be used as markers in your augmented reality applications.

In Chapter 10, *Machine Learning with OpenCV*, you will be introduced to the world of machine learning, and you will see how machine learning can be used in your computer vision projects.

Questions

1. Initialize the ORB detector, find keypoints, and compute descriptors in the loaded image image with ORB
2. Draw the previously detected keypoints
3. Create the BFMatcher object and match the descriptors_1 and descriptors_2, which have been previously calculated
4. Sort the matches calculated before and draw the first 20 matches
5. Detect markers using ArUco in the gray_frame image
6. Draw detected markers using ArUco
7. Draw rejected markers using ArUco
8. Detect and decode a QR code contained in the image image

Further reading

The following reference will help you dive deeper into augmented reality:

* *Augmented Reality for Developers (2017)* (https://www.packtpub.com/web-development/augmented-reality-developers)

Section 3: Machine Learning and Deep Learning in OpenCV

In this third section of the book, you'll get a taste of machine learning and deep learning. We will explore and make use of OpenCV's machine learning module. Additionally, you will learn how to create face processing projects using state-of-the-art algorithms in connection with face detection, tracking, and recognition. Finally, you will be introduced to the world of deep learning with OpenCV and also with some deep learning Python libraries (TensorFlow and Keras).

The following chapters will be covered in this section:

- Chapter 10, *Machine Learning with OpenCV*
- Chapter 11, *Face Detection, Tracking, and Recognition*
- Chapter 12, *Introduction to Deep Learning*

Machine Learning with OpenCV

10

Machine learning is an application of artificial intelligence that provides computers (and other systems with the certain capability of computation) with the capability to automatically make predictions or decisions from experience without being explicitly programmed to carry out the task. The concept of machine learning has been around for a long time, but it has been gaining momentum over the last several years mainly due to three key factors:

- There is enormously increased data.
- There are significantly improved algorithms.
- There is substantially more powerful computer hardware. Virtual personal assistants (for example, smart speakers or mobile apps), predictions while commuting (traffic predictions or navigation services), video systems (surveillance camera systems or license plate recognition systems), and e-commerce applications (recommendation systems or automatic price-comparison applications) are only a few examples of machine learning applications in our day-to-day life.

In this chapter, we are going to see some of the most common machine learning algorithms and techniques OpenCV provides to solve real-world problems, such as classification and regression problems, in your computer vision projects.

We will cover the following topics:

- An introduction to machine learning
- k-means clustering
- k-nearest neighbor
- Support vector machine

Technical requirements

The technical requirements are listed as follows:

- Python and OpenCV
- A Python-specific IDE
- The NumPy and Matplotlib packages
- The Git client

Further details about how to install these requirements are mentioned in `Chapter 1`, *Setting Up OpenCV*. The GitHub repository for *Mastering OpenCV 4 with Python*, which contains all the supporting project files necessary to work through this book from the first chapter to the last, can be accessed at `https://github.com/PacktPublishing/Mastering-OpenCV-4-with-Python`.

An introduction to machine learning

In `Chapter 1`, *Setting Up OpenCV*, we introduced the concepts of computer vision, artificial intelligence, machine learning, neural networks, and deep learning, which can be structured in a hierarchical way, as shown here:

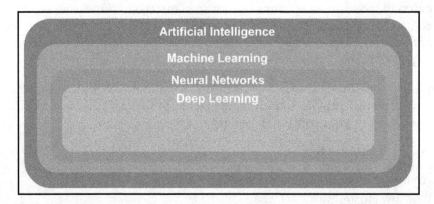

As can be seen, the **Artificial Intelligence** topic includes all of the other topics. In this chapter, we are going to focus on **Machine Learning**.

See `Chapter 1`, *Setting Up OpenCV*, if you want a refresher on these concepts.

Machine Learning is the process of programming computers to learn from historical data to make predictions on new data. **Machine Learning** is a sub-discipline of artificial intelligence and refers to statistical techniques, by which machines perform on the basis of learned interrelationships. On the basis of gathered or collected data, algorithms are independently *learned* by computers.

In the context of **Machine Learning**, there are three main approaches—**Supervised Machine Learning**, **Unsupervised Machine Learning**, and **Semi-Supervised Machine Learning** techniques. These approaches can be seen in the next diagram. To complete it, we have included the three most common techniques to solve **Classification**, **Regression**, and **Clustering** problems:

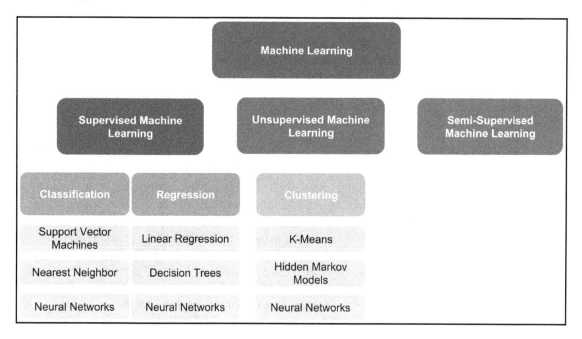

The main difference between these approaches is the learning procedure, which we'll discuss next.

Supervised machine learning

Supervised learning is performed using a collection of samples with the corresponding output values (desired output) for each sample. These machine learning methods are called **supervised** because we know the correct answer for each training example and the supervised learning algorithm analyzes the training data in order to make predictions on the training data. Besides, these predictions can be corrected based on the difference between the prediction and the corresponding desired output. Based on these corrections, the algorithm can learn from the mistakes to adjust its internal parameters. This way, in supervised learning, the algorithm iteratively adjusts a function, which best approximates the relationship between the collection of samples and the corresponding desired output.

Supervised learning problems can be further grouped into the following categories:

- **Classification:** When the output variable is a category, such as color (red, green, or blue), size (large, medium, or small), or gender (male or female), the problem can be considered as a classification problem. In a classification problem, the algorithm maps the input to output labels.
- **Regression**: When the output variable is a real value, such as age or weight, the supervised learning problem can be classified as a regression problem. In a regression problem, the algorithm maps the input to a continuous output.

In supervised learning, there are some major issues to take into account and for the sake of completeness are commented next:

- **Bias-variance trade-off**: Bias-variance trade-off is a common term in machine learning, which refers to the model—a model that underfits the data has a high bias, whereas a model that overfits the data has a high variance:
  - The **bias** can be seen as the error that occurs from erroneous assumptions in the learning algorithm and can be defined as the difference between the prediction of our model and the correct value we are trying to predict. This leads the algorithm to learn the wrong thing by not taking into account all of the information in the data (underfitting). Therefore, a model with a high bias failed to find all of the patterns in the data, so it does not fit the training set well and it will not fit the test set well either.

- The **variance** can be defined as the algorithm's tendency to learn the wrong things, irrespective of the real signal, by fitting models that follow the error/noise in the data too closely (overfitting). Therefore, a model with a high variance fits the training set very well, but it fails to generalize to the test set because it has also learned the error/noise in the data. Check out the following diagram for a better understanding:

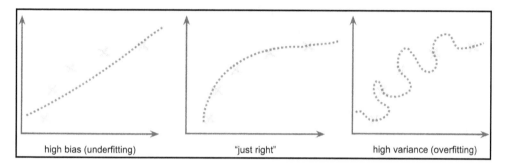

- **Function complexity and the amount of training data**: **Model complexity** refers to the complexity of the function the machine learning algorithm is attempting to learn in a similar fashion as the degree of a polynomial. The proper level of model complexity is generally determined by the nature of the training data. For example, if you have a small amount of data to train the model, a low-complexity model is preferable. This is because a high-complexity model will overfit the small training set.
- **Dimensionality of the input space**: When dealing with high-/very high-dimensional feature spaces, the learning problem can be very difficult because the many *extra* features can confuse the learning process, which results in a high variance. Therefore, when dealing with high-/very high-dimensional feature spaces, a common approach is to modify the learning algorithm to have a high bias and low variance. This problem is related to the **curse of dimensionality**, which refers to various aspects that arise when analyzing and organizing data in high-dimensional spaces that aren't found in low-dimensional spaces.
- **Noise in the output values**: If the desired output values are incorrect (due to human or sensor errors), overfitting can occur if the learning algorithm attempts to fit the data too closely. There are several common strategies that can be used to alleviate the effect of error/noise in the output values. For example, detecting and removing the noisy training examples before training the algorithm is a common approach. Another strategy is early stopping, which can be used to prevent overfitting.

Unsupervised machine learning

In unsupervised learning, there is no labeled output. In this sense, there is a collection of samples, but the corresponding output values for each sample are missing (the collection of samples has not been labeled, classified, or categorized). The goal of unsupervised learning is to model and infer the underlying structure or distribution in the collection of samples. Therefore, in unsupervised learning, the algorithm does not find out the right output, but it explores the data and can make inferences from the data trying to reveal hidden structures in it. Clustering, or dimensionality reduction, are two of the most common algorithms used in unsupervised learning.

Semi-supervised machine learning

As the name suggests, semi-supervised learning can be seen as a compromise between supervised and unsupervised learning because it uses both labeled and unlabeled data for training. In this sense, problems where you have a large amount of input data, and only some of the data is labeled, can be classified as semi-supervised learning problems.

Many real-world machine learning problems can be classified as semi-supervised because it can be very difficult, expensive, or time-consuming to label all of the data properly, whereas unlabeled data is easier to collect.

In these situations, only a small amount of the training data is labeled and you can explore both supervised and unsupervised learning techniques:

- You can use unsupervised learning techniques to discover and learn the structure in the input variables.
- You can use supervised learning techniques to train a classifier using the labeled data and, afterward, use this model to make predictions for the unlabeled data. At this point, you can feed that data back into the supervised learning algorithm as training data to iteratively increase the size of the labeled data and use the retrained model to make predictions on new unlabeled data.

k-means clustering

OpenCV provides the `cv2.kmeans()` function, which implements a k-means clustering algorithm, which finds centers of clusters and groups input samples around the clusters.

The objective of the k-means clustering algorithm is to partition (or cluster) *n* samples into `K` clusters where each sample will belong to the cluster with the nearest mean. The signature of the `cv2.kmeans()` function is as follows:

```
retval, bestLabels, centers=cv.kmeans(data, K, bestLabels, criteria,
attempts, flags[, centers])
```

`data` represents the input data for clustering. It should be of `np.float32` data type, and each feature should be placed in a single column. `K` specifies the number of clusters required at the end. The algorithm-termination criteria are specified with the `criteria` parameter, which sets the maximum number of iterations and/or the desired accuracy. When these criteria are satisfied, the algorithm terminates. `criteria` is a tuple of three parameters, `type`, `max_iterm`, and `epsilon`:

- `type`: This is the type of termination criteria. It has three flags:
    - `cv2.TERM_CRITERIA_EPS`: The algorithm stops when the specified accuracy, `epsilon`, is reached.
    - `cv2.TERM_CRITERIA_MAX_ITER`: The algorithm stops when the specified number of iterations, `max_iterm`, is reached.
    - `cv2.TERM_CRITERIA_EPS + cv2.TERM_CRITERIA_MAX_ITER`: The algorithm stops when any of the two conditions is reached.
- `max_iterm`: This is the maximum number of iterations.
- `epsilon`: This is the required accuracy.

An example of criteria can be the following:

```
criteria = (cv2.TERM_CRITERIA_EPS + cv2.TERM_CRITERIA_MAX_ITER, 20, 1.0)
```

In this case, the maximum number of iterations is set to `20` (`max_iterm = 20`) and the desired accuracy is `1.0` (`epsilon = 1.0`).

The `attempts` parameter specifies the number of times the algorithm is executed using different initial labelings. The algorithm returns the labels that yield the best compactness. The `flags` parameter specifies how initial centers are taken. The `cv2.KMEANS_RANDOM_CENTERS` flag selects random initial centers in each attempt. The `cv2.KMEANS_PP_CENTERS` flag uses the k-means++ center initialization proposed by Arthur and Vassilvitskii (see *k-means++: The Advantages of Careful Seeding* (2007)).

`cv2.kmeans()` returns the following:

- `bestLabels`: An integer array that stores the cluster indices for each sample
- `centers`: An array that contains the center for each cluster
- `compactness`: The sum of the squared distance from each point to their corresponding centers

In this section, we will see two examples of how to use the k-means clustering algorithm in OpenCV.

In the first example, an intuitive understanding of k-means clustering is expected to be achieved while, in the second example, k-means clustering will be applied to the problem of color quantization.

Understanding k-means clustering

In this example, we are going to cluster a set of 2D points using the k-means clustering algorithm. This set of 2D points can be seen as a collection of objects, which has been described using two features. This set of 2D points can be created and visualized with the `k_means_clustering_data_visualization.py` script.

The output of this script can be seen in the next screenshot:

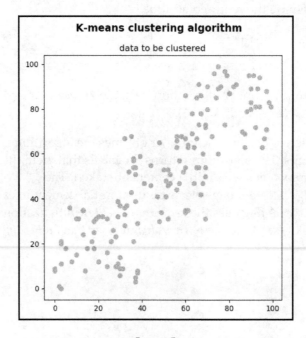

This set of 2D points consists of `150` points, created in this way:

```
data = np.float32(np.vstack(
    (np.random.randint(0, 40, (50, 2)), np.random.randint(30, 70, (50, 2)),
np.random.randint(60, 100, (50, 2)))))
```

This will represent the data for clustering. As previously mentioned, it should be of `np.float32` type and each feature should be placed in a single column.

In this case, there are two features corresponding to the *(x, y)* coordinates for each point. These coordinates can represent, for example, the height and weight for each of the `150` people, or the number of bedrooms and size for each of the `150` houses. In the first case, the k-means clustering algorithm will *decide* the size of the T-shirt (for example, small, medium, or large if `K=3`), while in the second case, the k-means clustering algorithm will *decide* the price of the house (for example, cheap, average, expensive, or very expensive if `K = 4`). In summary, `data` will be the input for our clustering algorithm.

In the next scripts, we will see how it can be clustered using different values of `K` and its corresponding visualization. To do so, we have coded three scripts:

- `k_means_clustering_k_2.py`: In this script, `data` has been clustered into two groups (`K = 2`).
- `k_means_clustering_k_3.py`: In this script, `data` has been clustered into three groups (`K = 3`).
- `k_means_clustering_k_4.py`: In this script, `data` has been clustered into four groups (`K = 4`).

In the `k_means_clustering_k_2.py` script, data has been clustered into 2 clusters. The first step is to define the algorithm-termination criteria. In this case, the maximum number of iterations is set to `20` (`max_iterm = 20`) and epsilon is set to `1.0` (`epsilon = 1.0`):

```
criteria = (cv2.TERM_CRITERIA_EPS + cv2.TERM_CRITERIA_MAX_ITER, 20, 1.0)
```

The next step is to apply the k-means algorithm using the `cv2.kmeans()` function:

```
ret, label, center = cv2.kmeans(data, 2, None, criteria, 10,
cv2.KMEANS_RANDOM_CENTERS)
```

At this point, we can separate the data using the `label` output, which stores the cluster indices for each sample. Therefore, we can split the data into different clusters depending on their labels:

```
A = data[label.ravel() == 0]
B = data[label.ravel() == 1]
```

The final step is to plot both A and B as well as the original data without being clustered for a better understanding of the clustering procedure:

```
# Create the dimensions of the figure and set title:
fig = plt.figure(figsize=(12, 6))
plt.suptitle("K-means clustering algorithm", fontsize=14,
fontweight='bold')
fig.patch.set_facecolor('silver')

# Plot the 'original' data:
ax = plt.subplot(1, 2, 1)
plt.scatter(data[:, 0], data[:, 1], c='c')
plt.title("data")

# Plot the 'clustered' data and the centroids
ax = plt.subplot(1, 2, 2)
plt.scatter(A[:, 0], A[:, 1], c='b')
plt.scatter(B[:, 0], B[:, 1], c='g')
plt.scatter(center[:, 0], center[:, 1], s=100, c='m', marker='s')
plt.title("clustered data and centroids (K = 2)")

# Show the Figure:
plt.show()
```

The output of this script can be seen in the next screenshot:

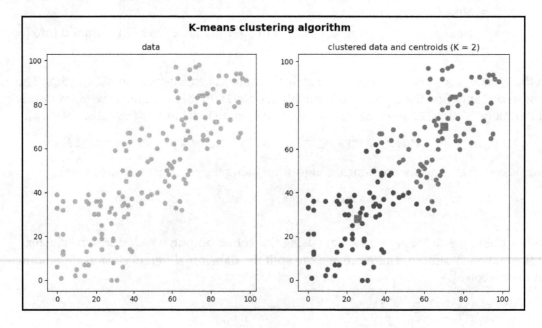

You can see that we have also plotted `center`, which is an array that contains the center for each cluster.

In the `k_means_clustering_k_3.py` script, the same procedure is applied to cluster the data, but we have decided to group the data into 3 clusters (`K` = 3). Therefore, when calling the `cv2.kmeans()` function, the `K` parameter is set to 3:

```
ret, label, center = cv2.kmeans(data, 3, None, criteria, 10,
cv2.KMEANS_RANDOM_CENTERS)
```

Additionally, when separating data using the `label` output, three groups are obtained:

```
A = data[label.ravel() == 0]
B = data[label.ravel() == 1]
C = data[label.ravel() == 2]
```

The final step is to show `A`, `B`, and `C`, as well as the centroids and the original data:

```
# Create the dimensions of the figure and set title:
fig = plt.figure(figsize=(12, 6))
plt.suptitle("K-means clustering algorithm", fontsize=14,
fontweight='bold')
fig.patch.set_facecolor('silver')

# Plot the 'original' data:
ax = plt.subplot(1, 2, 1)
plt.scatter(data[:, 0], data[:, 1], c='c')
plt.title("data")

# Plot the 'clustered' data and the centroids
ax = plt.subplot(1, 2, 2)
plt.scatter(A[:, 0], A[:, 1], c='b')
plt.scatter(B[:, 0], B[:, 1], c='g')
plt.scatter(C[:, 0], C[:, 1], c='r')
plt.scatter(center[:, 0], center[:, 1], s=100, c='m', marker='s')
plt.title("clustered data and centroids (K = 3)")

# Show the Figure:
plt.show()
```

In the previous snippet, we plot both the original data and the 'clustered' data and the centroids in the same figure. The output of this script can be seen in the next screenshot:

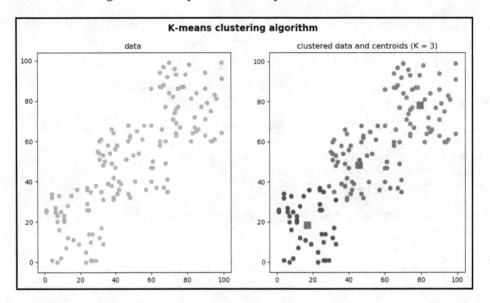

For the sake of completeness, we have also coded the `k_means_clustering_k_4.py` script, whose output can be seen in the next screenshot:

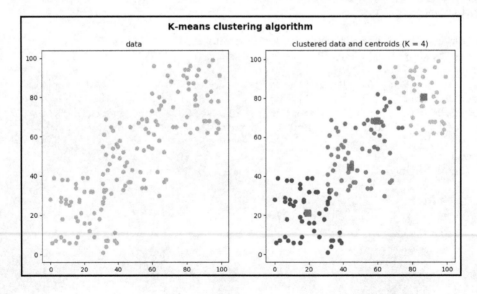

As can be seen, the number of clusters is set to 4 (K = 4).

Color quantization using k-means clustering

In this subsection, we will apply the k-means clustering algorithm to the problem of color quantization, which can be defined as the process of reducing the number of colors in an image. Color quantization is a critical point for displaying images on certain devices that can only display a limited number of colors (commonly due to memory restrictions). Therefore, a trade-off between the similarity and the reduction in the number of colors is usually necessary. This trade-off is established by setting the K parameter properly, as we will see in the next examples.

In the k_means_color_quantization.py script, we perform the k-means clustering algorithm to perform color quantization. In this case, each element of the data is composed of 3 features, which correspond to the B, G, and R values for each of the pixels of the image. Therefore, the key step is to transform the image into data this way:

```
data = np.float32(image).reshape((-1, 3))
```

Here, image is the image we previously loaded.

In this script, we performed the clustering procedure using several values of K (3, 5, 10, 20, and 40) in order to see how the resulting image changes. For example, if we want the resulting image with only 3 colors (K = 3), we must perform the following:

1. Load the BGR image:

```
img = cv2.imread('landscape_1.jpg')
```

2. Perform color quantization using the color_quantization() function:

```
color_3 = color_quantization(img, 3)
```

3. Show both images in order to see the results.
   The color_quantization() function performs the color quantization procedure:

```
def color_quantization(image, k):
    """Performs color quantization using K-means clustering
algorithm"""

    # Transform image into 'data':
    data = np.float32(image).reshape((-1, 3))
    # print(data.shape)
```

```
    # Define the algorithm termination criteria (maximum number of
iterations and/or required accuracy):
    # In this case the maximum number of iterations is set to 20 and
epsilon = 1.0
    criteria = (cv2.TERM_CRITERIA_EPS + cv2.TERM_CRITERIA_MAX_ITER, 20,
1.0)

    # Apply K-means clustering algorithm:
    ret, label, center = cv2.kmeans(data, k, None, criteria, 10,
cv2.KMEANS_RANDOM_CENTERS)

    # At this point we can make the image with k colors
    # Convert center to uint8:
    center = np.uint8(center)
    # Replace pixel values with their center value:
    result = center[label.flatten()]
    result = result.reshape(img.shape)
    return result
```

In the previous function, the key point is to make use of `cv2.kmeans()` method. Finally, we can build the image with k colors replacing each pixel value with their corresponding center value. The output of this script can be seen in the next screenshot:

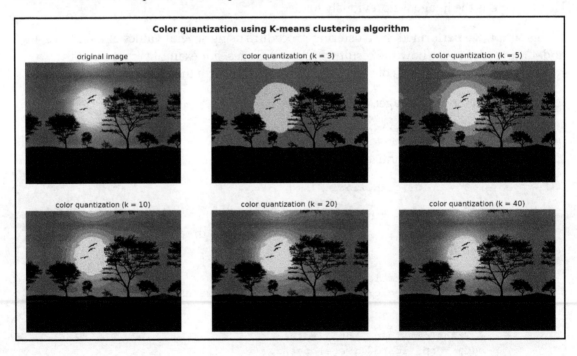

The previous script can be extended to include an interesting functionality, which shows the number of pixels assigned to each center value. This can be seen in the `k_means_color_quantization_distribution.py` script.

The `color_quantization()` function has been modified to include this functionality:

```
def color_quantization(image, k):
    """Performs color quantization using K-means clustering algorithm"""

    # Transform image into 'data':
    data = np.float32(image).reshape((-1, 3))
    # print(data.shape)

    # Define the algorithm termination criteria (the maximum number of
iterations and/or the desired accuracy):
    # In this case the maximum number of iterations is set to 20 and
epsilon = 1.0
    criteria = (cv2.TERM_CRITERIA_EPS + cv2.TERM_CRITERIA_MAX_ITER, 20,
1.0)

    # Apply K-means clustering algorithm:
    ret, label, center = cv2.kmeans(data, k, None, criteria, 10,
cv2.KMEANS_RANDOM_CENTERS)

    # At this point we can make the image with k colors
    # Convert center to uint8:
    center = np.uint8(center)
    # Replace pixel values with their center value:
    result = center[label.flatten()]
    result = result.reshape(img.shape)

    # Build the 'color_distribution' legend.
    # We will use the number of pixels assigned to each center value:
    counter = collections.Counter(label.flatten())
    print(counter)

    # Calculate the total number of pixels of the input image:
    total = img.shape[0] * img.shape[1]

    # Assign width and height to the color_distribution image:
    desired_width = img.shape[1]
    # The difference between 'desired_height' and 'desired_height_colors'
    # will be the separation between the images
    desired_height = 70
    desired_height_colors = 50

    # Initialize the color_distribution image:
    color_distribution = np.ones((desired_height, desired_width, 3),
```

```
dtype="uint8") * 255
    # Initialize start:
    start = 0

    for key, value in counter.items():
        # Calculate the normalized value:
        value_normalized = value / total * desired_width

        # Move end to the right position:
        end = start + value_normalized

        # Draw rectangle corresponding to the current color:
        cv2.rectangle(color_distribution, (int(start), 0), (int(end),
desired_height_colors), center[key].tolist(), -1)
        # Update start:
        start = end

    return np.vstack((color_distribution, result))
```

As you can see, we make use of `collections.Counter()` to count the number of pixels assigned to each center value:

```
counter = collections.Counter(label.flatten())
```

For example, if K = 3—Counter({0: 175300, 2: 114788, 1: 109912}). Once the color-distribution image has been built, the final step is to concatenate both images:

```
np.vstack((color_distribution, result))
```

The output of this script can be seen in the next screenshot:

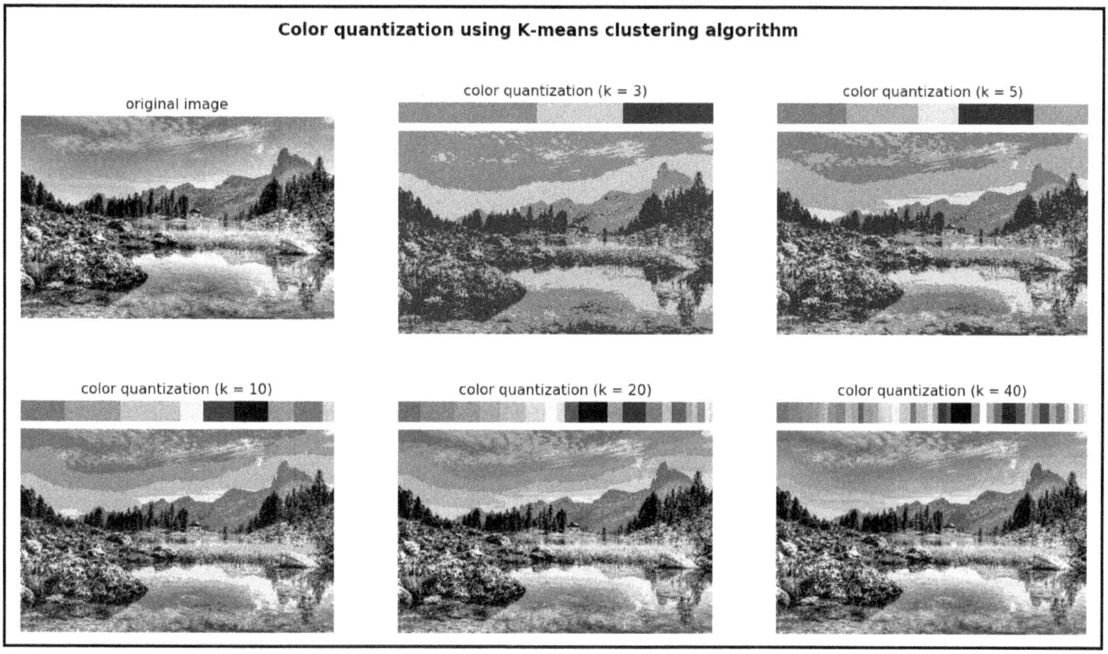

In the previous screenshot you can see the result of applying color quantization using k-means clustering algorithm varying the parameter k (3, 5, 10, 20, and 40). A bigger value of k means a more realistic image.

k-nearest neighbor

k-nearest neighbours (kNN) is considered one of the simplest algorithms in the category of supervised learning. kNN can be used for both classification and regression problems. In the training phase, kNN stores both the feature vectors and class labels of all of the training samples. In the classification phase, an unlabeled vector (a query or test vector in the same multidimensional feature space as the training examples) is classified as the class label that is most frequent among the k training samples nearest to the unlabeled vector to be classified, where k is a user-defined constant.

This can be seen graphically in the next diagram:

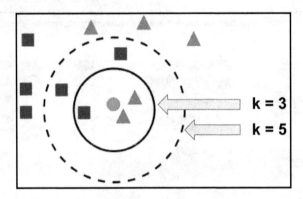

In the previous diagram, if **k = 3**, the green circle (the unlabeled test sample) will be classified as a *triangle* because there are two triangles and only one square inside the inner circle. If **k = 5**, the green circle will be classified as a *square* because there are three squares and only two triangles inside the dashed line circle.

In OpenCV, the first step to work with this classifier is to create it. The cv2.ml.KNearest_create() method creates an empty kNN classifier, which should be trained using the train() method to provide both the data and the labels. Finally, the findNearest() method is used to find the neighbors. The signature for this method is as follows:

```
retval, results, neighborResponses,
dist=cv2.ml_KNearest.findNearest(samples, k[, results[, neighborResponses[,
dist]]])
```

Here, samples is the input samples stored by rows, k sets the number of nearest neighbors (should be greater than one), results stores the predictions for each input sample, neighborResponses stores the corresponding neighbors, and dist stores the distances from the input samples to the corresponding neighbors.

In this section, we will see two examples in order to see how to use the kNN algorithm in OpenCV. In the first example, an intuitive understanding of kNN is expected to be achieved, while in the second example, kNN will be applied to the problem of handwritten digit recognition.

Understanding k-nearest neighbors

The `knn_introduction.py` script carries out a simple introduction to kNN, where a set of points are randomly created and assigned a label (0 or 1). Label 0 will represent red triangles, while label 1 will represent blue squares. We will use the kNN algorithm to classify a sample point based on the k nearest neighbors.

Hence, the first step is to create both the set of points with the corresponding label and the sample point to classify:

```
# The data is composed of 16 points:
data = np.random.randint(0, 100, (16, 2)).astype(np.float32)

# We create the labels (0: red, 1: blue) for each of the 16 points:
labels = np.random.randint(0, 2, (16, 1)).astype(np.float32)

# Create the sample point to be classified:
sample = np.random.randint(0, 100, (1, 2)).astype(np.float32)
```

The next step is to create the kNN classifier, train the classifier, and find the k nearest neighbors:

```
# k-NN creation:
knn = cv2.ml.KNearest_create()
# k-NN training:
knn.train(data, cv2.ml.ROW_SAMPLE, labels)
# k-NN find nearest:
k = 3
ret, results, neighbours, dist = knn.findNearest(sample, k)

# Print results:
print("result: {}".format(results))
print("neighbours: {}".format(neighbours))
print("distance: {}".format(dist))
```

In this case, and corresponding to the following screenshot, the obtained results are as follows:

```
result: [[0.]]
neighbours: [[0. 0. 0.]]
distance: [[ 80. 100. 196.]]
```

Therefore, the green point is classified as a red triangle. This can be seen in the next diagram:

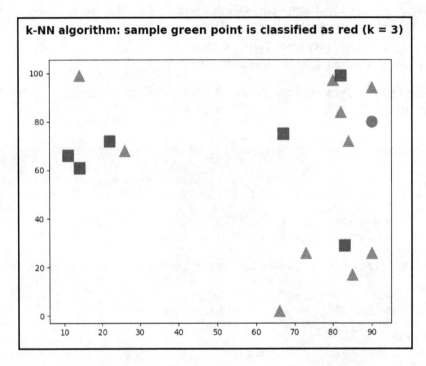

The previous screenshot gives you an intuitive understanding of kNN. In the next example, we are going to apply kNN to the problem of handwritten digit recognition.

Recognizing handwritten digits using k-nearest neighbor

We are going to see how to perform handwritten digit recognition using the kNN classifier. We will start with a *basic* script that achieves an acceptable accuracy, and we will modify it to increase its performance.

In these scripts, the training data is composed of handwritten digits. Instead of having many images, OpenCV provides a *big* image with handwritten digits inside. This image has a size of 2,000 x 1,000 pixels. Each digit is 20 x 20 pixels. Therefore, we have a total of 5,000 digits (100 x 50):

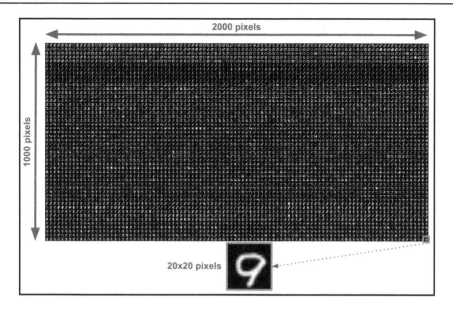

In the `knn_handwritten_digits_recognition_introduction.py` script, we are going to perform our first approach trying to recognize digits using the kNN classifier. In this first approach, we will use raw pixel values as features. This way, each descriptor will be a size of 400 (20 x 20).

The first step is to load all digits from the big image and to assign the corresponding label for each digit. This is performed with the `load_digits_and_labels()` function:

```
digits, labels = load_digits_and_labels('digits.png')
```

The code for the `load_digits_and_labels()` function is as follows:

```
def load_digits_and_labels(big_image):
    """Returns all the digits from the 'big' image and creates the
corresponding labels for each image"""

    # Load the 'big' image containing all the digits:
    digits_img = cv2.imread(big_image, 0)

    # Get all the digit images from the 'big' image:
    number_rows = digits_img.shape[1] / SIZE_IMAGE
    rows = np.vsplit(digits_img, digits_img.shape[0] / SIZE_IMAGE)

    digits = []
    for row in rows:
        row_cells = np.hsplit(row, number_rows)
        for digit in row_cells:
```

```
                digits.append(digit)
        digits = np.array(digits)

        # Create the labels for each image:
        labels = np.repeat(np.arange(NUMBER_CLASSES), len(digits) /
    NUMBER_CLASSES)
        return digits, labels
```

In the previous function, we first load the 'big' image and, afterwards, we get all the digits inside it. The last step of the previous function is to create the labels for each of the digits.

The next step performed in the script is to compute the descriptors for each image. In this case, the raw pixels are the feature descriptors:

```
    # Compute the descriptors for all the images.
    # In this case, the raw pixels are the feature descriptors
    raw_descriptors = []
    for img in digits:
        raw_descriptors.append(np.float32(raw_pixels(img)))
    raw_descriptors = np.squeeze(raw_descriptors)
```

At this point, we split the data into training and testing (50% for each). Therefore, 2,500 digits will be used to train the classifier, and 2,500 digits will be used to test the trained classifier:

```
    partition = int(0.5 * len(raw_descriptors))
    raw_descriptors_train, raw_descriptors_test = np.split(raw_descriptors,
    [partition])
    labels_train, labels_test = np.split(labels, [partition])
```

Now, we can train the kNN model using `knn.train()` method and test it using `get_accuracy()` function:

```
    # Train the KNN model:
    print('Training KNN model - raw pixels as features')
    knn = cv2.ml.KNearest_create()
    knn.train(raw_descriptors_train, cv2.ml.ROW_SAMPLE, labels_train)

    # Test the created model:
    k = 5
    ret, result, neighbours, dist = knn.findNearest(raw_descriptors_test, k)

    # Compute the accuracy:
    acc = get_accuracy(result, labels_test)
    print("Accuracy: {}".format(acc))
```

As we can see, k = 5. We obtain an accuracy of 92.60, but I think it can be improved.

The first thing we can do is to try with different values of k, which is a key parameter in the kNN classifier. This modification is carried out in the knn_handwritten_digits_recognition_k.py script.

In this script, we will create a dictionary to store accuracy when testing different values of k:

```
results = defaultdict(list)
```

Note that we have imported defaultdict from collections:

```
from collections import defaultdict
```

The next step is to compute the knn.findNearest() method, varying the k parameter (in this case, in the range of (1-9)) and storing the results in the dictionary:

```
for k in np.arange(1, 10):
    ret, result, neighbours, dist = knn.findNearest(raw_descriptors_test,
k)
    acc = get_accuracy(result, labels_test)
    print(" {}".format("%.2f" % acc))
    results['50'].append(acc)
```

The final step is to plot the result:

```
# Show all results using matplotlib capabilities:
fig, ax = plt.subplots(1, 1)
ax.set_xlim(0, 10)
dim = np.arange(1, 10)

for key in results:
    ax.plot(dim, results[key], linestyle='--', marker='o', label="50%")

plt.legend(loc='upper left', title="% training")
plt.title('Accuracy of the KNN model varying k')
plt.xlabel("number of k")
plt.ylabel("accuracy")
plt.show()
```

To show the results, we make you of matplotlib capabilities to plot the figure. The output of this script can be seen in the next screenshot:

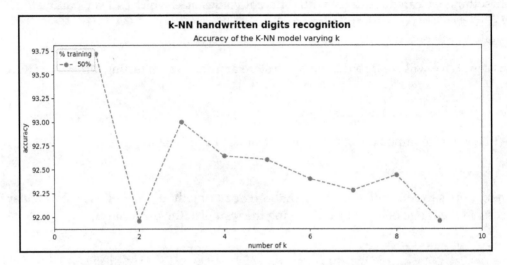

As you can see in the previous screenshot, the obtained accuracies by varying the `k` parameter are—`k=1`—`93.72`, `k=2`—`91.96`, `k=3`—`93.00`, `k=4`—`92.64`, `k=5`—`92.60`, `k=6`—`92.40`, `k=7`—`92.28`, `k=8`—`92.44`, and `k=9`—`91.96`.

 As seen previously, there are some differences in the obtained accuracy. Hence, do not forget to adjust the `k` parameter properly in your applications.

In these examples, we have been training and testing the model with 2,500 digits each.

In machine learning, training the classifiers with more data is usually a good idea because the classifier can better learn the structure of the features. In connection with the kNN classifier, increasing the number of training digits will also increase the probability to find the correct match of test data in the feature space.

In the `knn_handwritten_digits_recognition_k_training_testing.py` script, we have modified the percentage of images to train and test the model, as follows:

```
# Split data into training/testing:
split_values = np.arange(0.1, 1, 0.1)

for split_value in split_values:
    # Split the data into training and testing:
    partition = int(split_value * len(raw_descriptors))
```

```
    raw_descriptors_train, raw_descriptors_test = np.split(raw_descriptors,
[partition])
    labels_train, labels_test = np.split(labels, [partition])

    # Train KNN model
    print('Training KNN model - raw pixels as features')
    knn.train(raw_descriptors_train, cv2.ml.ROW_SAMPLE, labels_train)

    # Store the accuracy when testing:
    for k in np.arange(1, 10):
        ret, result, neighbours, dist =
knn.findNearest(raw_descriptors_test, k)
        acc = get_accuracy(result, labels_test)
        print(" {}".format("%.2f" % acc))
        results[int(split_value * 100)].append(acc)
```

As can be seen, the percentage of digits to train the algorithm are 10%, 20%, ..., 90%, and the percentage of digits to test the algorithm are 90%, 80%, ..., 10%.

And finally, we plot the results:

```
# Show all results using matplotlib capabilities:
# Create the dimensions of the figure and set title:
fig = plt.figure(figsize=(12, 5))
plt.suptitle("k-NN handwritten digits recognition", fontsize=14,
fontweight='bold')
fig.patch.set_facecolor('silver')

ax = plt.subplot(1, 1, 1)
ax.set_xlim(0, 10)
dim = np.arange(1, 10)

for key in results:
    ax.plot(dim, results[key], linestyle='--', marker='o', label=str(key) +
"%")

plt.legend(loc='upper left', title="% training")
plt.title('Accuracy of the KNN model varying both k and the percentage of
images to train/test')
plt.xlabel("number of k")
plt.ylabel("accuracy")
plt.show()
```

The output of
the `knn_handwritten_digits_recognition_k_training_testing.py` script can be
seen in the next screenshot:

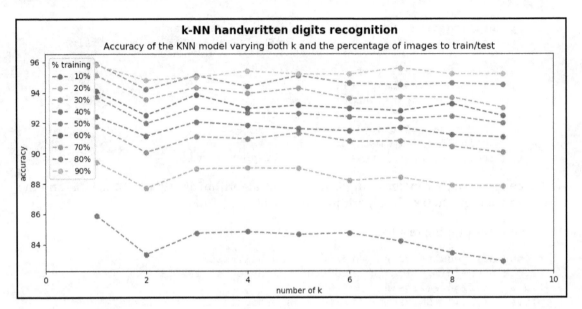

As the number of training images increases, the accuracy increases. Additionally, when we
are training the classifier with 90% of the digits, we are testing the classifier with the
remaining 10% of the digits, which is equivalent to testing the classifier with `500` digits, a
significant number for testing.

So far, we have been training the classifier with raw pixel values as features. In machine
learning, a common procedure before training the classifier is to perform some kind of
preprocessing to the input data helping the classifier when training. In the
`knn_handwritten_digits_recognition_k_training_testing_preprocessing.py`
script, we are applying a preprocessing in order to reduce the variability in the input digits.

This preprocessing is performed in the `deskew()` function:

```
def deskew(img):
    """Pre-processing of the images"""

    m = cv2.moments(img)
    if abs(m['mu02']) < 1e-2:
        return img.copy()
    skew = m['mu11'] / m['mu02']
    M = np.float32([[1, skew, -0.5 * SIZE_IMAGE * skew], [0, 1, 0]])
```

```
    img = cv2.warpAffine(img, M, (SIZE_IMAGE, SIZE_IMAGE),
flags=cv2.WARP_INVERSE_MAP | cv2.INTER_LINEAR)
    return img
```

The `deskew()` function de-skews the digit by using its second-order moments. More specifically, a measure of the skew can be calculated by the ratio of the two central moments (`mu11/mu02`). The calculated skew is used in calculating an affine transformation, which de-skews the digits. See the next screenshot to appreciate the effect of this preprocessing. In the top part of the screenshot, the original digits (blue border) are shown, while in the bottom part of the screenshot, the preprocessed digits (green border) are shown:

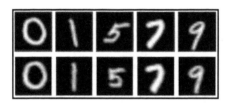

By applying this preprocessing, the recognition rate is increased, as can be seen in the next screenshot, where the recognition rates are plotted:

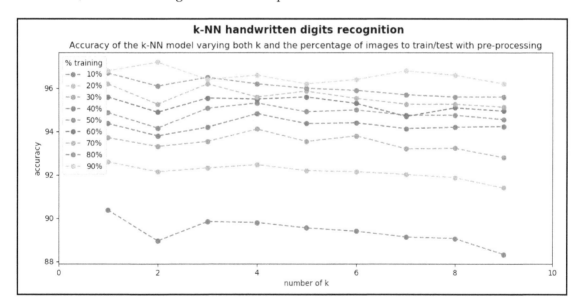

If you compare the accuracy obtained in this script, which performs a preprocessing in the input data and the previous script, which does not carry out any preprocessing, you can see that the overall accuracy has been increased.

In all of these scripts, we have been using the raw pixel values as feature descriptors. In machine learning, a common approach is to use more advanced descriptors. **Histogram of Oriented Gradients** (**HOG**) is a popular image descriptor.

 A feature descriptor is a representation of an image that simplifies the image by extracting useful information that describes elementary characteristics, such as the shape, color, texture, or motion. Typically, a feature descriptor converts an image into a feature vector/array of length n.

HOG is a popular feature descriptor used in computer vision, which was first used for human detection in static images.

In the knn_handwritten_digits_recognition_k_training_testing_preprocessin g_hog.py script, we will use HOG features instead of raw pixel values.

We have defined the get_hog() function, which gets the HOG descriptor:

```
def get_hog():
    """Get hog descriptor"""

    # cv2.HOGDescriptor(winSize, blockSize, blockStride, cellSize, nbins,
derivAperture, winSigma, histogramNormType,
    # L2HysThreshold, gammaCorrection, nlevels, signedGradient)
    hog = cv2.HOGDescriptor((SIZE_IMAGE, SIZE_IMAGE), (8, 8), (4, 4), (8,
8), 9, 1, -1, 0, 0.2, 1, 64, True)
    print("hog descriptor size: '{}'".format(hog.getDescriptorSize()))
    return hog
```

In this case, the feature descriptor for every image is size 144. In order to compute the HOG descriptor to every image, we must perform the following:

```
# Compute the descriptors for all the images.
# In this case, the HoG descriptor is calculated
hog_descriptors = []
for img in digits:
    hog_descriptors.append(hog.compute(deskew(img)))
hog_descriptors = np.squeeze(hog_descriptors)
```

As you can see, we apply hog.compute() to every de-skewed digit.

The results can be seen in the next screenshot:

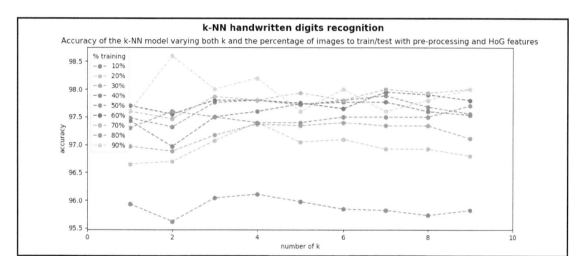

An accuracy of 98.60% is achieved when k=2 and 90% of the digits are used for training and 10% of the digits are used for testing. Therefore, we have increased the recognition rate from 92.60% (obtained in the first script of this subsection) to 98.60% (obtained in the previous script).

A good approach when you code your machine learning models and applications is to start with a basic approximation that tries to tackle the problem as soon as possible. Then, you can iteratively improve the model by adding a better preprocessing, more advanced feature descriptors, or other machine learning techniques if the obtained accuracy is not good enough. Finally, don't forget to collect more data for training and testing your models if necessary.

Support vector machine

A **Support Vector Machine** (**SVM**) is a supervised learning technique that constructs a hyperplane or a set of hyperplanes in a high-dimensional space by best separating the training examples according to its assigned class.

This can be seen in the next diagram, where the green line is the representation of the hyperplane that best separates the two classes because the distance to the nearest element of each of the two classes is the largest:

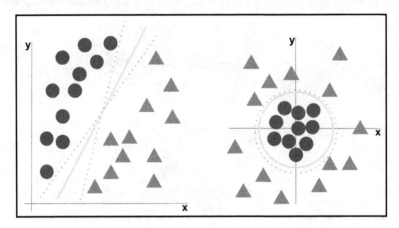

In the first case, the decision boundary is a line while, in the second case, the decision boundary is a circumference. The dashed lines and the dashed circumference represent other decision boundaries, but they do not best separate both classes.

SVM implementation in OpenCV is based on *LIBSVM: A library for support vector machines (2011)* (https://www.csie.ntu.edu.tw/~cjlin/libsvm/). To create an empty model, the cv2.ml.SVM_create() function is used. Next, the main parameters should be assigned to the model:

- svmType: This sets the type of the SVM. See LibSVM for details. Possible values are as follows:
    - SVM_C_SVC: C-support vector classification that can be used for n-class classification ($n \geq 2$)
    - NU_SVC: ν-support vector classification
    - ONE_CLASS: Distribution estimation (one-class SVM)
    - EPS_SVR: ϵ-support vector regression
    - NU_SVR: ν-support vector regression
- kernelType: This sets the kernel type of the SVM. See LibSVM for details. Possible values are as follows:
    - LINEAR: Linear kernel
    - POLY: Polynomial kernel
    - RBF: **Radial Basis Function (RBF)**, a good choice in most cases

- SIGMOID: Sigmoid kernel
- CHI2: Exponential Chi2 kernel, similar to the RBF kernel
- INTER: Histogram intersection kernel; a fast kernel

Kernel function selection can be tricky and is dataset dependent. In this sense, the RBF kernel is considered, in general, a good first choice because this kernel nonlinearly maps samples into a higher dimensional space dealing with cases when the relation between class labels and attributes is nonlinear. See *A Practical Guide to Support Vector Classification (2003)* for further details.

- degree: Parameter degree of a kernel function (POLY)
- gamma: The γ parameter of a kernel function (POLY/RBF/SIGMOID/CHI2)
- coef0: The coef0 parameter of a kernel function (POLY/SIGMOID)
- Cvalue: The C parameter of an SVM optimization problem (C_SVC/EPS_SVR/NU_SVR)

- nu: The ν parameter of a SVM optimization problem (NU_SVC/ONE_CLASS/NU_SVR)
- p: The ϵ parameter of an SVM optimization problem (EPS_SVR)
- classWeights: Optional weights in the C_SVC problem, assigned to particular classes
- termCrit: Termination criteria of the iterative SVM training procedure

The default constructor initializes the structure with the following values:

```
svmType: C_SVC, kernelType: RBF, degree: 0, gamma: 1, coef0: 0, C: 1, nu:
0, p: 0, classWeights: 0, termCrit: TermCriteria(MAX_ITER+EPS, 1000,
FLT_EPSILON )
```

In this section, we will see two examples of how to use SVM in OpenCV. In the first example, an intuitive understanding of SVM will be given, and in the second example, SVM will be applied to the problem of handwritten digit recognition.

Understanding SVM

The `svm_introduction.py` script carries out a simple example in order to see how to use SVMs in OpenCV. First of all, we create the training data and the labels:

```
# Set up training data:
labels = np.array([1, 1, -1, -1, -1])
data = np.matrix([[500, 10], [550, 100], [300, 10], [500, 300], [10, 600]],
dtype=np.float32)
```

As you can see, five points are created. The first two points are assigned the 1 class, while the other three points are assigned the -1 class. The next step is to initialize the SVM model using the `svm_init()` function:

```
# Initialize the SVM model:
svm_model = svm_init(C=12.5, gamma=0.50625)
```

The `svm_init()` function creates an empty model and assigns the main parameters and returns the model:

```
def svm_init(C=12.5, gamma=0.50625):
    """Creates empty model and assigns main parameters"""

    model = cv2.ml.SVM_create()
    model.setGamma(gamma)
    model.setC(C)
    model.setKernel(cv2.ml.SVM_LINEAR)
    model.setType(cv2.ml.SVM_C_SVC)
    model.setTermCriteria((cv2.TERM_CRITERIA_MAX_ITER, 100, 1e-6))

    return model
```

In this case, the SVM kernel type is set to LINEAR (no mapping is done) and the type of SVM is set to C_SVC (can be used for *n*-class classification where n ≥ 2).

Then, we train the SVM using the `svm_train()` function:

```
# Train the SVM:
svm_train(svm_model, data, labels)
```

Here, the `svm_train()` function trains the model using both the samples and the responses, and then returns the trained model:

```
def svm_train(model, samples, responses):
    """Trains the model using the samples and the responses"""

    model.train(samples, cv2.ml.ROW_SAMPLE, responses)
    return model
```

The next step is to create an image where the SVM response will be drawn:

```
# Create the canvas (black image with three channels)
# This image will be used to show the prediction for every pixel:
img_output = np.zeros((640, 640, 3), dtype="uint8")
```

And finally, we show the SVM response using the `show_svm_response()` function:

```
# Show the SVM response:
show_svm_response(svm_model, img_output)
```

Therefore, the `img_ouput` image shows the SVM response. The code for the `show_svm_response()` function is as follows:

```
def show_svm_response(model, image):
    """Show the prediction for every pixel of the image, the training data
and the support vectors"""

    colors = {1: (255, 255, 0), -1: (0, 255, 255)}

    # Show the prediction for every pixel of the image:
    for i in range(image.shape[0]):
        for j in range(image.shape[1]):
            sample = np.matrix([[j, i]], dtype=np.float32)
            response = svm_predict(model, sample)

            image[i, j] = colors[response.item(0)]

    # Show the training data:
    # Show samples with class 1:
    cv2.circle(image, (500, 10), 10, (255, 0, 0), -1)
    cv2.circle(image, (550, 100), 10, (255, 0, 0), -1)
    # Show samples with class -1:
    cv2.circle(image, (300, 10), 10, (0, 255, 0), -1)
    cv2.circle(image, (500, 300), 10, (0, 255, 0), -1)
    cv2.circle(image, (10, 600), 10, (0, 255, 0), -1)

    # Show the support vectors:
    support_vectors = model.getUncompressedSupportVectors()
```

```
        for i in range(support_vectors.shape[0]):
            cv2.circle(image, (support_vectors[i, 0], support_vectors[i, 1]),
   15, (0, 0, 255), 6)
```

As can be seen, the function shows the following:

- The predictions for every pixel of the image
- All five training data points
- The support vectors (the vectors that define the hyperplane are called **support vectors**)

The output of this script can be seen in the next screenshot:

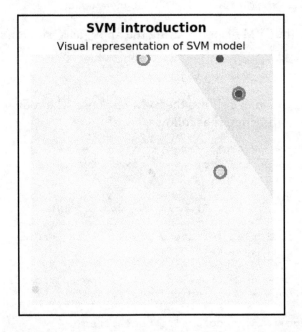

As you can see, the SVM has been trained using the training data and the labels composed of five points (two points are assigned class 1, while the other three points are assigned class -1) and it is later used to classify all of the pixels in the image. This classification results in a division of the image in a yellow and a cyan region. Additionally, you can see that the boundary between both regions corresponds to the optimal separation between the two classes because the distance to the nearest element of each of the two classes is the largest. The support vectors are shown with a red line border.

Handwritten digit recognition using SVM

We just saw how to perform handwritten digit recognition using the kNN classifier. The best accuracy was obtained by preprocessing the digits (recall the `deskew()` function) and computing the HOG descriptor as the feature vector used to describe each digit. Therefore, for the sake of simplicity, the next scripts, which are going to make use of SVM to classify the digits, will use the aforementioned approximation (preprocessing and HOG features).

The `svm_handwritten_digits_recognition_preprocessing_hog.py` script performs the handwritten digit recognition using SVM classification. The key code is shown as follows:

```
# Load all the digits and the corresponding labels:
digits, labels = load_digits_and_labels('digits.png')

# Shuffle data
# Constructs a random number generator:
rand = np.random.RandomState(1234)
# Randomly permute the sequence:
shuffle = rand.permutation(len(digits))
digits, labels = digits[shuffle], labels[shuffle]

# HoG feature descriptor:
hog = get_hog()

# Compute the descriptors for all the images.
# In this case, the HoG descriptor is calculated
hog_descriptors = []
for img in digits:
    hog_descriptors.append(hog.compute(deskew(img)))
hog_descriptors = np.squeeze(hog_descriptors)

# At this point we split the data into training and testing (50% for each
one):
partition = int(0.5 * len(hog_descriptors))
hog_descriptors_train, hog_descriptors_test = np.split(hog_descriptors,
[partition])
labels_train, labels_test = np.split(labels, [partition])

print('Training SVM model ...')
model = svm_init(C=12.5, gamma=0.50625)
svm_train(model, hog_descriptors_train, labels_train)

print('Evaluating model ... ')
svm_evaluate(model, hog_descriptors_test, labels_test)
```

In this case, we have used an RBF kernel:

```
def svm_init(C=12.5, gamma=0.50625):
    """Creates empty model and assigns main parameters"""

    model = cv2.ml.SVM_create()
    model.setGamma(gamma)
    model.setC(C)
    model.setKernel(cv2.ml.SVM_RBF)
    model.setType(cv2.ml.SVM_C_SVC)
    model.setTermCriteria((cv2.TERM_CRITERIA_MAX_ITER, 100, 1e-6))

    return model
```

The obtained accuracy is 98.60%, using only 50% of the digits to train the algorithm.

Additionally, when using the RBF kernel, there are two important parameters—C and γ. In this case, C=12.5 and γ=0.50625. As before, C and γ are unknown as the best for a given problem (dataset dependent). Therefore, some kind of parameter search must be done. Hence, the goal is to identify good (C and γ) where a *grid-search* on C and γ is recommended.

In the svm_handwritten_digits_recognition_preprocessing_hog_c_gamma.py script, two modifications are carried out in comparison with the svm_handwritten_digits_recognition_preprocessing_hog.py script. The first one is that the model is trained with 90% of the digits, and the remaining 10% is used for testing. The second modification is that a grid-search on C and γ is performed:

```
# Create a dictionary to store the accuracy when testing:
results = defaultdict(list)

for C in [1, 10, 100, 1000]:
    for gamma in [0.1, 0.3, 0.5, 0.7, 0.9, 1.1, 1.3, 1.5]:
        model = svm_init(C, gamma)
        svm_train(model, hog_descriptors_train, labels_train)
        acc = svm_evaluate(model, hog_descriptors_test, labels_test)
        print(" {}".format("%.2f" % acc))
        results[C].append(acc)
```

And finally, this is the result:

```
# Create the dimensions of the figure and set title:
fig = plt.figure(figsize=(10, 6))
plt.suptitle("SVM handwritten digits recognition", fontsize=14,
fontweight='bold')
fig.patch.set_facecolor('silver')
```

```
# Show all results using matplotlib capabilities:
ax = plt.subplot(1, 1, 1)
ax.set_xlim(0, 1.5)
dim = [0.1, 0.3, 0.5, 0.7, 0.9, 1.1, 1.3, 1.5]

for key in results:
    ax.plot(dim, results[key], linestyle='--', marker='o', label=str(key))

plt.legend(loc='upper left', title="C")
plt.title('Accuracy of the SVM model varying both C and gamma')
plt.xlabel("gamma")
plt.ylabel("accuracy")
plt.show()
```

The output of this script can be seen in the next screenshot:

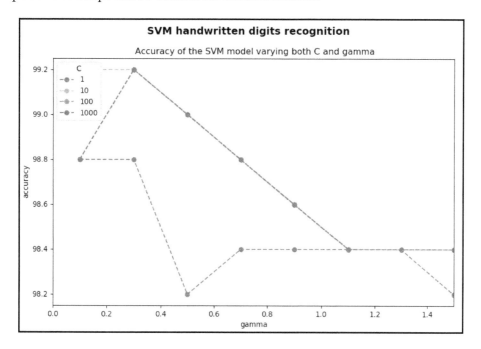

As shown, an accuracy of 99.20% is obtained in several cases.

By comparing the kNN classifier and SVM for handwritten digit recognition, we can conclude that SVM outperforms the kNN classifier.

Summary

In this chapter, we covered a complete introduction to machine learning.

In the first section, we contextualized the concept of machine learning and how it is related to other hot topics, such as artificial intelligence, neural networks, and deep learning. Additionally, we summarized the three main approaches in machine learning and discussed the three most common techniques to solve classification, regression, and clustering problems. Then, we applied the most common machine learning techniques to solve some real-world problems. More specifically, we looked at the k-means clustering algorithm, the k-nearest neighbor classifier, and SVM.

In the next chapter, we will explore how to create face-processing projects using state-of-the-art algorithms in connection with face detection, tracking, and recognition.

Questions

1. What are the three main approaches in the context of machine learning?
2. What is the difference between a classification and a regression problem?
3. What function does OpenCV provide to implement a k-means clustering algorithm?
4. What function does OpenCV provide to create a kNN classifier?
5. What function does OpenCV provide to find the nearest neighbors?
6. What function does OpenCV provide to create an SVM classifier?
7. What is a reasonable first choice for an SVM kernel?

Further reading

Check out the following resource if you'd like to dive deeper into machine learning:

- *Machine Learning for OpenCV (2017) by Michael Beyeler* (`https://www.packtpub.com/big-data-and-business-intelligence/machine-learning-opencv`)

11
Face Detection, Tracking, and Recognition

Face processing is a hot topic in artificial intelligence because a lot of information can be automatically extracted from faces using computer vision algorithms. The face plays an important role in visual communication because a great deal of non-verbal information, such as identity, intent, and emotion, can be extracted from human faces. Face processing is a really interesting topic for computer vision learners because it touches on different areas of expertise, such as object detection, image processing, and landmark detection or object tracking.

In this chapter, you will be introduced to the main topics related to face processing using state-of-the-art algorithms and techniques in order to achieve impressive results.

We will cover the following topics:

- Face processing introduction
- Face detection
- Detecting facial landmarks
- Face tracking
- Face recognition

In this chapter, you will learn how to create face processing projects using state-of-the-art algorithms in connection with face detection, tracking, and recognition. In `Chapter 12`, *Introduction to Deep Learning*, you will be introduced to the world of deep learning with OpenCV and to some deep learning Python libraries (TensorFlow and Keras).

Technical requirements

The technical requirements are listed as follows:

- Python and OpenCV
- A Python-specific IDE
- The NumPy and Matplotlib packages
- The Git client
- The Dlib package
- The `face_processing` package

Further details about how to install these requirements are mentioned in Chapter 1, *Setting Up OpenCV*. The GitHub repository for *Mastering OpenCV 4 with Python*, which contains all the supporting project files necessary to work through the book, from the first chapter to the last, can be accessed at `https://github.com/PacktPublishing/Mastering-OpenCV-4-with-Python`.

Installing dlib

Dlib (`http://dlib.net/python/index.html`) is a C++ software library that contains computer vision, machine learning, and deep learning algorithms. Dlib can also be used in your Python applications. In order to install `dlib` with the Python interface (`https://pypi.org/project/dlib/`), use the following command:

```
$ pip install dlib
```

Alternatively, if you want to compile `dlib` yourself, go into the `dlib` root folder and run the following command:

```
$ python setup.py install
```

Once that command has finished running, you are ready to use `dlib` from Python.

Note that you need to have both CMake and a C++ compiler installed for this to work properly. Also note that various optional features, such as GUI support (for example, `dlib.image_window`) and CUDA acceleration, will be either enabled or disabled based on what is available on your computer.

A third option for installing `dlib` is to access `http://pypi.fcio.net/simple/dlib/` and install the required `dlib` wheel package. In my case, I have downloaded the `dlib-19.8.1-cp36-cp36m-win_amd64.whl` file and installed it with the following command:

```
$ pip install dlib-19.8.1-cp36-cp36m-win_amd64.whl
```

The wheel filename is `{distribution}-{version}(-{build tag})?-{python tag}-{abi tag}-{platform tag}.whl`. For example, `distribution-1.0-1-py27-none-any.whl` is the first build of a package called **distribution**, and it is compatible with Python 2.7 (any Python 2.7 implementation), with no ABI (pure Python), on any CPU architecture. See `https://www.python.org/dev/peps/pep-0427/` for further details about the wheel binary package format.

To confirm that the installation has been performed correctly, just open a Python shell and try to import the `dlib` library:

```
python
import dlib
```

Remember that a recommended approach is to install packages in virtual environments. See `Chapter 1`, *Setting Up OpenCV*, for information on how to create and manage virtual environments.

For example, in this case, we will install `dlib` in a virtual environment using Anaconda Prompt:

1. Create a virtual environment:

```
(base) $ conda create -n dlib-env python=3.6
```

2. Activate the environment:

```
(base) $ activate dlib-env
```

See how `(dlib-env)` appears before the prompt after this command. This indicates that the virtual environment has been activated.

3. Install `dlib` using the following commands:

```
(dlib-env) $ pip install dlib
```

Installing the face_recognition package

In order to install the face_recognition package (https://pypi.org/project/face_recognition/), execute the following command:

```
$ pip install face_recognition
```

To check that the installation has been performed correctly, just open a Python shell and try to import the face_recognition library:

```
python
import face_recognition
```

Installing the cvlib package

To install the cvlib package (https://pypi.org/project/cvlib/), first install the required packages (numpy, opencv-python, requests, progressbar, pillow, tensorflow, keras) using the following command:

```
$ pip install -r requirements.txt
```

Then, install the cvlib package:

```
$ pip install cvlib
```

To upgrade to the newest version, enter the following command:

```
pip install --upgrade cvlib
```

Note that if you are using a GPU, you can edit the requirements.txt file to include tensorflow-gpu instead of tensorflow.

To check that the installation has been performed correctly, just open a Python shell and try to import the face_recognition library:

```
python
import cvlib
```

Face processing introduction

In this chapter, we will cover the main topics in connection with face processing. In order to do so, we will be using the **OpenCV** library, but also the `dlib` (`http://dlib.net/python/index.html`, `https://pypi.org/project/dlib/`, `https://github.com/davisking/dlib`), `face_recognition` (`https://pypi.org/project/face_recognition/`, `https://github.com/ageitgey/face_recognition`) and `cvlib` (`https://pypi.org/project/cvlib/`, `https://github.com/arunponnusamy/cvlib`, `https://www.cvlib.net/`) Python packages. In the previous section, you saw how to install these packages.

In order to introduce this chapter, we will be using different approaches throughout all the sections to see the different possibilities you have at hand to solve a concrete face processing task, and it can be helpful to have a high-level overview of all of these alternatives.

This diagram attempts to capture the concept of the previously mentioned topics:

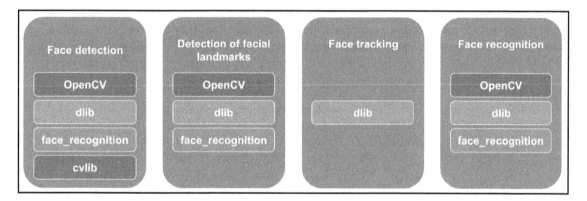

As you can see, four main points are going to be tackled here:

- **Face detection** is a specific case of object detection, where the task is to find both the locations and sizes of all the faces in an image.
- **Facial landmarks detection** is a specific case of landmarks detection, where the task is to locate the main landmarks in a face.
- **Face tracking** is a specific case of object tracking, where the task is to find both the locations and sizes of all the moving faces in a video by taking into account the extra information that can be extracted in consecutive frames of the video.

- **Face recognition** is a specific case of object recognition, where a person is identified or verified from an image or video using the information extracted from the face:
  - **Face identification** (1:N): The task is to find the closest match from an unknown person in a collection of known faces.
  - **Face verification** (1:1): The task is to check whether the person is who they claim to be.

As you can see in the previous diagram, **OpenCV**, **dlib**, **face_recognition**, and **cvlib**, are going to be used throughout this chapter.

Face detection

Face detection, which can be defined as the task of determining the location and size of faces in digital images, is usually the first key step when building face processing applications (for example, facial expression recognition, drowsiness detection, gender classification, face recognition, head-pose estimation, or human-computer interaction). This is because the aforementioned applications requires as an input the location and size of the detected faces. Therefore, automatic face detection plays a critical role, and is one of the most studied topics in the artificial intelligence community.

Face detection seems like an effortless task for a human, but it is a very challenging task for computers because many problems/challenges are usually involved (for example, appearance variations, scale, rotation, facial expressions, occlusion, or lighting condition). Face detection has made impressive progress after the work proposed by Viola and Jones (https://docs.opencv.org/4.0.1/d7/d8b/tutorial_py_face_detection.html). In this section, we will see some of the most popular face detection techniques that the OpenCV library and the dlib and face_processing packages provide, including the aforementioned Viola and Jones algorithm, and other machine learning and deep learning approaches.

Face detection with OpenCV

OpenCV provides two approaches for face detection:

- Haar cascade based face detectors
- Deep learning-based face detectors

The framework proposed by Viola and Jones (see *Rapid Object Detection Using a Boosted Cascade of Simple Features (2001)*) is an effective object detection method. This framework is very popular because OpenCV provides face detection algorithms based on this framework. Additionally, this framework can also be used for detecting other objects rather than faces (for example, full body detector, plate number detector, upper body detector, or cat face detector). In this section, we will see how to detect faces using this framework.

The `face_detection_opencv_haar.py` script performs face detection using haar feature-based cascade classifiers. In this sense, OpenCV provides four cascade classifiers to use for (frontal) face detection:

- `haarcascade_frontalface_alt.xml` (**FA1**): 22 stages and *20 x 20* haar features
- `haarcascade_frontalface_alt2.xml` (**FA2**): 20 stages and *20 x 20* haar features
- `haarcascade_frontalface_alt_tree.xml` (**FAT**): 47 stages and *20 x 20* haar features
- `haarcascade_frontalface_default.xml` (**FD**): 25 stages and *24 x 24* haar features

In some available publications, the authors evaluated the performance of these cascade classifiers using different criteria and datasets. Overall, it can be concluded that these classifiers achieve similar accuracy. That is why, in this script, we will be using two of them (to simplify things). More specifically, in this script, two cascade classifiers (the previously introduced `FA2` and `FD`) are loaded:

```
# Load cascade classifiers:
cas_alt2 = cv2.CascadeClassifier("haarcascade_frontalface_alt2.xml")
cas_default = cv2.CascadeClassifier("haarcascade_frontalface_default.xml")
```

The `cv2.CascadeClassifier()` function is used to load a classifier from a file. You can download these cascade classifier files from the OpenCV repository: `https://github.com/opencv/opencv/tree/master/data/haarcascades`. Moreover, we have included the two loaded cascade classifier files in the GitHub repository (`haarcascade_frontalface_alt2.xml` and `haarcascade_frontalface_default.xml`).

The next step is to perform the detection:

```
faces_alt2 = cas_alt2.detectMultiScale(gray)
faces_default = cas_default.detectMultiScale(gray)
```

The `cv2.CascadeClassifier.detectMultiScale()` function detects objects and returns them as a list of rectangles. The final step is to correlate the results using the `show_detection()` function:

```
img_faces_alt2 = show_detection(img.copy(), faces_alt2)
img_faces_default = show_detection(img.copy(), faces_default)
```

The `show_detection()` function draws a rectangle over each detected face:

```
def show_detection(image, faces):
    """Draws a rectangle over each detected face"""

    for (x, y, w, h) in faces:
        cv2.rectangle(image, (x, y), (x + w, y + h), (255, 0, 0), 5)
    return image
```

OpenCV also provides the `cv2.face.getFacesHAAR()` function to detect faces:

```
retval, faces_haar_alt2 = cv2.face.getFacesHAAR(img,
"haarcascade_frontalface_alt2.xml")
retval, faces_haar_default = cv2.face.getFacesHAAR(img,
"haarcascade_frontalface_default.xml")
```

It should be noted that `cv2.CascadeClassifier.detectMultiScale()` needs a grayscale image, while `cv2.face.getFacesHAAR()` needs a BGR image as an input. Moreover, `cv2.CascadeClassifier.detectMultiScale()` outputs the detected faces as a list of rectangles. For example, the output for two detected faces will be like this:

```
[[332 93 364 364] [695 104 256 256]]
```

The `cv2.face.getFacesHAAR()` function returns the faces in a similar format:

```
[[[298 524 61 61]] [[88 72 315 315]]]
```

To get rid of the useless one-dimension arrays, call `np.squeeze()`:

```
faces_haar_alt2 = np.squeeze(faces_haar_alt2)
faces_haar_default = np.squeeze(faces_haar_default)
```

The full code for detecting and drawing the faces in the loaded image is as follows:

```
# Load image and convert to grayscale:
img = cv2.imread("test_face_detection.jpg")
gray = cv2.cvtColor(img, cv2.COLOR_BGR2GRAY)

# Load cascade classifiers:
cas_alt2 = cv2.CascadeClassifier("haarcascade_frontalface_alt2.xml")
cas_default = cv2.CascadeClassifier("haarcascade_frontalface_default.xml")
```

```
# Detect faces:
faces_alt2 = cas_alt2.detectMultiScale(gray)
faces_default = cas_default.detectMultiScale(gray)
retval, faces_haar_alt2 = cv2.face.getFacesHAAR(img,
"haarcascade_frontalface_alt2.xml")
faces_haar_alt2 = np.squeeze(faces_haar_alt2)
retval, faces_haar_default = cv2.face.getFacesHAAR(img,
"haarcascade_frontalface_default.xml")
faces_haar_default = np.squeeze(faces_haar_default)


# Draw face detections:
img_faces_alt2 = show_detection(img.copy(), faces_alt2)
img_faces_default = show_detection(img.copy(), faces_default)
img_faces_haar_alt2 = show_detection(img.copy(), faces_haar_alt2)
img_faces_haar_default = show_detection(img.copy(), faces_haar_default)
```

The final step is to show the four created images by using OpenCV, or Matplotlib in this case. The full code can be seen in the `face_detection_opencv_haar.py` script. The output of this script can be seen in the following screenshot:

As you can see, the detected faces vary using the four aforementioned approximations by using haar feature-based cascade classifiers. Finally, it should also be commented that the `cv2.CascadeClassifier.detectMultiScale()` function has the `minSize` and `maxSize` parameters in order to establish the minimum size (objects smaller than `minSize` will not be detected) and the maximum size (objects larger than `maxSize` will not be detected), respectively. On the contrary, the `cv2.face.getFacesHAAR()` function does not offer this possibility.

Haar feature-based cascade classifiers can be used to detect objects other than human faces. The OpenCV library also provides two cascade files to use for cat face detection.

For the sake of completeness, the `cat_face_detection_opencv_haar.py` script loads two cascade files, which have been trained to detect frontal cat faces in images. This script is pretty similar to the `face_detection_opencv_haar.py` script. Indeed, the key modification is the two cascade files that have been loaded. In this case, here are the two loaded cascade files:

- `haarcascade_frontalcatface.xml`: A frontal cat face detector using the basic set of haar features with 20 stages and *24 x 24* haar features
- `haarcascade_frontalcatface_extended.xml`: A frontal cat face detector using the full set of haar features with 20 stages and *24 x 24* haar features

For more information about these cascade files, check out Joseph Howse's *OpenCV for Secret Agents, Packt Publishing, January 2015.* You can download these cascade classifier files from the OpenCV repository: `https://github.com/opencv/opencv/tree/master/data/haarcascades`. Moreover, we have included these two cascade classifier files in the GitHub repository.

The output of this script can be seen in the following screenshot:

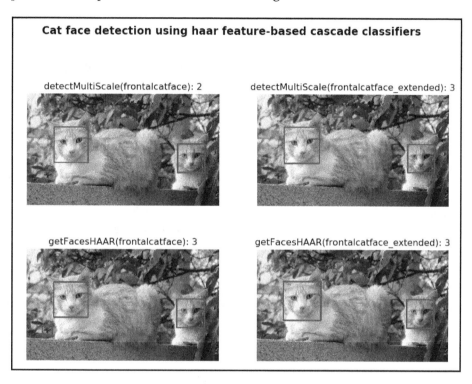

Additionally, OpenCV provides a deep learning-based face detector (`https://github.com/opencv/opencv/tree/master/samples/dnn/face_detector`). More specifically, the OpenCV **deep neural network** (**DNN**) face detector is based on the **Single Shot MultiBox Detector** (**SSD**) framework using a ResNet-10 network.

Since OpenCV 3.1, there is the DNN module, which implements a forward pass (inferencing) with pre-trained deep networks using popular deep learning frameworks, such as Caffe, TensorFlow, Torch, and Darknet. In OpenCV 3.3, the module has been promoted from the `opencv_contrib` repository to the main repository (`https://github.com/opencv/opencv/tree/master/modules/dnn`) and accelerated significantly. This means that we can use the pre-trained networks to perform a complete forward pass and utilize the output to make a prediction within our application rather than spend hours training the network. In `Chapter 12`, *Introduction to Deep Learning*, we will further explore the DNN module; in this chapter, we will focus on the deep learning face detector.

In this section, we will perform face detection using pre-trained deep learning face detector models, which are included in the library.

OpenCV provides two models for this face detector:

- **Face detector (FP16)**: Floating-point 16 version of the original Caffe implementation (5.1 MB)
- **Face detector (UINT8)**: 8-bit quantized version using TensorFlow (2.6 MB)

In each case, you will need two sets of files: the model file and the configuration file. In the case of the Caffe model, these files are the following:

- `res10_300x300_ssd_iter_140000_fp16.caffemodel`: This file contains the weights for the actual layers. It can be downloaded from `https://github.com/opencv/opencv_3rdparty/raw/19512576c112aa2c7b6328cb0e8d589a4a90a26d/res10_300x300_ssd_iter_140000_fp16.caffemodel` and it is also included in the GitHub repository of the book.
- `deploy.prototxt`: This file defines the model architecture. It can be downloaded from `https://github.com/opencv/opencv/blob/master/samples/dnn/face_detector/deploy.prototxt` and is included in the GitHub repository of the book.

If you're using the TensorFlow model, you'll need these files:

- `opencv_face_detector_uint8.pb`: This file contains the weights for the actual layers. This file can be downloaded from `https://github.com/opencv/opencv_3rdparty/raw/8033c2bc31b3256f0d461c919ecc01c2428ca03b/opencv_face_detector_uint8.pb` and is included in the GitHub repository of the book.
- `opencv_face_detector.pbtxt`: This file defines the model architecture. It can be downloaded from `https://github.com/opencv/opencv_extra/blob/master/testdata/dnn/opencv_face_detector.pbtxt` and is included in the GitHub repository of the book.

The `face_detection_opencv_dnn.py` script shows you how to detect faces by using face detection and pre-trained deep learning face detector models. The first step is to load the pre-trained model:

```
# Load pre-trained model:
net = cv2.dnn.readNetFromCaffe("deploy.prototxt",
"res10_300x300_ssd_iter_140000_fp16.caffemodel")
# net = cv2.dnn.readNetFromTensorflow("opencv_face_detector_uint8.pb",
"opencv_face_detector.pbtxt")
```

As you can see, in this example, the floating-point 16 version of the original Caffe implementation is loaded. To achieve the best accuracy, we must run the model on BGR images resized to *300 x 300* by applying mean subtraction of values of (104, 177, 123) for the blue, green, and red channels, respectively. This preprocessing is performed with the cv2.dnn.blobFromImage() OpenCV function:

```
blob = cv2.dnn.blobFromImage(image, 1.0, (300, 300), [104., 117., 123.],
False, False)
```

In Chapter 12, *Introduction to Deep Learning*, we will look at this function in more depth.

The next step is to set the blob as an input to obtain the results, performing a forward pass for the whole network to compute the output:

```
# Set the blob as input and obtain the detections:
net.setInput(blob)
detections = net.forward()
```

The final step is to iterate over all the detections and draw the results, only considering detections if the corresponding confidence is greater than a fixed minimum threshold:

```
# Iterate over all detections:
for i in range(0, detections.shape[2]):
    # Get the confidence (probability) of the current detection:
    confidence = detections[0, 0, i, 2]

    # Only consider detections if confidence is greater than a fixed
minimum confidence:
    if confidence > 0.7:
        # Increment the number of detected faces:
        detected_faces += 1
        # Get the coordinates of the current detection:
        box = detections[0, 0, i, 3:7] * np.array([w, h, w, h])
        (startX, startY, endX, endY) = box.astype("int")

        # Draw the detection and the confidence:
        text = "{:.3f}%".format(confidence * 100)
        y = startY - 10 if startY - 10 > 10 else startY + 10
        cv2.rectangle(image, (startX, startY), (endX, endY), (255, 0, 0),
3)
        cv2.putText(image, text, (startX, y), cv2.FONT_HERSHEY_SIMPLEX,
0.9, (0, 0, 255), 2)
```

The output of the `face_detection_opencv_dnn.py` script can be seen in the next screenshot:

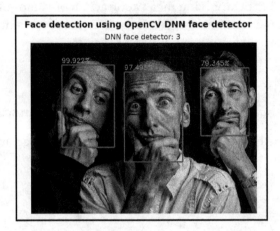

As can be seen, the three faces are detected with high confidence.

Face detection with dlib

You can use `dlib.get_frontal_face_detector()` to create a frontal face detector, which is based on **Histogram of Oriented Gradients** (**HOG**) features and a linear classifier in a sliding window detection approach. In particular, the HOG trainer uses a structural SVM-based training algorithm that enables the trainer to train in all the sub-windows in every training image. This face detector has been trained using 3,000 images from the *Labeled Faces in the Wild* (`http://vis-www.cs.umass.edu/lfw/`) dataset. It should be noted that this detector can also be used to spot objects other than faces. You can check out the `train_object_detector.py` script, which is included in the `dlib` library (`http://dlib.net/train_object_detector.py.html`), to see how to easily train your own object detectors using only a few training images. For example, you can train a great stop-sign detector using only eight images of stop signs.

The `face_detection_dlib_hog.py` script detects faces using the aforementioned `dlib` frontal face detector. The first step is to load the frontal face detector from `dlib`:

```
detector = dlib.get_frontal_face_detector()
```

The next step is to perform the detection:

```
rects_1 = detector(gray, 0)
rects_2 = detector(gray, 1)
```

The second argument indicates that the image is upsampled 1 time before the detection process is carried out, allowing the detector to detect more faces because the image is bigger. On the contrary, the execution time will be increased. Therefore, this should be taken into account for performance purposes.

The output of this script can be seen in the following screenshot:

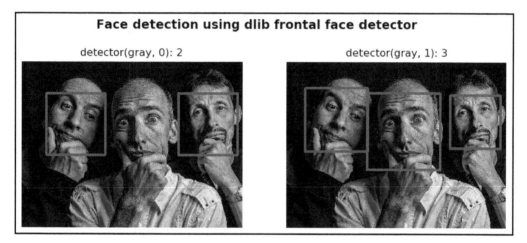

As you can see, if we detect faces using the original grayscale image (`rects_1 = detector(gray, 0)`), only two faces are found. However, if we detect faces using the grayscale image upsampled 1 time (`rects_2 = detector(gray, 1)`), the three faces are correctly detected.

The dlib library also offers a CNN face detector. You can use `dlib.cnn_face_detection_model_v1()` to create the CNN face detector. The constructor loads the face detection model from a file. You can download a pre-trained model (712 KB) from `http://dlib.net/files/mmod_human_face_detector.dat.bz2`. When creating the CNN face detector, the corresponding pre-trained model should be passed to this method:

```
cnn_face_detector =
dlib.cnn_face_detection_model_v1("mmod_human_face_detector.dat")
```

At this point, we are ready to spot faces using this detector:

```
rects = cnn_face_detector(img, 0)
```

This detector spots a `mmod_rectangles` object, which is a list of `mmod_rectangle` objects, and the `mmod_rectangle` object has two member variables—a `dlib.rectangle` object, and a `confidence` score. Therefore, to show the detections, the `show_detection()` function is coded:

```
def show_detection(image, faces):
    """Draws a rectangle over each detected face"""

    # faces contains a list of mmod_rectangle objects
    # The mmod_rectangle object has two member variables, a dlib.rectangle
object, and a confidence score
    # Therefore, we iterate over the detected mmod_rectangle objects
accessing dlib.rect to draw the rectangle

    for face in faces:
        cv2.rectangle(image, (face.rect.left(), face.rect.top()),
(face.rect.right(), face.rect.bottom()), (255, 0, 0), 10)
    return image
```

The `show_detection()` function should be called like this:

```
img_faces = show_detection(img.copy(), rects)
```

The full code is in the `face_detection_dlib_cnn.py` script. The output of this script can be seen in the next screenshot:

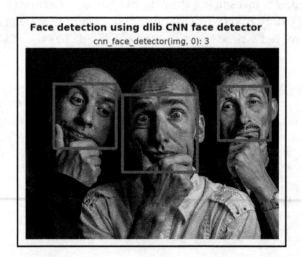

The dlib CNN face detector is much more accurate than the dlib HOG face detector, but it takes much more computational power to run. For example, for a *600 x 400* image, the HOG face detector takes around 0.25 seconds, while CNN face detector takes around 5. Indeed, the CNN face detector is meant to be executed on a GPU in order to attain a reasonable speed.

If you have GPU, you can enable CUDA, which should speed up the execution. To do so, you will need to compile dlib from source.

Face detection with face_recognition

With the aim of detecting faces using face_recognition, the face_locations() function should be called:

```
rects_1 = face_recognition.face_locations(rgb, 0, "hog")
rects_2 = face_recognition.face_locations(rgb, 1, "hog")
```

The first parameter is the input (RGB) image. The second parameter sets how many times the input image is upsampled before the detection process has been carried out. The third parameter determines which face detection model will be used.

In this case, the hog detection model will be used. The full code for this example can be seen in the face_detection_fr_hog.py script.

Additionally, face_processing can be configured to detect faces using the cnn face detector:

```
rects_1 = face_recognition.face_locations(rgb, 0, "cnn")
rects_2 = face_recognition.face_locations(rgb, 1, "cnn")
```

You can see the face_detection_fr_hog.py and face_detection_fr_cnn.py scripts, which perform face recognition using the hog and the cnn face detectors, respectively, if further details are required.

Remember that the face_processing library internally uses both the HOG and CNN dlib face detectors.

Face detection with cvlib

For the sake of completeness, we are introducing the `cvlib` package in this section because it also provides an algorithm for face detection. This library is a simple, high-level and easy-to-use open source computer vision library for Python (`https://github.com/arunponnusamy/cvlib`). In order to detect faces with `cvlib`, you can use the `detect_face()` function, which will return the bounding boxes and corresponding confidences for all detected faces:

```
import cvlib as cv
faces, confidences = cv.detect_face(image)
```

Under the hood, this function is using the OpenCV DNN face detector with pre-trained Caffe models (`https://github.com/arunponnusamy/cvlib/blob/master/cvlib/face_detection.py`).

Refer to the `face_detection_cvlib_dnn.py` script for further details.

Detecting facial landmarks

In computer vision, the localization of the fiducial facial key points (also called **facial landmarks**) is usually a key step in a lot of facial analysis methods and algorithms. Facial expression recognition, head pose estimation algorithms, and drowsiness detection systems are only a few examples, relying heavily on the facial shape information provided by the detection of facial landmarks.

A facial landmark detection algorithm aims to automatically identify the locations of the facial landmark points in images or videos. More specifically, those key points are either the dominant points that describe the unique location of a facial component (for example, corners of mouth or eyes) or an interpolated point that connects those dominant points around the facial components and facial contour. Formally, given a facial image denoted as *I*, a landmark detection algorithm detects the locations of *D* landmarks $x = \{x1, y1, x2, y2, ..., xD, yD\}$, where *x* and *y* represent the image coordinates of the facial landmarks. In this section, we are going to see how to detect facial landmarks using both OpenCV and dlib.

Detecting facial landmarks with OpenCV

The OpenCV facial landmark API is called **Facemark** (https://docs.opencv.org/4.0.1/ db/dd8/classcv_1_1face_1_1Facemark.html). It has three different implementations of landmark detection based on three different papers:

- **FacemarkLBF**
- **FacemarkKamezi**
- **FacemarkAAM**

The following example shows how to detect facial landmarks using these algorithms:

```
# Import required packages:
import cv2
import numpy as np

# Load image:
image = cv2.imread("my_image.png",0)

# Find faces:
cas = cv2.CascadeClassifier("haarcascade_frontalface_alt2.xml")
faces = cas.detectMultiScale(image , 1.5, 5)
print("faces", faces)

# At this point, we create landmark detectors and test them:
print("testing LBF")
facemark = cv2.face.createFacemarkLBF()
facemark .loadModel("lbfmodel.yaml")
ok, landmarks = facemark.fit(image , faces)
print ("landmarks LBF", ok, landmarks)

print("testing AAM")
facemark = cv2.face.createFacemarkAAM()
facemark .loadModel("aam.xml")
ok, landmarks = facemark.fit(image , faces)
print ("landmarks AAM", ok, landmarks)

print("testing Kazemi")
facemark = cv2.face.createFacemarkKazemi()
facemark .loadModel("face_landmark_model.dat")
ok, landmarks = facemark.fit(image , faces)
print ("landmarks Kazemi", ok, landmarks)
```

This example should detect the facial landmarks using the three different algorithms provided by OpenCV. *However, the generated Python wrappers for the* `fit()` *function are not correct.* Therefore, at the time of writing, and using `OpenCV 4.0`, this script does not work in Python.

To solve this problem, we need to modify the C++ code of the `fit()` function and install OpenCV from the source code. For example, here's the actual code for the `FacemarkLBFImpl::fit()` method:

```
// C++ code

bool FacemarkLBFImpl::fit( InputArray image, InputArray roi,
OutputArrayOfArrays _landmarks )
{
    // FIXIT
    std::vector<Rect> & faces = *(std::vector<Rect> *)roi.getObj();
    if (faces.empty()) return false;

    std::vector<std::vector<Point2f> > & landmarks =
        *(std::vector<std::vector<Point2f> >*) _landmarks.getObj();

    landmarks.resize(faces.size());

    for(unsigned i=0; i<faces.size();i++){
        params.detectROI = faces[i];
        fitImpl(image.getMat(), landmarks[i]);
    }

    return true;
}
```

It should be modified using the following code:

```
// C++ code

bool FacemarkLBFImpl::fit( InputArray image, InputArray roi,
OutputArrayOfArrays _landmarks )
{
    Mat roimat = roi.getMat();
    std::vector<Rect> faces = roimat.reshape(4,roimat.rows);
    if (faces.empty()) return false;

    std::vector<std::vector<Point2f> > landmarks(faces.size());

    for (unsigned i=0; i<faces.size();i++){
        params.detectROI = faces[i];
        fitImpl(image.getMat(), landmarks[i]);
```

```
    }

    if (_landmarks.isMatVector()) { // python
        std::vector<Mat> &v = *(std::vector<Mat>*) _landmarks.getObj();
        for (size_t i=0; i<faces.size(); i++)
            v.push_back(Mat(landmarks[i]));
    } else { // c++, java
        std::vector<std::vector<Point2f> > &v =
*(std::vector<std::vector<Point2f> >*) _landmarks.getObj();
        v = landmarks;
    }
    return true;
}
```

This way, the generated Python wrappers for the `fit()` function should be correct. *It should be noted that the Python code provided to detect facial landmarks using the three algorithms is correct and only the Python wrappers do not produce the correct code.* See these two links for further information about this issue:

- **Using Facemark API (Python), Version 4.0.0 - pre : bad alloc error**: `https://github.com/opencv/opencv_contrib/issues/1661`
- **Using the Facemark API Python**: `http://answers.opencv.org/question/206275/using-the-facemark-api-python/`

Detecting facial landmarks with dlib

Another option is to use the `dlib` library to detect facial landmarks. In the `landmarks_detection_dlib.py` script, we detected facial landmarks using `dlib`. More specifically, we used the images taken from the webcam to perform face detection using `dlib` frontal face detection. We also offer the possibility of taking the image from a test image. The next step is to get the shape using the shape predictor:

```
p = "shape_predictor_68_face_landmarks.dat"
predictor = dlib.shape_predictor(p)
shape = predictor(gray, rect)
```

The following step is to transform `shape` into a `numpy` array. In this sense, `shape` is a dlib `full_object_detection` object, which represents the location of an object in an image with the positions of all the parts. The `shape_to_np()` function carries out this transformation:

```
def shape_to_np(dlib_shape, dtype="int"):
    """Converts dlib shape object to numpy array"""

    # Initialize the list of (x,y) coordinates
    coordinates = np.zeros((dlib_shape.num_parts, 2), dtype=dtype)

    # Loop over all facial landmarks and convert them to a tuple with (x,y)
coordinates:
    for i in range(0, dlib_shape.num_parts):
        coordinates[i] = (dlib_shape.part(i).x, dlib_shape.part(i).y)

    # Return the list of (x,y) coordinates:
    return coordinates
```

Finally, we draw the 68 facial landmarks in the image. To draw the landmarks in the image, we have coded several functions that offer a flexible way to draw the required landmarks with the desired format. The next screenshot shows you the different possibilities when drawing the detected facial landmarks:

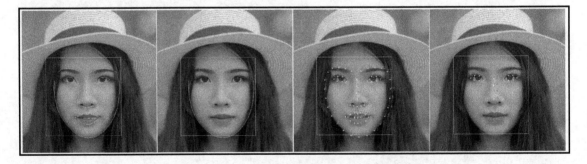

From left to right, to draw the landmarks in every image, we performed the following:

- **First image**: `draw_shape_lines_all(shape, frame)`
- **Second image**: `draw_shape_lines_range(shape, frame, JAWLINE_POINTS)`
- **Third image**: `draw_shape_points_pos(shape, frame)`
- **Fourth image**: `draw_shape_points_pos_range(shape, frame, LEFT_EYE_POINTS + RIGHT_EYE_POINTS + NOSE_BRIDGE_POINTS)`

It should be noted that `dlib` also offers the possibility of detecting 5 facial landmarks that correspond to the locations of both eyes and the tip of the nose. Therefore, if we want to use this shape predictor, we should load it accordingly:

```
p = "shape_predictor_5_face_landmarks.dat"
```

Detecting facial landmarks with face_recognition

The `landmarks_detection_fr.py` script shows you how to both detect and draw facial landmarks using the `face_recognition` package.

In order to detect landmarks, the `face_recognition.face_landmarks()` function is called, as follows:

```
# Detect 68 landmarks:
face_landmarks_list_68 = face_recognition.face_landmarks(rgb)
```

This function returns a dictionary of facial landmarks (for example, eyes and nose) for each face in the image. For example, if we print the detected landmarks, the output is as follows:

```
[{'chin': [(113, 251), (111, 283), (115, 315), (122, 346), (136, 376),
(154, 402), (177, 425), (203, 442), (231, 447), (260, 442), (285, 426),
(306, 403), (323, 377), (334, 347), (340, 315), (343, 282), (343, 251)],
'left_eyebrow': [(123, 223), (140, 211), (163, 208), (185, 211), (206,
220)], 'right_eyebrow': [(240, 221), (263, 212), (288, 209), (312, 211),
(332, 223)], 'nose_bridge': [(225, 249), (225, 272), (225, 295), (226,
319)], 'nose_tip': [(201, 337), (213, 340), (226, 343), (239, 339), (252,
336)], 'left_eye': [(144, 248), (158, 239), (175, 240), (188, 254), (173,
255), (156, 254)], 'right_eye': [(262, 254), (276, 240), (293, 239), (308,
248), (295, 254), (278, 255)], 'top_lip': [(185, 377), (200, 370), (216,
364), (226, 367), (238, 364), (255, 370), (274, 377), (267, 378), (238,
378), (227, 380), (215, 379), (192, 378)], 'bottom_lip': [(274, 377), (257,
391), (240, 399), (228, 400), (215, 398), (200, 391), (185, 377), (192,
378), (215, 381), (227, 382), (239, 380), (267, 378)]}]
```

The final step is to draw the detected landmarks:

```
# Draw all detected landmarks:
for face_landmarks in face_landmarks_list_68:
    for facial_feature in face_landmarks.keys():
        for p in face_landmarks[facial_feature]:
            cv2.circle(image_68, p, 2, (0, 255, 0), -1)
```

It should be noted that the signature of
the `face_recognition.face_landmarks()` method is as follows:

```
face_landmarks(face_image, face_locations=None, model="large")
```

Therefore, by default, the 68 feature points are detected. If `model="small"`, only 5 feature points will be detected:

```
# Detect 5 landmarks:
face_landmarks_list_5 = face_recognition.face_landmarks(rgb, None, "small")
```

If we print `face_landmarks_list_5`, we get the following output:

```
[{'nose_tip': [(227, 343)], 'left_eye': [(145, 248), (191, 253)],
'right_eye': [(307, 248), (262, 252)]}]
```

In this case, the dictionary only contains facial feature locations for both eyes and the tip of the nose.

The output of the `landmarks_detection_fr.py` script can be seen in the following screenshot:

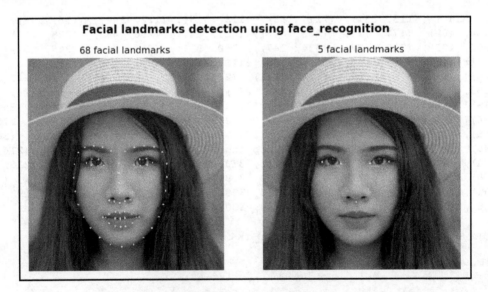

In the screenshot above, you can see the result of drawing both the detected 68 and 5 facial landmarks using `face_recognition` package.

Face tracking

Object tracking tries to estimate the trajectory of the target throughout the video sequence where only the initial location of a target is known. This task is really challenging on account of several factors, such as appearance variations, occlusions, fast motion, motion blur, and scale variations.

In this sense, **discriminative correlation filter** (**DCF**)-based visual trackers provide state-of-the-art performance. Additionally, these trackers are computationally efficient, which is critical in real-time applications. Indeed, the state-of-the-art performance of DCF-based trackers can be seen in the results of the **visual object tracking** (**VOT**) 2014 Challenge. In the VOT2014 Challenge, the top three trackers are based on correlation filters. VOT2014 evaluated 38 trackers (33 submitted trackers and 5 baselines from the VOT2014 committee: `http://www.votchallenge.net/vot2014/download/vot_2014_presentation.pdf`). Therefore, DCF trackers are currently a very popular method of choice for bounding box-based tracking.

The dlib library implements a DCF-based tracker, which is easy to use for object tracking. In this section, we will see how to use this tracker for both face tracking and for tracking an arbitrary object selected by the user. In the literature, this method is also known as **Discriminative Scale Space Tracker** (**DSST**). The only required input (other than the raw video) is a bounding box on the first frame (the initial location of a target) and, then, the tracker automatically predicts the trajectory of the target.

Face tracking with the dlib DCF-based tracker

In the `face_tracking_correlation_filters.py` script, we perform face tracking using the dlib frontal face detector for initialization and the `dlib` DCF-based tracker DSST for face tracking. In order to initialize the correlation tracker, we execute the following command:

```
tracker = dlib.correlation_tracker()
```

This initializes the tracker with default values (`filter_size` = 6, `num_scale_levels` = 5, `scale_window_size` = 23, `regularizer_space` = 0.001, `nu_space` = 0.025, `regularizer_scale` = 0.001, `nu_scale` = 0.025, and `scale_pyramid_alpha` = 1.020). A higher value of `filter_size` and `num_scale_levels` increases tracking accuracy, but it requires more computational power, increasing CPU processing. The recommended values for `filter_size` are 5, 6, and 7, and for `num_scale_levels`, 4, 5, and 6.

To begin tracking the method, `tracker.start_track()` is used. In this case, we perform face detection. If successful, we will pass the position of the face to this method, as follows:

```
if tracking_face is False:
    gray = cv2.cvtColor(frame, cv2.COLOR_BGR2GRAY)
    # Try to detect a face to initialize the tracker:
    rects = detector(gray, 0)
    # Check if we can start tracking (if we detected a face):
    if len(rects) > 0:
        # Start tracking:
        tracker.start_track(frame, rects[0])
        tracking_face = True
```

This way, the object tracker will start tracking what is inside the bounding box, which, in this case, is the detected face.

Additionally, to update the position of the tracked object, the `tracker.update()` method is called:

```
tracker.update(frame)
```

This method updates the tracker and returns the peak-to-side-lobe ratio, which is a metric that measures how confident the tracker is. Larger values of this metric indicate high confidence. This metric can be used to reinitialize the tracker with frontal face detection.

To get the position of the tracked object, the `tracker.get_position()` method is called:

```
pos = tracker.get_position()
```

This method returns the position of the object being tracked. Finally, we can draw the predicted position of the face:

```
cv2.rectangle(frame, (int(pos.left()), int(pos.top())), (int(pos.right()),
int(pos.bottom())), (0, 255, 0), 3)
```

In this script, we coded the option to reinitialize the tracker if the number *1* is pressed. If this number is pressed, we reinitialize the tracker trying to detect a frontal face. To clarify how this script works, the following two screenshots are included.

In the first screenshot, the tracking algorithm is waiting until a frontal face detection is performed to initialize the tracking:

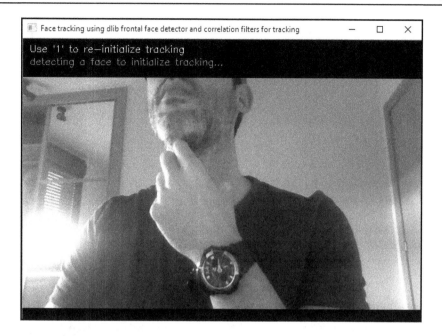

In the second screenshot, the tracking algorithm is currently tracking a previously detected face:

In the previous screenshot you can see that the algorithm is currently tracking the detected face. You can also see that you can also press the number *1* in order to re-initialize the tracking.

Object tracking with the dlib DCF-based tracker

The `face_tracking_correlation_filters.py` script can be modified to track an arbitrary object. In this case, we will use the mouse to select the object to track. If we press *1*, the algorithm will start tracking the object inside the pre-defined bounding box. Additionally, if we press *2*, the pre-defined bounding box will be emptied and the tracking algorithm will be stopped, allowing the user to select another bounding box.

To clarify how the `face_tracking_correlation_filters.py` script works, we have included the next two screenshots. In the first one, we can see that we need to select a bounding box to start the tracking:

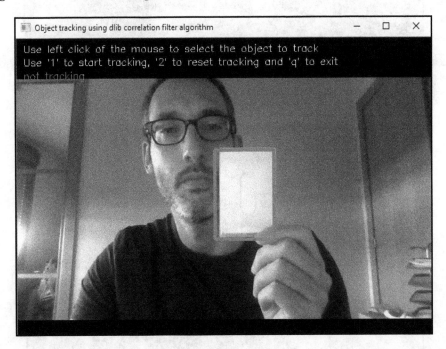

In the second one, we can see the output of an arbitrary frame when the algorithm is tracking the object:

As you can see in the previous screenshot, the algorithm is tracking the object inside the bounding box.

Face recognition

With the development of computer vision, machine learning, and deep learning, face recognition has become a hot topic. Face recognition can be applied to a wide range of uses, including crime prevention, surveillance, forensic applications, biometrics, and, more recently, in social networks. Automatic face recognition has various challenges, such as occlusions, appearance variations, expression, aging, and scale variations. Following its success with object recognition, CNNs have been widely used for face recognition.

In this chapter, we will see the functionality that OpenCV offers in connection with face recognition, and will also explore some deep learning approaches, which can be easily integrated into your computer vision projects to perform state-of-the-art face recognition results.

Face recognition with OpenCV

OpenCV provides support to perform face recognition (https://docs.opencv.org/4.0.1/ dd/d65/classcv_1_1face_1_1FaceRecognizer.html). Indeed, OpenCV provides three different implementations to use:

- **Eigenfaces**
- **Fisherfaces**
- **Local Binary Patterns Histograms** (LBPH)

These implementations perform the recognition in different ways. However, you can use any of them by changing only the way the recognizers are created. More specifically, to create these recognizers, the following code is necessary:

```
face_recognizer = cv2.face.LBPHFaceRecognizer_create()
face_recognizer = cv2.face.EigenFaceRecognizer_create()
face_recognizer = cv2.face.FisherFaceRecognizer_create()
```

Once created, and independently of the specific internal algorithm OpenCV is going to use to perform the face recognition, the two key methods, `train()` and `predict()`, should be used to perform both the training and the testing of the face recognition system, and it should be noted that the way we use these methods is independent of the recognizer created.

Therefore, it is very easy to try the three recognizers and select the one that offers the best performance for a specific task. Having said that, LBPH should provide better results than the other two methods when recognizing images *in the wild*, where different environments and lighting conditions are usually involved. Additionally, the LBPH face recognizer supports the `update()` method, where you can update the face recognizer given new data. For the Eigenfaces and Fisherfaces methods, this functionality is not possible.

In order to train the recognizer, the `train()` method should be called:

```
face_recognizer.train(faces, labels)
```

The `cv2.face_FaceRecognizer.train(src, labels)` method trains the specific face recognizer, where `src` corresponds to the training set of images (faces), and parameter labels set the corresponding label for each image in the training set.

To recognize a new face, the `predict()` method should be called:

```
label, confidence = face_recognizer.predict(face)
```

The `cv2.face_FaceRecognizer.predict(src)` method outputs (predicts) the recognition of the new `src` image by outputting the predicted label and the associated confidence.

Finally, OpenCV also provides the `write()` and `read()` methods to save the created model and to load a previously created model, respectively. For both methods, the `filename` parameter sets the name of the model to save or load:

```
cv2.face_FaceRecognizer.write(filename)
cv2.face_FaceRecognizer.read(filename)
```

As mentioned, the LBPH face recognizer can be updated using the `update()` method:

```
cv2.face_FaceRecognizer.update(src, labels)
```

Here, `src` and `labels` set the new training examples that are going to be used to update the LBPH recognizer.

Face recognition with dlib

Dlib offers a high-quality face recognition algorithm based on deep learning. Dlib implements a face recognition algorithm that offers state-of-the-art accuracy. More specifically, the model has an accuracy of 99.38% on the labeled faces in the wild database.

The implementation of this algorithm is based on the ResNet-34 network proposed in the paper *Deep Residual Learning for Image Recognition (2016)*, which was trained using three million faces. The created model (21.4 MB) can be downloaded from `https://github.com/davisking/dlib-models/blob/master/dlib_face_recognition_resnet_model_v1.dat.bz2`.

This network is trained in a way that generates a 128-dimensional (128D) descriptor, used to quantify the face. The training step is performed using *triplets*. A single *triplet* training example is composed of three images. Two of them correspond to the same person. The network generates the 128D descriptor for each of the images, slightly modifying the neural network weights in order to make the two vectors that correspond to the same person closer and the feature vector from the other person further away. The triplet loss function formalizes this and tries to *push* the 128D descriptor of two images of the same person closer together, while *pulling* the 128D descriptor of two images of different people further apart.

This process is repeated millions of times for millions of images of thousands of different people and finally, it is able to generate a 128D descriptor for each person. So, the final 128D descriptor is good encoding for the following reasons:

- The generated 128D descriptors of two images of the same person are quite similar to each other.
- The generated 128D descriptors of two images of different people are very different.

Therefore, making use of the `dlib` functionality, we can use a pre-trained model to map a face into a 128D descriptor. Afterward, we can use these feature vectors to perform face recognition.

The `encode_face_dlib.py` script shows how to calculate the 128D descriptor, used to quantify the face. The process is quite simple, as shown in the following code:

```
# Load image:
image = cv2.imread("jared_1.jpg")

# Convert image from BGR (OpenCV format) to RGB (dlib format):
rgb = image[:, :, ::-1]

# Calculate the encodings for every face of the image:
encodings = face_encodings(rgb)

# Show the first encoding:
print(encodings[0])
```

As you can guess, the `face_encodings()` function returns the 128D descriptor for each face in the image:

```
pose_predictor_5_point =
dlib.shape_predictor("shape_predictor_5_face_landmarks.dat")
face_encoder =
dlib.face_recognition_model_v1("dlib_face_recognition_resnet_model_v1.dat")
detector = dlib.get_frontal_face_detector()

def face_encodings(face_image, number_of_times_to_upsample=1,
num_jitters=1):
    """Returns the 128D descriptor for each face in the image"""

    # Detect faces:
    face_locations = detector(face_image, number_of_times_to_upsample)
    # Detected landmarks:
    raw_landmarks = [pose_predictor_5_point(face_image, face_location) for
face_location in face_locations]
```

```
    # Calculate the face encoding for every detected face using the
detected landmarks for each one:
    return [np.array(face_encoder.compute_face_descriptor(face_image,
raw_landmark_set, num_jitters)) for
            raw_landmark_set in raw_landmarks]
```

As you can see, the key point is to calculate the face encoding for every detected face using the detected landmarks for each one, calling dlib the `face_encoder.compute_face_descriptor()` function.

The `num_jitters` parameter sets the number of times each face will be randomly jittered, and the average 128D descriptor calculated each time will be returned. In this case, the output (encoding 128D descriptor) is as follows:

```
[-0.08550473 0.14213498 0.01144615 -0.05947386 -0.05831585 0.01127038
 -0.05497809 -0.03466939 0.14322688 -0.1001832 0.17384697 0.02444006
 -0.25994921 0.13708787 -0.08945534 0.11796272 -0.25426617 -0.0829383
 -0.05489913 -0.10409787 0.07074109 0.05810066 -0.03349853 0.07649824
 -0.07817822 -0.29932317 -0.15986916 -0.087205 0.10356752 -0.12659372
 0.01795856 -0.01736169 -0.17094864 -0.01318233 -0.00201829 0.0104903
 -0.02453734 -0.11754096 0.2014133 0.12671679 -0.0271306 -0.02350519
 0.08327188 0.36815098 0.12599576 0.04692561 0.03585262 -0.03999642
 0.23675609 -0.28394884 0.11896492 0.11870296 0.20243752 0.2106981
 0.03092775 -0.14315812 0.07708532 0.16536239 -0.19648902 0.22793224
 0.06825032 -0.00117573 0.00304667 -0.01902146 0.2539638 0.09768397
 -0.13558105 -0.15079053 0.11357955 -0.14893037 -0.09028706 0.03625216
 -0.13004847 -0.16567475 -0.21958281 0.08687183 0.35941613 0.16637127
 -0.08334676 0.02806632 -0.09188357 -0.10760318 0.02889947 0.08376379
 -0.11524356 -0.00998984 -0.05582509 0.09372396 0.30287758 -0.01063644
 -0.07903813 0.30418509 -0.01998731 0.0752025 -0.00424637 0.07463965
 -0.12972119 -0.04034984 -0.08435905 -0.01642537 0.00847361 -0.09549874
 -0.07568903 0.06476583 -0.19202243 0.16904426 -0.01247451 0.03941975
 -0.01960869 0.02145611 -0.25607404 -0.03039071 0.20248309 -0.25835767
 0.21397503 0.19302645 0.07284702 0.07879912 0.06171442 0.02366752
 0.06781606 -0.06446165 -0.14713687 -0.0714087 0.11978403 -0.01525984
 -0.04687868 0.00167655]
```

Once the faces are encoded, the next step is to perform the recognition.

The recognition can be easily computed using some kind of distance metrics computed using the 128D descriptors. Indeed, if two face descriptor vectors have a Euclidean distance between them that is less than 0.6, they can be considered to belong to the same person. Otherwise, they are from different people.

The Euclidean distance can be calculated using `numpy.linalg.norm()`.

In the `compare_faces_dlib.py` script, we compare four images against another image. To compare the faces, we have coded two functions: `compare_faces()` and `compare_faces_ordered()`. The `compare_faces()` function returns the distance when comparing a list of face encodings against a candidate to check:

```
def compare_faces(face_encodings, encoding_to_check):
    """Returns the distances when comparing a list of face encodings
against a candidate to check"""

    return list(np.linalg.norm(face_encodings - encoding_to_check, axis=1))
```

The `compare_faces_ordered()` function returns the ordered distances and the corresponding names when comparing a list of face encodings against a candidate to check:

```
def compare_faces_ordered(face_encodings, face_names, encoding_to_check):
    """Returns the ordered distances and names when comparing a list of
face encodings against a candidate to check"""

    distances = list(np.linalg.norm(face_encodings - encoding_to_check,
axis=1))
    return zip(*sorted(zip(distances, face_names)))
```

Therefore, the first step in comparing four images against another image is to load all of them and convert to RGB (`dlib format`):

```
# Load images:
known_image_1 = cv2.imread("jared_1.jpg")
known_image_2 = cv2.imread("jared_2.jpg")
known_image_3 = cv2.imread("jared_3.jpg")
known_image_4 = cv2.imread("obama.jpg")
unknown_image = cv2.imread("jared_4.jpg")

# Convert image from BGR (OpenCV format) to RGB (dlib format):
known_image_1 = known_image_1[:, :, ::-1]
known_image_2 = known_image_2[:, :, ::-1]
known_image_3 = known_image_3[:, :, ::-1]
known_image_4 = known_image_4[:, :, ::-1]
unknown_image = unknown_image[:, :, ::-1]

# Crate names for each loaded image:
names = ["jared_1.jpg", "jared_2.jpg", "jared_3.jpg", "obama.jpg"]
```

The next step is to compute the encodings for each image:

```
# Create the encodings:
known_image_1_encoding = face_encodings(known_image_1)[0]
known_image_2_encoding = face_encodings(known_image_2)[0]
known_image_3_encoding = face_encodings(known_image_3)[0]
known_image_4_encoding = face_encodings(known_image_4)[0]
known_encodings = [known_image_1_encoding, known_image_2_encoding,
known_image_3_encoding, known_image_4_encoding]
unknown_encoding = face_encodings(unknown_image)[0]
```

And finally, you can compare the faces using the previous functions. For example, let's make use of the `compare_faces_ordered()` function:

```
computed_distances_ordered, ordered_names =
compare_faces_ordered(known_encodings, names, unknown_encoding)
print(computed_distances_ordered)
print(ordered_names)
```

Doing so will give us the following:

```
(0.3913191431497527, 0.39983264838593896, 0.4104153683230741,
0.9053700273411349)
('jared_3.jpg', 'jared_1.jpg', 'jared_2.jpg', 'obama.jpg')
```

The first three values (0.3913191431497527, 0.39983264838593896, 0.4104153683230741) are less than 0.6. This means that the first three images ('jared_3.jpg', 'jared_1.jpg', 'jared_2.jpg') can be considered from the same person as the image to check ('jared_4.jpg'). The fourth value obtained (0.9053700273411349) means that the fourth image ('obama.jpg') is not the same person as the image to check.

This can be seen in the next screenshot:

In the previous screenshot, you can see that the first three images can be considered from the same person (the obtained values are less than 0.6), while the fourth image can be considered from another person (the obtained value is greater than 0.6).

Face recognition with face_recognition

Face recognition with `face_recognition` uses the `dlib` functionality for both encoding the faces and calculating the distances for the encoded faces. Therefore, you do not need to code the `face_encodings()` and `compare_faces()` functions, but just make use of them.

The `encode_face_fr.py` script shows you how to create the 128D descriptor that makes use of the `face_recognition.face_encodings()` function:

```
# Load image:
image = cv2.imread("jared_1.jpg")

# Convert image from BGR (OpenCV format) to RGB (face_recognition format):
image = image[:, :, ::-1]

# Calculate the encodings for every face of the image:
encodings = face_recognition.face_encodings(image)

# Show the first encoding:
print(encodings[0])
```

To see how to compare faces using `face_recognition`, the `compare_faces_fr.py` script has been coded. The code is as follows:

```
# Load known images (remember that these images are loaded in RGB order):
known_image_1 = face_recognition.load_image_file("jared_1.jpg")
known_image_2 = face_recognition.load_image_file("jared_2.jpg")
known_image_3 = face_recognition.load_image_file("jared_3.jpg")
known_image_4 = face_recognition.load_image_file("obama.jpg")

# Crate names for each loaded image:
names = ["jared_1.jpg", "jared_2.jpg", "jared_3.jpg", "obama.jpg"]

# Load unknown image (this image is going to be compared against all the
previous loaded images):
unknown_image = face_recognition.load_image_file("jared_4.jpg")

# Calculate the encodings for every of the images:
known_image_1_encoding = face_recognition.face_encodings(known_image_1)[0]
known_image_2_encoding = face_recognition.face_encodings(known_image_2)[0]
known_image_3_encoding = face_recognition.face_encodings(known_image_3)[0]
known_image_4_encoding = face_recognition.face_encodings(known_image_4)[0]
known_encodings = [known_image_1_encoding, known_image_2_encoding,
known_image_3_encoding, known_image_4_encoding]
unknown_encoding = face_recognition.face_encodings(unknown_image)[0]

# Compare the faces:
results = face_recognition.compare_faces(known_encodings, unknown_encoding)

# Print the results:
print(results)
```

The results obtained are [True, True, True, False]. Therefore, the first three loaded images ("jared_1.jpg", "jared_2.jpg", and "jared_3.jpg") are considered to be the same person as the unknown image ("jared_4.jpg"), while the fourth loaded image ("obama.jpg") is considered to be a different person.

Summary

In this chapter, we looked at state-of-the-art algorithms and techniques for face detection, detecting facial landmarks, face tracking, and face recognition. We reviewed the methods the main Python libraries and packages offer for face processing. More specifically, OpenCV, dlib, face_processing, and cvlib were introduced in the context of face processing. Some of these reviewed methods are based on deep learning techniques.

In the next chapter, we will explore deep learning in depth.

Questions

1. What packages and libraries were reviewed in this chapter in connection with face processing?
2. What is the main difference between face identification and face verification?
3. What does the `cv2.face.getFacesHAAR()` OpenCV function do?
4. What does the `cv2.dnn.blobFromImage()` function do?
5. What function does the `cvlib` package provide to detect faces?
6. What function does `face_recognition` provide to detect facial landmarks?
7. What function does `dlib` provide to initialize the correlation tracker?
8. What function does `dlib` provide to start the correlation tracker?
9. What function does `dlib` provide to get the position of the tracked object?
10. Calculate the 128D descriptor to perform face recognition of the `image` BGR image with `dlib`.

Further reading

The following resource will help you dive deeper into face processing with Python:

- *Artificial Intelligence with Python*, by Prateek Joshi (2017) (`https://subscription.packtpub.com/book/big_data_and_business_intelligence/9781786464392`)

Introduction to Deep Learning

12

Nowadays, **deep learning** is the most popular and fastest growing area in machine learning. Deep learning has been surpassing traditional approaches for machine learning applications since 2012. This is the reason why a lot of deep learning architectures have been applied to a great number of fields, including computer vision. Common applications of deep learning include automatic speech recognition, image recognition, visual art processing, natural language processing, recommendation systems, bioinformatics, and image restoration. Most modern deep learning architectures are based on an artificial neural network, and the *deep* in *deep learning* refers to the number of layers of the architecture.

In this chapter, you will be introduced to deep learning by looking at the differences with traditional machine learning approaches, which were covered in the Chapter 10, *Machine Learning with OpenCV* . Additionally, you will see some of the common deep learning architectures applied to both image classification and object detection. Finally, two deep learning Python libraries (TensorFlow and Keras) will be introduced.

More specifically, the following topics will be tackled in this chapter:

- Deep learning overview for computer vision tasks
- Deep learning in OpenCV
- TensorFlow library
- Keras library

In this chapter, you will be introduced to the world of deep learning with OpenCV, and also with some deep learning Python libraries (TensorFlow and Keras). In Chapter 13, *Mobile and Web Computer Vision with Python and OpenCV*, you will learn how to create computer vision and deep learning web applications.

Technical requirements

The technical requirements are listed here:

- Python and OpenCV
- Python-specific IDE
- NumPy and Matplotlib packages
- Git client
- TensorFlow library (see the following section on how to install TensorFlow)
- Keras library (see the following section on how to install Keras)

Further details about how to install these requirements are covered in Chapter 1, *Setting Up OpenCV*. The GitHub repository for *Mastering OpenCV 4 with Python*, which contains all the supporting project files necessary to work through the book from the first chapter to the last, can be accessed in `https://github.com/PacktPublishing/Mastering-OpenCV-4-with-Python`.

Installing TensorFlow

In order to install TensorFlow (`https://www.tensorflow.org/install/`), use the following command:

```
$ pip install tensorflow
```

To check whether the installation has been performed correctly, just open a Python shell and try to import the TensorFlow library as follows:

```
python
import tensorflow
```

Installing Keras

In order to install Keras (`https://keras.io/`), use the following command:

```
$ pip install keras
```

To check whether the installation has been performed correctly, just open a Python shell and try to import the Keras library as follows:

```
python
import keras
```

Remember that a recommended approach is to install packages in virtual environments. Refer to `Chapter 1`, *Setting Up OpenCV*, in order to see how to create and manage virtual environments.

Deep learning overview for computer vision tasks

Deep learning added an impressive boost to the field of computer vision. In this section of the chapter, some key concepts are tackled in order to introduce you to the world of deep learning.

Deep learning characteristics

Deep learning has some key differences when compared with traditional machine learning approaches. Additionally, deep learning techniques surpass machine learning in many computer vision tasks, but some key considerations should be taken into account in order to know when to apply each technique to accomplish a certain computation task. All of these considerations are briefly summarized as follows:

- Deep learning algorithms need to have a high-end infrastructure to train properly, contrary to machine learning techniques that can run on low-end machines. Indeed, deep learning algorithms inherently perform a large amount of computation that can be optimized using a GPU.
- When there is a lack of domain understanding for both feature introspection and engineering, deep learning techniques outperform other techniques because you have to worry less about feature engineering. Feature engineering can be defined as the process of applying domain knowledge to the creation of both feature detectors and extractors, with the objective of reducing the complexity of the data, allowing the traditional machine learning approaches to learn properly. Therefore, the performance of these machine learning algorithms relies on how accurately the features are identified and extracted. On the other hand, deep learning techniques try to extract high-level features from data, which makes deep learning much more advanced than traditional machine learning approaches. In deep learning, the task of finding relevant features is part of the algorithm, and it is automated by reducing the task of feature introspection and engineering for every problem.

- Both machine learning and deep learning are able to handle massive dataset sizes. However, machine learning methods make much more sense when dealing with small datasets. In this sense, the key difference between both approaches is its performance as the scale of data increases. For example, when working with small datasets, deep learning algorithms struggle to find patterns in the data and do not perform well because they need a large amount of data to adjust their internal parameters. A rule of thumb is to consider that deep learning outperforms other techniques if the data size is large, and traditional machine learning algorithms are preferable when the dataset is small.

In the next diagram, we have tried to summarize these aforementioned key points so as to remember them easily:

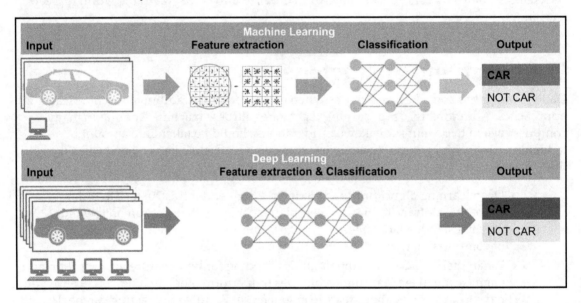

The key points elaborated on in the diagram are as follows:

- Computational resources (deep learning – high-end machines versus machine learning – low-end machines)
- Feature engineering (deep learning – feature extraction and classification in the same step versus machine learning – feature extraction and classification in separate steps)
- Dataset sizes (deep learning – large/very large datasets versus machine learning – medium/large datasets)

Deep learning explosion

The concept of deep learning is not new, as it was introduced to the machine learning domain and to **Artificial Neural Networks** by Rina Dechter in 1986, and by Igor Aizenberg and colleagues in 2000, respectively. However, it was not until 2012, when the deep learning revolution took place, that some outstanding works having a significant impact on the research community appeared. In connection with computer vision, the **AlexNet** architecture (the name of the convolutional neural network that the authors designed) was the winner of the **ImageNet Large Scale Visual Recognition Challenge** (ILSVRC) 2012, with a remarkably low error rate, beating all other competitors by an enormous (15.3% versus 26.2% (second place)) error rate. ImageNet (`http://image-net.org/`) is a large visual database, containing over 14 million labeled high-resolution images. These images were labeled by humans. ImageNet contains more than 20,000 categories. Therefore, the 2012 breakthrough in solving the *ILSVRC 2012* by AlexNet is often considered to be the beginning of the deep learning revolution of the 2010s.

Deep learning for image classification

Following the success of AlexNet in this competition, many other deep learning architectures have been submitted to the ImageNet challenge in order to accomplish better performance. In this sense, the next diagram shows one-crop accuracies of the most relevant deep learning approaches submitted to the ImageNet challenge, including the AlexNet (2012) architecture on the far left, to the best performing Inception-V4 (2016) on the far right:

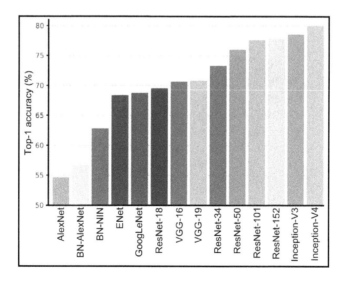

The main aspects of these deep learning architectures are briefly commented on as follows, highlighting the key aspects they introduce.

Additionally, we also include the reference to each publication in case further details are required:

- **AlexNet (2012)**:
    - **Description**: AlexNet was the winner of LSVRC-2012, and is a simple, yet powerful, network architecture with convolutional and pooling layers one on top of the other, followed by fully connected layers at the top. This architecture is commonly used as a starting point when applying a deep learning approach to computer vision tasks.
    - **Reference**: Alex Krizhevsky, Ilya Sutskever, and Geoffrey E Hinton. *ImageNet classification with deep convolutional neural networks.* In *Advances in neural information processing systems*, pp. 1097–1105, 2012.

- **VGG-16 and -19 (2014)**:
    - **Description**: VGGNet was proposed by the **Visual Geometry Group (VGG)** from the University of Oxford. The VGGNet model was placed second in the LSVRC-2014 by using only *3 x 3* filters throughout the whole network instead of using large-size filters (such as *7 x 7*, and *11 x 11*). The main contribution of this work is that it shows that the depth of a network is a critical component in achieving better recognition or classification accuracy in convolutional neural networks. VGGNet is considered a good architecture for benchmarking on a particular task. However, its main disadvantages are that it is very slow to train and its network architecture weights are quite large (533 MB for VGG-16 and 574 MB for VGG-19). VGGNet-19 uses 138 million parameters.
    - **Reference**: Simonyan, K., and Zisserman, A. (2014). *Very deep convolutional networks for large-scale image recognition.* arXiv preprint arXiv:1409.1556.

- **GoogLeNet/Inception V1 (2014):**
    - **Description:** **GoogLeNet** (also known as **Inception V1**) was the winner of LSVRC-2014, achieving a top-5 error rate of 6.67%, which is very close to human-level performance. This architecture is even deeper than VGGNet. However, it uses only one-tenth of the number of parameters of AlexNet (from 60 million to only 4 million parameters) due to the architecture of 9 parallel modules, the inception module, which is based on several very small convolutions with the objective of reducing the number of parameters.
    - **Reference:** Szegedy, C., Liu, W., Jia, Y., Sermanet, P., Reed, S., Anguelov, D., Dumitru, .E, Vincent, .V, and Rabinovich, A. (2015). *Going deeper with convolutions.* In *Proceedings of the IEEE conference on computer vision and pattern recognition* (pp. 1-9).

- **ResNet-18, -34, -50, -101 and -152 (2015):**
    - **Description:** Microsoft's **Residual Networks** (**ResNets**) was the winner of LSVRC-2015, and is the deepest network so far, with 153 convolution layers achieving a top-5 classification error of 4.9% (which is slightly better than human accuracy). This architecture includes *skip connections*, also known as **gate units** or **gated recurrent units**, enabling incremental learning changes. ResNet-34 uses 21.8 million parameters, ResNet-50 uses 25.6 million parameters, ResNet-101 uses 44.5 million, and, finally, ResNet-152 uses 60.2 million parameters.
    - **Reference:** He, K., Zhang, X., Ren, S., and Sun, J. (2016). *Deep residual learning for image recognition.* In *Proceedings of the IEEE conference on computer vision and pattern recognition* (pp. 770-778).

- **Inception V3 (2015):**
    - **Description:** As shown before, the inception architecture was introduced as GoogLeNet (also known as **Inception V1**). Later, this architecture was modified to introduce batch normalization (Inception-V2). The Inception V3 architecture includes additional factorization ideas whose objective is to reduce the number of connections/parameters without decreasing network efficiency.
    - **Reference:** Szegedy, C., Vanhoucke, V., Ioffe, S., Shlens, J., and Wojna, Z. (2016). *Rethinking the inception architecture for computer vision.* In *Proceedings of the IEEE conference on computer vision and pattern recognition* (pp. 2818-2826).

- **Inception V4 (2016)**:
    - **Description**: Inception V4, evolved from GoogLeNet. Additionally, this architecture has a more uniform simplified architecture and more inception modules than **Inception-V3**. **Inception-V4** was able to achieve 80.2% top-1 accuracy and 95.2% top-5 accuracy on the LSVRC.
    - **Reference**: Szegedy, C., Ioffe, S., Vanhoucke, V., and Alemi, A. A. (2017, February). *Inception-V4, inception-resnet and the impact of residual connections on learning.* In *AAAI* (Vol. 4, p. 12).

Deep learning for object detection

Object detection is a hot topic in deep learning that is suited for identifying and locating multiple relevant objects in a single image. To benchmark object detection algorithms, three databases are commonly used. The first one is the **PASCAL Visual Object Classification** (**PASCAL VOC**) dataset (`http://host.robots.ox.ac.uk/pascal/VOC/`), which consists of 20 categories and 10,000 images for training and validation, containing bounding boxes with objects. **ImageNet** has released an object detection dataset since 2013, and it is composed of around 500,000 images for training only and 200 categories. Finally, **Common Objects in Context** (**COCO**) (`http://cocodataset.org/`) is a large-scale object detection, segmentation, and captioning dataset with a total of 2.5 million labeled instances in 328,000 images. For more information about COCO datasets, you can read the publication *Microsoft COCO: Common objects in context (2014)*. To evaluate object detection algorithms, **mean Average Precision** (**mAP**) is commonly used, which is calculated by taking the mAP over all classes and/or over all **Intersection over Union** (**IoU**) thresholds, depending on the competition. In binary classification, the **Average Precision** (**AP**) metric corresponds to the summary of the **precision** (positive predictive value) - **recall** (sensitivity) **curve**, and the IoU metric is the overlapping area between the predicted box and the ground truth box. The following are examples of this:

- PASCAL VOC2007 challenge – only one IoU threshold was considered. For the PASCAL VOC challenge, a prediction is positive if IoU > 0.5. So, the mAP was averaged over all 20 object classes.
- For the COCO 2017 challenge, the mAP was averaged over all 80 object categories and all 10 IoU thresholds (from 0.5 to 0.95 with a step size of 0.05).

 Averaging over the 10 IoU thresholds (from 0.5 to 0.95 with a step size of 0.05) rather than only considering one threshold of $IoU \geq 0.5$ tends to reward models that are better at precise localization.

In the next table, you can see state-of-the-art deep learning algorithms for object detection evaluated with the three aforementioned datasets, where the mAP scores on both the PASCAL VOC and COCO datasets are shown:

Model	PASCAL VOC 2007 (%)	PASCAL VOC 2010 (%)	PASCAL VOC 2012 (%)	COCO 2015 (IoU=0.5) (%)	COCO 2015 (IoU=0.75) (%)	COCO 2015 (Official Metric) (%)	COCO 2016 (IoU=0.5) (%)	COCO 2016 (IoU=0.75) (%)	COCO 2016 (Official Metric) (%)	Real Time
R-CNN (2014)	-	62.4	-	-	-	-	-	-	-	No
Fast R-CNN (2015)	70.0	68.8	68.4	-	-	-	-	-	-	No
Faster R-CNN (2015)	78.8	-	75.9	-	-	-	-	-	-	No
R-FCN (2016)	82.0	-	-	53.2	-	31.5	-	-	-	No
YOLO (2016)	63.7	-	57.9	-	-	-	-	-	-	Yes
SDD (2016)	83.2	-	82.2	48.5	30.3	31.5	-	-	-	No
YOLO V2 (2016)	78.6	-	-	44.0	19.2	21.6	-	-	-	Yes
NASNet (2016)	-	-	-	43.1	-	-	-	-	-	No
Mask R-CNN (2017)	-	-	-	-	-	-	62.3	43.3	39.8	No

An introduction about the state-of-the-art deep learning algorithms for object detection is included below:

- **R-CNN (2014)**:
    - **Description**: **Region-based Convolutional Network** (**R-CNN**) is one of the first approaches using convolutional neural networks for object detection, showing that a convolutional neural network can lead to a higher object detection performance compared to systems based on simpler HOG-like features. This algorithm can be decomposed into the following three steps:
        1. Creating a set of region proposals
        2. Performing a forward pass through a modified version of AlexNet for every region proposal to extract feature vectors
        3. Potential objects are detected by means of several SVM classifiers and, also, a linear regressor changes the coordinates of the bounding box

- **Reference**: Girshick, R., Donahue, J., Darrell, T., and Malik, J. (2014). *Rich feature hierarchies for accurate object detection and semantic segmentation.* In *Proceedings of the IEEE conference on computer vision and pattern recognition* (pp. 580-587).

- **Fast R-CNN (2015)**:
  - **Description**: The **Fast Region-based Convolutional Network** (**Fast R-CNN**) method is a modification of the previous method to efficiently classify object proposals. Additionally, Fast R-CNN employs several innovations to improve training and testing speed while also increasing detection accuracy.
  - **Reference**: Girshick, R. (2015). *Fast r-cnn.* In *Proceedings of the IEEE international conference on computer vision and pattern recognition* (pp. 1440-1448).

- **Faster R-CNN (2015)**:
  - **Description**: Faster R-CNN is a modification of Fast R-CNN that introduces a **region proposal network** (**RPN**) sharing full-image convolutional features with the detection network, thus enabling nearly cost-free region proposals.
  - **Reference**: Ren, S., He, K., Girshick, R., and Sun, J. (2015). *Faster R-CNN – Towards real-time object detection with region proposal networks.* In *Advances in neural information processing systems* (pp. 91-99).

- **R-FCN (2016)**:
  - **Description**: **Region-based Fully Convolutional Network** (**R-FCN**) is a framework with only convolutional layers allowing complete backpropagation for training and inference for accurate and efficient object detection.
  - **Reference**: Dai, J., Li, Y., He, K., and Sun, J. (2016). *R-FCN: Object Detection via Region-based Fully Convolutional Networks.* In *Advances in neural information processing systems* (pp. 379-387).

- **YOLO (2016)**:
  - **Description**: **You only look once** (**YOLO**) is a deep learning architecture that predicts both bounding boxes and class probabilities in a single step. Compared to other deep learning detectors, YOLO makes more localization errors, but it is less likely to predict false positives in the background.
  - **Reference**: Redmon, J., Divvala, S., Girshick, R., and Farhadi, A. (2016). *You only look once: Unified, Real-Time Object Detection.* In *Proceedings of the IEEE conference on computer vision and pattern recognition* (pp. 779-788).

- **SSD (2016)**:
  - **Description**: **Single Shot MultiBox Detector** (**SSD**) is a single deep neural network developed to predict both the bounding boxes and the class probabilities at the same time by means of an end-to-end convolutional neural network architecture.
  - **Reference**: Liu, W., Anguelov, D., Erhan, D., Szegedy, C., Reed, S., Fu, C. Y., and Berg, A. C. (2016, October). *SSD: Single Shot Multibox Detector*. In *European conference on Computer Vision* (pp. 21-37). Springer, Cham.

- **YOLO V2 (2016)**:
  - **Description**: Authors introduced YOLO9000 and also YOLO V2 in the same publication. YOLO9000 is a real-time object detection system that can detect over 9,000 object categories, and YOLO V2 is an improved version of YOLO focused on improving accuracy while still being a fast detector.
  - **Reference**: Redmon, J., and Farhadi, A. (2017). *YOLO9000: Better, Faster, Stronger*. arXiv preprint.

- **NASNet (2016)**:
  - **Description**: The authors introduced a neural network search, which is the idea of using a recurrent neural network to compose neural network architectures. **Neural architecture search net** (**NASNet**) consists of learning the architecture of a model in order to optimize the number of layers, while also improving the accuracy.
  - **Reference**: Zoph, B., and Le, Q. V. (2016). *Neural Architecture Search with Reinforcement Learning*. arXiv preprint arXiv:1611.01578.

- **Mask R-CNN (2017)**:
  - **Description**: **Mask Region-based Convolutional Network** (**Mask R-CNN**) is another extension of the Faster R-CNN model that adds a parallel branch to the bounding box detection with the objective of predicting the object mask. The object mask is its segmentation by pixel in an image allowing object instance segmentation.
  - **Reference**: He, K., Gkioxari, G., Dollár, P., and Girshick, R. (2017, October). *Mask r-cnn. In Computer Vision (ICCV), 2017 IEEE International Conference* on *Computer Vision* (pp. 2980-2988). IEEE.

Deep learning in OpenCV

Since OpenCV 3.1, there has been a **deep neural networks** (**DNN**) module in the library, implementing forward pass (inferencing) with deep networks, pre-trained using some popular deep learning frameworks, such as **Caffe** (`http://caffe.berkeleyvision.org/`), **TensorFlow** (`https://www.tensorflow.org/`), **Torch/Pytorch** (`http://torch.ch/`), **Darknet** (`https://pjreddie.com/darknet/`), and models in **ONNX** (`https://onnx.ai/`) format. In OpenCV 3.3, the module has been promoted from an `opencv_contrib` repository to the main repository (`https://github.com/opencv/opencv/tree/master/modules/dnn`) and has been accelerated significantly. Therefore, since OpenCV 3.3, pre-trained networks can be used to make a prediction within our application, and many of the popular network architectures, which were introduced in the previous section, are compatible with OpenCV 3.3.

In this section, we will see how to apply some of these architectures to both object detection and image classification, but before we cover this, a number of functions that OpenCV provides in the DNN module should be reviewed.

Understanding cv2.dnn.blobFromImage()

In `Chapter 11`, *Face Detection, Tracking, and Recognition*, we have seen some examples involving deep learning computation. For example, in the `face_detection_opencv_dnn.py` script, a deep-learning based face detector (`https://github.com/opencv/opencv/tree/master/samples/dnn/face_detector`) was used to detect faces in images. The first step was to load pre-trained models as follows:

```
net = cv2.dnn.readNetFromCaffe("deploy.prototxt",
 "res10_300x300_ssd_iter_140000_fp16.caffemodel")
```

As a reminder, the `deploy.prototxt` file defines the model architecture, and the `res10_300x300_ssd_iter_140000_fp16.caffemodel` file contains the weights for the actual layers. In order to perform a forward pass for the whole network to compute the output, the input to the network should be a blob. The blob can be seen as a collection of images that have been adequately preprocessed to be fed to the network.

This pre-processing is composed of several operations – resizing, cropping, subtracting mean values, scaling, and swapping blue and red channels.

For example, in the aforementioned face detection example, we performed the following command:

```
# Load image:
image = cv2.imread("test_face_detection.jpg")

# Create 4-dimensional blob from image:
blob = cv2.dnn.blobFromImage(image, 1.0, (300, 300), [104., 117., 123.],
False, False)
```

In this case, this means we want to run the model on BGR images resized to *300 x 300,*
applying a mean subtraction of (104, 117, 123) values for the blue, green, and red channels, respectively. This can be summarized in the following table:

Model	Scale	Size WxH	Mean subtraction	Channels order
OpenCV face detector	1.0	*300 x 300*	104, 177, 123	BGR

At this point, we can set the blob as input and obtain the detections as follows:

```
# Set the blob as input and obtain the detections:
net.setInput(blob)
detections = net.forward()
```

See the `face_detection_opencv_dnn.py` script for further details.

Now, we are going to see the `cv2.dnn.blobFromImage()`
and `cv2.dnn.blobFromImages()` functions in detail. In order to do so, we are first going
to see the signature of both functions, and we are going to see the `blob_from_image.py`
and `blob_from_images.py` scripts. These scripts can be helpful when understanding
these functions. Additionally, in these scripts, we are also going to make use of the
OpenCV `cv2.dnn.imagesFromBlob()` function.

The signature of `cv2.dnn.blobFromImage()` is as follows:

```
retval=cv2.dnn.blobFromImage(image[, scalefactor[, size[, mean[, swapRB[,
crop[, ddepth]]]]]])
```

This function creates a four-dimensional blob from `image`. Additionally, it optionally
resizes the image to `size`, and crops the input image from center, subtracts `mean` values,
scales values by `scalefactor`, and swaps blue and red channels:

- `image`: This is the input image to preprocess.
- `scalefactor`: This is a multiplier for `image` values. This value can be used to
  scale our images. The default value is `1.0`, which means that no scaling is
  performed.

- `size`: This is the spatial size for the output image.
- `mean`: This is the scalar with mean values subtracted from the image. If you are performing mean subtraction, the values are intended to be (mean-R, mean-G, mean-B) when utilizing `swapRB =True`.
- `swapRB`: This flag can be used to swap the R and B channels in the image by setting this flag to `True`.
- `crop`: This is a flag that indicates whether the image will be cropped after resizing or not.
- `ddepth`: The depth of the output blob. You can choose between CV_32F or CV_8U.
- If `crop=False`, the resize of the image is performed without cropping. Otherwise, if (`crop=True`), the resize is applied first and then, the image is cropped from the center.
- Default values are `scalefactor=1.0`, `size = Size()`, `mean = Scalar()`, `swapRB = false`, `crop = false`, and `ddepth = CV_32F`.

The signature of `cv.dnn.blobFromImages()` is as follows:

```
retval=cv.dnn.blobFromImages(images[, scalefactor[, size[, mean[, swapRB[,
crop[, ddepth]]]]]])
```

This function creates a four-dimensional blob from multiple images. This way, you can perform a forward pass for the whole network to compute the output of several images at once. The following code shows you how to use this function properly:

```
# Create a list of images:
images = [image, image2]

# Call cv2.dnn.blobFromImages():
blob_images = cv2.dnn.blobFromImages(images, 1.0, (300, 300), [104., 117.,
123.], False, False)

# Set the blob as input and obtain the detections:
net.setInput(blob_images)
detections = net.forward()
```

At this point, we have introduced the `cv2.dnn.blobFromImage()` and `cv2.dnn.blobFromImages()` functions. So, we are ready to see the `blob_from_image.py` and `blob_from_images.py` scripts.

In the `blob_from_image.py` script, we first load a BGR image, and create a four-dimensional blob making use of the `cv2.dnn.blobFromImage()` function. You can check that the shape of the created blob is `(1, 3, 300, 300)`. Then, we call the `get_image_from_blob()` function, which can be used to perform the inverse preprocessing transformations in order to get the input image again. This way, you will get a better understanding of this preprocessing. The code of the `get_image_from_blob` function is as follows:

```
def get_image_from_blob(blob_img, scalefactor, dim, mean, swap_rb,
mean_added):
    """Returns image from blob assuming that the blob is from only one
image"""
    images_from_blob = cv2.dnn.imagesFromBlob(blob_img)
    image_from_blob = np.reshape(images_from_blob[0], dim) / scalefactor
    image_from_blob_mean = np.uint8(image_from_blob)
    image_from_blob = image_from_blob_mean + np.uint8(mean)

    if mean_added is True:
        if swap_rb:
            image_from_blob = image_from_blob[:, :, ::-1]
        return image_from_blob
    else:
        if swap_rb:
            image_from_blob_mean = image_from_blob_mean[:, :, ::-1]
        return image_from_blob_mean
```

In the script, we make use of this function to get different images from the blob, as demonstrated in the following code snippet:

```
# Load image:
image = cv2.imread("face_test.jpg")

# Call cv2.dnn.blobFromImage():
blob_image = cv2.dnn.blobFromImage(image, 1.0, (300, 300), [104., 117.,
123.], False, False)

# The shape of the blob_image will be (1, 3, 300, 300):
print(blob_image.shape)

# Get different images from the blob:
img_from_blob = get_image_from_blob(blob_image, 1.0, (300, 300, 3), [104.,
117., 123.], False, True)
```

```
img_from_blob_swap = get_image_from_blob(blob_image, 1.0, (300, 300, 3),
[104., 117., 123.], True, True)
img_from_blob_mean = get_image_from_blob(blob_image, 1.0, (300, 300, 3),
[104., 117., 123.], False, False)
img_from_blob_mean_swap = get_image_from_blob(blob_image, 1.0, (300, 300,
3), [104., 117., 123.], True, False)
```

The created images are explained as follows:

- The `img_from_blob` image corresponds to the original BGR image resized to `(300,300)`.
- The `img_from_blob_swap` image corresponds to the original BGR image resized to `(300,300)`, and the blue and red channels have been swapped.
- The `img_from_blob_mean` image corresponds to the original BGR image resized to `(300,300)`, where the scalar with mean values has not been added to the image.
- The `img_from_blob_mean_swap` image corresponds to the original BGR image resized to `(300,300)`, where the scalar with mean values has not been added to the image and the blue and red channels have been swapped.

The output of this script can be seen in the following screenshot:

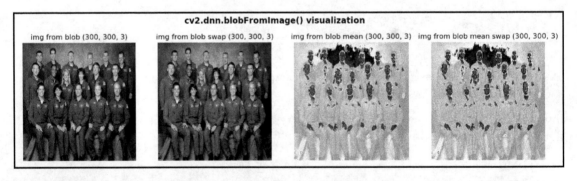

In the previous screenshot, we can see the four obtained (`img_from_blob`, `img_from_blob_swap`, `img_from_blob_mean`, and `img_from_blob_mean_swap`) images.

In the `blob_from_images.py` script, we first load two BGR images, create a four-dimensional blob making use of the `cv2.dnn.blobFromImages()` function. You can check that the shape of the created blob is `(2, 3, 300, 300)`. Then, we call the `get_images_from_blob()` function, which can be used to perform the inverse pre-processing transformations in order to get the input images again.

The code for the `get_images_from_blob` function is as follows:

```
def get_images_from_blob(blob_imgs, scalefactor, dim, mean, swap_rb,
mean_added):
    """Returns images from blob"""

    images_from_blob = cv2.dnn.imagesFromBlob(blob_imgs)
    imgs = []

    for image_blob in images_from_blob:
        image_from_blob = np.reshape(image_blob, dim) / scalefactor
        image_from_blob_mean = np.uint8(image_from_blob)
        image_from_blob = image_from_blob_mean + np.uint8(mean)
        if mean_added is True:
            if swap_rb:
                image_from_blob = image_from_blob[:, :, ::-1]
            imgs.append(image_from_blob)
        else:
            if swap_rb:
                image_from_blob_mean = image_from_blob_mean[:, :, ::-1]
            imgs.append(image_from_blob_mean)

    return imgs
```

As previously shown, the `get_images_from_blob()` function returns the images from the blob making use of the OpenCV `cv2.dnn.imagesFromBlob()` function. In the script, we make use of this function to get different images from the blob as follows:

```
# Load images and get the list of images:
image = cv2.imread("face_test.jpg")
image2 = cv2.imread("face_test_2.jpg")
images = [image, image2]

# Call cv2.dnn.blobFromImages():
blob_images = cv2.dnn.blobFromImages(images, 1.0, (300, 300), [104., 117.,
123.], False, False)
# The shape of the blob_image will be (2, 3, 300, 300):
print(blob_images.shape)

# Get different images from the blob:
imgs_from_blob = get_images_from_blob(blob_images, 1.0, (300, 300, 3),
[104., 117., 123.], False, True)
imgs_from_blob_swap = get_images_from_blob(blob_images, 1.0, (300, 300, 3),
[104., 117., 123.], True, True)
imgs_from_blob_mean = get_images_from_blob(blob_images, 1.0, (300, 300, 3),
[104., 117., 123.], False, False)
imgs_from_blob_mean_swap = get_images_from_blob(blob_images, 1.0, (300,
300, 3), [104., 117., 123.], True, False)
```

In the previous code, we make use of the `get_images_from_blob()` function to get different images from the blob. The created images are explained as follows:

- The `imgs_from_blob` images correspond to the original BGR images resized to `(300,300)`.
- The `imgs_from_blob_swap` images correspond to the original BGR images resized to `(300,300)`, and the blue and red channels have been swapped.
- The `imgs_from_blob_mean` images correspond to the original BGR images resized to `(300,300)`, where the scalar with mean values has not been added to the image.
- The `imgs_from_blob_mean_swap` images correspond to the original BGR images resized to `(300,300)`, where the scalar with mean values has not been added to the image and the blue and red channels have been swapped.

The output of this script can be seen in the following screenshot:

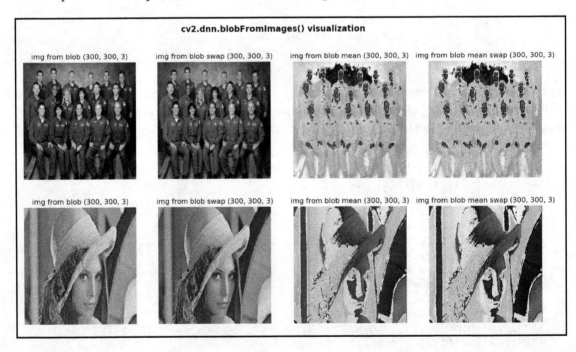

One final consideration with both `cv2.dnn.blobFromImage()` and `cv2.dnn.blobFromImages()` is the `crop` parameter, which indicates whether the image is cropped. In the case of cropping, the image is cropped from the center, as indicated in the following screenshot:

As you can see, the cropping is performed from the center of the image, indicated by the yellow line. To replicate the cropping that OpenCV performs inside the `cv2.dnn.blobFromImage()` and `cv2.dnn.blobFromImages()` functions, we have coded the `get_cropped_img()` function as follows:

```python
def get_cropped_img(img):
    """Returns the cropped image"""

    # calculate size of resulting image:
    size = min(img.shape[1], img.shape[0])

    # calculate x1, and y1
    x1 = int(0.5 * (img.shape[1] - size))
    y1 = int(0.5 * (img.shape[0] - size))

    # crop and return the image
    return img[y1:(y1 + size), x1:(x1 + size)]
```

As you can see, the size of the cropped image will be based on the minimum dimension of the original image. Therefore, in the previous example, the cropped image will have a size of (482, 482).

In the blob_from_images_cropping.py script, we see the effect of cropping, and we also replicate the cropping procedure in the get_cropped_img() function:

```
# Load images and get the list of images:
image = cv2.imread("face_test.jpg")
image2 = cv2.imread("face_test_2.jpg")
images = [image, image2]

# To see how cropping works, we are going to perform the cropping
formulation that
# both blobFromImage() and blobFromImages() perform applying it to one of
the input images:
cropped_img = get_cropped_img(image)
# cv2.imwrite("cropped_img.jpg", cropped_img)

# Call cv2.dnn.blobFromImages():
blob_images = cv2.dnn.blobFromImages(images, 1.0, (300, 300), [104., 117.,
123.], False, False)
blob_blob_images_cropped = cv2.dnn.blobFromImages(images, 1.0, (300, 300),
[104., 117., 123.], False, True)

# Get different images from the blob:
imgs_from_blob = get_images_from_blob(blob_images, 1.0, (300, 300, 3),
[104., 117., 123.], False, True)
imgs_from_blob_cropped = get_images_from_blob(blob_blob_images_cropped,
1.0, (300, 300, 3), [104., 117., 123.], False, True)
```

The output of the blob_from_images_cropping.py script can be seen in the following screenshot:

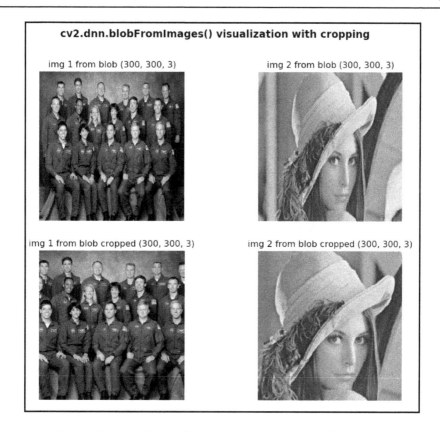

The effect of cropping in the two loaded images can be seen, and we can also appreciate that the aspect ratio is maintained.

Complete examples using the OpenCV DNN face detector

Next, we will see how to modify the `face_detection_opencv_dnn.py` script (from `Chapter 11`, *Face Detection, Tracking, and Recognition*) in order to do the following:

- Compute the output when several images (with possible different sizes) are fed to the network – the `face_detection_opencv_cnn_images.py` script

- Compute the output when several images (with possible different sizes) are fed to the network when the `crop=True` parameter in the `cv2.dnn.blobFromImages()` function—the `face_detection_opencv_cnn_images_crop.py` script

The output of the `face_detection_opencv_cnn_images.py` script is shown in the following screenshot:

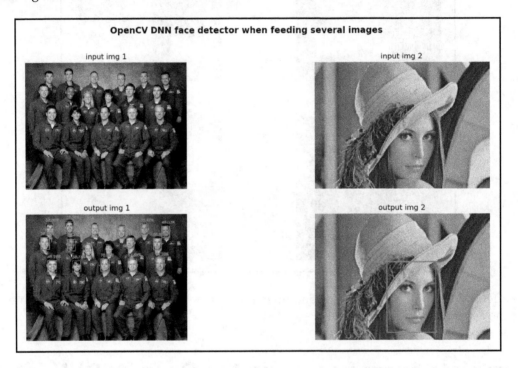

The output of the `face_detection_opencv_cnn_images_crop.py` script is shown in the following screenshot:

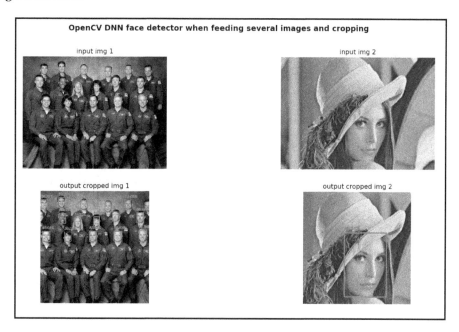

In the previous screenshot, you can clearly see the difference when the images have been cropped from the center.

OpenCV deep learning classification

Several examples of how to perform image classification using different pre-trained models will be covered in this section. Note that you can get the inference time by using the `net.getPerfProfile()` method as follows:

```
# Feed the input blob to the network, perform inference and get the output:
net.setInput(blob)
preds = net.forward()

# Get inference time:
t, _ = net.getPerfProfile()
print('Inference time: %.2f ms' % (t * 1000.0 / cv2.getTickFrequency()))
```

As you can see, the `net.getPerfProfile()` method is called after performing the inference.

The `net.getPerfProfile()` method returns overall time for inference and timings (in ticks) for the layers. This way, you can compare the inference time using different deep learning architectures.

We will see the main deep learning classification architectures, starting from the AlexNet architecture, which is shown in the next subsection.

AlexNet for image classification

Image classification using the OpenCV DNN module by using AlexNet and Caffe pre-trained models is performed in the `image_classification_opencv_alexnet_caffe.py` script. The first step is to load the name of the classes. The second step is to load the serialized Caffe model from disk. The third step is to load the input image to classify. The fourth step is to create the blob with a size of `(227, 2327)` and the `(104, 117, 123)` mean subtraction values. The fifth step is to feed the input blob to the network, perform inference, and get the output. The sixth step is to get the 10 indexes with the highest probability (in descending order). This way, the index with the highest probability (top prediction) will be the first. Finally, we will draw the class and the probability associated with the top prediction on the image. The output of this script can be seen in the following screenshot:

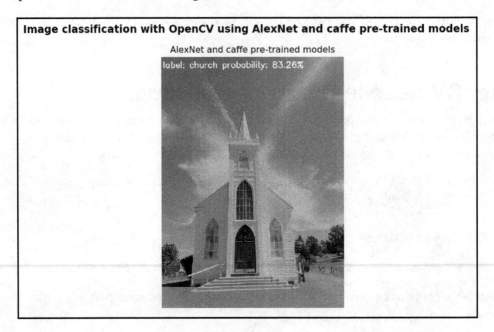

As shown in the previous screenshot, the top prediction corresponds to a church with a probability of 0.8325679898.

The top 10 predictions are as follows:

- 1. label: church, probability: 0.8325679898
- 2. label: monastery, probability: 0.043678388
- 3. label: mosque, probability: 0.03827961534
- 4. label: bell cote, probability: 0.02479489893
- 5. label: beacon, probability: 0.01249620412
- 6. label: dome, probability: 0.01223050058
- 7. label: missile, probability: 0.006323920097
- 8. label: projectile, probability: 0.005275635514
- 9. label: palace, probability: 0.004289720673
- 10. label: castle, probability: 0.003241452388

It should also be noted that we perform the following when drawing the class and probability:

```
text = "label: {} probability: {:.2f}%".format(classes[indexes[0]],
preds[0][indexes[0]] * 100)
print(text)
y0, dy = 30, 30
for i, line in enumerate(text.split('\n')):
    y = y0 + i * dy
    cv2.putText(image, line, (5, y), cv2.FONT_HERSHEY_SIMPLEX, 0.8, (0,
255, 255), 2)
```

This way, the text can be split and drawn in different lines in the image. For example, if we execute the following code, the text will be drawn in two lines:

```
text = "label: {}\nprobability: {:.2f}%".format(classes[indexes[0]],
preds[0][indexes[0]] * 100)
```

It should be noted that the bvlc_alexnet.caffemodel file is not included in the repository of this book because it exceeds GitHub's file size limit of 100.00 MB. You have to download it from http://dl.caffe.berkeleyvision.org/bvlc_alexnet.caffemodel.

Therefore, you have to download the bvlc_alexnet.caffemodel file before running the script.

GoogLeNet for image classification

In a similar fashion to the previous script, image classification using the OpenCV CNN module using GoogLeNet and Caffe pre-trained models is performed in the `image_classification_opencv_googlenet_caffe.py` script.

The output of this script can be seen in the following screenshot:

As shown in the previous screenshot, the top prediction corresponds to a church with a probability of 0.9082632661.

The top 10 predictions are as follows:

- 1. label: church, probability: 0.9082632661
- 2. label: bell cote, probability: 0.06350905448
- 3. label: monastery, probability: 0.02046923898
- 4. label: dome, probability: 0.002624791814
- 5. label: mosque, probability: 0.001077500987
- 6. label: fountain, probability: 0.001011475339
- 7. label: palace, probability: 0.0007750992081

- 8. label: castle, probability: 0.0002349214483
- 9. label: pedestal, probability: 0.0002306570677
- 10. label: analog clock, probability: 0.0002107089822

ResNet for image classification

The ResNet for image classification script
(`image_classification_opencv_restnet_50_caffe.py`) will use ResNet-50 with
Caffe pre-trained models to perform image classification.

The output can be seen in the following screenshot:

As shown in the previous screenshot, the top prediction corresponds to a church with a
probability of 0.9955400825.

The top 10 predictions are as follows:

- 1. label: church, probability: 0.9955400825
- 2. label: dome, probability: 0.002429900225
- 3. label: bell cote, probability: 0.0007424423238
- 4. label: monastery, probability: 0.0003768313909
- 5. label: picket fence, probability: 0.0003282549733

- 6. label: mosque, probability: 0.000258318265
- 7. label: mobile home, probability: 0.0001083607058
- 8. label: stupa, probability: 2.96174203e-05
- 9. label: palace, probability: 2.621001659e-05
- 10. label: beacon, probability: 2.02897063e-05

SqueezeNet for image classification

In the image_classification_opencv_squeezenet_caffe.py script, we perform image classification using the SqueezeNet architecture, which provides AlexNet-level accuracy with 50x fewer parameters. The output of this script can be seen in the following screenshot:

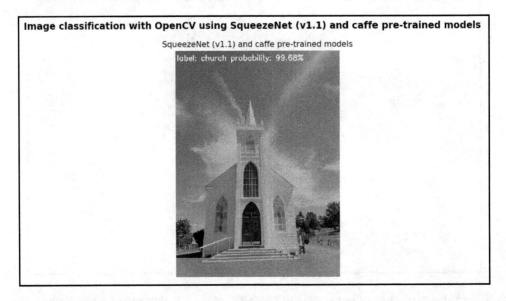

As shown in the previous screenshot, the top prediction corresponds to a church with a probability of 0.9967952371.

In this script, we are using SqueezeNet v1.1, which has *2.4x* less computation than v1.0, but without sacrificing any accuracy.

The top 10 predictions are as follows:

- 1. label: church, probability: 0.9967952371
- 2. label: monastery, probability: 0.001899079769
- 3. label: bell cote, probability: 0.0006924766349
- 4. label: mosque, probability: 0.0002616141282
- 5. label: dome, probability: 0.0001891527208
- 6. label: palace, probability: 0.0001046952093
- 7. label: stupa, probability: 8.239243471e-06
- 8. label: vault, probability: 7.135886335e-06
- 9. label: triumphal arch, probability: 6.732503152e-06
- 10. label: cinema, probability: 4.201304819e-06

OpenCV deep learning object detection

Several examples of how to perform object detection using different pre-trained models will be covered in this section. Object detection tries to detect instances of semantic objects of predefined classes (for example, cats, cars, and humans) in images or videos.

MobileNet-SSD for object detection

We are going to use a MobileNet architecture combined with an SSD framework. MobileNets can be seen as efficient convolutional neural networks for mobile vision applications.

The MobileNet-SSD was trained on the COCO dataset and fine-tuned on PASCAL VOC reaching 72.27% mAP (see the table summarizing mAP for object detection algorithms to put this metric in context). When fine-tuned on PASCAL VOC, 20 object classes can be detected as follows:

- **Person**: Person
- **Animal**: Bird, cat, cow, dog, horse, and sheep
- **Vehicle**: Aeroplane, bicycle, boat, bus, car, motorbike, and train
- **Indoor**: Bottle, chair, dining table, potted plant, sofa, and TV/monitor

In the `object_detection_opencv_mobilenet_caffe.py` script, we perform object detection using the OpenCV DNN module by using MobileNet-SSD and Caffe pre-trained models.

The output of this script can be seen in the following screenshot:

As shown in the previous screenshot, all objects were correctly detected with high accuracy.

YOLO for object detection

In the `object_detection_opencv_yolo_darknet.py` script, object detection is carried out using YOLO v3. YOLO v3 uses a few tricks to improve training and increase performance, including multi-scale predictions and a better backbone classifier, among others.

The output of this script can be seen in the following screenshot:

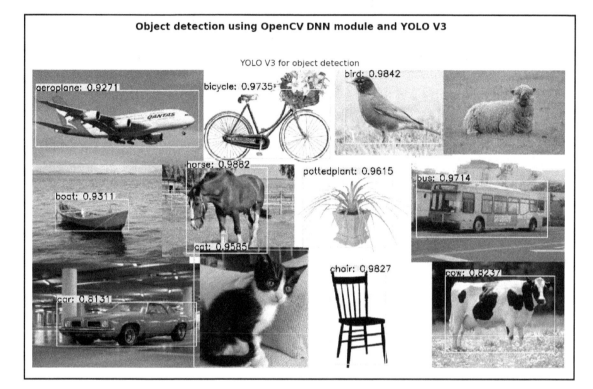

As shown in the previous screenshot, all objects but one (the sheep) were correctly detected with high accuracy. Therefore, you have to download the `yolov3.weights` file before running the script.

It should be noted that the `yolov3.weights` file is not included in the repository of this book because it exceeds GitHub's file size limit of 100.00 MB. You have to download it from `https://pjreddie.com/media/files/yolov3.weights`.

The TensorFlow library

TensorFlow is an open source software platform for machine learning and deep learning that was developed by the Google Brain team for internal use. Later on, TensorFlow was released under the Apache license in 2015. In this section, we will see some examples in order to introduce you to the TensorFlow library.

Introduction example to TensorFlow

The TensorFlow library represents the computation to perform by linking operations into a computation graph. Once this computation graph is created, you can open a TensorFlow session and execute the computation graph to get the results. This procedure can be seen in the `tensorflow_basic_op.py` script, which performs a multiplication operation defined inside a computation graph as follows:

```
# path to the folder that we want to save the logs for Tensorboard
logs_path = "./logs"

# Define placeholders:
X_1 = tf.placeholder(tf.int16, name="X_1")
X_2 = tf.placeholder(tf.int16, name="X_2")

# Define a multiplication operation:
multiply = tf.multiply(X_1, X_2, name="my_multiplication")
```

The values for placeholders are provided when the graph is run in a session, as demonstrated in the following code snippet:

```
# Start the session and run the operation with different inputs:
with tf.Session() as sess:
    summary_writer = tf.summary.FileWriter(logs_path, sess.graph)

    print("2 x 3 = {}".format(sess.run(multiply, feed_dict={X_1: 2, X_2:
3})))
    print("[2, 3] x [3, 4] = {}".format(sess.run(multiply, feed_dict={X_1:
[2, 3], X_2: [3, 4]})))
```

As you can see, the computational graph is parametrized to access external inputs, known as **placeholders**. In the same session, we are performing two multiplications with different inputs. As the computational graph is a key point in TensorFlow, the graph visualization can help you to both understand and debug them using TensorBoard, which is a visualization software that comes with any standard TensorFlow installation. To visualize the computation graph with TensorBoard, you need to write log files of the program using `tf.summary.FileWriter()`, as shown previously. If you execute this script, the `logs` directory will be created in the same location where you executed this script. To run TensorBoard, you should execute the following code:

```
$ tensorboard --logdir="./logs"
```

This will generate a link (`http://localhost:6006/`) for you to enter in your browser, and you will see the **TensorBoard** page, which can be seen in the following screenshot:

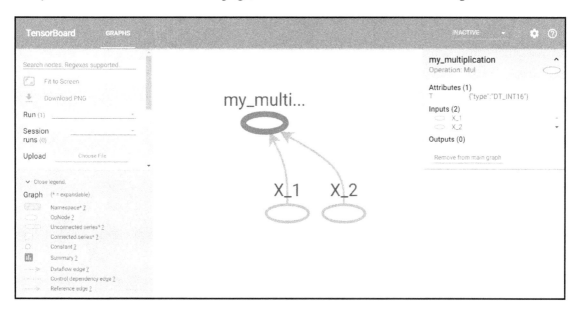

You can see the computation graph of the previous script. Additionally, as TensorFlow graphs can have many thousands of nodes, scopes can be created to simplify the visualization, and **TensorBoard** uses this information to define a hierarchy on the nodes in the graph. This idea is shown in the `tensorflow_basic_ops_scope.py` script, where we define two operations (addition and multiplication) inside the `Operations` scope as follows:

```
with tf.name_scope('Operations'):
    addition = tf.add(X_1, X_2, name="my_addition")
    multiply = tf.multiply(X_1, X_2, name="my_multiplication")
```

If you execute the script and repeat the previous steps, the computational graph shown in **TensorBoard** can be seen in the following screenshot:

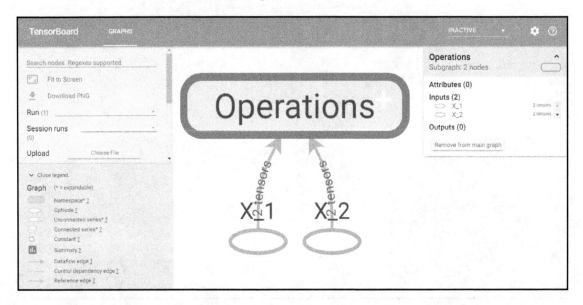

Note that you can also use constants (`tf.Constant`) and variables (`tf.Variable`) in your scripts. The difference between `tf.Variable` and `tf.placeholder` consists in the time when the values are passed. As you have seen in these previous examples, with `tf.placeholder`, you do not have to provide an initial value, and the values are specified at runtime with the `feed_dict` argument inside a session. On the other hand, if you use a `tf.Variable` variable, you have to provide an initial value when you declare it.

 A placeholder is simply a variable to which data will be assigned afterward. When training/testing an algorithm, placeholders are commonly used for feeding training/testing data into the computation graph.

For the sake of simplification, we are not going to show the created computational graphs for the next script, but it is a recommended approach for visualizing the computational graphs using **TensorBoard**, because it will help you understand (and also validate) what computations are performed.

Linear regression in TensorFlow

In the next examples, we are going to perform linear regression using TensorFlow, helping you understand additional concepts you will need when training and testing your deep learning algorithms.

More specifically, we are going to see three scripts. In each script, we are going to cover the following topics:

- `tensorflow_linear_regression_training.py`: This script generates the linear regression model.
- `tensorflow_linear_regression_testing.py`: This script loads the created model and uses it to make new predictions.
- `tensorflow_save_and_load_using_model_builder.py`: This script loads the created model and exports it for inference using `SavedModelBuilder()`. Additionally, this script also loads the final model to make new predictions.

Linear regression is a very common statistical method that allows us to model the relationship from a given set of two-dimensional sample points. In this case, the model function is as follows:

$$y = Wx + b$$

This describes a line with the `W` slope and *y*-intercept `b`. Therefore, the goal is to find the values for the `W` and `b` parameters that would provide the best fit in some sense (for example, minimizing the mean square error) for the two-dimensional sample points.

When training a linear regression model (see `tensorflow_linear_regression_training.py`), the first step is to generate some data to use for training the algorithm as follows:

```
x = np.linspace(0, N, N)
y = 3 * np.linspace(0, N, N) + np.random.uniform(-10, 10, N)
```

The next step is to define the placeholders in order to feed our training data into the optimizer during the training process as follows:

```
X = tf.placeholder("float", name='X')
Y = tf.placeholder("float", name='Y')
```

At this point, we declare two variables (randomly initialized) for the weights and bias as follows:

```
W = tf.Variable(np.random.randn(), name="W")
b = tf.Variable(np.random.randn(), name="b")
```

The next step is to construct a linear model as follows:

```
y_model = tf.add(tf.multiply(X, W), b, name="y_model")
```

We also define the cost function. In this case, we will use the mean squared error `cost` function, as demonstrated in the following code snippet:

```
cost = tf.reduce_sum(tf.pow(y_model - Y, 2)) / (2 * N)
```

Now, we create the gradient descent optimizer that is going to minimize the `cost` function modifying the values of the `W` and `b` variables.

The traditional optimizer is called **gradient descent** (iterative optimization algorithm with the aim of finding the minimum of a function), and is shown here:

```
optimizer = tf.train.GradientDescentOptimizer(learning_rate).minimize(cost)
```

The learning rate parameter controls how much the coefficients change on each update of the gradient descent algorithm. As commented before, the gradient descent is an iterative optimization algorithm and, hence, in each iteration, the parameters are modified according to the learning rate parameter.

The final step when creating the model is to perform the initialization of the variables as follows:

```
init = tf.global_variables_initializer()
```

At this point, we can begin the training process inside a session, as demonstrated in the following code snippet:

```
# Start the training procedure inside a TensorFlow Session:
with tf.Session() as sess:
    # Run the initializer:
    sess.run(init)

    # Uncomment if you want to see the created graph
    # summary_writer = tf.summary.FileWriter(logs_path, sess.graph)

    # Iterate over all defined epochs:
    for epoch in range(training_epochs):
```

```
    # Feed each training data point into the optimizer:
    for (_x, _y) in zip(x, y):
        sess.run(optimizer, feed_dict={X: _x, Y: _y})

    # Display the results every 'display_step' epochs:
    if (epoch + 1) % disp_step == 0:
        # Calculate the actual cost, W and b:
        c = sess.run(cost, feed_dict={X: x, Y: y})
        w_est = sess.run(W)
        b_est = sess.run(b)
        print("Epoch", (epoch + 1), ": cost =", c, "W =", w_est, "b =",
b_est)

    # Save the final model
    saver.save(sess, './linear_regression')

    # Storing necessary values to be used outside the session
    training_cost = sess.run(cost, feed_dict={X: x, Y: y})
    weight = sess.run(W)
    bias = sess.run(b)

print("Training finished!")
```

As shown in the preceding code snippet, once the session is started, we run the initializer, and then we iterate over all defined epochs to train the linear regression model. Additionally, we print the results for every `display_step` epochs. Finally, when the training is done, we save the final model.

At this point, the training is finished and we can show the results, which can be seen in the following screenshot:

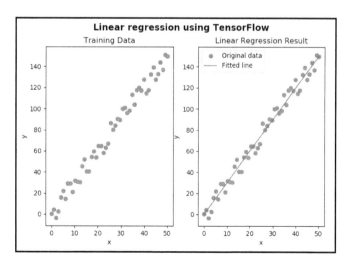

In the preceding diagram, we can see both the training data (left) and the fitted line corresponding to the linear regression model (right).

When saving the final model (`saver.save(sess, './linear_regression')`), four files are created:

- `.meta` file: Contain the TensorFlow graph
- `.data` file: Contain the values of the weights, biases, gradients, and all the other variables saved
- `.index` file: Identify the checkpoint
- `checkpoint` file: Keeps a record of the latest checkpoint files saved

At this point, we can load a pre-trained model and use it for prediction purposes. This is performed in the `tensorflow_linear_regression_testing.py` script. The first thing to do when loading a model is to load the graph from the `.meta` file as follows:

```
tf.reset_default_graph()
imported_meta = tf.train.import_meta_graph("linear_regression.meta")
```

The second step is to load the values of the variables (note that values only exist within a session). We also run the model to get the values of W, b, and new prediction values as follows:

```
with tf.Session() as sess:
    imported_meta.restore(sess, './linear_regression')
    # Run the model to get the values of the variables W, b and new
prediction values:
    W_estimated = sess.run('W:0')
    b_estimated = sess.run('b:0')
    new_predictions = sess.run(['y_model:0'], {'X:0': new_x})
```

At this point, we can show the training data, the regression line, and the newly obtained predictions, which can be seen in the following screenshot:

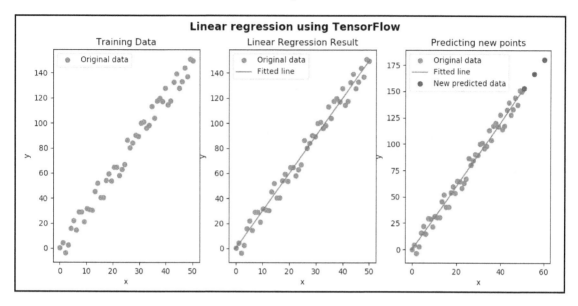

As shown in the previous screenshot, we have used the pre-trained model for making new predictions (blue points). However, when serving a model in production, we just want our model and its weights nicely packaged in one file, facilitating storage, versioning, and updates of your different models. The result will be a binary file with a `.pb` extension, containing both topology and weights of the trained network. The process of creating this binary file, and how to use it for inference, is performed in the `tensorflow_save_and_load_using_model_builder.py` script.

In this script, we have coded the `export_model()` function to export the trained model using SaveModel (https://www.tensorflow.org/guide/saved_model) as follows:

```
def export_model():
    """Exports the model"""

    trained_checkpoint_prefix = 'linear_regression'

    loaded_graph = tf.Graph()
    with tf.Session(graph=loaded_graph) as sess:
        sess.run(tf.global_variables_initializer())

        # Restore from checkpoint
        loader = tf.train.import_meta_graph(trained_checkpoint_prefix +
'.meta')
```

```
        loader.restore(sess, trained_checkpoint_prefix)

        # Add signature:
        ...
        signature_map =
{signature_constants.DEFAULT_SERVING_SIGNATURE_DEF_KEY: signature}

        # Export model:
        builder = tf.saved_model.builder.SavedModelBuilder('./my_model')
        builder.add_meta_graph_and_variables(sess,
signature_def_map=signature_map,
tags=[tf.saved_model.tag_constants.SERVING])
        builder.save()
```

This will create `saved_model.pb` inside the `my_model` folder. At this point, in order to verify whether the exported model has been generated correctly, we can both import and use it in order to make new predictions as follows:

```
with tf.Session(graph=tf.Graph()) as sess:
    tf.saved_model.loader.load(sess,
[tf.saved_model.tag_constants.SERVING], './my_model')
    graph = tf.get_default_graph()
    x = graph.get_tensor_by_name('X:0')
    model = graph.get_tensor_by_name('y_model:0')
    print(sess.run(model, {x: new_x}))
```

After calling the `load` function, the graph will be loaded as the default graph. Additionally, the variables are also loaded, so you can start running inference on any new data. This will output the `[153.04472 166.54755 180.05037]` array, which corresponds to the predicted values generated by our model.

Handwritten digits recognition using TensorFlow

In this example, we are going to classify images using TensorFlow. More specifically, we are going to create a simple model (a softmax regression model) for learning and predicting handwritten digits in images using the MNIST dataset.

Softmax regression is a generalization of logistic regression we can use for multi-class classification. The MNIST dataset (`http://yann.lecun.com/exdb/mnist/`) contains a variety of handwritten digital images:

The `mnist_tensorflow_save_model.py` script creates the model for learning and predicting handwritten digits in images.

The main steps are shown as follows. You can use the following code to automatically import this dataset:

```
from tensorflow.examples.tutorials.mnist import input_data
data = input_data.read_data_sets("MNIST/", one_hot=True)
```

The downloaded data set is composed of three parts – 55,000 rows of `mnist.train` training data, 10,000 rows of `mnist.test` test data, and 5,000 rows of `mnist.validation` validation data. Additionally, training, testing, and validation parts contain the corresponding label for each digit. For example, the training data is composed of `mnist.train.images` (training dataset images) and `mnist.train.labels` (training dataset labels). Each image is composed of *28 x 28* pixels, resulting in a `784` element array. The `one_hot=True` option means that the labels will be represented in a way that only one bit will be `1` for a specific digit. For example, for `9`, the corresponding label will be `[0 0 0 0 0 0 0 0 0 1]`.

This technique is called **one-hot encoding**, meaning that labels have been converted from a single number to a vector, whose length is equal to the number of possible classes. This way, all elements of the vector will be set to zero, except the i element, whose value will be 1 corresponding to the i class.

When defining the placeholders, we need to match their shapes and types in order to feed the data into the following variables:

```
x = tf.placeholder(tf.float32, shape=[None, 784], name='myInput')
y = tf.placeholder(tf.float32, shape=[None, 10], name='Y')
```

When we assign None to a placeholder, it means the placeholder can be fed with as many examples as necessary. In this case, the x placeholder can be fed with any 784-dimensional vector. Therefore, the shape of this tensor is [None, 784]. Additionally, we also create the y placeholder for feeding the true label. In this case, the shape of this tensor will be [None, 10].

At this point, we can start building the computation graph. The first step is to create the W and b variables as follows:

```
W = tf.Variable(tf.zeros([784, 10]))
b = tf.Variable(tf.zeros([10]))
```

The W and b variables are created and will be initialized with zeros because TensorFlow will optimize these values when training. The dimension of W is [784, 10] because we want to multiply it by a 784-dimensional array corresponding to the representation of a certain image in order to get a 10-dimensional output vector.

Now, we can implement our model as follows:

```
output_logits = tf.matmul(x, W) + b
y_pred = tf.nn.softmax(output_logits, name='myOutput')
```

tf.matmul() is used for matrix multiplication and tf.nn.softmax() is used to apply the softmax function to an input tensor, meaning that the output is normalized and can be interpreted as probabilities. At this point, we can define the loss function, the optimizer (in this case, AdamOptimizer (https://www.tensorflow.org/api_docs/python/tf/train/AdamOptimizer) is created), and the accuracy of the model as follows:

```
# Define the loss function, optimizer, and accuracy
loss = tf.reduce_mean(tf.nn.softmax_cross_entropy_with_logits_v2(labels=y,
logits=output_logits), name='loss')
optimizer = tf.train.AdamOptimizer(learning_rate=learning_rate, name='Adam-
op').minimize(loss)
```

```
correct_prediction = tf.equal(tf.argmax(output_logits, 1), tf.argmax(y, 1),
name='correct_pred')
accuracy = tf.reduce_mean(tf.cast(correct_prediction, tf.float32),
name='accuracy')
```

Finally, we can train the model, validate it with the `mnist.validation` validation data, and also save the model as follows:

```
with tf.Session() as sess:
    sess.run(tf.global_variables_initializer())
    for i in range(num_steps):
        # Get a batch of training examples and their corresponding labels.
        x_batch, y_true_batch = data.train.next_batch(batch_size)

        # Put the batch into a dict to be fed into the placeholders
        feed_dict_train = {x: x_batch, y: y_true_batch}
        sess.run(optimizer, feed_dict=feed_dict_train)

    # Validation:
    feed_dict_validation = {x: data.validation.images, y:
data.validation.labels}
    loss_test, acc_test = sess.run([loss, accuracy],
feed_dict=feed_dict_validation)
    print("Validation loss: {}, Validation accuracy: {}".format(loss_test,
acc_test))

    # Save model:
    saved_path_model = saver.save(sess, './softmax_regression_model_mnist')
    print('Model has been saved in {}'.format(saved_path_model))
```

Once the model has been saved, we can use it to recognize handwritten digits in images. In the `mnist_save_and_load_model_builder.py` script, we are going to create `saved_model.pb` inside the `my_model` folder and use this model for making new predictions for loading images using OpenCV. To save the model, we make use of the `export_model()` function that was introduced in the previous section. To make new predictions, we use the following code:

```
# Load some test images:
test_digit_0 = load_digit("digit_0.png")
test_digit_1 = load_digit("digit_1.png")
test_digit_2 = load_digit("digit_2.png")
test_digit_3 = load_digit("digit_3.png")

with tf.Session(graph=tf.Graph()) as sess:
    tf.saved_model.loader.load(sess,
[tf.saved_model.tag_constants.SERVING], './my_model')
    graph = tf.get_default_graph()
```

```
    x = graph.get_tensor_by_name('myInput:0')
    model = graph.get_tensor_by_name('myOutput:0')
    output = sess.run(model, {x: [test_digit_0, test_digit_1, test_digit_2,
test_digit_3]})
    print("predicted labels: {}".format(np.argmax(output, axis=1)))
```

Here, `test_digit_0`, `test_digit_1`, `test_digit_2`, and `test_digit_3` are four loaded images containing one digit each. To load each image, we make use of the `load_digit()` function as follows:

```
def load_digit(image_name):
    """Loads a digit and pre-process in order to have the proper format"""

    gray = cv2.imread(image_name, cv2.IMREAD_GRAYSCALE)
    gray = cv2.resize(gray, (28, 28))
    flatten = gray.flatten() / 255.0
    return flatten
```

As you can see, we have to preprocess each image in order to have the proper format, corresponding with the format of the MNIST database images. If we execute this script, we will get the following predicted class for each image:

```
predicted labels: [0 1 2 3]
```

The Keras library

Keras (`https://keras.io/`) is an open source, high-level neural network API written in Python (compatible with Python 2.7-3.6). It is capable of running on top of TensorFlow, Microsoft Cognitive Toolkit, Theano, or PlaidML, and was developed with a focus on enabling fast experimentation. In this section, we are going to see two examples. In the first example, we are going to see how to solve a linear regression problem using the same input data as the TensorFlow example in the previous section. In the second example, we will classify some handwritten digits using the MNIST dataset in the same way we also performed in the previous section with TensorFlow. This way, you can clearly see the differences between the two libraries when solving the same kind of problems.

Linear regression in Keras

The `linear_regression_keras_training.py` dataset performs the training of a linear regression model. The first step is to create the data to be used for training/testing the algorithm as follows:

```
# Generate random data composed by 50 (N = 50) points:
x = np.linspace(0, N, N)
y = 3 * np.linspace(0, N, N) + np.random.uniform(-10, 10, N)
```

The next step is to create the model. To do so, we have created the `create_model()` function, as demonstrated in the following code snippet:

```
def create_model():
    """Create the model using Sequencial model"""

    # Create a sequential model:
    model = Sequential()
    # All we need is a single connection so we use a Dense layer with
linear activation:
    model.add(Dense(input_dim=1, units=1, activation="linear",
kernel_initializer="uniform"))
    # Compile the model defining mean squared error(mse) as the loss
    model.compile(optimizer=Adam(lr=0.1), loss='mse')

    # Return the created model
    return model
```

When using Keras, the simplest type of model is the `Sequential` model, which can be seen as a linear stack of layers, and is used in this example to create the model. Additionally, for more complex architectures, the Keras functional API, which allows building arbitrary graphs of layers, can be used. So, using the `Sequential` model, we build the model by stacking layers using the `model.add()` method. In this example, we are using a single *dense* or *fully connected layer* with a *linear* activation function. Next, we can compile (or configure) the model defining the **mean squared error** (**MSE**) as the loss. In this case, the `Adam` optimizer is used and a learning rate of `0.1` is set.

At this point, we can now train the model feeding the data using the `model.fit()` method as follows:

```
linear_reg_model.fit(x, y, epochs=100, validation_split=0.2, verbose=1)
```

After training, we can get the values of both `w` and `b` (learned parameters), which are going to be used to calculate the predictions as follows:

```
w_final, b_final = get_weights(linear_reg_model)
```

The `get_weights()` function returns the values for these parameters as follows:

```
def get_weights(model):
    """Get weights of w and b"""

    w = model.get_weights()[0][0][0]
    b = model.get_weights()[1][0]
    return w, b
```

At this point, we can build the following predictions:

```
# Calculate the predictions:
predictions = w_final * x + b_final
```

We can also save the model as follows:

```
linear_reg_model.save_weights("my_model.h5")
```

The output of this script can be seen in the following screenshot:

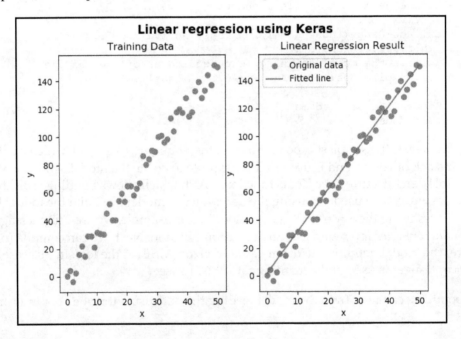

As shown in the previous screenshot, we can see both the training data (on the left) and the fitted line corresponding to the linear regression model (on the right).

We can load the pre-trained model to make predictions. This example can be seen in the `linear_regression_keras_testing.py` script. The first step is to load the weights as follows:

```
linear_reg_model.load_weights('my_model.h5')
```

Using the `get_weights()` function, we can get the learned parameters as follows:

```
m_final, b_final = get_weights(linear_reg_model)
```

At this point, we get the following predictions of the training data and also get new predictions:

```
predictions = linear_reg_model.predict(x)
new_predictions = linear_reg_model.predict(new_x)
```

The final step is to show the results obtained, which can be seen in the following screenshot:

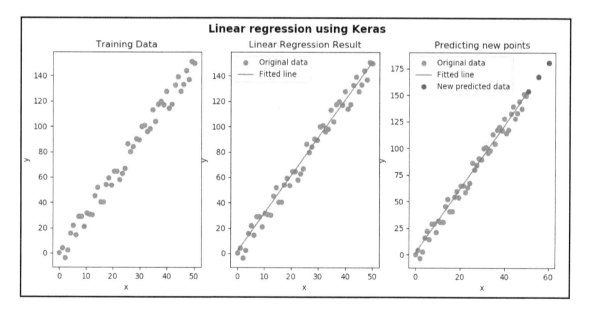

As shown in the previous screenshot, we have used the pre-trained model for making new predictions (blue points).

Handwritten digit recognition in Keras

In this example, we are going to see how to recognize handwritten digits using Keras. The `mnist_keras_training.py` script creates the model using a four-layer neural network, as demonstrated in the following code snippet:

```
def create_model():
    """Create the model using Sequencial model"""

    # Create a sequential model (a simple NN is created) adding a softmax
    activation at the end with 10 units:
    model = Sequential()
    model.add(Dense(units=128, activation="relu", input_shape=(784,)))
    model.add(Dense(units=128, activation="relu"))
    model.add(Dense(units=128, activation="relu"))
    model.add(Dense(units=10, activation="softmax"))

    # Compile the model using the loss function "categorical_crossentropy"
    and Stocastic Gradient Descent optimizer:
    model.compile(optimizer=SGD(0.001), loss="categorical_crossentropy",
    metrics=["accuracy"])

    # Return the created model
    return model
```

In this case, we have compiled the model using the `categorical_crossentropy` loss function, which is a loss function well-suited for comparing two probability distributions and using the **stochastic gradient descent** (**GSD**) optimizer.

To load the MNIST data, we have to use the following code:

```
(train_x, train_y), (test_x, test_y) = mnist.load_data()
```

Additionally, we have to reshape the loaded data to have the proper shape as follows:

```
train_x = train_x.reshape(60000, 784)
test_x = test_x.reshape(10000, 784)
train_y = keras.utils.to_categorical(train_y, 10)
test_y = keras.utils.to_categorical(test_y, 10)
```

At this point, we can create the model, train the model, save the created model, and also get the accuracy obtained when evaluating the testing data as follows:

```
# Create the model:
model = create_model()

# Use the created model for training:
```

```
model.fit(train_x, train_y, batch_size=32, epochs=10, verbose=1)

# Save the created model:
model.save("mnist-model.h5")

# Get the accuracy when testing:
accuracy = model.evaluate(x=test_x, y=test_y, batch_size=32)

# Show the accuracy:
print("Accuracy: ", accuracy[1])
```

At this point, we are ready to use the pre-trained model for predicting new handwritten digits in images. This is performed in the mnist_keras_predicting.py script as follows:

```
# Note: Images should have black background:
def load_digit(image_name):
    """Loads a digit and pre-process in order to have the proper format"""

    gray = cv2.imread(image_name, cv2.IMREAD_GRAYSCALE)
    gray = cv2.resize(gray, (28, 28))
    gray = gray.reshape((1, 784))

    return gray


# Create the model:
model = create_model()

# Load parameters of the model from the saved mode file:
model.load_weights("mnist-model.h5")

# Load some test images:
test_digit_0 = load_digit("digit_0.png")
test_digit_1 = load_digit("digit_1.png")
test_digit_2 = load_digit("digit_2.png")
test_digit_3 = load_digit("digit_3.png")
imgs = np.array([test_digit_0, test_digit_1, test_digit_2, test_digit_3])
imgs = imgs.reshape(4, 784)

# Predict the class of the loaded images
prediction_class = model.predict_classes(imgs)

# Print the predicted classes:
print("Class: ", prediction_class)
```

As you can see, we have loaded four images and we have used the trained model to predict the class of these images. The output obtained is the following:

```
Class:   [0 1 2 3]
```

Summary

In this chapter, we have performed an introduction to deep learning using some popular libraries, including OpenCV, TensorFlow, and Keras. In the first part of the chapter, we looked at an overview of the state-of-the-art deep learning architectures for both image classification and object detection. In the second part, we looked at deep learning modules in OpenCV that provide a DNN library implementing forward pass (inferencing) with deep networks that have been pre-trained by using some popular deep learning frameworks. Therefore, since OpenCV 3.3, pre-trained networks can be used to make a prediction within our application. Later on in this chapter, we had an introduction to TensorFlow, and, finally, we had an introduction to Keras.

In the next chapter, we will have an introduction to both mobile and web computer vision. More specifically, we will see how to create web computer vision as well as web deep learning applications, using OpenCV, Keras, and Flask and learned how to ingrate it with them to provide the web applications machine learning and deep learning capabilities.

Questions

1. What are the three main differences between machine learning and deep learning stated at the beginning of this chapter?
2. What year is considered the explosion of deep learning?
3. What does the following function perform?
   ```
   blob = cv2.dnn.blobFromImage(image, 1.0, (300, 300), [104.,
   117., 123.], False, False)
   ```
4. What do the following lines perform?
   ```
   net.setInput(blob).
   preds = net.forward()
   ```

5. What is a placeholder in TensorFlow?
6. When saving a model using `saver.save()` in TensorFlow, what four files are created?
7. What is the meaning of one-hot encoding?
8. What is a sequential model in Keras?
9. What is the purpose of `model.fit()` in Keras?

Further reading

The following reference will help you dive deeper into deep learning with Python:

- *Practical Convolutional Neural Networks, by Mohit Sewak, Md. Rezaul Karim, and Pradeep Pujari (2018)* (`https://www.packtpub.com/big-data-and-business-intelligence/practical-convolutional-neural-networks`)

Section 4: Mobile and Web Computer Vision

In this last section of the book, you will learn how to create computer vision and deep learning web applications using Flask, which is a small and powerful Python web framework available under the BSD license, in order to build computer vision and deep learning web applications. Additionally, you will learn how to deploy your Flask applications to the cloud.

The following chapter will be covered in this section:

- Chapter 13, *Mobile and Web Computer Vision with Python and OpenCV*

13
Mobile and Web Computer Vision with Python and OpenCV

Web computing is an interesting topic because it allows us to leverage cloud computing. In this sense, there are a lot of Python web frameworks that can be used to deploy your applications. These frameworks provide a collection of packages, allowing the developers to focus on the core logic of the application rather than having to handle low-level details (for example, protocols, sockets, or process and thread management, among others).

In this chapter, we are going to use Flask, which is a small and powerful Python web framework available under the BSD license, in order to build computer vision and deep learning web applications. Additionally, we are going to see how to deploy our applications to the cloud rather than run them on our computer, by leveraging cloud computing.

The main sections of this chapter are as follows:

- Introduction to Python web frameworks
- Introduction to Flask
- Web computer vision applications using OpenCV and Flask
- Deep learning API using Keras and Flask
- Deploying a Flask application to the cloud

Technical requirements

The technical requirements are as follows:

- Python and OpenCV
- Python-specific IDE
- NumPy and Matplotlib packages
- Git client
- Flask (see how to install Flask in the next subsection, *Installing the packages)*
- Keras (see how to install Keras in the next subsection, *Installing the packages*)
- TensorFlow (see how to install TensorFlow in the next subsection, *Installing the packages*)
- Requests (see how to install `requests` in the next subsection, *Installing the packages*)
- Pillow (see how to install Pillow in the next subsection, *Installing the packages*)

Further details about how to install these requirements are present in Chapter 1, *Setting Up OpenCV*. The GitHub repository for *Mastering OpenCV 4 with Python*, containing all the supporting project files necessary to work through the book from the first chapter to the last one, can be accessed in this URL: `https://github.com/PacktPublishing/Mastering-OpenCV-4-with-Python`.

In the next subsections, we will see how to install the necessary packages (Flask, Keras, TensorFlow, and requests) using `pip` commands.

Installing the packages

Let's quickly review how you can install the required packages:

- **Flask**: You can install Flask (`http://flask.pocoo.org/`) with the following command:

```
$ pip install flask
```

To check if the installation has been performed correctly, just open a Python shell and try to import the Flask library:

```
python
import Flask
```

- **TensorFlow**: You can install TensorFlow (`https://www.tensorflow.org/install/`) with the following command:

`$ pip install tensorflow`

To check if the installation has been performed correctly, just open a Python shell and try to import the TensorFlow library:

```
python
import tensorflow
```

- **Keras**: You can install Keras (`https://keras.io/`) with the following command:

`$ pip install keras`

To check if the installation has been performed correctly, just open a Python shell and try to import the Keras library:

```
python
import keras
```

- **Requests**: You can install Requests (`http://docs.python-requests.org/en/master/`) with the following command:

`$ pip install requests`

To check if the installation has been performed correctly, just open a Python shell and try to import the requests library:

```
python
import requests
```

- **Pillow**: In order to install Pillow (`https://pypi.org/project/Pillow/`), use the following command:

`pip install Pillow`

To check if the installation has been performed correctly, just open a Python shell and try to import the Pillow library:

```
python
import PIL
```

I would like to mention that the recommended approach is to install packages in virtual environments. See `Chapter 1`, *Setting Up OpenCV*, to learn more about creating and managing virtual environments.

Introduction to Python web frameworks

Python web frameworks (`https://wiki.python.org/moin/WebFrameworks`) provide a collection of packages that allow developers to focus on the core logic of the application rather than having to handle low-level details (for example, protocols, sockets or process, and thread management, among others). Furthermore, these frameworks can be categorized into full-stack and non-full-stack frameworks. **Django** and **Flask** are two popular web frameworks for Python, which we will discuss later on in this chapter:

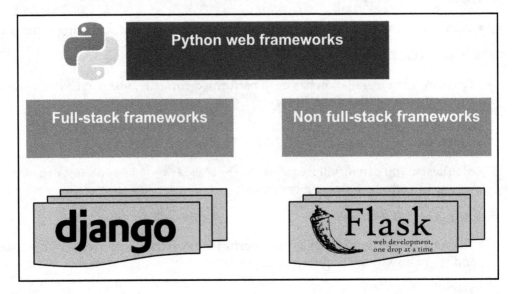

The perfect example of a **Full-stack frameworks** is Django (`https://www.djangoproject.com/`), which is a free, open source, full-stack Python framework, trying to include all the necessary features by default, as opposed to offering them as separate libraries. Django makes it easier to create web applications, and requires less time than other frameworks. It focuses on automating as much as possible by following the principle of **don't repeat yourself** (**DRY**). If you are interested in learning Django, we recommend you read this tutorial, which is about writing your first Django application (`https://docs.djangoproject.com/en/2.1/intro/tutorial01/`).

Flask, which is available under the BSD license, can be considered as the perfect example of **non-full-stack frameworks**. Indeed, Flask is considered a micro-framework, which is a framework with few or no dependencies on external libraries.

Flask has the following dependencies:

- Werkzeug WSGI toolkit (http://werkzeug.pocoo.org/):
    - A WSGI utility library
- Jinja2 (http://jinja.pocoo.org/):
    - A template engine

Both Django and Flask can be used to develop computer vision and deep learning applications. However, it is generally accepted that Django has a slightly steeper learning curve than Flask. Additionally, Flask focuses on minimalism and simplicity. For example, Flask's `Hello World` application is only a few lines of code. Moreover, Flask is also recommended for smaller and less complicated applications, whereas Django is commonly used for larger and more complex applications.

In this chapter, we are going to see how Flask can be used to create computer vision and deep learning web applications.

Introduction to Flask

Here is Flask's `Hello World` application which, as we mentioned, contains only a few lines of code. This can be seen in `hello.py` script, as follows:

```python
# Import required packages:
from flask import Flask

app = Flask(__name__)


@app.route("/")
def hello():
    return "Hello World!"


if __name__ == "__main__":
    app.run()
```

After importing the required package, we will create an instance of `Flask` class, which will be our **Web Server Gateway Interface (WSGI)** application. The `route()` decorator is used to indicate what URL should trigger the `hello()` function, which will print the message `Hello World!`.

In Flask, you can use the route() decorator to bind a function to a URL.

Execute this script with the following command:

```
$ python hello.py
```

You will see this message in your console, telling you that the web server has been started:

```
* Serving Flask app "hello" (lazy loading)
* Environment: production
WARNING: Do not use the development server in a production environment.
Use a production WSGI server instead.
* Debug mode: off
* Running on http://127.0.0.1:5000/ (Press CTRL+C to quit)
```

At this point, you can open your browser and input http://127.0.0.1:5000/. This will perform a GET request to our server, which will return the corresponding message, allowing us to see it in the browser. These steps can be summarized in the next screenshot:

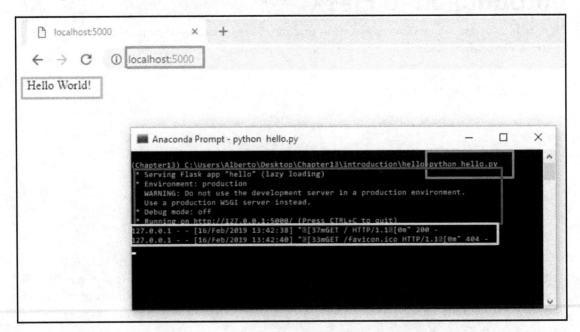

As you can see, the browser displays the Hello World! message.

In the previous example, the script is called `hello.py`. Make sure not to call your applications `flask.py` because this can cause a conflict with Flask itself.

In the previous example, the server was accessible only from our own computer, not from any other in the network. In order to make the server publicly available, the parameter `host=0.0.0.0` should be added when running the server application. This can be seen in the `hello_external.py` script:

```python
# Import required packages:
from flask import Flask

app = Flask(__name__)


@app.route("/")
def hello():
    return "Hello World!"


if __name__ == "__main__":
    # Add parameter host='0.0.0.0' to run on your machines IP address:
    app.run(host='0.0.0.0')
```

This way, we can perform the request from any other device connected to this network, which is illustrated in the next screenshot:

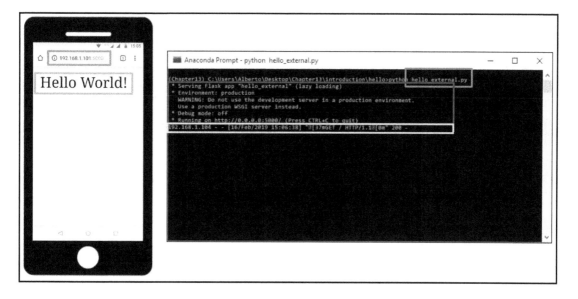

As previously mentioned, you can use the `route()` decorator to bind a function to a URL, as shown in the `hello_routes_external.py` script:

```python
# Import required packages:
from flask import Flask

app = Flask(__name__)


@app.route("/")
def hello():
    return "Hello World!"


@app.route("/user")
def hello_user():
    return "User: Hello World!"


if __name__ == "__main__":
    # Add parameter host='0.0.0.0' to run on your machines IP address:
    app.run(host='0.0.0.0')
```

This is illustrated in the next screenshot, where we request the `http://192.168.1.101:5000/user` URL and we get the `User: Hello World!` message:

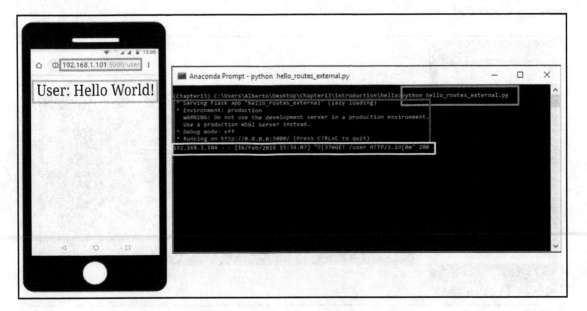

In this section, we have introduced some basic concepts that you must take into account when creating your applications with Flask.

In the next section, we will see different examples in order to understand how to create web computer vision applications using OpenCV and Flask.

Web computer vision applications using OpenCV and Flask

In this section, we will see how to create web computer vision applications using OpenCV and Flask. We will start with the equivalent Hello world application using OpenCV and Flask.

A minimal example to introduce OpenCV and Flask

Script hello_opencv.py is coded in order to show how you can use OpenCV to perform a very basic web computer vision application. The code of this script is shown next:

```
# Import required packages:
import cv2
from flask import Flask, request, make_response
import numpy as np
import urllib.request

app = Flask(__name__)


@app.route('/canny', methods=['GET'])
def canny_processing():
    # Get the image:
    with urllib.request.urlopen(request.args.get('url')) as url:
        image_array = np.asarray(bytearray(url.read()), dtype=np.uint8)

    # Convert the image to OpenCV format:
    img_opencv = cv2.imdecode(image_array, -1)

    # Convert image to grayscale:
    gray = cv2.cvtColor(img_opencv, cv2.COLOR_BGR2GRAY)

    # Perform canny edge detection:
```

```
edges = cv2.Canny(gray, 100, 200)

# Compress the image and store it in the memory buffer:
retval, buffer = cv2.imencode('.jpg', edges)

# Build the response:
response = make_response(buffer.tobytes())
response.headers['Content-Type'] = 'image/jpeg'

# Return the response:
return response


if __name__ == "__main__":
    # Add parameter host='0.0.0.0' to run on your machines IP address:
    app.run(host='0.0.0.0')
```

The previous code can be explained with the help of the following steps:

1. The first step is to import the required packages. In this example, we have used the `route()` decorator to bind the `canny_processing()` function to the `/canny` URL. Additionally, the `url` parameter is also needed to perform the GET request correctly. In order to get this parameter, the `request.args.get()` function is used.

2. The next step is to read the image this URL holds as follows:

```
with urllib.request.urlopen(request.args.get('url')) as url:
    image_array = np.asarray(bytearray(url.read()), dtype=np.uint8)
```

   This way, the image is read as an array.

3. The next step is to convert the image to OpenCV format and perform Canny edge processing, which should be performed on the corresponding grayscale image:

```
# Convert the image to OpenCV format:
img_opencv = cv2.imdecode(image_array, -1)

# Convet image to grayscale:
gray = cv2.cvtColor(img_opencv, cv2.COLOR_BGR2GRAY)

# Perform canny edge detection:
edges = cv2.Canny(gray, 100, 200)
```

4. The next step is to compress the image and store it in the memory buffer, shown as follows:

```
# Compress the image and store it in the memory buffer:
retval, buffer = cv2.imencode('.jpg', edges)
```

5. The final step is to build and return the response to the client, as follows:

```
# Build and return the response:
response = make_response(buffer.tobytes())
response.headers['Content-Type'] = 'image/jpeg'

# Return the response:
return response
```

If we run the script (`$ python hello_opencv.py`), the server will be running and, then, if we perform a GET request from a client (for example, our mobile phone), we will get the processed image, which can be seen in the next screenshot. Additionally, take into consideration that you may need to disable the firewall (on Windows) to be able to perform these requests:

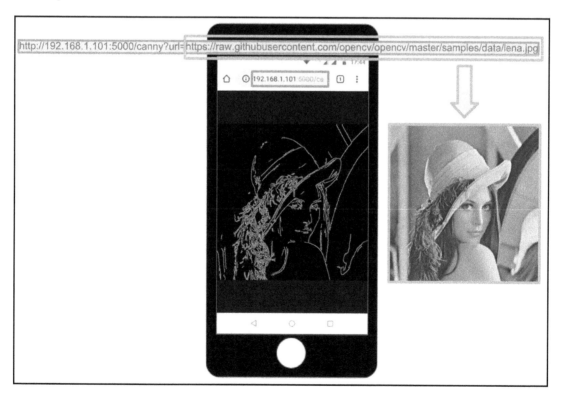

As shown, we have performed the following GET request:

```
http://192.168.1.101:5000/canny?url=https://raw.githubusercontent.com/openc
v/opencv/master/samples/data/lena.jpg
```

Here, `https://raw.githubusercontent.com/opencv/opencv/master/samples/data/lena.jpg` is the image we want to process with our web computing vision application.

Minimal face API using OpenCV

In this example, we will see how to create a web face API using OpenCV and Flask. The `minimal_face_api` project codes the web server application. The `main.py` script is responsible for parsing the requests and building the response to the client. The code of this script is as follows:

```python
# Import required packages:
from flask import Flask, request, jsonify
import urllib.request
from face_processing import FaceProcessing

# Initialize application and FaceProcessing():
app = Flask(__name__)
fc = FaceProcessing()


@app.errorhandler(400)
def bad_request(e):
    # return also the code error
    return jsonify({"status": "not ok", "message": "this server could not
understand your request"}), 400


@app.errorhandler(404)
def not_found(e):
    # return also the code error
    return jsonify({"status": "not found", "message": "route not found"}),
404


@app.errorhandler(500)
def not_found(e):
    # return also the code error
    return jsonify({"status": "internal error", "message": "internal error
occurred in server"}), 500
```

```
@app.route('/detect', methods=['GET', 'POST', 'PUT'])
def detect_human_faces():
    if request.method == 'GET':
        if request.args.get('url'):
            with urllib.request.urlopen(request.args.get('url')) as url:
                return jsonify({"status": "ok", "result":
fc.face_detection(url.read())}), 200
        else:
            return jsonify({"status": "bad request", "message": "Parameter
url is not present"}), 400
    elif request.method == 'POST':
        if request.files.get("image"):
            return jsonify({"status": "ok", "result":
fc.face_detection(request.files["image"].read())}), 200
        else:
            return jsonify({"status": "bad request", "message": "Parameter
image is not present"}), 400
    else:
        return jsonify({"status": "failure", "message": "PUT method not
supported for API"}), 405


if __name__ == "__main__":
    # Add parameter host='0.0.0.0' to run on your machines IP address:
    app.run(host='0.0.0.0')
```

As you can see, we make use of the jsonify() function to create the JSON representation of the given arguments, with an application/json MIME type. JSON can be considered the *de facto* standard for information exchange and, in this example, we will return a JSON response, rather than return an image as we have performed in the previous example. As you can also see, this API supports both GET and POST requests. Additionally, in the main.py script, we also register error handlers by decorating functions with errorhandler(). Remember also to set the error code when returning the response to the client.

The image processing is performed in the face_processing.py script, where the FaceProcessing() class is coded:

```
# Import required packages:
import cv2
import numpy as np
import os


class FaceProcessing(object):
    def __init__(self):
```

```
            self.file = os.path.join(os.path.join(os.path.dirname(__file__),
    "data"), "haarcascade_frontalface_alt.xml")
            self.face_cascade = cv2.CascadeClassifier(self.file)

    def face_detection(self, image):
        # Convert image to OpenCV format:
        image_array = np.asarray(bytearray(image), dtype=np.uint8)
        img_opencv = cv2.imdecode(image_array, -1)
        output = []
        # Detect faces and build output:
        gray = cv2.cvtColor(img_opencv, cv2.COLOR_BGR2GRAY)
        faces = self.face_cascade.detectMultiScale(gray, scaleFactor=1.1,
    minNeighbors=5, minSize=(25, 25))
        for face in faces:
            # face.tolist(): returns a copy of the array data as a Python
    list
            x, y, w, h = face.tolist()
            face = {"box": [x, y, x + w, y + h]}
            output.append(face)
        # Return output:
        return output
```

The `face_detection()` method performs face detection by using the OpenCV `detectMultiScale()` function. For every detected face, we will get its coordinates, `(x, y, w, h)`, and build the `box` by encoding the detection in a proper format:

```
face = {"box": [x, y, x + w, y + h]}
```

Finally, we add the encoded face detection to the `output`:

```
output.append(face)
```

When all the detected faces are added to the output, we will return it.

To make use of this API, we can perform a GET request from the browser in the same way as we performed in the previous examples. Additionally, as our API also supports POST requests, we have included two scripts to test the functionality of this API. These scripts perform both GET and POST requests to see how you can interact with the aforementioned face API. More specifically, `demo_request.py` performs several requests to the face API in order to obtain different responses and, also, to see how error handling works.

In this script, we first perform a GET request using an incorrect URL:

```
# Import required packages:
import requests

FACE_DETECTION_REST_API_URL = "http://localhost:5000/detect"
FACE_DETECTION_REST_API_URL_WRONG = "http://localhost:5000/process"
IMAGE_PATH = "test_face_processing.jpg"
URL_IMAGE =
"https://raw.githubusercontent.com/opencv/opencv/master/samples/data/lena.j
pg"

# Submit the GET request:
r = requests.get(FACE_DETECTION_REST_API_URL_WRONG)
# See the response:
print("status code: {}".format(r.status_code))
print("headers: {}".format(r.headers))
print("content: {}".format(r.json()))
```

In this case, we get the following:

```
status code: 404
 headers: {'Content-Type': 'application/json', 'Content-Length': '51',
'Server': 'Werkzeug/0.14.1 Python/3.6.6', 'Date': 'Sat, 16 Feb 2019
19:20:25 GMT'}
 content: {'message': 'route not found', 'status': 'not found'}
```

The obtained status code (404) means that the client could communicate with the server, but the server could not find what was requested. This is because the URL of the request (http://localhost:5000/process) is incorrect.

The second request we perform is a correct GET request:

```
# Submit the GET request:
payload = {'url': URL_IMAGE}
r = requests.get(FACE_DETECTION_REST_API_URL, params=payload)
# See the response:
print("status code: {}".format(r.status_code))
print("headers: {}".format(r.headers))
print("content: {}".format(r.json()))
```

In this case, we get the following:

```
status code: 200
 headers: {'Content-Type': 'application/json', 'Content-Length': '53',
'Server': 'Werkzeug/0.14.1 Python/3.6.6', 'Date': 'Sat, 16 Feb 2019
19:20:31 GMT'}
 content: {'result': [{'box': [213, 200, 391, 378]}], 'status': 'ok'}
```

The status code (200) indicates that the request has been performed successfully. Additionally, you can also see that one face has been detected corresponding to Lenna's face.

The third request we perform is also a GET request, but the payload is missing:

```
# Submit the GET request:
r = requests.get(FACE_DETECTION_REST_API_URL)
# See the response:
print("status code: {}".format(r.status_code))
print("headers: {}".format(r.headers))
print("content: {}".format(r.json()))
```

In this case, the response we get is as follows:

```
status code: 400
 headers: {'Content-Type': 'application/json', 'Content-Length': '66',
'Server': 'Werkzeug/0.14.1 Python/3.6.6', 'Date': 'Sat, 16 Feb 2019
19:20:32 GMT'}
 content: {'message': 'Parameter url is not present', 'status': 'bad
request'}
```

The status code (400) means a bad request. As you can see, the url parameter is missing.

The fourth request we perform is a POST request with the correct payload:

```
# Load the image and construct the payload:
image = open(IMAGE_PATH, "rb").read()
payload = {"image": image}

# Submit the POST request:
r = requests.post(FACE_DETECTION_REST_API_URL, files=payload)
# See the response:
print("status code: {}".format(r.status_code))
print("headers: {}".format(r.headers))
print("content: {}".format(r.json()))
```

We get the following response:

```
status code: 200
 headers: {'Content-Type': 'application/json', 'Content-Length': '449',
'Server': 'Werkzeug/0.14.1 Python/3.6.6', 'Date': 'Sat, 16 Feb 2019
19:20:34 GMT'}
 content: {'result': [{'box': [151, 29, 193, 71]}, {'box': [77, 38, 115,
76]}, {'box': [448, 37, 490, 79]}, {'box': [81, 172, 127, 218]}, {'box':
[536, 47, 574, 85]}, {'box': [288, 173, 331, 216]}, {'box': [509, 170, 553,
214]}, {'box': [357, 48, 399, 90]}, {'box': [182, 179, 219, 216]}, {'box':
[251, 38, 293, 80]}, {'box': [400, 174, 444, 218]}, {'box': [390, 87, 430,
127]}, {'box': [54, 89, 97, 132]}, {'box': [499, 91, 542, 134]}, {'box':
[159, 95, 198, 134]}, {'box': [310, 115, 344, 149]}, {'box': [225, 116,
265, 156]}], 'status': 'ok'}
```

As you can see, many faces are detected. This is because `test_face_processing.jpg`
contains a lot of faces.

The final request is `PUT` request:

```
# Submit the PUT request:
r = requests.put(FACE_DETECTION_REST_API_URL, files=payload)
# See the response:
print("status code: {}".format(r.status_code))
print("headers: {}".format(r.headers))
print("content: {}".format(r.json()))
```

We get the following output:

```
status code: 405
 headers: {'Content-Type': 'application/json', 'Content-Length': '66',
'Server': 'Werkzeug/0.14.1 Python/3.6.6', 'Date': 'Sat, 16 Feb 2019
19:20:35 GMT'}
 content: {'message': 'PUT method not supported for API', 'status':
'failure'}
```

As you can see, the `PUT` method is not supported. This face API only supports `GET` and
`POST` methods.

As you could see in the previous responses, when the request was performed successfully, we got the detected faces as JSON data. In order to see how to parse the response and use it to draw the detected faces, we can code the script `demo_request_drawing.py` as follows:

```python
# Import required packages:
import cv2
import numpy as np
import requests
from matplotlib import pyplot as plt


def show_img_with_matplotlib(color_img, title, pos):
    """Shows an image using matplotlib capabilities"""

    img_RGB = color_img[:, :, ::-1]

    ax = plt.subplot(1, 1, pos)
    plt.imshow(img_RGB)
    plt.title(title)
    plt.axis('off')


FACE_DETECTION_REST_API_URL = "http://localhost:5000/detect"
IMAGE_PATH = "test_face_processing.jpg"

# Load the image and construct the payload:
image = open(IMAGE_PATH, "rb").read()
payload = {"image": image}

# Submit the POST request:
r = requests.post(FACE_DETECTION_REST_API_URL, files=payload)

# See the response:
print("status code: {}".format(r.status_code))
print("headers: {}".format(r.headers))
print("content: {}".format(r.json()))

# Get JSON data from the response and get 'result':
json_data = r.json()
result = json_data['result']

# Convert the loaded image to the OpenCV format:
image_array = np.asarray(bytearray(image), dtype=np.uint8)
img_opencv = cv2.imdecode(image_array, -1)

# Draw faces in the OpenCV image:
for face in result:
    left, top, right, bottom = face['box']
```

```
    # To draw a rectangle, you need top-left corner and bottom-right corner
of rectangle:
    cv2.rectangle(img_opencv, (left, top), (right, bottom), (0, 255, 255),
2)
    # Draw top-left corner and bottom-right corner (checking):
    cv2.circle(img_opencv, (left, top), 5, (0, 0, 255), -1)
    cv2.circle(img_opencv, (right, bottom), 5, (255, 0, 0), -1)

# Create the dimensions of the figure and set title:
fig = plt.figure(figsize=(8, 8))
plt.suptitle("Using face detection API", fontsize=14, fontweight='bold')
fig.patch.set_facecolor('silver')

# Show the output image
show_img_with_matplotlib(img_opencv, "face detection", 1)

# Show the Figure:
plt.show()
```

As it can be seen above, we first load the image and construct the payload. Then, we perform a POST request. Afterwards, we get the JSON data from the response and get the result:

```
# Get JSON data from the response and get 'result':
json_data = r.json()
result = json_data['result']
```

At this point, we can draw the detected faces, iterating over all the detected faces, as follows:

```
# Draw faces in the OpenCV image:
for face in result:
    left, top, right, bottom = face['box']
    # To draw a rectangle, you need top-left corner and bottom-right corner
of rectangle:
    cv2.rectangle(img_opencv, (left, top), (right, bottom), (0, 255, 255),
2)
    # Draw top-left corner and bottom-right corner (checking):
    cv2.circle(img_opencv, (left, top), 5, (0, 0, 255), -1)
    cv2.circle(img_opencv, (right, bottom), 5, (255, 0, 0), -1)
```

For each detected face we draw a rectangle and also top-left and bottom-right points. The output of this script can be seen in the next screenshot:

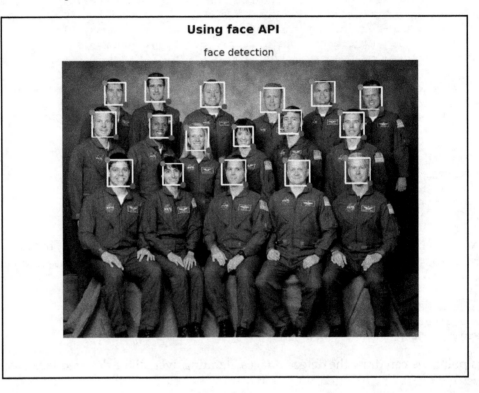

Faces detected with API using OpenCV

As shown in the previous screenshot, all the faces have been detected.

Deep learning cat detection API using OpenCV

Following the same approach we performed in the previous example-Minimal face API using OpenCV, we are going to create a deep learning API using OpenCV. More specifically, we will see how to create a deep learning cat detection API. The `cat_detection_api` project codes the web server application. The `main.py` script is responsible for parsing the requests and for building the response to the client. The code of this script is as follows:

```
# Import required packages:
from flask import Flask, request, jsonify
import urllib.request
from image_processing import ImageProcessing
```

```
app = Flask(__name__)
ip = ImageProcessing()


@app.errorhandler(400)
def bad_request(e):
    # return also the code error
    return jsonify({"status": "not ok", "message": "this server could not
understand your request"}), 400


@app.errorhandler(404)
def not_found(e):
    # return also the code error
    return jsonify({"status": "not found", "message": "route not found"}),
404


@app.errorhandler(500)
def not_found(e):
    # return also the code error
    return jsonify({"status": "internal error", "message": "internal error
occurred in server"}), 500


@app.route('/catfacedetection', methods=['GET', 'POST', 'PUT'])
def detect_cat_faces():
    if request.method == 'GET':
        if request.args.get('url'):
            with urllib.request.urlopen(request.args.get('url')) as url:
                return jsonify({"status": "ok", "result":
ip.cat_face_detection(url.read())}), 200
        else:
            return jsonify({"status": "bad request", "message": "Parameter
url is not present"}), 400
    elif request.method == 'POST':
        if request.files.get("image"):
            return jsonify({"status": "ok", "result":
ip.cat_face_detection(request.files["image"].read())}), 200
        else:
            return jsonify({"status": "bad request", "message": "Parameter
image is not present"}), 400
    else:
        return jsonify({"status": "failure", "message": "PUT method not
supported for API"}), 405


@app.route('/catdetection', methods=['GET', 'POST', 'PUT'])
```

```
def detect_cats():
    if request.method == 'GET':
        if request.args.get('url'):
            with urllib.request.urlopen(request.args.get('url')) as url:
                return jsonify({"status": "ok", "result":
ip.cat_detection(url.read())}), 200
        else:
            return jsonify({"status": "bad request", "message": "Parameter
url is not present"}), 400
    elif request.method == 'POST':
        if request.files.get("image"):
            return jsonify({"status": "ok", "result":
ip.cat_detection(request.files["image"].read())}), 200
        else:
            return jsonify({"status": "bad request", "message": "Parameter
image is not present"}), 400
    else:
        return jsonify({"status": "failure", "message": "PUT method not
supported for API"}), 405


if __name__ == "__main__":
    # Add parameter host='0.0.0.0' to run on your machines IP address:
    app.run(host='0.0.0.0')
```

As you can see, we make use of the `route()` decorator to bind the `detect_cat_faces()` function to the `/catfacedetection` URL and, also, to bind the `detect_cats()` function to the `/catdetection` URL. Additionally, we make use of the `jsonify()` function to create the JSON representation of the given arguments with an `application/json` MIME type. As you can also see, this API supports both GET and POST requests. Additionally, in `main.py` script, we also register error handlers by decorating functions with `errorhandler()`. Remember to also set the error code when returning the response to the client.

The image processing is performed in the `image_processing.py` script, where the `ImageProcessing()` class is coded. In this sense, only the `cat_face_detection()` and `cat_detection()` methods are shown:

```
class ImageProcessing(object):
    def __init__(self):
        ...
        ...

    def cat_face_detection(self, image):
        image_array = np.asarray(bytearray(image), dtype=np.uint8)
        img_opencv = cv2.imdecode(image_array, -1)
```

```
        output = []
        gray = cv2.cvtColor(img_opencv, cv2.COLOR_BGR2GRAY)
        cats = self.cat_cascade.detectMultiScale(gray, scaleFactor=1.1,
minNeighbors=5, minSize=(25, 25))
        for cat in cats:
            # face.tolist(): returns a copy of the array data as a Python
list
            x, y, w, h = cat.tolist()
            face = {"box": [x, y, x + w, y + h]}
            output.append(face)
        return output

    def cat_detection(self, image):
        image_array = np.asarray(bytearray(image), dtype=np.uint8)
        img_opencv = cv2.imdecode(image_array, -1)
        # Create the blob with a size of (300,300), mean subtraction values
(127.5, 127.5, 127.5):
        # and also a scalefactor of 0.007843:
        blob = cv2.dnn.blobFromImage(img_opencv, 0.007843, (300, 300),
(127.5, 127.5, 127.5))

        # Feed the input blob to the network, perform inference and ghe the
output:
        self.net.setInput(blob)
        detections = self.net.forward()

        # Size of frame resize (300x300)
        dim = 300

        output = []

        # Process all detections:
        for i in range(detections.shape[2]):
            # Get the confidence of the prediction:
            confidence = detections[0, 0, i, 2]

            # Filter predictions by confidence:
            if confidence > 0.1:
                # Get the class label:
                class_id = int(detections[0, 0, i, 1])

                # Get the coordinates of the object location:
                left = int(detections[0, 0, i, 3] * dim)
                top = int(detections[0, 0, i, 4] * dim)
                right = int(detections[0, 0, i, 5] * dim)
                bottom = int(detections[0, 0, i, 6] * dim)

                # Factor for scale to original size of frame
```

```
        heightFactor = img_opencv.shape[0] / dim
        widthFactor = img_opencv.shape[1] / dim

        # Scale object detection to frame
        left = int(widthFactor * left)
        top = int(heightFactor * top)
        right = int(widthFactor * right)
        bottom = int(heightFactor * bottom)

        # Check if we have detected a cat:
        if self.classes[class_id] == 'cat':
            cat = {"box": [left, top, right, bottom]}
            output.append(cat)
    return output
```

As seen here, two methods are implemented. The `cat_face_detection()` method performs cat face detection using the OpenCV `detectMultiScale()` function.

The `cat_detection()` method performs cat detection using MobileNet SSD object detection, which was trained in Cafe-SSD framework, and it can detect 20 classes. In this example, we will be detecting cats. Therefore, if `class_id` is a cat, we will add the detection to the output. For more information about how to process detections and use pre-trained deep learning models, we recommend Chapter 12, *Introduction to Deep Learning*, which is focused on deep learning. The entire code can be found at https://github.com/PacktPublishing/Mastering-OpenCV-4-with-Python/blob/master/Chapter13/01-chapter-content/opencv_examples/cat_detection_api_axample/cat_detection_api/image_processing.py.

In order to test this API, the `demo_request_drawing.py` script can be used, which is as follows:

```
# Import required packages:
import cv2
import numpy as np
import requests
from matplotlib import pyplot as plt


def show_img_with_matplotlib(color_img, title, pos):
    """Shows an image using matplotlib capabilities"""

    img_RGB = color_img[:, :, ::-1]

    ax = plt.subplot(1, 1, pos)
    plt.imshow(img_RGB)
    plt.title(title)
```

```
    plt.axis('off')


CAT_FACE_DETECTION_REST_API_URL = "http://localhost:5000/catfacedetection"
CAT_DETECTION_REST_API_URL = "http://localhost:5000/catdetection"
IMAGE_PATH = "cat.jpg"

# Load the image and construct the payload:
image = open(IMAGE_PATH, "rb").read()
payload = {"image": image}

# Convert the loaded image to the OpenCV format:
image_array = np.asarray(bytearray(image), dtype=np.uint8)
img_opencv = cv2.imdecode(image_array, -1)

# Submit the POST request:
r = requests.post(CAT_DETECTION_REST_API_URL, files=payload)

# See the response:
print("status code: {}".format(r.status_code))
print("headers: {}".format(r.headers))
print("content: {}".format(r.json()))

# Get JSON data from the response and get 'result':
json_data = r.json()
result = json_data['result']

# Draw cats in the OpenCV image:
for cat in result:
    left, top, right, bottom = cat['box']
    # To draw a rectangle, you need top-left corner and bottom-right corner
of rectangle:
    cv2.rectangle(img_opencv, (left, top), (right, bottom), (0, 255, 0), 2)
    # Draw top-left corner and bottom-right corner (checking):
    cv2.circle(img_opencv, (left, top), 10, (0, 0, 255), -1)
    cv2.circle(img_opencv, (right, bottom), 10, (255, 0, 0), -1)

# Submit the POST request:
r = requests.post(CAT_FACE_DETECTION_REST_API_URL, files=payload)

# See the response:
print("status code: {}".format(r.status_code))
print("headers: {}".format(r.headers))
print("content: {}".format(r.json()))

# Get JSON data from the response and get 'result':
json_data = r.json()
result = json_data['result']
```

```
# Draw cat faces in the OpenCV image:
for face in result:
    left, top, right, bottom = face['box']
    # To draw a rectangle, you need top-left corner and bottom-right corner
of rectangle:
    cv2.rectangle(img_opencv, (left, top), (right, bottom), (0, 255, 255),
2)
    # Draw top-left corner and bottom-right corner (checking):
    cv2.circle(img_opencv, (left, top), 10, (0, 0, 255), -1)
    cv2.circle(img_opencv, (right, bottom), 10, (255, 0, 0), -1)

# Create the dimensions of the figure and set title:
fig = plt.figure(figsize=(6, 7))
plt.suptitle("Using cat detection API", fontsize=14, fontweight='bold')
fig.patch.set_facecolor('silver')

# Show the output image
show_img_with_matplotlib(img_opencv, "cat detection", 1)

# Show the Figure:
plt.show()
```

In the previous script, we perform two POST requests in order to detect both the cat faces and, also, the cats in the cat.jpg image. Additionally, we also parse the response from both requests and draw the results, which can be seen in the output of this script, as shown in the following screenshot:

As shown in the previous screenshot, both the cat face detection and the full-body cat detection are drawn.

Deep learning API using Keras and Flask

In `Chapter 12`, *Introduction to Deep Learning*, we saw how to create deep learning applications using both TensorFlow and Keras. In this section, we will see how to create a deep learning API using both Keras and Flask.

More specifically, we are going to see how to work with pre-trained deep learning architectures included in Keras and, then, we will see how to create a deep learning API using these pre-trained deep learning architectures.

Keras applications

Keras Applications (`https://keras.io/applications/`, compatible with Python 2.7-3.6 and distributed under the MIT license) is the application module of the Keras deep learning library, providing both deep learning model definitions and pre-trained weights for a number of popular architectures (for example, VGG16, ResNet50, Xception, and MobileNet, among others), which can be used for prediction, feature extraction, and fine-tuning.

Model architectures are downloaded during **Keras** installation, but pre-trained weights are downloaded automatically when instantiating a model. Additionally, all of these deep learning architectures are compatible with all backends (TensorFlow, Theano, and CNTK).

These deep learning architectures are trained and validated on the ImageNet dataset (`http://image-net.org/`) for classifying images into one of 1,000 categories or classes:

Model	Size	Top-1 Accuracy	Top-5 Accuracy	Parameters	Depth
Xception	88 MB	0.790	0.945	22,910,480	126
VGG16	528 MB	0.713	0.901	138,357,544	23
VGG19	549 MB	0.713	0.900	143,667,240	26
ResNet50	99 MB	0.749	0.921	25,636,712	168
InceptionV3	92 MB	0.779	0.937	23,851,784	159
InceptionResNetV2	215 MB	0.803	0.953	55,873,736	572
MobileNet	16 MB	0.704	0.895	4,253,864	88
MobileNetV2	14 MB	0.713	0.901	3,538,984	88
DenseNet121	33 MB	0.750	0.923	8,062,504	121
DenseNet169	57 MB	0.762	0.932	14,307,880	169
DenseNet201	80 MB	0.773	0.936	20,242,984	201
NASNetMobile	23 MB	0.744	0.919	5,326,716	.
NASNetLarge	343 MB	0.825	0.960	88,949,818	.

Keras Applications: Models for image classification with weights trained on ImageNet

In the previous screenshot, you can see the documentation for individual models available in the **Keras Applications** module:

- **Xception**: Xception V1 model, with weights pre-trained on ImageNet
- **VGG16**: VGG16 model, with weights pre-trained on ImageNet
- **VGG19**: VGG19 model, with weights pre-trained on ImageNet
- **ResNet50**: ResNet50 model, with weights pre-trained on ImageNet
- **InceptionV3**: InceptionV3 model, with weights pre-trained on ImageNet
- **InceptionResNetV2**: InceptionResNetV2 model, with weights pre-trained on ImageNet
- **MobileNet**: MobileNet model, with weights pre-trained on ImageNet
- **MobileNetV2**: MobileNetV2 model, with weights pre-trained on ImageNet
- **DenseNet121**: DenseNet121 model, with weights pre-trained on ImageNet
- **DenseNet169**: DenseNet169 model, with weights pre-trained on ImageNet
- **DenseNet201**: DenseNet201 model, with weights pre-trained on ImageNet
- **NASNetMobile**: NASNetMobile model, with weights pre-trained on ImageNet
- **NASNetLarge**: NASNetLarge model, with weights pre-trained on ImageNet

In the `classification_keras_pretrained_imagenet_models.py` script, we show how you can use these pre-trained models for prediction purposes.

 These pre-trained models can also be used for feature extraction (for example, feature extraction from an arbitrary intermediate layer), and fine-tuning (for example, fine-tuning a pre-trained model on a new set of classes).

The key code for the `classification_keras_pretrained_imagenet_models.py` script can be seen next. It should be noted that this script takes a long time to execute. The full code can be found at `https://github.com/PacktPublishing/Mastering-OpenCV-4-with-Python/blob/master/Chapter13/01-chapter-content/keras/keras_classification_pretrained_models/classification_keras_pretrained_imagenet_models.py`:

```
# Import required packages
...

def preprocessing_image(img_path, target_size, architecture):
    """Image preprocessing to be used for each Deep Learning
architecture"""

    # Load image in PIL format
    img = image.load_img(img_path, target_size=target_size)
    # Convert PIL format to numpy array:
```

```
        x = image.img_to_array(img)
        # Convert the image/images into batch format:
        x = np.expand_dims(x, axis=0)
        # Pre-process (prepare) the image using the specific architecture:
        x = architecture.preprocess_input(x)
        return x


def put_text(img, model_name, decoded_preds, y_pos):
    """Show the predicted results in the image"""

    cv2.putText(img, "{}: {}, {:.2f}".format(model_name,
decoded_preds[0][0][1], decoded_preds[0][0][2]),
                (20, y_pos), cv2.FONT_HERSHEY_SIMPLEX, 0.6, (255, 0, 255),
2)


# Path of the input image to be classified:
img_path = 'car.jpg'

# Load some available models:
model_inception_v3 = inception_v3.InceptionV3(weights='imagenet')
model_vgg_16 = vgg16.VGG16(weights='imagenet')
model_vgg_19 = vgg19.VGG19(weights='imagenet')
model_resnet_50 = resnet50.ResNet50(weights='imagenet')
model_mobilenet = mobilenet.MobileNet(weights='imagenet')
model_xception = xception.Xception(weights='imagenet')
model_nasnet_mobile = nasnet.NASNetMobile(weights='imagenet')
model_densenet_121 = densenet.DenseNet121(weights='imagenet')

# Prepare the image for the corresponding architecture:
x_inception_v3 = preprocessing_image(img_path, (299, 299), inception_v3)
x_vgg_16 = preprocessing_image(img_path, (224, 224), vgg16)
x_vgg_19 = preprocessing_image(img_path, (224, 224), vgg19)
x_resnet_50 = preprocessing_image(img_path, (224, 224), resnet50)
x_mobilenet = preprocessing_image(img_path, (224, 224), mobilenet)
x_xception = preprocessing_image(img_path, (299, 299), xception)
x_nasnet_mobile = preprocessing_image(img_path, (224, 224), nasnet)
x_densenet_121 = preprocessing_image(img_path, (224, 224), densenet)

# Get the predicted probabilities:
preds_inception_v3 = model_inception_v3.predict(x_inception_v3)
preds_vgg_16 = model_vgg_16.predict(x_vgg_16)
preds_vgg_19 = model_vgg_19.predict(x_vgg_19)
preds_resnet_50 = model_resnet_50.predict(x_resnet_50)
preds_mobilenet = model_mobilenet.predict(x_mobilenet)
preds_xception = model_xception.predict(x_xception)
preds_nasnet_mobile = model_nasnet_mobile.predict(x_nasnet_mobile)
```

```
preds_densenet_121 = model_nasnet_mobile.predict(x_densenet_121)

# Print the results (class, description, probability):
print('Predicted InceptionV3:', decode_predictions(preds_inception_v3,
top=5)[0])
print('Predicted VGG16:', decode_predictions(preds_vgg_16, top=5)[0])
print('Predicted VGG19:', decode_predictions(preds_vgg_19, top=5)[0])
print('Predicted ResNet50:', decode_predictions(preds_resnet_50, top=5)[0])
print('Predicted MobileNet:', decode_predictions(preds_mobilenet,
top=5)[0])
print('Predicted Xception:', decode_predictions(preds_xception, top=5)[0])
print('Predicted NASNetMobile:', decode_predictions(preds_nasnet_mobile,
top=5)[0])
print('Predicted DenseNet121:', decode_predictions(preds_densenet_121,
top=5)[0])

# Show results:
numpy_image = np.uint8(image.img_to_array(image.load_img(img_path))).copy()
numpy_image = cv2.resize(numpy_image, (500, 500))
numpy_image_res = numpy_image.copy()

put_text(numpy_image_res, "InceptionV3",
decode_predictions(preds_inception_v3), 40)
put_text(numpy_image_res, "VGG16", decode_predictions(preds_vgg_16), 65)
put_text(numpy_image_res, "VGG19", decode_predictions(preds_vgg_19), 90)
put_text(numpy_image_res, "ResNet50", decode_predictions(preds_resnet_50),
115)
put_text(numpy_image_res, "MobileNet", decode_predictions(preds_mobilenet),
140)
put_text(numpy_image_res, "Xception", decode_predictions(preds_xception),
165)
put_text(numpy_image_res, "NASNetMobile",
decode_predictions(preds_nasnet_mobile), 190)
put_text(numpy_image_res, "DenseNet121",
decode_predictions(preds_densenet_121), 215)
```

The first step is to import the required packages, as shown:

```
from keras.preprocessing import image
from keras.applications import inception_v3, vgg16, vgg19, resnet50,
mobilenet, xception, nasnet, densenet
from keras.applications.imagenet_utils import decode_predictions
```

The second step is to instantiate the different model architectures, as follows:

```
# Load some available models:
model_inception_v3 = inception_v3.InceptionV3(weights='imagenet')
model_vgg_16 = vgg16.VGG16(weights='imagenet')
model_vgg_19 = vgg19.VGG19(weights='imagenet')
model_resnet_50 = resnet50.ResNet50(weights='imagenet')
model_mobilenet = mobilenet.MobileNet(weights='imagenet')
model_xception = xception.Xception(weights='imagenet')
model_nasnet_mobile = nasnet.NASNetMobile(weights='imagenet')
model_densenet_121 = densenet.DenseNet121(weights='imagenet')
```

The third step is to both load and pre-process the image/images to classify. For this purpose, we have the `preprocessing_image()` function:

```
def preprocessing_image(img_path, target_size, architecture):
    """Image preprocessing to be used for each Deep Learning
architecture"""

    # Load image in PIL format
    img = image.load_img(img_path, target_size=target_size)
    # Convert PIL format to numpy array:
    x = image.img_to_array(img)
    # Convert the image/images into batch format:
    x = np.expand_dims(x, axis=0)
    # Pre-process (prepare) the image using the specific architecture:
    x = architecture.preprocess_input(x)
    return x
```

The first step of the `preprocessing_image()` function is to load the image by using the `image.load_img()` function, specifying the target size. It should be noted that Keras loads the image in PIL format (`width, height`), which should be converted into NumPy format (`height, width, channels`) using the `image.img_to_array()` function. Then, the input image should be converted to a four-dimensional Tensor (`batchsize, height, width, channels`) using NumPy's `expand_dims()` function. The final step when pre-processing an image is to normalize the image, which is specific for each architecture. This is achieved calling the `preprocess_input()` function.

We make use of the aforementioned `preprocessing_image()`, as follows:

```
# Prepare the image for the corresponding architecture:
x_inception_v3 = preprocessing_image(img_path, (299, 299), inception_v3)
x_vgg_16 = preprocessing_image(img_path, (224, 224), vgg16)
x_vgg_19 = preprocessing_image(img_path, (224, 224), vgg19)
x_resnet_50 = preprocessing_image(img_path, (224, 224), resnet50)
x_mobilenet = preprocessing_image(img_path, (224, 224), mobilenet)
x_xception = preprocessing_image(img_path, (299, 299), xception)
x_nasnet_mobile = preprocessing_image(img_path, (224, 224), nasnet)
x_densenet_121 = preprocessing_image(img_path, (224, 224), densenet)
```

Once the image/images have been pre-processed, we can use `model.predict()` to get the classification results (predicted probabilities for each class):

```
# Get the predicted probabilities:
preds_inception_v3 = model_inception_v3.predict(x_inception_v3)
preds_vgg_16 = model_vgg_16.predict(x_vgg_16)
preds_vgg_19 = model_vgg_19.predict(x_vgg_19)
preds_resnet_50 = model_resnet_50.predict(x_resnet_50)
preds_mobilenet = model_mobilenet.predict(x_mobilenet)
preds_xception = model_xception.predict(x_xception)
preds_nasnet_mobile = model_nasnet_mobile.predict(x_nasnet_mobile)
preds_densenet_121 = model_nasnet_mobile.predict(x_densenet_121)
```

The predicted values can be decoded into a list of tuples (`class ID`, `description`, and `confidence of prediction`):

```
# Print the results (class, description, probability):
print('Predicted InceptionV3:', decode_predictions(preds_inception_v3,
top=5)[0])
print('Predicted VGG16:', decode_predictions(preds_vgg_16, top=5)[0])
print('Predicted VGG19:', decode_predictions(preds_vgg_19, top=5)[0])
print('Predicted ResNet50:', decode_predictions(preds_resnet_50, top=5)[0])
print('Predicted MobileNet:', decode_predictions(preds_mobilenet,
top=5)[0])
print('Predicted Xception:', decode_predictions(preds_xception, top=5)[0])
print('Predicted NASNetMobile:', decode_predictions(preds_nasnet_mobile,
top=5)[0])
print('Predicted DenseNet121:', decode_predictions(preds_densenet_121,
top=5)[0])
```

It should be noted that we obtain one list of tuples (`class ID`, `description`, and `confidence of prediction`) for each image in the batch.

In this case, only one image is used as an input. The obtained output is as follows:

```
Predicted InceptionV3: [('n04285008', 'sports_car', 0.5347126),
('n03459775', 'grille', 0.26265427), ('n03100240', 'convertible',
0.04198084), ('n03770679', 'minivan', 0.030852199), ('n02814533',
'beach_wagon', 0.01985116)]
 Predicted VGG16: [('n03770679', 'minivan', 0.38101497), ('n04285008',
'sports_car', 0.11982699), ('n04037443', 'racer', 0.079280525),
('n02930766', 'cab', 0.063257575), ('n02974003', 'car_wheel', 0.058513235)]
 Predicted VGG19: [('n03770679', 'minivan', 0.23455109), ('n04285008',
'sports_car', 0.22764407), ('n04037443', 'racer', 0.091262065),
('n02930766', 'cab', 0.082842484), ('n02974003', 'car_wheel', 0.07619765)]
 Predicted ResNet50: [('n04285008', 'sports_car', 0.2878513), ('n03770679',
'minivan', 0.27558535), ('n03459775', 'grille', 0.14996652), ('n02974003',
'car_wheel', 0.07796249), ('n04037443', 'racer', 0.050856136)]
 Predicted MobileNet: [('n04285008', 'sports_car', 0.2911019),
('n03770679', 'minivan', 0.24308795), ('n04037443', 'racer', 0.17548184),
('n02814533', 'beach_wagon', 0.12273211), ('n02974003', 'car_wheel',
0.065000646)]
 Predicted Xception: [('n04285008', 'sports_car', 0.3404192), ('n03770679',
'minivan', 0.12870753), ('n03459775', 'grille', 0.11251074), ('n03100240',
'convertible', 0.068289846), ('n03670208', 'limousine', 0.056636304)]
 Predicted NASNetMobile: [('n04285008', 'sports_car', 0.54606944),
('n03100240', 'convertible', 0.2797665), ('n03459775', 'grille',
0.037253976), ('n02974003', 'car_wheel', 0.02682667), ('n02814533',
'beach_wagon', 0.014193514)]
 Predicted DenseNet121: [('n04285008', 'sports_car', 0.65400195),
('n02974003', 'car_wheel', 0.076283), ('n03459775', 'grille', 0.06899618),
('n03100240', 'convertible', 0.058678553), ('n04037443', 'racer',
0.051732656)]
```

Finally, we show the obtained results (best prediction) for each architecture in the image using the `put_text()` function:

```
put_text(numpy_image_res, "InceptionV3",
decode_predictions(preds_inception_v3), 40)
put_text(numpy_image_res, "VGG16", decode_predictions(preds_vgg_16), 65)
put_text(numpy_image_res, "VGG19", decode_predictions(preds_vgg_19), 90)
put_text(numpy_image_res, "ResNet50", decode_predictions(preds_resnet_50),
115)
put_text(numpy_image_res, "MobileNet", decode_predictions(preds_mobilenet),
140)
put_text(numpy_image_res, "Xception", decode_predictions(preds_xception),
165)
put_text(numpy_image_res, "NASNetMobile",
decode_predictions(preds_nasnet_mobile), 190)
put_text(numpy_image_res, "DenseNet121",
decode_predictions(preds_densenet_121), 215)
```

The `put_text()` function code is as follows:

```
def put_text(img, model_name, decoded_preds, y_pos):
    """Show the predicted results in the image"""

    cv2.putText(img, "{}: {}, {:.2f}".format(model_name,
decoded_preds[0][0][1], decoded_preds[0][0][2]),
                (20, y_pos), cv2.FONT_HERSHEY_SIMPLEX, 0.6, (255, 0, 255),
    2)
```

In `put_text()` function, we call the `cv2.putText()` function to render the corresponding string in the image.

The output for the `classification_keras_pretrained_imagenet_models.py` script can be seen in the next screenshot:

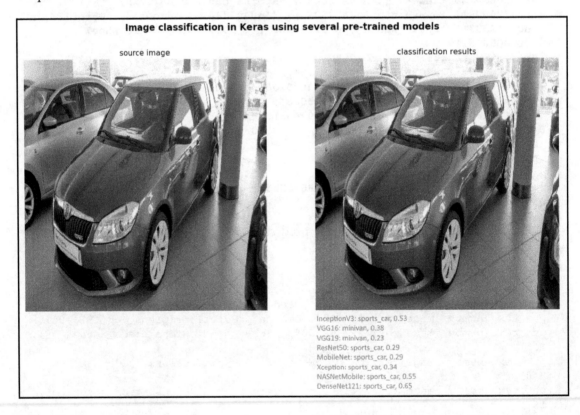

As shown in the preceding screenshot, most models classify this image as a `sport_car`; however, VGG models (VGG16 and VGG19) classify this image as a `minivan`, maybe due to the height of the car.

If we run the script with another input image (`cat.jpg` in this case), the output is shown in the next screenshot:

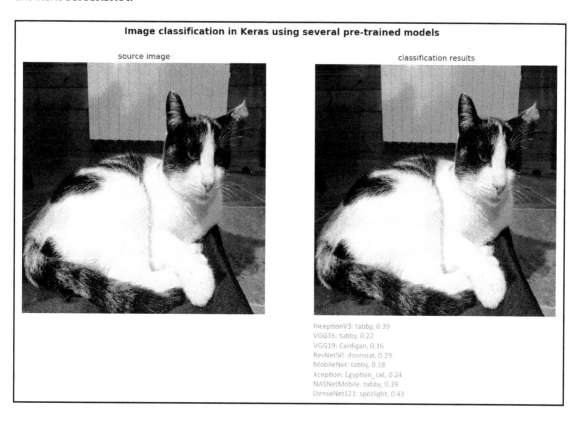

In this case, most models classify this image as `tabby`, which is a domestic cat (tabby cat). The Xception model classifies this image as `Egyptian_cat`.

Deep learning REST API using Keras Applications

In the previous subsection, we have seen how to work with the applications module of the Keras deep learning library, providing both deep learning model definitions and pre-trained weights for a number of popular architectures.

In this subsection, we are going to see how to create a deep learning REST API based on one of these pre-trained architectures.

The Keras deep learning REST API is a single file named `keras_server.py`. The code for this script can be seen next:

```
# Import required packages:
from keras.applications import nasnet, NASNetMobile
from keras.preprocessing.image import img_to_array
from keras.applications import imagenet_utils
from PIL import Image
import numpy as np
import flask
import io
import tensorflow as tf

# Initialize Flask app, Keras model and graph:
app = flask.Flask(__name__)
graph = None
model = None


def load_model():
    # Get default graph:
    global graph
    graph = tf.get_default_graph()
    # Load the pre-trained Keras model(pre-trained on ImageNet):
    global model
    model = NASNetMobile(weights="imagenet")


def preprocessing_image(image, target):
    # Make sure the image mode is RGB:
    if image.mode != "RGB":
        image = image.convert("RGB")

    # Resize the input image:
    image = image.resize(target)
    # Convert PIL format to numpy array:
```

```
        image = img_to_array(image)
        # Convert the image/images into batch format:
        image = np.expand_dims(image, axis=0)
        # Pre-process (prepare) the image using the specific architecture:
        image = nasnet.preprocess_input(image)
        # Return the image:
        return image


@app.route("/predict", methods=["POST"])
def predict():
    # Initialize result:
    result = {"success": False}

    if flask.request.method == "POST":
        if flask.request.files.get("image"):
            # Read input image in PIL format:
            image = flask.request.files["image"].read()
            image = Image.open(io.BytesIO(image))

            # Pre-process the image to be classified:
            image = preprocessing_image(image, target=(224, 224))

            # Classify the input image:
            with graph.as_default():
                predictions = model.predict(image)
            results = imagenet_utils.decode_predictions(predictions)
            result["predictions"] = []

            # Add the predictions to the result:
            for (imagenet_id, label, prob) in results[0]:
                r = {"label": label, "probability": float(prob)}
                result["predictions"].append(r)

            # At this point we can say that the request was dispatched
successfully:
            result["success"] = True

    # Return result as a JSON response:
    return flask.jsonify(result)


@app.route("/")
def home():
    # Initialize result:
    result = {"success": True}
    # Return result as a JSON response:
    return flask.jsonify(result)
```

```
if __name__ == "__main__":
    print("Loading Keras pre-trained model")
    load_model()
    print("Starting")
    app.run()
```

The first step is to import the required packages, as follows:

```
# Import required packages:
from keras.applications import nasnet, NASNetMobile
from keras.preprocessing.image import img_to_array
from keras.applications import imagenet_utils
from PIL import Image
import numpy as np
import flask
import io
import tensorflow as tf
```

The next step is to initialize the Flask application, our model, and the computation graph, like so:

```
# Initialize Flask app, Keras model and graph:
app = flask.Flask(__name__)
graph = None
model = None
```

We define the `load_model()` function, which is responsible for creating the architecture and loading the required weights:

```
def load_model():
    # Get default graph:
    global graph
    graph = tf.get_default_graph()
    # Load the pre-trained Keras model(pre-trained on ImageNet):
    global model
    model = NASNetMobile(weights="imagenet")
```

As it can be seen, NASNetMobile weights are loaded.

We also define the `preprocessing_image()` function, as follows:

```
def preprocessing_image(image, target):
    # Make sure the image mode is RGB:
    if image.mode != "RGB":
        image = image.convert("RGB")

    # Resize the input image:
    image = image.resize(target)
    # Convert PIL format to numpy array:
    image = img_to_array(image)
    # Convert the image/images into batch format:
    image = np.expand_dims(image, axis=0)
    # Pre-process (prepare) the image using the specific architecture:
    image = nasnet.preprocess_input(image)
    # Return the image:
    return image
```

This function prepares the input image—converts the image to RGB, resizes it, converts the image/images into the batch format and, finally, preprocesses it using the specific architecture.

Finally, we use the `route()` decorator to bind `predict()` function to the `/predict` URL. `predict()` function processes the requests and returns the predictions to the clients, like so:

```
@app.route("/predict", methods=["POST"])
def predict():
    # Initialize result:
    result = {"success": False}

    if flask.request.method == "POST":
        if flask.request.files.get("image"):
            # Read input image in PIL format:
            image = flask.request.files["image"].read()
            image = Image.open(io.BytesIO(image))

            # Pre-process the image to be classified:
            image = preprocessing_image(image, target=(224, 224))

            # Classify the input image:
            with graph.as_default():
                predictions = model.predict(image)
            results = imagenet_utils.decode_predictions(predictions)
            result["predictions"] = []

            # Add the predictions to the result:
```

```
        for (imagenet_id, label, prob) in results[0]:
            r = {"label": label, "probability": float(prob)}
            result["predictions"].append(r)

        # At this point we can say that the request was dispatched
successfully:
            result["success"] = True

    # Return result as a JSON response:
    return flask.jsonify(result)
```

The first step when processing the image—in the `predict()` function—is to read the input image in PIL format. Next, we preprocess the image and pass it through the network to get the predictions. Finally, we add the predictions to the result, and return the result as a JSON response.

In the same way as we did in previous sections, we have coded two scripts in order to perform a POST request to the Keras deep learning REST API.
The `request_keras_rest_api.py` script performs the POST request and prints the results. The `request_keras_rest_api_drawing.py` script performs the POST request, prints the results, and also creates an image to render the obtained results. For the sake of simplification, only the `request_keras_rest_api_drawing.py` script is shown, as follows:

```
# Import required packages:
import cv2
import numpy as np
import requests
from matplotlib import pyplot as plt


def show_img_with_matplotlib(color_img, title, pos):
    """Shows an image using matplotlib capabilities"""

    img_RGB = color_img[:, :, ::-1]

    ax = plt.subplot(1, 1, pos)
    plt.imshow(img_RGB)
    plt.title(title)
    plt.axis('off')


KERAS_REST_API_URL = "http://localhost:5000/predict"
IMAGE_PATH = "car.jpg"

# Load the image and construct the payload:
```

```
image = open(IMAGE_PATH, "rb").read()
payload = {"image": image}

# Submit the POST request:
r = requests.post(KERAS_REST_API_URL, files=payload).json()

# Convert the loaded image to the OpenCV format:
image_array = np.asarray(bytearray(image), dtype=np.uint8)
img_opencv = cv2.imdecode(image_array, -1)
img_opencv = cv2.resize(img_opencv, (500, 500))

y_pos = 40

# Show the results:
if r["success"]:
    # Iterate over the predictions
    for (i, result) in enumerate(r["predictions"]):
        # Print the results:
        print("{}. {}: {:.4f}".format(i + 1, result["label"],
result["probability"]))
        # Render the results in the image:
        cv2.putText(img_opencv, "{}. {}: {:.4f}".format(i + 1,
result["label"], result["probability"]),
                    (20, y_pos), cv2.FONT_HERSHEY_SIMPLEX, 0.6, (255, 0,
255), 2)
        y_pos += 30
else:
    print("Request failed")

# Create the dimensions of the figure and set title:
fig = plt.figure(figsize=(8, 6))
plt.suptitle("Using Keras Deep Learning REST API", fontsize=14,
fontweight='bold')
fig.patch.set_facecolor('silver')

# Show the output image
show_img_with_matplotlib(img_opencv, "Classification results
(NASNetMobile)", 1)

# Show the Figure:
plt.show()
```

As you can see, we perform a POST request to the Keras deep learning REST API. In order to show the results, we iterate over the obtained predictions. For each prediction, we both print the results and render the results in the image.

The output of this script can be seen in the next screenshot:

In the previous screenshot, you can see the top 5 predictions corresponding to the input car.jpg image.

Deploying a Flask application to the cloud

If you have developed a Flask application you can run in your computer, you can easily make it public by deploying it to the cloud. There are a lot of options if you want to deploy your application to the cloud (for example, Google App Engine: `https://cloud.google.com/appengine/`, Microsoft Azure: `https://azure.microsoft.com`, Heroku: `https://devcenter.heroku.com/`, and Amazon Web Services: `https://aws.amazon.com`, among others). Additionally, you can also use *PythonAnywhere* (`www.pythonanywhere.com`), which is a Python online **integrated development environment** (**IDE**) and web hosting environment, making it easy to create and run Python programs in the cloud.

PythonAnywhere is very simple, and also the recommended way of hosting machine learning-based web applications. PythonAnywhere provides some interesting features, such as WSGI-based web hosting (for example, Django, Flask, and Web2py).

In this section, we will see how to create a Flask application and how to deploy it on PythonAnywhere.

To show you how to deploy a Flask application to the cloud using PythonAnywhere, we are going to use the code of the `mysite` project. This code is very similar (with minor modifications) to the minimal face API we have previously seen in this chapter. These modifications will be explained after creating the site:

1. The first step is to create a PythonAnywhere account. For this example, a *beginner* account is enough (`https://www.pythonanywhere.com/pricing/`):

2. After registering, you will have access to your dashboard. This can be seen in the next screenshot:

As you can see, I have created the user `opencv`.

3. The next step is to click on **Web** menu and then, click the **Add new web app** button, as shown in the next screenshot:

4. At this point, you are ready to create the new web app, as shown in the next screenshot:

5. Click **Next** and then, click **Flask** and also, click on the latest version of Python. Finally, click **Next** to accept the project path:

This will create a `Hello world` Flask application that you can see if you visit `https://your_user_name.pythonanywhere.com`. In my case, the URL will be `https://opencv.pythonanywhere.com`.

6. At this point, we are ready to upload our own project. The first step is to click on **Go to directory** in the **Code** section of the **Web** menu, as shown in the next screenshot:

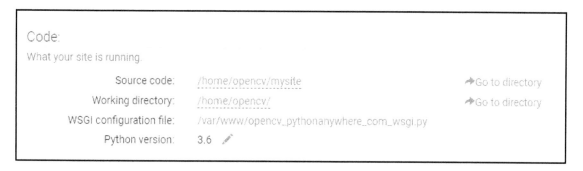

7. We can upload files to our site using the **Upload a file** button. We have uploaded three files, as follows:

- flask_app.py
- face_processing.py
- haarcascade_frontalface_alt.xml

This can be seen in the next screenshot:

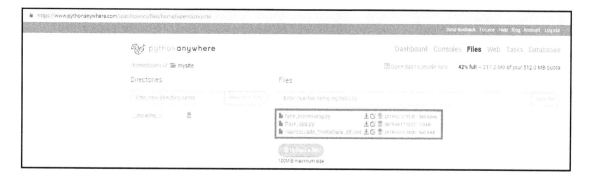

You can see the uploaded content of these files by clicking the **download icon**. In this case, you can see the content of these files in the following URLs:

- The `flask_app.py`: https://www.pythonanywhere.com/user/opencv/files/home/opencv/mysite/flask_app.py
- The `face_processing.py`: https://www.pythonanywhere.com/user/opencv/files/home/opencv/mysite/face_processing.py
- The `haarcascade_frontalface_alt.xml`: https://www.pythonanywhere.com/user/opencv/files/home/opencv/mysite/haarcascade_frontalface_alt.xml

8. Next step is to set up the virtual environment. To accomplish this, a bash console should be opened by clicking on **Open Bash console here** (see the previous screenshot). Once it's opened, run the following command:

```
$ mkvirtualenv --python=/usr/bin/python3.6 my-virtualenv
```

You will see the prompt changes from $ to (my-virtualenv) $. This means that the virtual environment has been activated. At this point, we will install all the required packages (`flask` and `opencv-contrib-python`):

```
(my-virtualenv) $ pip install flask
```

```
(my-virtualenv) $ pip install opencv-contrib-python
```

You can see that `numpy` is also installed. All these steps can be seen in the next screenshot:

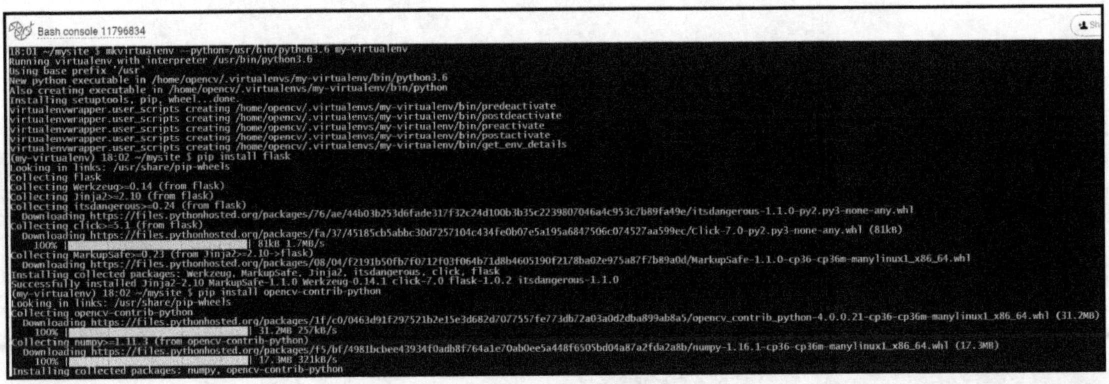

If you want to install additional packages, do not forget to activate the virtual environment you have created. You can reactivate it with the following command:

```
$ workon my-virtualenv
  (my-virtualenv)$
```

9. At this point, we have almost finished. The final step is to reload the uploaded project by clicking on the **Web** option in the menu and reloading the site, which can be seen in the next screenshot:

Hence, we are ready to test the face API uploaded to PythonAnywhere, which can be accessed using `https://opencv.pythonanywhere.com/`. You will see something like the following screenshot:

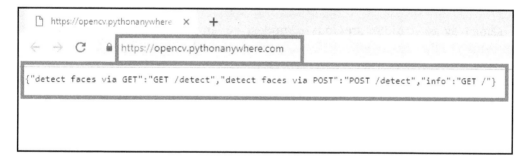

You can see a JSON response. This JSON response is obtained because we have used the `route()` decorator to bind the `info_view()` function to the URL /. This is one of the modifications we have performed in this example in comparison with the minimal face API we have seen in this chapter. Therefore, we have modified the `flask_app.py` script to include:

```
@app.route('/', methods=["GET"])
def info_view():
    # List of routes for this API:
```

```
output = {
    'info': 'GET /',
    'detect faces via POST': 'POST /detect',
    'detect faces via GET': 'GET /detect',
}
return jsonify(output), 200
```

This way, when accessing `https://opencv.pythonanywhere.com/`, we will get the list of routes for this API. This is helpful when uploading a project to PythonAnywhere in order to see that everything is working fine. The second (and final) modification is performed in the `face_processing.py` script. In this script, we have changed the path of the `haarcascade_frontalface_alt.xml` file, which is used by the face detector:

```
class FaceProcessing(object):
    def __init__(self):
        self.file = "/home/opencv/mysite/haarcascade_frontalface_alt.xml"
        self.face_cascade = cv2.CascadeClassifier(self.file)
```

See the path of the file, which matches with the new path assigned when uploading the `haarcascade_frontalface_alt.xml` file to PythonAnywhere.

 This path should be changed according to the username (`opencv` in this case).

In the same way as we did in previous examples, we can perform a `POST` request to the face API uploaded to PythonAnywhere. This is performed in the `demo_request.py` script:

```
# Import required packages:
import cv2
import numpy as np
import requests
from matplotlib import pyplot as plt


def show_img_with_matplotlib(color_img, title, pos):
    """Shows an image using matplotlib capabilities"""

    img_RGB = color_img[:, :, ::-1]

    ax = plt.subplot(1, 1, pos)
    plt.imshow(img_RGB)
    plt.title(title)
    plt.axis('off')
```

```
FACE_DETECTION_REST_API_URL = "http://opencv.pythonanywhere.com/detect"
IMAGE_PATH = "test_face_processing.jpg"

# Load the image and construct the payload:
image = open(IMAGE_PATH, "rb").read()
payload = {"image": image}

# Submit the POST request:
r = requests.post(FACE_DETECTION_REST_API_URL, files=payload)

# See the response:
print("status code: {}".format(r.status_code))
print("headers: {}".format(r.headers))
print("content: {}".format(r.json()))

# Get JSON data from the response and get 'result':
json_data = r.json()
result = json_data['result']

# Convert the loaded image to the OpenCV format:
image_array = np.asarray(bytearray(image), dtype=np.uint8)
img_opencv = cv2.imdecode(image_array, -1)

# Draw faces in the OpenCV image:
for face in result:
    left, top, right, bottom = face['box']
    # To draw a rectangle, you need top-left corner and bottom-right corner
of rectangle:
    cv2.rectangle(img_opencv, (left, top), (right, bottom), (0, 255, 255),
2)
    # Draw top-left corner and bottom-right corner (checking):
    cv2.circle(img_opencv, (left, top), 5, (0, 0, 255), -1)
    cv2.circle(img_opencv, (right, bottom), 5, (255, 0, 0), -1)

# Create the dimensions of the figure and set title:
fig = plt.figure(figsize=(8, 6))
plt.suptitle("Using face API", fontsize=14, fontweight='bold')
fig.patch.set_facecolor('silver')

# Show the output image
show_img_with_matplotlib(img_opencv, "face detection", 1)

# Show the Figure:
plt.show()
```

There is nothing new in this script, with the exception of the following line:

```
FACE_DETECTION_REST_API_URL = "http://opencv.pythonanywhere.com/detect"
```

Note that we are requesting our cloud API. The output of this script can be seen in the next screenshot:

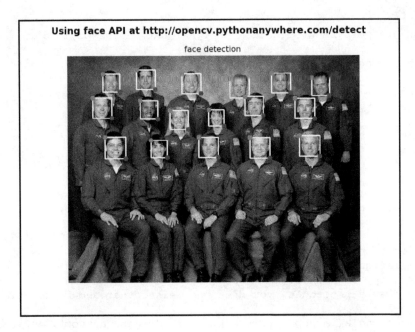

This way we can confirm that our cloud API is up and running.

Summary

In this last chapter of the book, we have seen how to create web applications using Python web frameworks and discovered the potential of web frameworks like Flask. More specifically, we have developed several web computer vision and web deep learning applications using OpenCV, Keras, and Flask and learned how to ingrate it with them to provide the web applications machine learning and deep learning capabilities. Additionally, we have also covered how to deploy a Flask application to the cloud using PythonAnywhere, which provides capabilities for web hosting. Finally, we have also seen how to perform requests (for example, GET and POST) from the browser (GET requests) and, also, programmatically (GET and POST requests) to create a web face API using OpenCV and Flask, and to create a deep learning API using OpenCV.

Questions

- What two main categories of web frameworks exist?
- What is the purpose of the `route()` decorator in Flask?
- How can you run the Flask server application to be accessible from any other computer on the network?
- What is the purpose of the `jsonify()` function?
- What is the purpose of the `errorhandler()` decorator in Flask?
- What is Keras Applications?
- What is PythonAnywhere?

Further reading

The following references will help you dive deeper into Flask (and also Django):

- *Mastering Flask Web Development – Second Edition* by Daniel Gaspar and Jack Stouffer (`https://www.packtpub.com/web-development/mastering-flask-web-development-second-edition`)
- *Flask – Building Web Applications* (`https://www.packtpub.com/web-development/flask-building-web-applications`)
- *Flask By Example* by Gareth Dwyer (`https://www.packtpub.com/web-development/flask-example`)
- *Python web development: Django vs Flask in 2018* by Aaron Lazar (`https://hub.packtpub.com/python-web-development-django-vs-flask-2018/`)

Assessments

Chapter 1

1. The main purpose of Python virtual environments is to create an isolated environment for Python projects. This means that each project can have its own dependencies, regardless of what dependencies every other project has. In other words, it is an isolated working copy of Python that allows you to work on a specific project without worry of affecting other projects.

2. The connection between `pip`, `virtualenv`, `pipenv`, Anaconda, and `conda` is as follows:

    - `pip`: The Python Package Manager:
        - The PyPA recommended tool for installing Python packages
        - You can find and publish Python packages using PyPI: The Python Package Index (`https://pypi.python.org/pypi`)

    - `pyenv`: Python Version Manager:
        - pyenv lets you easily switch between multiple versions of Python
        - If you need to use different versions of Python, `pyenv` lets you manage this easily

    - `virtualenv`: Python Environment Manager:
        - The `virtualenv` is a tool to create isolated Python environments
        - To create a `virtualenv`, simply invoke `virtualenv ENV`, where ENV is a directory in which to place the new virtual environment
        - To initialize the `virtualenv`, you need to source `ENV/bin/activate`
        - To stop using `virtualenv`, simply call `deactivate`
        - Once you activate the `virtualenv`, you can install all of a workspace's package requirements by running `pip install -r requirements.txt`

- `anaconda`: Package Manager, Environment Manager, and Additional Scientific Libraries:
    - Anaconda includes an easy installation of Python and updates of over 100 prebuilt and tested scientific and analytic Python packages that include NumPy, Pandas, SciPy, Matplotlib, and IPython, with over 620 more packages available via a simple `conda install <packagename>`.
    - `conda` is an open source package management system and environment management system (provides virtual environment capabilities) included in the Anaconda distribution. Therefore, you can create virtual environments with `conda`.
    - While `conda` allows you to install packages, these packages are separate to PyPI packages, so you may still need to use `pip` additionally depending on the types of packages you need to install.

3. Notebook documents are documents that are produced by the Jupyter Notebook App, which contain both computer code and rich text elements. Because of this mix of code and text elements, notebooks are the ideal place to bring together both an analysis description and its results. Moreover, they can be executed to perform data analysis in real time. The Jupyter Notebook App is a server-client application that allows for the editing and running of notebook documents via a web browser. The name Jupyter is an acronym that stands for the three languages it was designed for—Julia , Python, and R. It comes included in the Anaconda distribution.

4. To work with images, the main packages that you need are as follows: Numpy, opencv, scikit-image, PIL, Pillow, SimpleCV, Mahotas, and ilastik. Additionally, to work in machine learning problems, you can also use pandas, scikit-learn, Orange, PyBrain, or Milk. Finally, if your computer vision project involves deep learning techniques, you can also use TensorFlow, Pytorch, Theano, or Keras.

5. To install packages using `pip` according to the `requirements.txt` file from a local directory, we should execute `pip install -r requirements.txt` to install all the packages contained in this file. You can also create a virtual environment first, and then install all the required packages:

   - `cd` to the directory where `requirements.txt` is located
   - Activate your `virtualenv`
   - Run `pip install -r requirements.txt`

6. An **integrated development environment** (**IDE**) is a software application that provides comprehensive facilities to computer programmers for software development. An IDE normally consists of a source code editor, build automation tools, and a debugger. Most modern IDEs have intelligent code completion. Python IDE is the first thing you need to get started with Python programming. You can get started with Python programming in a basic text editor such as Notepad, but it is much better to use a complete and feature rich Python IDE.

   PyCharm is a professional Python IDE, and comes in two flavors:

   - **Professional**: Full-featured IDE for Python and web development (free trial)
   - **Community**: Lightweight IDE for Python and scientific development (free, open source)

   Most of its features are available in the Community flavor, including intelligent code completion, intuitive project navigation, on the fly error checking and fixing, code quality with PEP8 checks and smart refactoring, a graphical debugger, and test runner. It also integrates with IPython notebook, and supports Anaconda as well as other scientific packages such as Matplotlib and NumPy.

7. OpenCV is released under a BSD license. Therefore, it is free for both commercial and academic use (`https://www.opencv.org/license.html`). BSD licenses can be grouped into three types:

   - Two-clause BSD license
   - Three-clause BSD license
   - Four-clause BSD license

OpenCV uses the three-clause BSD license. All of these clauses are listed as follows:

```
Redistribution and use in source and binary forms, with or without
modification, are permitted provided that the following conditions
are met:

(1) Redistributions of source code must retain the above copyright
notice, this list of conditions and the following disclaimer.

(2) Redistributions in binary form must reproduce the above
copyright notice, this list of conditions and the following
disclaimer in the documentation and/or other materials
provided with the distribution.

(3) Neither the name of the [organization] nor the names of its
contributors may be used to endorse or promote products derived
from this software without specific prior written permission.

(4) All advertising materials mentioning features or use of this
software must display the following acknowledgement: This product
includes software developed by the [organization].
```

Chapter 2

1. There are three image processing steps:
    1. Getting the necessary information to work with (for example, an image or video file, among others)
    2. Processing the image by applying image processing techniques
    3. Showing the results in the required way (for example, save the image to disk, show the image, and so forth)
2. The processing step can be broken down into three processing levels:
    1. Low-level processing
    2. Mid-level processing
    3. High-level processing

3. A grayscale image contains for every pixel of the image a value that is proportional to the brightness or gray levels of the image. This value is also called intensity or grayscale level. This value is $\in$ *[0, L-1]*, where *L = 256* (for an 8-bit image).

On the other hand, black and white images contain for every pixel of the image a value that can only take two values. Usually, these values are 0 (black) and 255 (white). In many cases, the black and white images are the result of some image processing steps and techniques (for example, the result of a thresholding operation).

4. A digital image is a representation of a 2D image as a finite set of digital values, which are called pixels. A pixel is the basic unit of programmable color in a digital image.

The image resolution can be seen as the detail an image holds. An image with a resolution of 800 × 1200 is a grid with 800 columns and 1200 rows, containing 800 × 1200 = 960,000 pixels.

5. OpenCV performs the following actions:

- Load (read) an image: `cv2.imread()`:
  - `img = cv2.imread('logo.png')`
  - `gray_img = cv2.imread('logo.png', cv2.IMREAD_GRAYSCALE)`
- Show an image: `cv2.imshow()`:
  - `cv2.imshow('bgr image', img )`
- Wait for a keystroke: `cv2.waitKey()`:
  - `cv2.waitKey(0)`
- Split the channels: `cv2.split()`:
  - `b, g, r = cv2.split(img)`
- Merge the channels: `cv2.merge()`:
  - `img = cv2.merge([r, g, b])`

6. `$ jupyter notebook.`

7. The following colors will be obtained:

   - (B = 0, G = 255, R = 255): Yellow
   - (B = 255, G = 255, R = 0): Cyan
   - (B = 255, G = 0, R = 255): Magenta
   - (B = 255, G = 255, R = 255): White

   You can further play with the RGB color chart at `https://www.rapidtables.com/web/color/RGB_Color.html`.

8. Whether an image is color or grayscale can be determined by its dimensions (`img.shape`). As we saw in this chapter, if a color image is loaded, the length of `img.shape` will be 3. On the other hand, if the loaded image is grayscale, the length of `img.shape` will be 2. The code is attached as follows:

```
# load OpenCV logo image:
img = cv2.imread('logo.png')

# Get the shape of the image:
dimensions = img.shape

# Check the length of dimensions
if len(dimensions) < 3:
 print("grayscale image!")
if len(dimensions) == 3:
 print("color image!")

# Load the same image but in grayscale:
gray_img = cv2.imread('logo.png', cv2.IMREAD_GRAYSCALE)

# Get again the img.shape properties:
dimensions = gray_img.shape

# Check the length of dimensions
if len(dimensions) < 3:
print("grayscale image!")
if len(dimensions) == 3:
print("color image!")
```

Chapter 3

1. The second element of the list is the first argument to the script, which is `sys.argv[1]`.

2. The code is as follows:

```
parser = argparse.ArgumentParser()
parser.add_argument("first_number", help="first number to be
added", type=int)
```

3. The code to save the image is as follows:

```
cv2.imwrite("image.png", img)
```

4. The `capture` object is created as follows:

```
capture = cv2.VideoCapture(0)
```

5. The `capture` object is created as follows:

```
capture = cv2.VideoCapture(0)
print("CV_CAP_PROP_FRAME_WIDTH:
'{}'".format(capture.get(cv2.CAP_PROP_FRAME_WIDTH)))
```

6. The code to read the image is as follows:

```
image = cv2.imread("logo.png")
cv2.imwrite("logo_copy.png", gray_image)
```

7. The script is written as follows:

```
"""

Example to introduce how to read a video file backwards and save it
"""

# Import the required packages
import cv2
import argparse

def decode_fourcc(fourcc):
"""Decodes the fourcc value to get the four chars identifying it

"""
fourcc_int = int(fourcc)

# We print the int value of fourcc
print("int value of fourcc: '{}'".format(fourcc_int))
```

```
# We can also perform this in one line:
# return "".join([chr((fourcc_int >> 8 * i) & 0xFF) for i in
range(4)])

fourcc_decode = ""
for i in range(4):
int_value = fourcc_int >> 8 * i & 0xFF
print("int_value: '{}'".format(int_value))
fourcc_decode += chr(int_value)
return fourcc_decode


# We first create the ArgumentParser object
# The created object 'parser' will have the necessary information
# to parse the command-line arguments into data types.
parser = argparse.ArgumentParser()

# We add 'video_path' argument using add_argument() including a
help.
parser.add_argument("video_path", help="path to the video file")

# We add 'output_video_path' argument using add_argument()
including a help.
parser.add_argument("output_video_path", help="path to the video
file to write")

args = parser.parse_args()

# Create a VideoCapture object and read from input file
# If the input is the camera, pass 0 instead of the video file name
capture = cv2.VideoCapture(args.video_path)

# Get some properties of VideoCapture (frame width, frame height
and frames per second (fps)):
frame_width = capture.get(cv2.CAP_PROP_FRAME_WIDTH)
frame_height = capture.get(cv2.CAP_PROP_FRAME_HEIGHT)
fps = capture.get(cv2.CAP_PROP_FPS)
codec = decode_fourcc(capture.get(cv2.CAP_PROP_FOURCC))

print("codec: '{}'".format(codec))

# FourCC is a 4-byte code used to specify the video codec and it is
platform dependent!
fourcc = cv2.VideoWriter_fourcc(*codec)


# Create VideoWriter object. We use the same properties as the
input camera.
```

```python
# Last argument is False to write the video in grayscale. True
otherwise (write the video in color)
out = cv2.VideoWriter(args.output_video_path, fourcc, int(fps),
(int(frame_width), int(frame_height)), True)

# Check if camera opened successfully
if capture.isOpened() is False:
print("Error opening video stream or file")

# We get the index of the last frame of the video file
frame_index = capture.get(cv2.CAP_PROP_FRAME_COUNT) - 1
# print("starting in frame: '{}'".format(frame_index))

# Read until video is completed
while capture.isOpened() and frame_index >= 0:

# We set the current frame position
capture.set(cv2.CAP_PROP_POS_FRAMES, frame_index)

# Capture frame-by-frame from the video file:
ret, frame = capture.read()

if ret is True:

# Print current frame number per iteration
# print("CAP_PROP_POS_FRAMES :
'{}'".format(capture.get(cv2.CAP_PROP_POS_FRAMES)))

# Get the timestamp of the current frame in milliseconds
# print("CAP_PROP_POS_MSEC :
'{}'".format(capture.get(cv2.CAP_PROP_POS_MSEC)))

# Display the resulting frame
cv2.imshow('Original frame', frame)

# Write the frame to the video
out.write(frame)

# Convert the frame to grayscale:
gray_frame = cv2.cvtColor(frame, cv2.COLOR_BGR2GRAY)

# Display the grayscale frame
cv2.imshow('Grayscale frame', gray_frame)

frame_index = frame_index - 1
# print("next index to read: '{}'".format(frame_index))

# Press q on keyboard to exit the program:
```

```
if cv2.waitKey(25) & 0xFF == ord('q'):
break
# Break the loop
else:
break

# Release everything:
capture.release()
out.release()
cv2.destroyAllWindows()
```

Chapter 4

1. The parameter thickness can take positive and negative values. If the value is positive, it indicates the thickness of the outline. A negative value (for example, -1) indicates that a filled shape will be drawn. For example, to draw a filled ellipse, note the following:

   ```
   cv2.ellipse(image, (80, 80), (60, 40), 0, 0, 360, colors['red'],
   -1)
   ```

   You can also use cv2.FILLED:

   ```
   cv2.ellipse(image, (80, 80), (60, 40), 0, 0, 360, colors['red'],
   cv2.FILLED)
   ```

2. The lineType parameter can take three values (cv2.LINE_4 == 4, cv2.LINE_AA == 16, cv2.LINE_8 == 8). To draw Anti Aliased lines, you must use cv2.LINE_AA:

   ```
   cv2.line(image, (0, 0), (20, 20), colors['red'], 1, cv2.LINE_AA)
   ```

3. The diagonal line is created with the help of the following code:

   ```
   cv2.line(image, (0, 0), (512, 512), colors['green'], 3)
   ```

4. The text is rendered as follows:

   ```
   cv2.putText(image, 'Hello OpenCV', (10, 30),
   cv2.FONT_HERSHEY_SIMPLEX, 0.9, colors['red'], 2, cv2.LINE_4)
   ```

5. The code for this exercise corresponds to the `circle_polygon.py` script. To get the coordinates, you can use the parametric equation of the circle (see `analog_clock_values.py`). The following figure shows you this polygon:

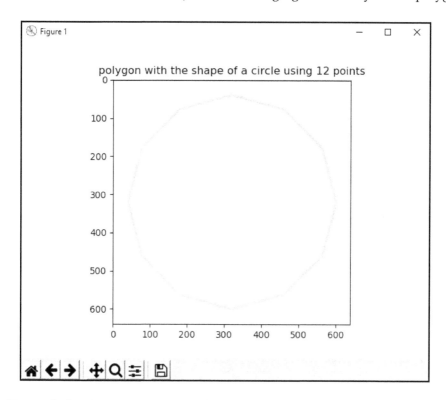

The code for the `circle_polygon.py` file is as follows:

```
"""
Example to show how to draw a circle polygon
"""

# Import required packages:
import cv2
import numpy as np
import matplotlib.pyplot as plt


def show_with_matplotlib(img, title):
    """Shows an image using matplotlib capabilities

    """
    # Convert BGR image to RGB
```

```
        img_RGB = img[:, :, ::-1]

        # Show the image using matplotlib:
        plt.imshow(img_RGB)
        plt.title(title)
        plt.show()


# Dictionary containing some colors
colors = {'blue': (255, 0, 0), 'green': (0, 255, 0), 'red': (0, 0,
255), 'yellow': (0, 255, 255),
        'magenta': (255, 0, 255), 'cyan': (255, 255, 0), 'white':
(255, 255, 255), 'black': (0, 0, 0),
        'gray': (125, 125, 125), 'rand': np.random.randint(0,
high=256, size=(3,)).tolist(),
        'dark_gray': (50, 50, 50), 'light_gray': (220, 220, 220)}

# We create the canvas to draw: 640 x 640 pixels, 3 channels, uint8
(8-bit unsigned integers)
# We set background to black using np.zeros()
image = np.zeros((640, 640, 3), dtype="uint8")

# If you want another background color you can do the following:
# image[:] = colors['light_gray']
image.fill(255)

pts = np.array(
    [(600, 320), (563, 460), (460, 562), (320, 600), (180, 563),
(78, 460), (40, 320), (77, 180), (179, 78), (319, 40),
    (459, 77), (562, 179)])

# Reshape to shape (number_vertex, 1, 2)
pts = pts.reshape((-1, 1, 2))

# Call cv2.polylines() to build the polygon:
cv2.polylines(image, [pts], True, colors['green'], 5)

# Show image:
show_with_matplotlib(image, 'polygon with the shape of a circle
using 12 points')
```

6. The code corresponds to the `matplotlib_mouse_events_rect.py` script.

The key point is how to capture the double left click:

- Double click: `event.dblclick`
- Left click: `event.button == 1`

The code for the `matplotlib_mouse_events_rect.py` file is as follows:

```
"""
Example to show how to capture a double left click with matplotlib
events to draw a rectangle
"""

# Import required packages:
import cv2
import numpy as np
import matplotlib as mpl
import matplotlib.pyplot as plt

# Dictionary containing some colors
colors = {'blue': (255, 0, 0), 'green': (0, 255, 0), 'red': (0, 0,
255), 'yellow': (0, 255, 255),
          'magenta': (255, 0, 255), 'cyan': (255, 255, 0), 'white':
(255, 255, 255), 'black': (0, 0, 0),
          'gray': (125, 125, 125), 'rand': np.random.randint(0,
high=256, size=(3,)).tolist(),
          'dark_gray': (50, 50, 50), 'light_gray': (220, 220, 220)}

# We create the canvas to draw: 400 x 400 pixels, 3 channels, uint8
(8-bit unsigned integers)
# We set the background to black using np.zeros()
image = np.zeros((400, 400, 3), dtype="uint8")

# If you want another background color you can do the following:
image[:] = colors['light_gray']


def update_img_with_matplotlib():
    """Updates an image using matplotlib capabilities

    """
    # Convert BGR to RGB image format
    img_RGB = image[:, :, ::-1]

    # Display the image:
    plt.imshow(img_RGB)

    # Redraw the Figure because the image has been updated:
    figure.canvas.draw()


# We define the event listener for the 'button_press_event':
def click_mouse_event(event):
    # Check if a double left click is performed:
```

```
        if event.dblclick and event.button == 1:
            # (event.xdata, event.ydata) contains the float coordinates
of the mouse click event:
            cv2.rectangle(image, (int(round(event.xdata)),
int(round(event.ydata))),
                            (int(round(event.xdata)) + 100,
int(round(event.ydata)) + 50), colors['blue'], cv2.FILLED)
        # Call 'update_image()' method to update the Figure:
        update_img_with_matplotlib()


# We create the Figure:
figure = plt.figure()
figure.add_subplot(111)

# To show the image until a click is performed:
update_img_with_matplotlib()

# 'button_press_event' is a MouseEvent where a mouse botton is
click (pressed)
# When this event happens the function 'click_mouse_event' is
called:
figure.canvas.mpl_connect('button_press_event', click_mouse_event)

# Display the figure:
plt.show()
```

7. The code corresponds to the meme_generator_opencv_python.py script. This is a simple script where an image is loaded, and afterwards, some text is rendered:

```
"""
Example to show how to draw basic memes with OpenCV
"""


# Import required packages:
import cv2
import numpy as np
import matplotlib.pyplot as plt


def show_with_matplotlib(img, title):
    """Shows an image using matplotlib capabilities

    """
    # Convert BGR image to RGB
    img_RGB = img[:, :, ::-1]
```

```
# Show the image using matplotlib:
plt.imshow(img_RGB)
plt.title(title)
plt.show()


# Dictionary containing some colors
colors = {'blue': (255, 0, 0), 'green': (0, 255, 0), 'red': (0, 0,
255), 'yellow': (0, 255, 255),
        'magenta': (255, 0, 255), 'cyan': (255, 255, 0), 'white':
(255, 255, 255), 'black': (0, 0, 0),
        'gray': (125, 125, 125), 'rand': np.random.randint(0,
high=256, size=(3,)).tolist(),
        'dark_gray': (50, 50, 50), 'light_gray': (220, 220, 220)}

# We load the image 'lenna.png':
image = cv2.imread("lenna.png")

# Write some text (up)
cv2.putText(image, 'Hello World', (10, 30),
cv2.FONT_HERSHEY_TRIPLEX, 0.8, colors['green'], 1, cv2.LINE_AA)

# Write some text (down)
cv2.putText(image, 'Goodbye World', (10, 200),
cv2.FONT_HERSHEY_TRIPLEX, 0.8, colors['red'], 1, cv2.LINE_AA)

# Show image:
show_with_matplotlib(image, 'very basic meme generator')
```

Chapter 5

1. The `cv2.split()` function splits the source multi-channel image into several single-channel images,
   `(b, g, r) = cv2.split(image)`.
2. The `cv2.merge()` function merges several single-channel images into a multi-channel image, `image = cv2.merge((b, g, r))`.
3. The image can be translated as follows:

   ```
   height, width = image.shape[:2]
   M = np.float32([[1, 0, 150], [0, 1, 300]])
   dst_image = cv2.warpAffine(image, M, (width, height))
   ```

4. The image can be rotated in the following manner:

```
height, width = image.shape[:2]
M = cv2.getRotationMatrix2D((width / 2.0, height / 2.0), 30, 1)
dst_image = cv2.warpAffine(image, M, (width, height))
```

5. The image can be built as follows:

```
kernel = np.ones((5, 5), np.float32) / 25
smooth_image = cv2.filter2D(image, -1, kernel)
```

6. The grayscale image is as follows:

```
M = np.ones(image.shape, dtype="uint8") * 40
added_image = cv2.add(image, M)
```

7. COLORMAP_JET can be applied as follows: img_COLORMAP_JET = cv2.applyColorMap(gray_img, cv2.COLORMAP_JET)

Chapter 6

1. An image histogram is a type of histogram that reflects the tonal distribution of the image. It plots the frequency (number of pixels) for each tonal value (commonly in the range of [0-255]).
2. In OpenCV, we make use of the cv2.calcHist() function to calculate the histogram of images. To calculate the histogram of a grayscale image using 64 bits, the code is as follows:

```
hist = cv2.calcHist([gray_image], [0], None, [64], [0, 256])
```

3. We first build the image, M, with the same shape as the grayscale image, gray_image, and we set the value, 50, for every pixel of this image. Afterwards, we add both images using cv2.add(). Finally, the histogram is computed using cv2.calcHist():

```
M = np.ones(gray_image.shape, dtype="uint8") * 50
added_image = cv2.add(gray_image, M)
hist_added_image = cv2.calcHist([added_image], [0], None, [256], [0, 256])
```

4. In a BGR image, the red channel is the third channel (index 2):

```
cv2.calcHist([img], [2], None, [256], [0, 256])
```

5. OpenCV provides `cv2.calcHist()`, numpy provides `np.histogram()`, and matplotlib provides `plt.hist()`. As we saw in this chapter, `cv2.calcHist()` is faster than both `np.histogram()` and `plt.hist()`.

6. We have defined a function, `get_brightness()`, which calculates the brightness of a given grayscale image. This function makes use of the numpy function, `np.mean()`, which returns the average of the array elements. Therefore, the code for this function is as follows:

```
def get_brightness(img):
    """Calculates the brightness of the image"""

    brightness = np.mean(img)
    return brightness
```

We have computed the brightness of the three images:

```
brightness_1 = get_brightness(gray_image)
brightness_2 = get_brightness(added_image)
brightness_3 = get_brightness(subtracted_image)
```

The full code for this example can be seen in the `grayscale_histogram_brightness.py` script.

7. First of all, we have to import `default_timer`:

```
from timeit import default_timer as timer
```

Then, we have to measure the execution time of both functions:

```
start = timer()
gray_image_eq = cv2.equalizeHist(gray_image)
end = timer()
exec_time_equalizeHist = (end - start) * 1000

start = timer()
gray_image_clahe = clahe.apply(gray_image)
end = timer()
exec_time_CLAHE = (end - start) * 1000
```

The full code for this example can be seen in the `comparing_hist_equalization_clahe_time.py.` script.

Chapter 7

1. `ret, thresh = cv2.threshold(gray_image, 100, 255, cv2.THRESH_BINARY)`

2. `thresh = cv2.adaptiveThreshold(gray_image, 255, cv2.ADAPTIVE_THRESH_GAUSSIAN_C, cv2.THRESH_BINARY, 9, 2)`

3. `ret, th = cv2.threshold(gray_image, 0, 255, cv2.THRESH_BINARY + cv2.THRESH_OTSU)`

4. `ret, th = cv2.threshold(gray_image, 0, 255, cv2.THRESH_BINARY + cv2.THRESH_TRIANGLE)`

5. Otsu's thresholding using scikit-image can be applied as follows:

```
thresh = threshold_otsu(gray_image)
binary = gray_image > thresh
binary = img_as_ubyte(binary)
```

Remember that the `threshold_otsu(gray_image)` function returns the threshold value based on Otsu's binarization algorithm. Afterwards, with this value, the binary image is constructed (`dtype= bool`), which should be converted into an 8-bit unsigned integer format (`dtype= uint8`) for proper visualization. The `img_as_ubyte()` function is used for this purpose.

6. Triangle thresholding using scikit-image can be applied as follows:

```
thresh_triangle = threshold_triangle(gray_image)
binary_triangle = gray_image > thresh_triangle
binary_triangle = img_as_ubyte(binary_triangle)
```

7. Niblack's thresholding using scikit-image can be applied as follows:

```
thresh_niblack = threshold_niblack(gray_image, window_size=25,
k=0.8)
binary_niblack = gray_image > thresh_niblack
binary_niblack = img_as_ubyte(binary_niblack)
```

This algorithm was originally designed for text recognition. See the publication, *An introduction to Digital Image Processing (1986)*, for further details.

8. Sauvola's thresholding using scikit-image and a window size of 25 can be applied as follows:

```
thresh_sauvola = threshold_sauvola(gray_image, window_size=25)
binary_sauvola = gray_image > thresh_sauvola
binary_sauvola = img_as_ubyte(binary_sauvola)
```

Two key points are worth noting:

- Sauvola is a modification of the Niblack technique
- This algorithm was originally designed for text recognition

See the publication, *Adaptive document image binarization (2000)*, for further details.

9. To get the array with the values for thresholding the image, we make use of `np.arange()`. As we want an array with values in the range [60-130] with step 10, the following line codes this functionality:

```
threshold_values = np.arange(start=60, stop=140, step=10)
```

Afterwards, we iterate to apply the `cv2.threshold()` function with the corresponding threshold value defined in `threshold_values`:

```
thresholded_images = []
for threshold in threshold_values:
    ret, thresh = cv2.threshold(gray_image, threshold, 255,
cv2.THRESH_BINARY)
    thresholded_images.append(thresh)
```

Finally, we show the thresholded images contained in the `thresholded_images` array. The full code can be seen in the `thresholding_example_arange.py` script.

Chapter 8

1. The `cv2.findContours()` function finds contours in a binary image (for example, the resulting image after a thresholding operation).
2. The four flags OpenCV provides for compressing contours are as follows:

- `cv2.CHAIN_APPROX_NONE`
- `cv2.CHAIN_APPROX_SIMPLE`
- `cv2.CHAIN_APPROX_TC89_KCOS`
- `cv2.CHAIN_APPROX_TC89_L1`

3. The `cv2.moments()` function calculates all of the moments up to the third order of a polygon or rasterized shape.

4. The moment, `m00`, gives the area of the contour.

5. OpenCV provides the `cv2.HuMoments()` function to calculate the seven Hu moment invariants.

6. The `cv2.approxPolyDP()` function returns a contour approximation of the given contour based on the given precision. This function uses the Douglas-Peucker algorithm. The `epsilon` parameter specifies the precision for establishing the maximum distance between the original curve and its approximation.

7. The `extreme_points()` function defined in the `contour_functionality.py` script can be rewritten in a more compact way, as follows:

```python
def extreme_points_2(contour):
    """Returns extreme points of the contour"""

    extreme_left = tuple(contour[contour[:, :, 0].argmin()][0])
    extreme_right = tuple(contour[contour[:, :, 0].argmax()][0])
    extreme_top = tuple(contour[contour[:, :, 1].argmin()][0])
    extreme_bottom = tuple(contour[contour[:, :, 1].argmax()][0])

    return extreme_left, extreme_right, extreme_top, extreme_bottom
```

8. OpenCV provides the `cv2.matchShapes()` function, which can be used to compare two contours using three comparison methods. All of these methods use the Hu moment invariants. The three implemented methods are `cv2.CONTOURS_MATCH_I1`, `cv2.CONTOURS_MATCH_I2` and `cv.CONTOURS_MATCH_I3`.

Chapter 9

1. Keypoints and compute descriptors in the loaded image, `image`, with ORB are as follows:

```python
orb = cv2.ORB()
keypoints = orb.detect(image, None)
keypoints, descriptors = orb.compute(image, keypoints)
```

2. Previously detected keypoints, `keypoints`, are as follows:

```
image_keypoints = cv2.drawKeypoints(image, keypoints, None,
color=(255, 0, 255), flags=0)
```

To draw detected keypoints, the `cv2.drawKeypoints()` function is used.

3. The `BFMatcher` object and matching of the descriptors, descriptors_1 and descriptors_2, which have been previously calculated, is created as follows:

```
bf_matcher = cv2.BFMatcher(cv2.NORM_HAMMING, crossCheck=True)
bf_matches = bf_matcher.match(descriptors_1, descriptors_2)
```

4. The first 20 matches of the matches that were sorted before is as follows:

```
bf_matches = sorted(bf_matches, key=lambda x: x.distance)
result = cv2.drawMatches(image_query, keypoints_1, image_scene,
keypoints_2, bf_matches[:20], None, matchColor=(255, 255, 0),
singlePointColor=(255, 0, 255), flags=0)
```

To draw the computed matches, `cv2.drawMatches()` is used.

5. Markers using ArUco in the image `gray_frame` are detected as follows:

```
corners, ids, rejected_corners =
cv2.aruco.detectMarkers(gray_frame, aruco_dictionary,
parameters=parameters)
```

To detect markers, the `cv2.aruco.detectMarkers()` function is used.

6. The detected markers when using ArUco are as follows:

```
frame = cv2.aruco.drawDetectedMarkers(image=frame, corners=corners,
ids=ids, borderColor=(0, 255, 0))
```

To draw markers, the `cv2.aruco.drawDetectedMarkers()` function is used.

7. The rejected markers when using Aruco are as follows:

```
frame = cv2.aruco.drawDetectedMarkers(image=frame,
corners=rejected_corners, borderColor=(0, 0, 255))
```

To draw markers, the `cv2.aruco.drawDetectedMarkers()` function is also used.

8. Detect and decode a QR code contained in the image with the following code:

```
data, bbox, rectified_qr_code =
qr_code_detector.detectAndDecode(image)
```

Chapter 10

1. In the context of machine learning, there are three main approaches and techniques: supervised, unsupervised, and semi-supervised machine learning.

2. Supervised learning problems can be further grouped into regression and classification problems. A classification problem happens when the output variable is a category, and a regression problem is when the output variable is a real value. For example, if we predict the possibility of rain in some regions and assign two labels (rain/no rain), this is a classification problem. On the other hand, if the output of our model is the probability associated with the rain, this is a regression problem.

3. OpenCV provides the `cv2.kmeans()` function, implementing a k-means clustering algorithm, which finds centers of clusters and groups input samples around the clusters. k-means is one of the most important clustering algorithms available for unsupervised learning.

4. The `cv2.ml.KNearest_create()` method creates an empty k-NN classifier, which should be trained using the `train()` method, providing both the data and the labels.

5. The `cv2.findNearest()` method is used to find the neighbors.

6. To create an empty model, the `cv2.ml.SVM_create()` function is used.

7. In general, the RBF kernel is a reasonable first choice. The RBF kernel non-linearly maps samples into a higher dimensional space, so that it, unlike the linear kernel, can handle the case when the relation between class labels and attributes is non-linear. See *A Practical Guide to Support Vector Classification (2003)* for further details.

Chapter 11

1. We have seen four libraries and packages: OpenCV library, but also the dlib (`http://dlib.net/python/index.html`, `https://pypi.org/project/dlib/`, `https://github.com/davisking/dlib`), `face_recognition` (`https://pypi.org/project/face_recognition/`, `https://github.com/ageitgey/face_recognition`), and cvlib (`https://pypi.org/project/cvlib/`, `https://github.com/arunponnusamy/cvlib`, `https://www.cvlib.net/`) Python packages.

2. Face recognition, which is a specific case of object recognition, where a person is identified or verified from an image or video using the information extracted from the face, can be decomposed into face identification and face verification:

   - **Face verification** is a 1:1 matching problem that tries to answer the question: *Is this the claimed person?* For instance, unlocking a mobile phone using your face is an example of face verification.
   - **Face identification** is a 1:N matching problem that tries to answer the question: *Who is this person?* For example, a face identification system can be installed in an office building to identify all the employees while they are entering the office.

3. The `cv2.face.getFacesHAAR()` function can be used to detect faces in images:

   ```
   retval, faces = cv2.face.getFacesHAAR(img,
   "haarcascade_frontalface_alt2.xml")
   ```

   Here, `img` is a BGR image and `"haarcascade_frontalface_alt2.xml"` is the string variable for the Haar Cascade file.

4. The `cv2.dnn.blobFromImage()` function is used to create a four-dimensional blob from the input image. Optionally, this function performs pre-processing, which is necessary to input the blob into the network to obtain the correct results. This function will be covered more in-depth in the next chapter.

5. The `cv.detect_face()` function can be used to detect faces using cvlib:

   ```
   import cvlib as cv
   faces, confidences = cv.detect_face(image)
   ```

   Under the hood, this function is using the OpenCV DNN face detector with pre-trained Caffe models (`https://github.com/arunponnusamy/cvlib/blob/master/cvlib/face_detection.py`). See the `face_detection_cvlib_dnn.py` script for further details.

6. To detect the landmarks, the `face_recognition.face_landmarks()` function should be called:

```
face_landmarks_list_68 = face_recognition.face_landmarks(rgb)
```

This function returns a dictionary of facial landmarks (for instance, eyes, nose, and so on) for each face in the image. It should be noted that the `face_recognition` package works with RGB images.

7. To initialize the correlation tracker, the `dlib.correlation_tracker()` function should be called:

```
tracker = dlib.correlation_tracker()
```

This initializes the tracker with default values.

8. To start tracking, the `tracker.start_track()` method is used and a bounding box containing the object to track is required:

```
tracker.start_track(image, rect)
```

Here, `rect` is the bounding box of the object to track.

9. To get the position of the tracked object, the `tracker.get_position()` method is called:

```
pos = tracker.get_position()
```

This method returns the position of the object being tracked.

10. The 128D descriptor to perform face recognition of the BGR image, `image`, with dlib is calculated as follows:

```
# Convert image from BGR (OpenCV format) to RGB (dlib format):
rgb = image[:, :, ::-1]
# Calculate the encodings for every face of the image:
encodings = face_encodings(rgb)
# Show the first encoding:
print(encodings[0])
```

Chapter 12

1. Three main differences between machine learning and deep learning are as follows:

   - Deep learning algorithms need to have a high-end infrastructure to train properly. Deep learning techniques heavily rely on high-end machines, contrary to traditional machine learning techniques, which can work on low-end machines.
   - When there is a lack of domain understanding for both feature introspection and engineering, deep learning techniques outperform other techniques because you have to worry less about feature engineering.
   - Both machine learning and deep learning are able to handle massive dataset sizes, however machine learning methods make much more sense when dealing with small datasets. A rule of thumb is to consider that deep learning outperforms other techniques if the data size is large, while traditional machine learning algorithms are preferable when the dataset is small.

2. In connection with computer vision, Alex Krizhevsky, Ilya Sutskever, and Geoff Hinton published *ImageNet Classification with Deep Convolutional Neural Networks (2012)*. This publication is also known as **AlexNet**, which is the name of the convolutional neural network the authors designed and is considered one of the most influential papers in computer vision. Therefore, the year 2012 is considered the explosion on deep learning.

3. This function creates a four-dimensional blob from the image, and means that we want to run the model on BGR images resized to 300x300, applying a mean subtraction of values (104, 117, 123) for each blue, green, and red channels, respectively.

4. The first line feeds the input blob to the network, while the second one performs inference, and when the inference is done, we get the predictions.

5. A placeholder is simply a variable that we will assign data to at a later date. When training/testing an algorithm, placeholders are commonly used for feeding training/testing data into the computation graph.

6. When saving the final model (for instance, `saver.save(sess, './linear_regression')`), four files are created:

   - `.meta` **files**: Contain the TensorFlow graph
   - `.data` **files**: Contain the values of the weights, biases, gradients, and all the other variables that were saved
   - `.index` **files**: Identify the checkpoint
   - `checkpoint` **file**: Keep a record of the latest checkpoint files that were saved

7. **One-hot encoding** means that labels have been converted from a single number into a vector whose length is equal to the number of possible classes. This way, all elements of the vector will be set to zero except the i element, whose value will be 1, corresponding to the class i.

8. When using Keras, the simplest type of model is the sequential model, which can be seen as a linear stack of layers and is used in this example to create the model. Additionally, for more complex architectures, the Keras functional API, which allows you to build arbitrary graphs of layers, can be used.

9. This method can be used for training the model for a fixed number of epochs (iterations on a dataset).

Chapter 13

1. Web frameworks can be categorized into full-stack and non full-stack frameworks. Django (`https://www.djangoproject.com/`) is a full-stack web framework for Python, while Flask (`http://flask.pocoo.org/`) is a non full-stack framerwork for Python.

2. In Flask, you can use the `route()` decorator to bind a function to a URL. In other words, the `route()` decorator is used to indicate to Flask what URL should trigger a specific function.

3. To make the server publicity available, the `host=0.0.0.0` parameter should be added when running the server application:

```
if __name__ == "__main__":
    # Add parameter host='0.0.0.0' to run on your machines IP
address:
    app.run(host='0.0.0.0')
```

4. The `jsonify()` function is used to create the JSON representation of the given arguments with an `application/json` mimetype. JSON can be considered the de facto standard for information exchange and, therefore, it is a good idea to return JSON data to the client.

5. We can register error handlers by decorating the functions with `errorhandler()`. For example, note the following:

```
@app.errorhandler(500)
def not_found(e):
    # return also the code error
    return jsonify({"status": "internal error", "message":
"internal error occurred in server"}), 500
```

If an internal error occurs in the server, the client will be given a 500 error code.

6. Keras Applications (`https://keras.io/applications/`) is the applications module of the Keras deep learning library, providing both deep learning model definitions and pre-trained weights for a number of popular architectures (for example, VGG16, ResNet50, Xception, and MobileNet, among others), which can be used for prediction, feature extraction, and fine-tuning. These deep learning architectures are trained and validated on the ImageNet dataset (`http://image-net.org/`) for classifying images into one of 1000 categories or classes.

7. PythonAnywhere (`www.pythonanywhere.com`) is a Python online integrated development environment (IDE) and web hosting environment, making it easy to create and run Python programs in the cloud.

Other Books You May Enjoy

If you enjoyed this book, you may be interested in these other books by Packt:

Learn OpenCV 4 By Building Projects - Second Edition
David Millán Escrivá, Vinícius G. Mendonça, Prateek Joshi

ISBN: 9781789341225

- Install OpenCV 4 on your operating system
- Create CMake scripts to compile your C++ application
- Understand basic image matrix formats and filters
- Explore segmentation and feature extraction techniques
- Remove backgrounds from static scenes to identify moving objects for surveillance
- Employ various techniques to track objects in a live video
- Work with new OpenCV functions for text detection and recognition with Tesseract
- Get acquainted with important deep learning tools for image classification

Mastering OpenCV 4 - Third Edition
Roy Shilkrot, David Millán Escrivá

ISBN: 9781789533576

- Build real-world computer vision problems with working OpenCV code samples
- Uncover best practices in engineering and maintaining OpenCV projects
- Explore algorithmic design approaches for complex computer vision tasks
- Work with OpenCV's most updated API (v4.0.0) through projects
- Understand 3D scene reconstruction and Structure from Motion (SfM)
- Study camera calibration and overlay AR using the ArUco Module

Leave a review - let other readers know what you think

Please share your thoughts on this book with others by leaving a review on the site that you bought it from. If you purchased the book from Amazon, please leave us an honest review on this book's Amazon page. This is vital so that other potential readers can see and use your unbiased opinion to make purchasing decisions, we can understand what our customers think about our products, and our authors can see your feedback on the title that they have worked with Packt to create. It will only take a few minutes of your time, but is valuable to other potential customers, our authors, and Packt. Thank you!

Index

M

machine learning
  about 16, 294, 295
  semi-supervised machine learning 298
  supervised machine learning 296
  unsupervised machine learning 298
Mahotas
  reference 40
marker-based augmented reality
  about 268
  augmentation 275
  camera calibration 272
  camera pose, estimating 274, 275, 277, 279
  dictionaries, creating 268
  markers, creating 268
  markers, detecting 270
markerless-based augmented reality
  about 261
  feature detection 262
  feature matching 264, 266
  homography computation, for finding objects 266
matchers
  Brute-Force (BF) matcher 264
  Fast Library for Approximate Nearest Neighbors
    matcher 264
Matplotlib histograms
  versus NumPy 185
  versus OpenCV 185
Matplotlib
  about 10
  reference 10, 41
  used, for event handling 129, 130
mean squared error (MSE) 413
Microsoft Azure
  reference 465
Milk
  reference 41
minimal face API
  creating, OpenCV used 434, 439
MIT license
  reference 45
model complexity 297
modulo operation 153
morphological transformations

about 158
applying, to images 160, 161
black hat operation 159
closing operation 159
dilation operation 158
erosion operation 158
gradient operation 159
hat operation 159
opening operation 158
structuring element 160
mouse events
  used, for dynamic drawing 127

N

Neural Networks 17
NLTK
  reference 41
node package
  reference 50
non-full-stack framework 426
NumPy
  reference 10, 40
  versus Matplotlib histograms 185
  versus OpenCV 185

O

object detection, deep learning
  about 397
  MobileNet-SSD 397
  YOLO 398
one-hot encoding 410
ONNX
  reference 380
OpenCV (Open Source Computer Vision)
  about 9
  accessing, with grayscale images 65
  algorithms and techniques 262
  BGR order 67, 69, 72, 73
  channels, merging 140
  channels, splitting 140
  code testing specifications 10, 14
  color maps 166
  coordinate system 61, 62
  example 431
  face detection 336, 338, 341, 343

Printed in the USA
CPSIA information can be obtained
at www.ICGtesting.com
JSHW052353100823
46345JS00002B/188